The *Corpus Iuris Civilis* in the Middle Ages

Brill's Studies in Intellectual History

VOLUME 147

The *Corpus Iuris Civilis* in the Middle Ages

Manuscripts and Transmission from the Sixth Century to the Juristic Revival

by
Charles M. Radding
and
Antonio Ciaralli

BRILL

LEIDEN • BOSTON
2007

On the cover: Cologne, Historisches Archiv, W. 328, f. 31r.

This book is printed on acid-free paper.

Library of Congress Cataloging-in-Publication data

A C.I.P. record for this book is available from the Library of Congress.

ISSN 0920-8607
ISBN-13: 978 90 04 15499 5
ISBN-10: 90 04 15499 X

For Armando Petrucci
and in memory of Paola Supino Martini

CONTENTS

ABBREVIATIONS

BIDR	*Bulletino dell'Istituto di Diritto Romano*
MGH	*Monumenta Germaniae Historica*
Capit.	*Capitularia regum Francorum*
Dipl.	*Diplomata*
Leges	*Leges*
PL	*Patrologia cursus completa, series Latina*, ed. J. P. Migne
ZRG	*Zeitschrift für Rechtsgeschichte*
ZSS	*Zeitschrift der Savigny-Stiftung für Rechtsgeschichte*
GA	*Germanistische Abteilung*
KA	*Kanonistische Abteilung*
RA	*Romanistische Abteilung*

LIST OF ILLUSTRATIONS

Tables

Plates

PREFACE

Although a survey of early legal manuscripts has long been overdue, it was not originally our purpose to conduct one. We began our study with a rather different objective: seeing what early legal manuscripts could tell us about the study of law during the eleventh and twelfth centuries. Our inspiration came from a few manuscripts of the Lombard law whose physical aspects had offered tantalizing glimpses of how they had been produced and read. One contained marginal notes roughly written in non-standard Latin from a time before vernacular was routinely written. Another used headings written in a script that belonged in documents rather than books. Such discoveries suggested that a careful look at other early legal manuscripts might shed more light than had been previously imagined on the people and their learning of this very early period of the juristic revival in Europe. Besides, no-one else was interested in these manuscripts. We decided to take a few months and see what we could find, extending our inquiries to manuscripts of the Roman law as well.

But once we began working through manuscripts available to us, the project took on a life of its own. It was not a surprise that many of the dates traditionally assigned to these manuscripts were wrong. Most of the work had been done in the nineteenth century, when paleography was still in its infancy and before the diffusion of photography had made it possible directly to compare manuscripts in different libraries. What we did not expect was that nearly all the errors would be in the same direction, so that the mistakes did not simply cancel each other out. A long list of "eleventh-century" manuscripts of Justinian's Code—all of those readily available to us in original or microfilm—turned out to be from the twelfth century. What about the rest? The census was no longer avoidable. We had to see them all.

Ordering microfilm of manuscripts or visiting them in person took time. Tracing the implications of the new datings took even longer, because the traditional account of the history of Justinian's *Corpus* turned out to have been built precisely upon those nineteenth-century dates we were now preparing to discard. Changing those dates, therefore, reopened a number of questions that had long seemed settled. What is the evidence for the circulation of the different works of the

Corpus in the early Middle Ages? When does study of Justinian's works begin again and by whom? How does the history of the Digest fit into the new chronology of the rest of the *Corpus*? How does the recovery of the works of the *Corpus* affect our understanding of the juristic renaissance generally?

Our account will attempt to address these issues in detail, surveying so far as possible all the relevant, available evidence on the subject. Possibly there are documents or texts that we have overlooked despite our best efforts. Possibly, too, other researchers may arrive at more precise localizations of some of the manuscripts—for example, by matching hands in manuscript books with those in documents in local archives that we were not able exhaustively to study. Yet the paleographical, documentary, and historical evidence agrees in so many details that we are confident that the main lines of our conclusions will survive the scrutiny that they will certainly receive in the future, even if further research discovers evidence that improves some of the details.

Division of the research between the authors has followed disciplinary lines, with Antonio Ciaralli responsible for manuscript descriptions, including all datings and the appendix, and Charles Radding for historical analysis. Radding is largely responsible for the text itself, and he translated the appendix from Ciaralli's original Italian. Both authors wish to acknowledge the advice and assistance they have received. Armando Petrucci and Paola Supino Martini, whose loss we feel most deeply, were generous throughout with their paleographical expertise and advice. Portions of the manuscript have been read and commented upon by Chris Wickham, Anders Winroth, and Ronald Witt; while scholars too numerous to mention have been generous with their expertise on a variety of specific points. Support for travel, microfilm, and other expenses has come from Michigan State University and the University of Verona, while a fellowship from the Institute for Advanced Studies provided Charles Radding with time and resources to complete much of the historical research. Responsibility for errors and omissions, and for conclusions that these readers may not share, of course, remains ours alone.

CHAPTER ONE

PALEOGRAPHY AND HISTORY

Although the works of the *Corpus Iuris Civilis* are not texts that appeal to a casual reader, they occupied an extraordinary place in European history between the late eleventh and nineteenth centuries. As school texts, they lay at the center of the activities of the *studium* of Bologna, one of the earliest and most important of the medieval universities. The prestige won in the classroom, moreover, made Justinian's works attractive to working jurists: Pisa made Roman law its local law as early as the 1160s.[1] By the end of the Middle Ages the Roman law-based *ius commune* had been adopted by courts throughout Europe.

By the eighteenth century, this long period of influence seemed to have run its course. The French civil code promulgated in 1804 drew heavily on the model provided by the Justinianic codification, but its enactment also severed the relationship between the *Corpus* and the daily operation of the law. The main exception was Germany, where a civil code was not enacted until 1900 and where an ongoing debate about legal reform led many scholars to seek inspiration in a return to the sources of Roman legal tradition.[2] Coinciding as it did with a boom in classical and medieval studies, this interest in the historical development of law led to the creation of a formidable body of scholarship—everything from broad surveys to critical editions—that largely set the terms within which Roman law would be studied throughout the twentieth century.

Stephan Kuttner's account from the early 1980s provides a succinct statement of the history of the *Corpus Iuris Civilis* that emerged from the nineteenth century. "Medieval philosophy would have blossomed," he wrote:

> even if Aristotle's Posterior Analytics had never been found. But it is unthinkable that a science of law could have taken shape in the medieval

[1] Chris Wickham, *Courts and Conflict in Twelfth-Century Tuscany* (Oxford, 2003), chap. 3.

[2] Peter Stein, *Roman Law in European History* (Cambridge, 1999); Manlio Bellomo, *The Common Legal Past of Europe 1000–1800*, trans. by Lydia G. Cochrane (Washington, D.C., 1995). For the Pandectists, see James Q. Whitman, *The Legacy of Roman Law in the German Romantic Era* (Princeton, 1990).

> West without the rediscovery of Justinian's Digest, about 1070 AD. The central monument of ancient Roman jurisprudence presented a model and a challenge to the medieval mind for which the eleventh-century reader was rather ill-prepared. To be sure, relics of the imposing structure of the laws of Rome existed . . . Lombard Italy and the formerly Byzantine regions of the peninsula had preserved portions of Justinian's Code (*Codex Justinianus*), his elementary *Institutiones*, and an abridged Latin version of his Greek *Novellae* (the *Epitome Juliani*).

But, he continued, there is no evidence from this period of law as "an intellectually coherent discipline," nor could there be until "the reappearance of the Digest itself, which marked indeed 'the beginning of everything,' a new epoch."[3]

> [T]he reappearance of the Digest itself [in some respects] was unique. First, everything 'hung by a slender thread,' since only a single complete manuscript of the book had survived, and lay unused until the latter part of the eleventh century. . . . [E]ach and every extant copy of the Digest (with the exception of one ninth-century fragment) is ultimately derived from the *codex Florentinus* (**F**). . . . After more than three centuries of debate, Theodor Mommsen's studies, culminating in his editio maior of 1870, demonstrated that all the differences from **F** which are common to the so-called vulgate manuscripts or littera Bononiensis can be reduced to a single, lost archetype, the codex secundus (S), and that this itself was an emended copy of F, written in Beneventan script. At times the 'redactor' of S erred in his conjectures, but on the whole his emendations show a respectable standard of critical and philological insights, which would place the book's presumable origin at the threshold of the 'new times': they bespeak an urge for learning and harmonization that would have been out of context before the last third of the eleventh century.[4]

Other historians make essentially the same points: that all the works of the *Corpus Iuris Civilis* except the Digest were known, at least partially, during the early Middle Ages, and that it was the recovery of that work in the late eleventh century that triggered the revival of jurisprudence.[5]

---

3 Stephan Kuttner, "The Revival of Jurisprudence," in *Renaissance and Renewal in the Twelfth Century*, ed. by Robert L. Benson and Giles Constable (Cambridge, Mass., 1982), pp. 299–300.

4 Ibid., pp. 300–1.

5 See, for example, Hermann Lange, *Römisches Recht im Mittelalter* (München, 1997), chap. 1; Ennio Cortese, *Il diritto nella storia medievale. I. L'alto medioevo* (Roma, 1995); and the earlier, classic text of Francesco Calasso, *Medio Evo del Diritto. Le fonti* (Milano, 1954).

The emphasis on the Digest itself is an echo of the nineteenth-century Pandectists who—as the name itself suggests—valued the Digest above all else. Much of the factual basis underlying this interpretation is similarly nineteenth-century in origin, including the manuscript work that prepared the way for Mommsen's and Krüger's editions of Justinian's Institutes, Code, and Digest. A great deal of this research was, by the standards of the time, at the very cutting edge of historical methodology; indeed, the enduring educational and practical importance of the *Corpus* had long meant that work on its texts often drew on the latest scholarly methods. Poliziano had brought the humanist's understanding of textual transmission to his study of manuscripts of the Digest; publishers in the early sixteenth century went back to early manuscripts for editions of the works of the *Corpus*; and later in that century Lelio Torelli, his son Francesco, and Antonio Agustín replicated the text of the *Florentina*, the unique codex of the Digest dating almost back to Justinian's time, in a meticulously produced printed edition.[6] In the same spirit, Mommsen and Krüger had drawn upon the newest techniques of manuscript study to produce their path-breaking editions of the Justinianic codification.

It is well known that Mommsen's and Krüger's editions are still in use a century and a quarter later, with no sign of being replaced anytime soon. Less well known is that many of the manuscript descriptions cited by Mommsen and Krüger are even earlier, dating back to the early decades of the nineteenth century. And almost entirely forgotten is the essential role these manuscript descriptions played in the formation of our understanding of the history of Justinian's *Corpus* in the Middle Ages. Our task in this chapter is to understand this interplay between paleography and history, and how it shaped the understanding of the history of Roman law in the Middle Ages that still dominates today.

---

[6] *Digestorum seu Pandectarum libri quinquaginta ex Florentinis Pandectis repraesentati* (Florentia, 1553). On this project, see Giovanni Gualandi, "Per la storia della *Editio Princeps* delle Pandette fiorentine di Lelio Torelli," in *Le Pandette di Giustiniano. Storia e fortuna di un codice illustre. Due giornate di studio Firenze 23–24 giugno 1983* [Accademia Toscana di Scienze e Lettere « La Colombaria », Studi LXXVI] (Firenze, 1986), pp. 143–98; and Hans Erich Troje, *Graeca Leguntur. Die Aneignung des byzantinischen Rechts und die Entstehung eines humanistischen Corpus iuris civilis in der Jurisprudenz des 16. Jahrhunderts* [Forschungen zur Neueren Privatrechtsgeschichte, Bd. 18] Köln/Wien, 1971, pp. 41–49.

The Editors

Savigny and Schrader

Although modern historians often invoke the work of Karl Friedrich von Savigny (d. 1861) as their historiographical point of departure, Savigny himself felt that he was working within a tradition that was already well-established. This can be seen, not only in the citation of published sources on nearly every page of his multi-volume *History of Roman Law during the Middle Ages*, but in his explanation of how his research evolved. After noting that his original intention had been to start with Irnerius, he continued by observing:

> If it were really true, as has been generally believed, that the Roman law perished with the Western Empire and revived by accident, after six hundred years of neglect, the above mentioned plan would unquestionably be the best... Many, however, have already refused their assent to this alleged subversion of Roman jurisprudence [... so that p]ersons convinced of the erroneousness of both opinions must at once see the advantage of commencing the present inquiry at a much earlier period, and endeavoring to discover how the jurisprudence of subsequent times, in so far as its condition depends on Roman influence, has arisen from the legislation of the Western Empire, by mere development and progressive change, without any total interruption.[7]

Savigny was also, as this passage suggests, far more cautious than modern historians in discounting the evidence for knowledge of Roman law in the early Middle Ages. He had little definite to say about the history of Justinian's *Corpus* in the early Middle Ages, but he clearly believed that even the Digest was available to some extent. Thus, for example, he suggested that a passage in the ninth-century author Agobard of Lyons might derive from the Digest (vol. 2, 279); he noted several possible references to the Digest in the Lombardist *Quaestiones ac monita* that he dated to ca. 1000 (vol. 2, pp. 244–49); and he placed the *Exceptiones Petri* (notable for its substantial collection of excerpts from the Digest) before the last quarter of the eleventh century. Since he never claimed that the Digest was unknown in the early Middle Ages, its reappearance was not a problem he studied; he was more interested by the odd fact that the post-1100 manu-

---

[7] Friedrich Karl von Savigny, *Geschichte des römischen Rechts im Mittelalter* 2nd ed. (Heidelberg, 1834), vol. 1, pp. vi–vii. Since the passage was unchanged from the first edition, we have been able to use E. Cathcart's translation (Edinburgh, 1829).

script tradition divided it into three distinct parts, each with its own name (vol. 3, pp. 422–42). Savigny saw the continuity of the legal tradition as especially marked in Italy, and he concluded his survey of the evidence with the observation that "Justinian's law was known and used in all periods of Lombard Italy."[8]

Rather than attributing to Savigny the currently dominant account of the history of the *Corpus Iuris Civilis*, it would be better to see its origins in the work of his contemporary, Eduard Schrader of the University of Tübingen. Schrader enjoyed a cooperative relationship with Savigny, with whom he exchanged information about manuscripts and legal texts of various kinds, but his own purpose was to produce new editions of the various works of the *Corpus*. To this end, he and his collaborators arranged for a survey of the surviving manuscripts, assigning a date to each and having copies and facsimiles made of those that they considered the most important. Necessarily in this age before photography, all this work was painstakingly done by hand. This massive effort may perhaps be best understood as the counterpart to the contemporary efforts that led to the founding of the *Monumenta Germaniae Historica* in the 1820s, and indeed some of the scholars involved in the early MGH also assisted Schrader. One of these was Frederick Bluhme, and some flavor of the work involved can be gotten from his earliest reports, which were organized almost as travelogues recounting his visits to libraries about whose holdings he may have known little before arriving.[9] Bluhme's account also makes it clear that legal manuscripts were one of the principal targets of these early researches, and indeed law codes and other legal enactments were among the earliest editions published by the MGH.

The first work produced by Schrader's group was his *Prodromus* of 1823, in which he and his collaborators laid out the intellectual basis for their work on Justinian's *Institutiones*.[10] The *Prodromus* described the Tübingen project in detail as well as the different sources that an edition would necessarily consider: notable previous editions as well as manuscripts. More than a hundred manuscripts of the *Institutiones* were listed and described, of which only three were thought to be

[8] "Das Justinianische Recht war in Lombardischen Italien zu allen Zeiten bekannt und geltend." vol. 2, pp. 269–70.

[9] "Bemerkungen über einzelne Handschriften und Urkunden" in *Archiv der Gesellschaft für ältere Deutschegeschictskunde* vol. 4 (1824); *Iter Italicum* (Berlin, 1824).

[10] E. Schrader, et al., *Prodromus corporis iuris civilis* (Berlin, 1823).

earlier than the twelfth century. These were Bamberg, Staatsbibliothek, Msc. Jur. 1 (formerly D.II.3), which was described as ninth or tenth century in the catalogue of manuscripts but later (p. 76) was referred to as ninth century; Turin, Biblioteca Nazionale Universitaria, D.III.13 (formerly (H.VI.4), the bulk of which was dated to the tenth century, with replacement leaves from the twelfth; and Paris, Bibliothèque Nationale, ms. lat. 4421, attributed to the eleventh century.

These dates were based on paleographical methods very different from those in use today. Although Schrader and his collaborators had considerable personal experience with manuscripts, their expertise fell well short of what would be achieved at the end of the century with Ludwig Traube's Munich school.[11] In Schrader's time, paleography was still dominated by the old-fashioned classificatory method, described by Bischoff as "the diligent collection of all known varieties of Latin handwriting and their arrangement according to a system."[12] This project had culminated decades earlier in the *Nouveau traité de diplomatique* by the Maurist Benedictines Charles Toustain and René-Prosper Tassin in which, as the title of that book suggests, paleography still took second place to diplomatics.[13] Reflecting this tradition, early nineteenth-century paleography consisted mainly of "various rules of thumb" for dating manuscripts.[14]

A more detailed understanding of German paleography during this period can be gained from Traube's own retrospective essay, written in the early twentieth century.[15] Traube made no great claims for this period of German paleography ("Gott schütze uns vor nationalem Hochmut!"), but singled out as worthy of mention Ulrich F. Kopp (1762–1834), who was primarily interested in deciphering the encrypted writing known as tironian notes, and Johann F. Massmann (1797–1874) and Karl Zangemeister of whom, however, he observed that the scripts they studied "are not very important for us," meaning

[11] See J. Authenrieth, "Die Münchener Schule. Ludwig Traube-Paul Lehmann-Bernard Bischoff," in *Un secolo di paleografia e diplomatica (1887–1986). Per il centenario dell'Istituto di paleografia dell'Università di Roma*, ed. A. Petrucci and A. Pratesi (Roma, [1988]), pp. 99–130.

[12] Bernard Bischoff, *Latin Paleography. Antiquity and the Middle Ages*, trans. by Dáibhí ó Cróinín and David Ganz (Cambridge, 1989), p. 1.

[13] *Nouveau traité de diplomatique, où l'on examine les fondamens de cet art... par deux religieux bénédictins de la Congregation de S. Maur* (Paris, 1750–1765).

[14] Bischoff, *Latin Paleography*, p. 2.

[15] Ludwig Traube, "Geschichte der Paläographie," in *Vorlesungen und Abhandlungen*, ed. by Franz Boll (München, 1909–20, repr. 1965), vol. 1, pp. 1–80, at pp. 71–76.

that they were specialists in cursive scripts used in documents rather than in the scripts used for books. In addition, Traube mentioned two schools within the German-speaking world, the earlier of which was linked to the *Monumenta Germaniae Historica.* Although the MGH is best known today for its series of published sources, in its earliest phase it was devoted to publishing descriptions of codices and documents in its official journal, the *Archiv der Gesellschaft für ältere deutsche Geschichtskunde* (1820–1831); Traube described the paleographers involved in this enterprise, Georg Pertz (1795–1876), Hans Bethmann, Philipp Jaffé, Wilhelm Wattenbach (1819–1897) as "die Männer der älteren Generation," with Wilhelm Arndt and Paul Ewald representing still later trends. The other paleographical school, founded by Theodor von Sickel (1826–1908), had ties to the *Institut für Österreichische Geschichtsforschung.*

In Traube's view, the most important of these scholars was Wattenbach ("der deutsche Paläograph par excellence") who in 1869—or 43 years after Schrader's *Prodromus*—had published the *Anleitung zur lateinische Palaeographie,* the first paleographical manual to provide clear and reliable guidelines for dating manuscripts.[16] Before this work was published, indeed, studying manuscripts meant long and patient immersion in monumental and expensive collections of facsimiles such as Sickel's *Monumenta graphica*[17] and the collection of writing samples organized by Pertz from the MGH. All of these conditions, of course, had been even worse when Schrader had been most actively collecting information on legal manuscripts.

The shift that produced modern paleography resulted in part from the invention of photography, which permitted the accurate reproduction of manuscripts, and in part from a reorientation of perspective toward seeing scripts as evolving over time rather than as static types. Wattenbach's manual had already made a practical step in this direction by providing plates devoted to the mutation of individual letter shapes between Roman times and the ninth century. But the essential theoretical breakthroughs came later: Léopold Delisle's use of the concept of *scriptorium* in his 1885 work on Tours, which directed scholars toward a recognition of the graphic, decorative,

---

[16] Wilhelm Wattenbach, *Anleitung zur lateinische Palaeographie* (Leipzig, 1869).

[17] *Monumenta graphica medii aevi ex archivis et bibliothecis imperii Austriaci collecta* (Vienna, 1858–82).

and other characteristics shared by manuscripts from the same center; and Traube's enunciation of a developmental history of handwriting (*Entwicklungsgeschichte der Schrift*) which he himself demonstrated in his studies of the history of abbreviations. In the twentieth century, the combination of this vision with photographic techniques has resulted in a proliferation of scholarly tools for the dating of manuscripts and the study of the history of scripts. Especially important is the series *Codices Latini Antiquiores* (= *CLA*), organized by Traube's student E. A. Lowe, that reproduces a portion of every known Latin book or manuscript fragment from the eighth century or earlier.[18] Other tools include reproductions of documents and of datable manuscripts, handbooks of abbreviations (noting not just how to decipher them but where and when they occur), and guides to codicology.

The logical extension of the idea of *scriptorium* was the concept of "scriptorial province" or "graphic area" as a region whose handwriting and manuscripts shared a definable specific set of characteristics. In effect this concept recognizes sub-types or derivations of a canonized script that were the common patrimony of a group of writers diffused over a specific geographical region. One such graphic type is the Beneventan script of southern Italy, whose characteristics were defined by Lowe in his book of 1914;[19] another is Roman minuscule, which was described twenty years ago by Paola Supino in an important book.[20] During the period between the late tenth and mid-twelfth centuries, this hand was used not only in the city of Rome itself, but in an area extending in the north toward Viterbo and Rieti and into Umbria as far as Foligno and Norcia and in the south to Velletri and the monastery of Subiaco.

One of the scribes who copied Bamberg Msc. Jur. 1, described as ninth or tenth century in the *Prodromus*, turns out to have written in a roman minuscule (*romanesca*) that Supino attributed to the end of the tenth century.[21] A dating to this period is not new among

---

[18] Elias Avery Lowe, *Codices Latini Antiquiores*, 1–11 and Suppl. (Oxford 1934–71); 2[2] (ibid. 1972). Addenda by B. Bischoff and V. Brown, *Mediaeval Studies*, 47 (1985): 317–66, with 18 plates. The impact of photography on art history, a field with many methodological similarities to paleography, was discussed by W. Benjamin, "Das Kunstwerk im Zeitalter seiner technischen Reproduzierbarkeit" [orig. pub. 1936] in Benjamin, *Illuminationen. Ausgewählte Schriften I*, (Frankfurt/M., 1977), pp. 136–69 and "Kleine Geschichte der Photographie" [orig. pub. 1931]).

[19] *The Beneventan Script* (Oxford, 1914).

[20] Paola Supino Martini, *Roma e l'area grafica romanesca (secoli X–XII)* [Biblioteca de Scrittura e Civilté, 1] (Alessandria, 1987).

[21] Supino Martini, *Roma e l'area grafica romanesca*, pp. 127–28.

paleographers: as early as 1914 Lowe proposed attributing this manuscript to the late tenth century or the beginning of the eleventh. There are even reasons to believe that the Bamberg Institutes may be slightly later. Observing that the manuscript appears paleographically too "advanced" (*fortgeschritten*) to belong to the period of Otto III, Bischoff suggested that it might have been Henry II rather than Otto who took the manuscript to Bamberg from Italy;[22] Armando Petrucci similarly dated this manuscript to the early eleventh century rather than the late tenth, in an unpublished talk of 1988.[23]

The dates for the other manuscripts singled out as early in Schrader's *Prodromus* are also wrong by a century and more. The older and more important section of Turin D.III.13, which was described by Schrader as dating from the tenth century, was written by a single scribe in a well-organized Caroline minuscule attributable to the later eleventh century.[24] Since the fame of this manuscript is due not just to the supposed age of the manuscript but also to the numerous glosses that enrich its margins, one should also mention that the oldest of these are essentially contemporary with the manuscript itself. Also misdated, finally, is the Paris ms. lat. 4421, which turns out to be from the second quarter of the twelfth century rather than the eleventh century.

Since Bamberg Msc. Jur. 1 is, in fact, the oldest of surviving Institutes manuscripts, its misdating to the ninth century did not in itself compromise Schrader's project. His editions failed, rather, because he was working in a period before principles for choosing among different manuscript readings had been clearly articulated. Collating numerous manuscripts in such circumstances had the effect merely of multiplying the number of known variants; it did not provide any

---

[22] B. Bischoff, "Italienische Handschriften des neunten bis elften Jahrhunderts in frühmittelalterlichen Bibliotheken außerhalb Italiens," in *Il libro e il testo. Atti del convegno internazionale. Urbino, 20–23 settembre 1982*, ed. by C. Questa and R. Raffaeli, (Università di Urbino, 1984), pp. 169–94 at 176.

[23] See also A. Ciaralli, "Produzione manoscritta e trasmissione dei testi di natura giuridica tra XI e XII secolo: due esempi," in *Juristische Buchproduktion im Mittelalter, Kolloquium 25. bis 28. Oktober 1998*, ed. by Vicenzo Colli (Frankfurt/Main, 2002), pp. 71–104 at 78–83. The authors express their gratitude to Petrucci for having given them access to his text.

[24] Petrucci had already indicated the eleventh century as the correct dating of this manuscript to C. G. Mor; see Mor, "Per la storia dei libri giustinianei nell'età preirneriana," as revised in Mor, *Scritti di storia giuridica altomedievale* (Pisa, 1977), pp. 11–23 at p. 13.

guidance for which ones were the best. In his 1832 edition of the Institutes,[25] Schrader generally solved this problem by selecting the reading that appeared in the greatest number of manuscripts but the result (as Krüger later remarked) was only to increase uncertainty about the text. The brute-force collation of manuscripts, moreover, proved simply impractical for the other works of the *Corpus*, all of which were much longer than the Institutes. Schrader made little progress toward editions of these works, although the transcriptions and other evidence he collected continued to be consulted by scholars for the rest of the nineteenth century.

Mommsen and Krüger

In practice, it was not until the mid-nineteenth century that the Lachmann or stemmatic method provided scholars with the techniques necessary for handling editorial problems on the scale posed by the major works of Roman law. This approach, which had been evolving for some time, was premised on reconstructing the *stemma codicum* or family tree of the manuscript tradition. The editor began by conducting a careful review (*recensio*) of all manuscripts to determine their content. First one manuscript, usually the oldest, and then others were carefully transcribed, the idea being "to look for what is in the codices without any interpretation, as Lachmann put it."[26] On the assumption that variations introduced in one manuscript would be perpetuated in those copied from it, the manuscripts were grouped into blocks according to shared errors or variations until the editor arrived at a hypothetical stemma or family tree of the codices. Dispensing with later manuscripts, the editor could then concentrate on manuscripts theoretically closer to the archetype, in this way even-

[25] *Corpus iuris civilis. Ad fidem codicum manuscriptorum aliorumque subsidiorum criticorum recensuit, commentario perpetuo instruxit Eduardus Schrader.* (Berlin, 1832).

[26] Leonard E. Boyle, "Optimist and Recensionist: 'Common errors' or 'common variations'?," in *Latin Script and Letters A.D. 400–900*, ed. by John J. O'Meara and Bernd Nauman (Leiden, 1976), pp. 264–74, at p. 267. A more detailed discussion, with particular reference to nineteenth century practices, may be found in Sebastiano Timpanaro, *La genesi del metodo del Lachmann*, 2nd ed. (Padova, 1985), now available in an English translation by Glenn Most (Chicago, 2006). Whether it worked that way even in Lachmann's hands has been doubted; see, for example, P. L. Schmidt, "Lachmann's Method: On the History of a Misunderstanding," in *The Uses of Latin and Greek*, ed. by A. C. Dionisotti, A. Grafton, and J. Kaye [Warburg Institute Surveys and Texts, 16] (London, 1988), pp. 227–36. See also Giovanni Fiesoli, *La genesi del lachmannismo* (Firenze, 2000).

tually reconstructing what the text looked like before the traditions began to diverge.

The effort to apply the Lachmann method to *Corpus Iuris Civilis* was led by Theodor Mommsen, who set the example in his own edition of the Digest. A new edition of the Digest had long been a priority among jurists, but bringing it to fruition had been complicated by disputes about the relative weight that should be given to the great sixth-century manuscript belonging to the Biblioteca Laurenziana in Florence and the much newer manuscripts in the medieval tradition. While the Florentina [= **F**] was much closer in date to the original publication of the Digest, its text is also obviously defective in places. For such passages, moreover, the later manuscripts often offered readings that made good sense. For some of these passages, indeed, if one looked in enough of the later manuscripts (of which there are hundreds) it was possible to find several different plausible readings. Some of these variants must have reflected conjectures by medieval scholars, but were they all simply later emendations? Could not some of them have traced back to an authentic ancient tradition, different from the Florentina and, for these particular passages, superior to it? Such questions—at once textual (which reading was authentic) and historical (how did the medieval tradition take shape)—had posed an effective barrier to a critical edition of the Digest for hundreds of years.

In 1862, when Mommsen laid out the editorial procedures that he planned to apply to the Digest, he drew upon not only the editorial principles articulated by Lachmann but also Savigny's work and the Schrader transcripts.[27] Regarding the critical problem of the "Bolognese" or (as they would later be known) Vulgata manuscripts, he noted, first, that much of the confusion in the medieval manuscripts was due to the activities of medieval scholars: Savigny had extensively documented how, for a period as early as the twelfth century, glossators both inserted reading borrowed directly from **F** into their own manuscripts, and proposed conjectural emendations to improve difficult passages. Mommsen conceded, however, that not every reading in the medieval manuscripts could be dismissed as a conjecture, because Savigny had also demonstrated that there were 18 passages, none later than book

[27] Theodor Mommsen, "Über die kritische Grundlage unseres Digestentextes," in *Gesammelte Schriften*, vol. 2 (Berlin, 1905) [orig. pub. 1862], pp. 107–40.

33, where readings could be confirmed by Greek versions preserved in the Byzantine collections known as *Basilica*. Balancing these contradictory pieces of evidence, Mommsen hypothesized an Ur-manuscript of the Bolognese tradition that was independent of **F** although "closely related" [*nächst verwandt*] (p. 128) to it, as evidenced by shared faults when compared with the (very brief) excerpts preserved in early medieval manuscripts; he also supposed that this Ur-manuscript was complete only to D. 35.2.82 or, put another way, that it lacked the second half of the *Infortiatum* (known in the Middle Ages as the *Tres partes*) and the *Digestum Novum*. He concluded that, although collation of the Bolognese tradition with **F** could not be neglected, the amount of conjecture and emendation that had been incorporated into those manuscripts meant that not much positive yield was to be expected from it. (p. 129) He proposed, accordingly, to select such manuscripts "in which there had been the least contribution of conjectural criticism and borrowings from the *littera pisana*," (as the Florentina was known between the twelfth and fifteenth centuries, while it was in Pisa). He even provided an initial list of which those manu-scripts were.

Although in 1862 Mommsen claimed no more than that the lost Ur-manuscript was closely related to the Florentina, in his *editio maior* of 1870 he described that manuscript in rather different terms.[28] To begin with, he asserted that the manuscript, which he now called the Codex Secundus (= **S**), was a complete copy of the Digest in three or four parts from which all of the so-called vulgata manuscripts descended: that is, he included all of the *Infortiatum* and the *Novum* in this derivation, rather than supposing an archetype truncated in book 35. (pp. lxiiii–lv) This manuscript could not have been **F** itself, because the page breaks were wrong for those we see in the medieval divisions of the Digest, and because, he argued, **S** must have been written in "langobardic minuscule" rather than in the "squared letters" (uncial) of **F**. But, he argued, **S** must have been copied from **F**, both because of the errors shared by both manuscripts and because of errors present in the Bolognese tradition caused by problems particular to **F** itself. The awkward problem of the "authentic" readings in the medieval tradition, which Torelli and Agustín had not had to deal with, Mommsen accounted for by positing a medieval

[28] *Digesta Iustiniani Augusti*, ed. Th. Mommsen (Berlin, 1870), Praefatio, pp. v–lxxx.

redactor—"either Irnerius or someone earlier than Irnerius unknown to us" (p. lxviii)—who corrected **F**'s obvious errors, aided in places by another hypothetical manuscript complete only to book 34.

For Mommsen, in 1870, this hypothesis had the additional benefit of justifying the procedure he had already adopted of relying principally on **F**, with a very partial collation of a small number of medieval manuscripts. The *editio maior*, when it was published, provided even less information about the medieval manuscripts than he had originally promised. Thus, for the portions encompassing the *Digestum Vetus*, Mommsen collated **F** with only one manuscript, Paris, Bibliothèque Nationale, ms. lat. 4450 [= **P**], checking the readings in the three other manuscripts he used for this section of the Digest only when **F** and **P** differed; for the rest of the Digest, the collation of medieval manuscripts was even more restricted.[29] Doubts about the adequacy of this procedure arose at once, and specialists in classical Roman law ever since have doubted the validity of his stemma and his description of the hypothetical manuscript **S**.[30]

Even as work proceeded on the Digest, which Mommsen published in parts throughout the 1860s before issuing his *editio maior* in 1870, his young collaborator Paul Krüger began work on Justinian's Institutes and Code. In 1867, when he was just 27, Krüger published both a new edition of the Institutes and a critical study of the Code that was to be the basis of a full edition.[31] In these early works, Krüger

---

[29] As discussed by Robert Röhle, "*Digestorum Editio Maior* und Theodor Mommsen," BIDR, vol. 73 (1970): 19–34, at pp. 22–23.

[30] For contemporary criticisms of Mommsen's stemma, see among others Adolf August Rudorff, "Mommsen's Pandektenausgabe," *ZRG*, 6 (1867): 418–47, and Zacharia von Lingenthal, review of Mommsen's edition in *ZRG*, 10 (1872): 165–78. Among more recent critics, see Juan Miquel, "Mechanische Fehler in der Überlieferung der Digesten," in ZSS RA, 80 (1963): 233–86; Röhle, "*Digestorum Editio Maior* und Theodor Mommsen"; Hans van de Wouw, "Zur Textgeschichte des Infortiatum und zu seiner Glossierung durch die frühen Bologneser Glossatoren," *Ius Commune*, 11 (1984): 231–80; Franz Wieacker, "Mommsens *Digestorum Editio Maior*: Aspekte und Aporien," in *Le Pandette di Giustiniano. Storia e fortuna di un codice illustre.* [Accademia Toscana di Scienze e Lettere "La Colombaria": Studi 76] (Firenze, 1986), pp. 199–214; and various essays by Pietro Pescani, most recently "Origine delle lezioni della litera Bononiensis superiori a quella della litera Florentina," BIDR, 85 (1982): 205–82.

[31] *Institutiones* (Berlin, 1867); *Kritik des Justinianischen Codex* (Berlin, 1867), *Codex Iustinianus* (Berlin, 1877). For Krüger's career, see the memoir by Fritz Schulz, "Paul Krüger. Ein Nachruf," in ZSS RA, 47 (1927): IX–XXXIX; Schulz underlines the difficulties Krüger had throughout his whole career because he lacked the means to travel to important manuscript collections.

also relied almost exclusively on the materials gathered for Schrader. Indeed, his dependence on others for research funds (for he had few resources of his own) meant that he could see few manuscripts in person until he received a travel grant from the Savigny-Stiftung in 1868. For the Institutes, Krüger could do little except repeat the dates already proposed for the manuscripts, mostly by Schrader's researchers:

Table 1: Manuscripts of the *Institutiones* (Krüger)

Verona, Bib. Cap., XXXVIII (36) [excerpt]	VI
Berlin, Staatsbib., lat. 269 [excerpt]	IX
Bamberg, Staatsbib., Msc. Jur. 1	IX or X
Turin D.III.13	IX or X
Vercelli, Bib. cap., 122 [excerpt]	IX or X
Monte Cassino, Comp. Jur.	X or XI
Paris, Bib. nat., lat. 4421	XI
Bamberg, Jur. 2	XI or XII
Cologne, Historisches Archiv W. 328	XII

The errors for Bamberg Jur. 1, Turin D.III.13, and Paris 4421 have already been noted, and the same tendency toward excessively early attributions can be seen in the other manuscripts Krüger listed. The Monte Cassino manuscript, which was reconstructed out of leaves later used to bind other manuscripts, today is more correctly attributed to the second half of the eleventh century. Vercelli 122, a manuscript of the *Epitome Juliani* of the Novels with excerpts of the Institutes and the Code, turns out to be another manuscript in *minuscula romanesca*, which Supino attributed to the mid-eleventh century.[32] In contrast, the datings for Bamberg Jur. 2 and Cologne 328 change little: the Bamberg manuscript would be more properly described as XIex./XIIin., that is, within 25 years of 1100, while Cologne 328 is perhaps slightly later, from the early twelfth century. The attribution of the Verona fragment to the sixth century and the Berlin excerpt to the ninth are correct.

Even as Krüger was finishing his edition of the Institutes, he was turning his attention to Justinian's Code. This work posed far more complex problems than the rest of Justinian's codification. Except for

[32] Ciaralli, "Produzione manoscritta," pp. 83–90.

a lengthy but still very partial palimpsest preserved at Verona, there were no ancient manuscripts comparable to **F** that might anchor an edition. Nor were the manuscripts from the medieval universities as complete as those of the Institutes, for they omitted all constitutions in Greek, most of the inscriptions and subscriptions stating the legislative circumstances for the individual laws, and books nine through twelve (which were transmitted separately as the *Tres Libri*). Nor was it even apparent how the vulgata manuscripts related to one another—an essential point for the Lachmann method—since they did not even agree on the order of presenting the constitutions. Krüger concluded that the university-era manuscripts, rather than having a direct lineage with antique manuscripts, instead derived from a shortened version of the Code, known as the *Epitome Codicis*, that survived in a handful of earlier manuscripts: evidently medieval scholars had taken the Epitome as a base text, reinserting previously omitted materials until they had reconstructed (with some errors) Justinian's original text. He proposed, therefore, to concentrate on the manuscripts of the *Epitome Codicis*, relying on a small selection of the earliest manuscripts of the restored version to fill in the missing details.

In the *Kritik*, and later in his edition, Krüger described three epitomized manuscripts: Pistoia Arch. Cap. 66 (now ms. 106), which he attributed to the tenth century in accordance to received datings (Mommsen had recently described it as "*spätestens aus dem zehnten Jahrhundert*");[33] Paris, BN ms. lat. 4516, which he attributed to the eleventh century; and Darmstadt, Universitäts- und Landesbibliothek, 2000, a manuscript discovered a few years earlier by Mommsen and attributed by Krüger to the twelfth century. All of these descriptions necessarily were made by other scholars, since Krüger still had seen none of the manuscripts himself. Thus he refers to the facsimile of the Pistoia manuscript (p. 10), and he had to rely on Mommsen's notes even for the Darmstadt manuscript (p. 131).

The description of Pistoia 106, in many ways the key manuscript of the group, manifested a variety of errors. To begin with, rather than being the work of one (or two) hands as described in the Schrader tradition and repeated by Krüger in his *Kritik*, eight scribes participated in the writing of this manuscript; the supplemental constitutions

[33] Theodor Mommsen, "Zeitfolge der Verordnungen Diocletians und seiner Mitregenten," [originally published in 1860] in *Schriften*, vol. 2, pp. 195–298, at p. 197.

found in the margins were the work of more than twenty other copyists, while still others contributed the marginal and interlinear glosses. All of these hands are to be attributed to the second half of the eleventh century.[34] Paris, Bib. Nat. ms. lat. 4516 can be attributed to the last quarter of the eleventh century, while Darmstadt 2000 was copied at the end of the eleventh century or the beginning of the twelfth.

After receiving a travel grant to see manuscripts in person, Krüger corrected his most important errors on the Pistoia manuscript. In his 1877 edition of the Code he described it (with only a slight inaccuracy) as the work of nine different scribes; later that same year, moreover, in the much abbreviated apparatus to the stereotype edition of the entire *Corpus*, he changed the dating to read *X vel XI*.[35] Yet neither of these corrections really entered the historiography. Thus, when Luigi Chiappelli edited the Pistoia glosses in 1885, he still referred to the manuscript as a tenth-century production whose base text was the work of one principal scribe.[36]

Chiappelli's publication, entitled *La Glossa pistoiese*, briefly provided a further occasion for discussing the paleography of the Pistoia manuscript. Reviewing it, Krüger acerbically noted numerous errors and omissions, observing parenthetically that Chiappelli was not only unschooled in paleography, but that he was evidently unfamiliar with Krüger's own, fully annotated edition.[37] Hermann Fitting, the reviewer for the *Zeitschrift für Rechtsgeschichte*, even challenged Chiappelli's dating of the Pistoia manuscript, reporting that a paleographer to whom he had shown the photograph published by Chiappelli had dated the copyist's hand to the end of tenth century and the glosses to the eleventh; Fitting also remarked on similarities in usage between the Pistoia glosses and those found in the works of the eleventh-century Lombard jurists as well as other eleventh-century glosses to the

[34] In a personal communication, Petrucci expressed his concurrence with this dating; this manuscript is ascribed to the mid-eleventh century in the new catalogue, *I manoscritti medievali della provincia di Pistoia*, ed. by G. Murano, G. Savino, S. Zamponi (Tavernuzze, 1998), p. 43, no. 46 plates LV and B; S. Zamponi kindly informs us that Bischoff also suggested a later date for this manuscript.

[35] *Codex Iustinianus*, p. VI; *Codex Iustinianus (Corpus Iuris Civilis, editio stereotypa, vol. 2)*.

[36] Luigi Chiappelli, *La Glossa pistoiese al Codice giustinianeo tratta dal manoscritto capitolare di Pistoia* (Torino, 1885). See also Chiappelli, "Nuovo esame del manoscritto pistoiese del Codice giustinianeo," in *Studi e documenti di storia e diritto*, 6 (1885): 189–244.

[37] P. Krüger, in *Kritischen Vierteljahresschrift für Gesetzgebung und Rechtswissenschaft*, 28 (1886): 220–26.

Roman law.[38] Chiappelli could do little but accept these criticisms, admitting that there were several strata of glosses and that the great majority of them were later than the tenth-century, but this exchange, too, appears to have been entirely forgotten by subsequent scholars.[39]

One reason why Krüger's revised description of the Pistoia codex was overlooked appears to have been that scholars had already made up their minds about the circulation of the works of the *Corpus* in the early Middle Ages. The consensus appears to have emerged in the 1860s. Although in 1862 Mommsen could write about the re-emergence of the Digest during the ninth or tenth centuries, his edition effectively pushed the rediscovery of the Digest back to the late eleventh.[40] In the absence of the Digest, as Rudorff wrote in 1867, other works—including the Institutes, Code, and *Epitome Juliani*—had an "unchallenged dominance in the field of law" between Gregory the Great and Gregory VII.[41] Thus, by the time Krüger had begun to re-evaluate the manuscript evidence on which this judgment was based, the broader question was taken as settled and a new generation of legal scholars was already turning their attention away from the manuscripts of the *Corpus* to other historical problems. Young scholars would henceforth encounter manuscripts of the works of the *Corpus* not as a problem for research but as established facts to be used for other purposes.

The Historians

Fitting and Conrat

With the problems surrounding the *Corpus* itself apparently solved, much new research in the last decades of the nineteenth century was directed toward publishing early glosses to the *Corpus*, such as those in the Pistoia *Epitome Codicis* and the Bamberg and Turin *Institutes*, as well as numerous freestanding treatises. Since these works were transmitted

---

[38] H. Fitting, "Über neue Beiträge zur Geschichte der Rechtswissenschaft im früheren Mittelalter," ZSS RA, 7 (1886): 1–26.

[39] L. Chiappelli, "Neue Bemerkungen über die pistoieser Glosse zum Justinianischen Codex," ZSS RA, 8 (1887): 86–99.

[40] Mommsen, "Über die kritische Grundlage," p. 126; "Praefatio," pp. XIII-XIV. See also H. H. Jakobs, "Die große Zeit der Glossatoren," ZSS RA, 116 (1999): 222–58, at pp. 233–35.

[41] Rudorff, "Mommsen's Pandektenausgabe," p. 419.

anonymously, situating them into the history of legal learning often depended on what historians thought that history was. In the 1870s that debate about these broader issues found its focus in response to the thesis, vigorously sustained by Fitting for over twenty-five years, that a law school at Rome had preserved the traditions of classical jurisprudence throughout the early Middle Ages and that Irnerius had received his own education there. The evidence he offered in support of this extraordinary claim was quite modest: really little more than Odofredo's thirteenth-century account of the *translatio studii* from Rome to Ravenna to Bologna, supplemented by the claim that certain works, all of which are now regarded as dating from the twelfth century, had actually been written at Rome during the eleventh and possibly even by Irnerius himself.[42] Reading Fitting now, it is hard to believe that a thesis based on such a slender body of evidence ever had any real chance of success. Thanks to his persistence, however, his work ended up framing the discussion, as other historians set out to refute him by disproving any claim that there had been significant learning in the law before the eleventh or even the twelfth century.

One of the works written in response to Fitting was the scholarly masterpiece of the late nineteenth century, Max Conrat's *Geschichte der Quellen und Literatur des römischen Rechts im frühen Mittelalter*.[43] In contrast to Fitting's slim, lightly footnoted volumes, Conrat produced an exhaustive survey of the knowledge of Roman law between the fifth and twelfth centuries in 600 densely written, printed, and annotated pages. The scope of Conrat's inquiry went well beyond the circulation and use of Justinian's *Corpus*, because he examined any evidence suspected of revealing the survival of Roman law, including the influence of Roman legal rules and procedures on ecclesiastical and Germanic law and the circulation of Roman law compilations (notably the *Brevarium*) produced in Germanic Europe. Even by the standards of legal history, the result made for difficult reading (as the reviewer

[42] Among Fitting's works, the most important for his general thesis are: *Über die sogenannte Turiner Institutionenglosse und den sogenannten Brachylogus. Ein Beitrag zu der Geschichte des römischen Rechtes vom sechsten bis zum elften Jahrhundert* (Halle, 1870; repr. 1967); *Die Anfänge der Rechtsschule zu Bologna* (Berlin and Leipzig, 1888); and *Questiones de iuris subtilitatibus des Irnerius* (Berlin, 1894).

[43] Max Conrat, *Geschichte der Quellen und Literatur des römischen Rechts im frühen Mittelalter* (Leipzig, 1891).

for the *Zeitschrift der Savigny-Stiftung für Rechtsgeschichte* noted),[44] because while Conrat examined each individual piece of evidence, noting and discussing uncertainties about place and date of origin, he only rarely attempted to link different pieces of evidence or to provide general conclusions. Working back and forth through his analysis, moreover, is substantially complicated by the fact that this massive volume lacks an index: it had been deferred to a planned second volume that was never written. Nevertheless, Conrat's analysis may be taken as the definitive statement of how the evidence for the early medieval circulation of Justinian's texts seemed in the late nineteenth century, and in most respects it has not yet been superseded.

Although Conrat devoted three hundred pages to the period from the sixth to the tenth centuries, most of the evidence he found derived from sources other than the Justinianic codification. Conrat observed, for example, that outside of Italy Roman law was known almost exclusively through the Visigothic *Brevarium* and, to a lesser extent, the Latin collection of Novels known as the *Epitome Juliani*. For the rest of the *Corpus*, however, Conrat found only very limited evidence of its circulation.

1) In discussing the Code, Conrat commented that: "For the earlier period, the transmission of the first nine books of the Code is witnessed only by the sixth-century Veronese fragment that was written over in the seventh or eighth century and a few (*wenigen*) manuscripts of the *Epitome Codicis*, Pistoia 66 (10th century) and Paris 4516 (11th century), which lacked the *Tres Libri*. There are also only a small number of older manuscripts with excerpts from the Code." (Conrat cited here two manuscripts of the *Epitome Juliani* [Vercelli 122 and the *Codex Utinensis*, now Leipzig, Universitätsbibliothek 3493 & 3494 = Hänel 8 & 9], Paris 4421 of the Institutes [he refers to Schrader for the description], and a Viennese canon law manuscript in which one constitution from the Code had later been copied.)[45] Finally, one manuscript survives of the drastically shortened version of the Code known as the *Summa Perusina*.

2) For the Institutes, Conrat acknowledged that there were only a few excerpts to be found in other lawbooks; he cited Berlin lat.

---

[44] L. Seuffert in ZSS RA, 13 (1892): 366–76 at p. 366.

[45] *Geschichte*, p. 54. Although the Viennese manuscript mentioned by Conrat, ÖNB ms. 2147, is indeed a ninth-century manuscript, C. 7.38.2 was written on the bottom of f. 4r only in the eleventh century.

269, a ninth-century manuscript of the *Epitome Juliani* that contained brief excerpts from both the Institutes and the Digest, and the *codex Utinensis*. The manuscript tradition itself, moreover, was "scanty" (*dürftig*), because with the sixth-century fragment in Verona having been palimpsested at an early date "only two manuscripts can be said with confidence to have survived from before the eleventh century: Bamberg D.II.13 [= Jur. 1] (IX/X century) and Turin D.III.15 (IX century)."[46]

3) For documentary evidence, charters, and letters, Conrat could do no more than cite a few pages of Savigny's *Geschichte* discussing four documents ranging in date from the eighth to tenth century that mention laws contained in Justinian's legislation. Conrat further noted that, although Rome was one of the few cities where Roman law remained in force, papal documents mentioned Lombard law more frequently than they did Roman law.[47] Finally, he noticed that the *Summa Perusina* is cited in a handful of documents from around Rome from the late tenth and early eleventh century.

4) The Novels and some passages from the first four books of the Code and from the Institutes, were excerpted in three collections apparently for ecclesiastical use, all from the ninth century: the *Lex Romana canonice compta*, which itself appears to have been the source for the Roman material in the *Collectio Anselmo dedicata*, and the so-called Bobbio excerpts. The Novels alone were used in two other collections evidently compiled for the use of the clergy.

5) Finally, for literature on Justinian's law-books, Conrat was forced back again to the glosses in the earliest manuscripts of the Code and Institutes. For the Institutes, he could cite only the glosses contained in the Bamberg and Turin manuscripts, although he believed that some of these originated in the sixth century, having been copied with the text of the Institutes, and that others should be attributed to the eleventh century. In addition to the glosses, he found worth mentioning only an epitome of the Institutes, of unknown origin, contained in a ninth-century manuscript; but he concluded that the collection

---

[46] *Geschichte*, p. 57.

[47] Conrat, *Geschichte*, p. 51 and n. 2, which cites Savigny, vol. ii, pp. 227–29, 232–38, in which most of the documents were subsequent to 1000. The document cited in note *a* on p. 226 is now attributed to the twelfth rather than the eighth century; see E. Besta, "Il diritto romano nella contesa tra i vescovi di Siena e di Arezzo," in *Archivio storico italiano*, 5th ser. 37 (1906): 61–92.

was of little legal or historical significance because the text was seriously corrupted and lacked even an indication of the source from which the material was taken. For the Code, except for the *Summa Perusina*, all of the evidence came from the Pistoia, Paris, and Darmstadt manuscripts of the *Epitome Codicis*, which Conrat considered both for the glosses and for the effort to reconstitute the complete text by reinserting the missing legislation. As usual, the evidence for the *Epitome Juliani* was more abundant; Vercelli ms. 122, misattributed to the tenth century, played a role here as well, but the bulk of Conrat's material was drawn from other, authentically ninth- and tenth-century manuscripts.

To assess the effect of the earlier manuscript work on the first part of Conrat's *History*, one need only compare Table 2, giving the dates he used, with Table 3 [see p. 22] summarizing the results of our work on the same manuscripts. Virtually all of the evidence for the circulation of the *Corpus* (excepting always the *Epitome Juliani*) disappears: there are no manuscripts of the Institutes from before the early eleventh century nor of the Code before the mid-eleventh. The absence of manuscript evidence is rendered more important, moreover, by the modest quantity of other evidence that Conrat was able to find for the circulation of either the Institutes and Code: only a tiny handful of documents (one of the most important of which is now held to be eleventh century) and a few compilations for ecclesiastical use. Conrat himself felt the disparity in his evidence, expressing some perplexity that the work that had gone into copying and commenting on the surviving manuscripts of the *Corpus*, "which were prepared for juristic ends and predestined to open juristic discussion," had so little echo elsewhere. All in all, he concluded, "the early medieval literature to the Justinian enactment turns out to be at a very low level."[48]

[48] "Man darf danach Produkte wie jene Glossen nicht direkt zur Charakteristik der juristische Literatur des früheren Mittelalters zu den Rechtsbüchern Justinians verwenden. Dass indes die Handschriften der Rechtsbücher, welche doch zu juristischen Zwecken angefertigt wurden und zur Aufnahme juristischer Erörterungen über die Rechtbücher prädestiniert waren, jenem Umsetzungs- und Ergänzungsprozesse, und dazu mit so wenig Erfolg unterworfen werden konnten, lässt darauf schliessen, was wir von den juristischen Erörterungen zu erwarten haben; zugleich aber zeigen sie uns im Verhältnis zu den Handschriften, welche zur Verfügung stehen, wie spärlich die juristischen Erörterungen im Vergleich zu jenen exoterischen vertreten sind und zudem, wie nahe die ersteren den letzteren stehen. Alles in allem befindet sich sonach die Literatur des früheren Mittelalters zur Justinianischen Gesetzgebung auf einer sehr niedrigen Stufe." *Geschichte*, p. 204.

Table 2: Nineteenth-century ms. datings (Schrader/Mommsen/Krüger)

	IX	IX/X	X	X/XI	XI	XI/XII	XII
Institutiones	Bamb. Jur. 1 Turin D.III.13 Berlin 269 *Vercelli 122* *Leip. 3493/3494*		*M. Cassino Comp.		Bamb. Jur. 2 Paris lat. 4421	Cologne 328	
Codex	*Vercelli 122* *Leip. 3493/3494*		†Pistoia 106		†Paris lat. 4516	M. Cassino 49 Berlin 273	†Darmst. 2000
Digesta	*Berlin 269*					Paris lat. 4450 Vat. lat 1406 *M. Cassino 49* *Berlin 273*	

Table 3: Corrected datings of manuscripts known in the nineteenth century

	IX	IX/X	X	X/XI	XI	XI/XII	XII
Institutiones	Berlin 269 *Leip. 3493/3494*				Turin D.III.13 *M. Cassino Comp.	Bamb. Jur. 2	Paris 4421 Cologne 328
Codex	*Leip. 3493/3494*				†Pistoia 106 †Paris 4516 *Vercelli 122*	Berlin 273 †Darmst. 2000	M. Cassino 49
Digesta	*Berlin 269*				Vat. lat. 1406 Paris lat. 4450 (XI ex.)	*Berlin 273*	

Excerpt *Fragment †Epitome Codicis

The misattributions of these manuscripts to the earlier period had a second, less obvious effect on Conrat's work, because they could not be given their proper weight in his consideration of the eleventh-century—the period he called the Übergangzeit in recognition of the importance of that period. Much of this section, which comprises nearly half of the entire book, was concerned with showing that the *Brachylogus* and *Exceptiones Petri*, which some scholars (notably Fitting, but also Savigny) had believed early medieval in origin, in fact dated from the twelfth century. Even after removing those works from consideration, however, Conrat found a great deal of other evidence to demonstrate that the study of Roman law was undergoing a substantial revival in the eleventh century. The evidence of particular importance to his discussion included:

1) the glosses and other materials in Cologne Historisches Archiv ms. W 328, a manuscript containing the Institutes and *Epitome Juliani.* These evidently were written by a jurist in the Lombardist tradition and, in addition to demonstrating that the Institutes were being studied, also cite the Code and Digest as well as the Novels.[49]

2) the glosses to the Turin Institutes, some of which he believed must date from the eleventh or early twelfth century.[50]

3) the references to the *Corpus* in a series of works devoted to the Lombard law collection known as the *Liber Legis Langobardorum* or *Liber Papiensis.* These included, in addition to marginal glosses contained in the manuscripts of these works, a handful of citations in a group of opuscula known as the *Quaestiones ac monita*, and the numerous citations to all four works of the *Corpus* found in two book-length commentaries from the second half of the eleventh century, the *Walcausina* and *Expositio.*[51]

4) a literature on the Roman law in the form of freestanding brief treatises, such as those on the *actio mutui* and the varieties of legal actions included in Cologne ms. 328, again evidently originating with the jurists of Lombard law.[52]

---

[49] *Geschichte*, pp. 333–40, esp. pp. 333–35; on the relationship between the Cologne glosses and lombardist jurisprudence, see pp. 419–20.

[50] *Geschichte*, pp. 340–45.

[51] For the Walcausina and the *Expositio*, see Radding, *The Origins of Medieval Jurisprudence: Pavia and Bologna, 850–1150* (Yale University Press, 1988), with citations to the earlier literature. For the Walcausina in particular, see Radding, "*Petre te appellat Martinus.* Eleventh-century judicial procedure as seen through the glosses of Walcausus," in *La Giustizia nell'Alto medioevo II (secoli IX–XI), XLIV Settimana di studio sull'Alto Medioevo, Spoleto, 11–17 aprile 1996* (Spoleto, 1997), pp. 827–61.

[52] *Geschichte*, pp. 595–600.

5) from the last fifteen years of the eleventh century, the incorporation of some passages from the Roman law into canonistic literature. Examples include some excerpts from the Code that were incorporated into a canon law collection attributed to Anselm of Lucca in the 1080s, and excerpts from the Digest in the *Collectio Britannica* of the 1090s. Conrat, however, concluded that the employment of Roman law in Italian canon law literature was still sparse ("*nur spärliche*").[53]

With this evidence in mind, and despite the exclusion of important manuscript evidence and glosses misdated to an earlier period, Conrat underlined the importance of the eleventh century on the final page of his great work.

> The literature of the *Übergangzeit* is essentially a literature . . . on the Justinianic law-books, and as such not merely abbreviated and glossed but with source material also restored, especially from the Digest. Demonstrably [*nachweislich*] it was on the soil of Lombardist northern Italy that such a literature developed, and even a Romanist literature, which in its form is independent of the law-books, and finally a literature in which Roman sources were placed in service of Lombardist legal collections. All these branches of Lombardist production give the picture of a progressive literary development. Thus one may describe the eleventh century as the period when a Renaissance of Roman law occurred in Lombardy.[54]

In contrast, he found little evidence of any significant juristic activity in contemporary Ravenna.

For Conrat, therefore, the essential contrast between the early Middle Ages and the eleventh century lay in the evidence that Justinian's *Corpus* had found readers among legal professionals. For them, Justinian's works represented not merely texts to be quoted (as the popes occasionally had done in their letters) but legal principles to be understood and applied. Nor had he any doubt who these legal professionals were. Although he conceded that some of this literature was produced for ecclesiastical purposes, the developments he thought most important took place among the eleventh century Lombardists who brought new pieces of the Corpus back into circulation, employed it in their interpretations of Lombard law, and studied it for its own sake. What made their work especially important, moreover, was the

[53] *Geschichte*, p. 378.
[54] *Geschichte*, p. 626.

increase over time in the complexity and skill of this literature, evidence that the scholars who produced it were not simply repeating a static body of knowledge.

The message was not lost on early readers of Conrat's work,[55] and it appears to have been the dominant view at the time. Thus Krüger, writing in 1888, similarly stressed the importance of the Lombardist jurists.[56] But it turned out that this first volume was virtually Conrat's last word on the subject. Turning his attention to the earlier period of Roman law, he left the early Middle Ages and the juristic renaissance to others.

Kantorowicz and After

Although the evidence available for discussing the circulation of the *Corpus Iuris Civilis* is little changed now from what it was when Conrat wrote, it will also be obvious that his own conclusions are rather different from what is usually taught today. Although Conrat was attentive to the Digest, and skeptical about the extent of its circulation in the early Middle Ages, he did not see its reappearance as in itself marking a break. Rather, his designation of the eleventh century as the "period of transition" rested on the sudden abundance of many kinds of evidence attesting to the revival of legal studies.

In fact, the "modern" interpretation emerged only in the next generation of scholars, those who came of age around or after 1890. The concerns of these scholars differed from those of their predecessors in several important ways. To begin with, unlike Conrat, Krüger, and still earlier historians, they were not immersed in the manuscripts of the *Corpus*; that work had been done, and they accepted the results without feeling it necessary to work through all of the evidence themselves. They were also, naturally enough, more reverential toward their intellectual predecessors than those men's contemporaries had been. Mommsen's hypothesis of the Codex Secundus had been received with open skepticism at the time he proposed it, even by Rudorff to whom his edition was eventually dedicated; but to the young men of the early twentieth century he was not a colleague but a legend. It is also significant that Fitting's theories, despite having been thoroughly

---

[55] See, for example, Seuffert's review, p. 376.
[56] *Geschichte*, p. 381.

discredited by 1890, continued to exercise a hold on the imaginations of scholars, serving them as a straw man for the entire twentieth century.

Sharing in all of these attitudes was the man who emerged as the dominant force in the new generation of legal historians, and who was personally largely responsible for shaping the modern orthodoxy on the juristic renaissance: Hermann Kantorowicz (1877–1940).[57] Kantorowicz was a jurist with wide interests who made important contributions to the philosophy and sociology of law and, during the interwar period, to the debate on international politics. His reputation in these areas doubtless lent authority to his work on legal history, which was merely a sideline for him; indeed, a recent biography of him barely mentions it at all.[58] And his training in medieval history appears to have been modest because, despite the confidence with which he wrote about technical issues in paleography and codicology, his work in those areas is marked with the most elementary errors. For example, he boldly explained the peculiar fact that the earliest manuscripts of the *Digestum Vetus* ended in mid-sentence by a *horror vacui* on the part of a scribe who could not leave any space blank; in actual practice, since books were not bound until the copying was complete, scribes simply added additional fascicles as needed to arrive at the end of the book.[59] But the impact of Kantorowicz's work on legal history is undeniable, and the emphasis on the Digest typical of the twentieth century can be traced directly to him.

Kantorowicz's first major work in legal history, published in two parts in 1909 and 1910, dealt with the transmission of the Digest.[60] Sub-titling his monograph *Ergänzungen zu Mommsen* (supplements to Mommsen), Kantorowicz remarked in his introduction that Mommsen's thesis remained inviolable in its main points," and that he intended

[57] A biographical note on Kantorowicz is included in Gerd Kleinheyer and Jan Schneider, *Deutsche Juristen aus fünf Jahrhunderten*, 3. Auflage (Heidelberg, 1989), pp. 146–50; it is an indication of Kantorowicz's importance that he is the youngest jurist included and the only one from the twentieth century.

[58] Karlheinz Muscheler, *Hermann Ulrich Kantorowicz. Eine Biographie* (Berlin, 1984).

[59] For a devastating critique of the paleography Kantorowicz put forth in his last book, see the review by F. Patetta, a near contemporary of Kantorowicz and a connoisseur and collector of medieval manuscripts, in BIDR, vol. 5 n.s.: 436–44 [repr. in *Studi sulle fonti giuridiche medievali*, G. Astuti, ed. (Torino, 1967), pp. 1011–19.]

[60] Hermann Kantorowicz, *Über die Entstehung der Digestenvulgata* (Weimar, 1910) [originally published as a two-part article in ZSS RA, 30 (1909): 183–271 and 31 (1910): 14–88].

to provide a better grounding for Mommsen's authoritative opinions.[61] Although as part of his discussion Kantorowicz also reexamined the Florentina, the bulk of his work was dedicated to the hypothetical Codex Secundus: the manuscript on which it was based, where and when it was produced, the emendations introduced by its hypothetical redactor, and its eventual division into three parts to produce the Digest as it was studied in the Middle Ages. For the most part, Kantorowicz based his account of the Codex Secundus on a comparison between the readings reported by Mommsen's edition for the Florentina and the earliest manuscripts in the later medieval tradition; he did little new work on the manuscripts themselves, nor had he much to add to Conrat's discussion of the pre-1100 literature.

What made Kantorowicz's work important was his bold linking of the fate of the Digest with the studium of Bologna. He saw the rediscovery of the Digest not only as the key event in the juristic revival, but as one that owed nothing to previous developments. This event, moreover, he saw inextricably linked to the *studium* of Bologna itself, even suggesting (despite real implausibility in dating) that the unknown scholar who had produced the codex Secundus was none other than Irnerius himself. Kantorowicz found few scholars willing to accept this last conclusion, but many of the points he made in support of it did enter the subsequent scholarly literature. Notably successful was his confident description of the unknown redactor as a "philologist" (taking up a suggestion of Mommsen, and with an eye to Odofredo's thirteenth-century description of Irnerius as a "master of the arts"): readers familiar with eleventh-century culture might have pounced on the idea that eleventh-century rhetoric or grammar was remotely similar to "philology," but this characterization won a wide circulation among legal historians. Similarly influential was Kantorowicz's rejection of Conrat's conclusion that the Digest had begun to circulate among Lombardist jurists soon after 1050—a date much too early for Irnerius.

Kantorowicz's ability to present his most radical innovations as a return to the great masters of the past, already evident in the monograph on the Digest, was employed still more dramatically in his 1912 obituary of Max Conrat. Praising Conrat generously—"[who would write legal history henceforth] must build on Conrat's ground, using

[61] *Digestenvulgata*, pp. 2–3.

Conrat's materials, and following Conrat's methods"[62]—he at the same time transformed Conrat's masterpiece into an image of his own ideas. The idea of an Übergangzeit, which had been central to Conrat's book, Kantorowicz dismissed out of hand as a "vague and false opinion" that failed adequately to recognize the importance of "the discovery of the Digest and the appearance of the genius Irnerius."[63] More astonishing, perhaps, is that when summarizing the results of Conrat's *Geschichte* Kantorowicz not only omitted any reference to Conrat's conclusions pointing toward the Lombardist jurists of the eleventh century; he actually attributed to Conrat the position that the "great moment" of legal history came "when the Codex Pisanus [= F] rose from the grave and created the first of the Bolognese masters, with no teacher to call their own except the ancient Romans themselves."[64] The last phrase evidently was a formulation Kantorowicz particularly liked, because he would restate it years later near the end of his life in his book on the bolognese glossators.[65]

In 1914, Kantorowicz made his ideas explicit in a bold essay on the periods of legal history. Describing the rediscovery of the Florentine Digest, which by chance had survived intact, he continued:

> And a further chance was that a copy of this manuscript, which today is found in Florence, fell into the hands of a genius, whom some have tried to identify as the same grammarian Guarnerius of Bologna who would later . . . be known as Irnerius. At first, this man studied the book with the eyes of a philologist: he compared his text with a collection of excerpts dating back to Justinian's time, and with excellent judgment combined them in a new text, the vulgate of the Digest, which was to remain valuable until the nineteenth century. From this manuscript there then derived all [subsequent] Digest manuscripts without exception. But one who reads and understands the Digest is known as a jurist, and thus our philological jurist wrote down the results of his studies in numerous glosses.[66]

---

[62] H. Kantorowicz, "Max Conrat (Cohn) und die mediävistische Forschung," ZSS RA, 33 (1912): 417–73, at p. 473.

[63] "Max Conrat," 440–41.

[64] ". . . nach der Mitte des elften Jahrhunderts der große Moment ein großes Geschlecht: der Codex Pisanus steigt aus dem Grabe, und die ältesten Bolognesen erschaffen, ohne andere Lehrmeister zu besitzen als die Römer . . .," Kantorowicz, "Max Conrat," p. 448.

[65] *Studies in the Glossators of the Roman Law* (Cambridge, 1938), p. 3.

[66] "Die Epochen der Rechtswissenschaft" (1914), repr. in H. Kantorowicz, *Rechtshistorische Schriften*, ed. Helmut Coing and Gerhard Immel (Karlsruhe, 1970), p. 3.

From the Digest, Kantorowicz explained, Irnerius eventually moved on to the Code, which previously had been known only in excerpts, until the enterprise of legal study had been set on a firm footing.

By the mid-1910s, therefore, virtually all elements linking the Digest to the juristic revival were in place except one—the Beneventan script of the hypothetical Codex Secundus. The practice of determining the script of a lost manuscript was a feature of the Lachmann method, the idea being that a scribe might misread certain letters or combinations of letters written in a script he was unfamiliar with. In imitation of this practice, Mommsen had suggested that the Codex Secundus had been written in "langobardic" script.[67] We shall see in chapter six that Mommsen's evidence on this point fell well short of what would have been needed to make it, but at the time his remarks were significant only as a minor piece in his argument that the Bolognese tradition derived from an intermediate manuscript rather than directly from **F**: he offered the suggestion in a brief passage, and employed it not at all in choosing readings for his edition. His ascription to langobardic script was then occasionally repeated by subsequent writers, and Kantorowicz discussed it in detail in his work on the vulgate Digest.

What gave Mommsen's hypothesis historical significance was Lowe's description in 1914 of "Beneventan" script, a pre-caroline or (in nineteenth-century terminology) "langobardic" script that remained in use in southern Italy into the thirteenth century and beyond. Describing the Codex Secundus as written in Beneventan script was a subtle error, because Beneventan was not a new name for the nineteenth-century "langobardic" but rather a subset of it; yet it had the important effect of attributing the Codex Secundus to a specific geographical provenance. The next step was taken in the 1960s when, at the end of a long article dealing with copying errors in the textual tradition of the Digest, Juan Miquel observed that if Codex Secundus were written in Beneventan, a likely provenance for it would be the great scriptorium of Monte Cassino under Abbot Desiderius.[68] Other than the later use of the Digest by Ivo of Chartres, an author who like Desiderius was close to the papal reform movement,[69] Miquel

---

[67] *Digesta Iustiniani Augusti*, Praefatio, p. LXV.
[68] Miquel, "Mechanische Fehler," pp. 282–83.
[69] The suggestion of a link between the papal reform movement and the rediscovery

offered no real evidence in support of this suggestion. Nonetheless, it was an idea that entered the standard interpretation of the juristic renaissance, being repeated by prominent legal historians including Peter Weimar,[70] and eventually Kuttner. Other historians, such as Ennio Cortese, have been less satisfied with the evidence for Mommsen's Codex Secundus, but they too have continued to repeat Kantorowicz's insistence that the rediscovery of the Digest marked a crucial moment in the juristic renaissance.

Although literature on the Digest has proliferated during the twentieth century to the extent that it defies any brief summary, scholarly opinion on the rest of the *Corpus Iuris Civilis* stands virtually where it did when Conrat wrote a century ago. Throughout the twentieth century, indeed, the leading authorities on legal history continued to assert that, even if the Digest was unknown in the early Middle Ages, Justinian's other works circulated during those centuries, at least in Italy,[71] and this continues to be the view universally held today. Even the evidence cited remains the same as it was in Conrat's time: the manuscripts or rather the datings assigned to them in the early nineteenth century. Thus, in the 1950s, F. Calasso confidently discussed the Pistoia Code and its glosses as evidence that the Code was being studied in the tenth century and perhaps even earlier, noting that the glosses may have been copied from another source.[72] In his own recent survey, Cortese similarly documents the circulation of the *Epitome Codicis* in the tenth century with a reference to Pistoia 106 and (citing articles published a century ago), he continued commenting that Bamberg and Turin manuscripts of the Institutes may have been only a little earlier.[73] The nineteenth-century datings survive in a

of the Digest had been made before, by the noted historian of canon law Paul Fournier, "Un tournant de l'histoire du droit, 1060–1140," *Nouvelle Revue historique de droit français et étranger*, 41 (1917): 129–80 at 151–53. Miquel does not, however, cite Fournier's article.

[70] Peter Weimar, "Die legistische Literatur der Glossatorenzeit," in *Handbuch der Quellen und Literatur der neueren europäischen Privatrechtsgeschichte, I. Mittelalter (1100–1500). Die Gelehrten Rechte und die Gesetzebung*, ed. by Helmut Coing (Munich, 1973), pp. 129–260.

[71] See, for example, Calasso, *Medio Evo del Diritto*, pp. 285–94; G. Astuti, "Tradizione dei testi del Corpus Iuris Civilis nell'alto medio evo", in *Tradizione romanistica e civiltà giuridica europea*, ed. Giovanni Diurni [Ius Nostrum. Studi e testi pubblicati dall'Istituto del Diritto Italiano dell'Università di Roma, 2a serie, 1] (Rome, 1984), pp. 171–236, at pp. 182–200;

[72] *Medio Evo del Diritto*, pp. 289–90.

[73] Cortese, *Diritto nella storia medievale*, pp. 239–40, 242. Similarly Lange, *Römisches Recht*, pp. 10–15, 60–86.

perfect state of preservation even in the more technical literature, such as the lengthy appendix of a recent article by G. Santini.[74]

A final irony comes from the fact that, despite the crucial role played by a small group of manuscripts in the historiography of the *Corpus Iuris Civilis*, there has also been a continuous discussion doubting whether those same manuscripts have been dated correctly. Already in the 1870s, as we have seen, Krüger acknowledged the possibility that the Pistoia *Epitome Codicis* could be as late as the eleventh century. Then, at the turn of the century, Patetta suggested that the Bamberg and Pistoia codices could all be as late as the eleventh century;[75] Patetta's remarks, however, took the form of individual asides to discussions of the glosses in those manuscripts and he seems never to have recognized the implications that such dates might have on broader questions. More recently, in an article published posthumously on the transmission of Justinian's corpus, Guido Astuti echoed Patetta's doubts about the dating of the Bamberg and Pistoia codices, going on to remark that the Turin and the reconstructed Monte Cassino manuscripts of the Institutes might also more properly be attributed to the eleventh century.[76] None of those doubts had any impact on his overall interpretation of the history of those works, however, and he confidently reasserted that traditional view that the Institutes and Code circulated in early medieval Italy.

Conclusion: From Paleography to History

During the twentieth century, legal historians have been virtually unanimous in repeating a history of Roman law that contrasts the near total obscurity of the Digest between the sixth and eleventh centuries with the broader circulation of the other books of the *Corpus Iuris Civilis*. We have seen in this chapter, however, that even as this history has achieved the status of a received wisdom, the facts on which

[74] G. Santini, "Il sapere giuridico occidentale e la sua trasmissione dal VI all'XI secolo," *Rivista di Storia del Diritto Italiano*, 67 (1994): 91–205.

[75] On Bamberg Jur. 1, see "Contributi alla storia del diritto romano," BIDR, 4 (1892): 249–86 at 265 [*Studi*, p. 137]; on Pistoia 106, see "Di un nuovo manoscritto del Codice Epitomato," BIDR, 7 (1895): 203–24, at p. 205 n. 1 [*Studi*. p. 221]. Patetta makes it clear that he understood the previous discussion of this last manuscript to have placed it no earlier than the *late* tenth century.

[76] "Tradizione dei testi," pp. 184–85, 189.

it was originally based appear to have receded from the consciousness of scholars. Few appear to realize that the manuscript datings still cited today were the work of scholars from the first third of the nineteenth century: Schrader's *équipe*. Nor does it even seem to be remembered how little other evidence there is for the circulation of the Code and Institutes before the eleventh century, so that scholars in one place can narrate the standard history of the Corpus, while in another they express their doubts about the very manuscript datings on which that history was based. Many of these doubts have been confirmed by our own census of the early manuscripts of the *Corpus Iuris Civilis*.

It should not be thought that one of our purposes in undertaking this census was to introduce paleographical issues into the study of legal history. The paleography was always there—for Conrat as well as for Mommsen and Krüger. Nor does the census itself tell us what circulation the different works of the *Corpus* had. That would be claiming too much, because surviving manuscripts are just one category of evidence showing that texts were known and read. Yet the census does reopen a wide range of historical questions. The narrowest concerns the texts: when and where were they known? how intensively were they studied? With these particular texts, however, or at least with the Code and Digest, the questions do not stop there. One must also try to understand how history accounts for the complexities of the surviving manuscripts—the same problem that made them so difficult to edit when that was last done in the nineteenth century. Finally, and most generally, one must attempt to relate the history of these important texts to the history of medieval learning generally. What led to these works, difficult as they are, being taken up again in the eleventh and twelfth centuries? who did the work? what attracted them to these texts? and how did their background affect the shape they gave the texts as they passed them on to the later Middle Ages and eventually to us?

In addressing these historical problems, our focus throughout will be on the three works of the Justinianic codification: the Institutes, the Code, and the Digest. Less attention will be given to the Novels, the fourth work making up what is now known as the *Corpus Iuris Civilis*, which circulated in the version known as the *Epitome Juliani* until the twelfth century. Not only has the *Epitome Juliani* recently been the subject of a detailed monograph by Wolfgang Kaiser,[77] but its history in the early Middle Ages was (as we shall see) very different from that of the rest of the *Corpus*. Our first task will be understanding how that history looks when the manuscript evidence has been brought up to date.

[77] Wolfgang Kaiser, *Die Epitome Iuliani: Beiträge zum römischen Recht im frühen Mittelalter und zum byzantinischen Rechtsunterricht* (Frankfurt/Main, 2004).

CHAPTER TWO

THE *CORPUS IURIS CIVILIS* IN THE EARLY MIDDLE AGES

Justinian's project of codifying Roman law began in 528, shortly after his accession to the throne. The original idea was to replace earlier compilations such as the *Codex Theodosianus* from 438 with a new one that would include more recent constitutions while eliminating contradictions and obsolete rules. The commission of ten jurists appointed to carry out this task must have worked quickly, because the emperor was able to enact his *Novus Codex Justinianus* into law in April 529.

Evidently pleased with his role as a legislator, Justinian constituted a second law commission in December 530. Led by the jurist Tribonian, who had participated in the compilation of the *Novus Codex Justinianus*, this commission was charged with collecting and organizing the work of earlier jurisconsults, the most important of whom had been active before 250 AD. The work of this commission was still going on when Justinian additionally directed it to prepare an introduction to the law appropriate for students just beginning their studies. This work, the *Institutiones* or Institutes, was issued in November 533, a month before the *Digesta* or *Pandectae* in fifty books was itself brought to completion. Tribonian and his associates then revised the Code, incorporating legislation issued since 529 and making it consistent with the Institutes and Digest. This second edition of the Code (the *Codex repetitae praelectionis*), issued in November 534, is what is now known as the *Codex Justinianus*.

Distinct from Justinian's codification are the collections of his later legislation known as the Novels. Unlike the Institutes, the Code, and the Digest, these were private collections. The version that circulated in early medieval Europe was the *Epitome Juliani*, a Latin version of 124 laws from 535 to 555 compiled by a Julian who taught law in Constantinople.[1] The *Epitome Juliani* won, as we shall see, a considerable circulation in early medieval Europe, although it would be supplanted during the twelfth century by a somewhat larger collection

---

[1] Gustav Haenel, *Iuliani Epitome latina Novellarum Iustiniani* (Lipsiae, 1873).

of 134 novels, also in Latin, known as the *Authenticum*. The fifteenth century would bring west two other, Greek collections but these, as well as the *Authenticum*, lie outside the scope of this study. It was only after the Middle Ages that the Justinianic law books—the Institutes, Code, Digest, and Novels—came to be known as the *Corpus Iuris Civilis*, a term we adopt here for ease in discussion.

Justinian's legislation was not formally applied to Italy until the Pragmatic Sanction of 554, nearly twenty years after the original reconquest, although some historians think that it may have begun to circulate there possibly as early as 540.[2] We know, too, that the texts themselves arrived in Italy because the majority of the surviving sixth-century evidence has links to Italy. The *Codices Latini Antiquiores*, E. A. Lowe's authoritative catalog of pre-ninth-century Latin books, lists twelve sixth-century books and book fragments of the various works of the Justinianic codification, plus another described as *saec. VI–VII* from the turn of the sixth to seventh centuries. Of these, six are of the Digest, four of the Code (including one of the first editions of the Code), and one of the Institutes. [See Table 4]

If fragments recovered in Egypt are excluded from Lowe's list, the remaining six manuscripts all appear to have spent time in Italy; except for the Pommersfelden fragment of the Digest (*CLA* 1351), they are still there today. The three palimpsests (*CLA* 495, 513, 1167) were all rewritten in Italy in the early Middle Ages. The Florentina (*CLA* 293), similarly, was in Italy at an early date, although it apparently was not copied there.[3] The Pommersfelden fragment of five leaves from a papyrus Digest, finally, comes to us as part of a collection of materials that apparently originated in Ravenna.[4] It is also worth noting that the Digest is the best-represented work of the four within the *Corpus*, a fact that should caution us against assuming that because the Digest was difficult it must have been rare.

---

[2] Cortese, *Diritto nella storia medievale*, pp. 109–12.

[3] The case for an Italian origin of the Florentina was argued by Guglielmo Cavallo and Francesco Magistrale, "Libri e scritture del diritto nell'età di Giustiniano," *Index*, 15 (1987): 97–110, at pp. 105–6, but Wolfgang Kaiser's demonstration that eight correctors worked on the manuscript, as well as four readers who offered emendations, suggests that it originated in an administrative center larger than any that can readily be imagined for Byzantine Italy. See Kaiser, "Schreiber und Korrektoren des Codex Florentinus," ZSS RA, 118 (2001): 133–219.

[4] J.-O. Tjäder, "Ein Verhandlungsprotokol aus dem J. 433 n. Chr.," *Scriptorium*, 12 (1958): 3–43.

Table 4: Manuscripts and fragments of the *Corpus Iuris Civilis* listed in the *Codices Latini Antiquiores*

Institutes

CLA IV, 495: Verona, Bib. cap. XXXVIII (36) 3 leaves, rewritten in Verona, saec. IX.	Uncial, saec. VI–VII

Code

CLA III, 293: Florence, Bib. Laur. P.S. I., S.N. Fragment from a papyrus codex containing the first edition of Justinian's code.	Uncial, saec. VI
CLA IV, 513: Verona, Bib. cap. LXII (60) [fol. 4–81] Palimpsest, primary script VI saec., rewritten in VIII saec. in north Italian center, probably Verona.	Uncial, saec. VI
CLA V, 700: Paris, Sorbonne, Inst. de papyrologie, *Pap. Reinach 2219* Fragment of Cod., book XII.	Uncial, saec. VIII
CLA VIII, 1167: Hist. arch. GB Kasten B.ro. 130 Palimpsest rewritten in saec. VII, probably in Italy.	Uncial, saec. VI
Supp., 1713: London, Egypt Explorations Society *Pap. Oxy. 1814* Fragment of index to *Ius. Codex*,	Uncial, AD 525–535

Digest

CLA III, 295: Florence, Bib. Laur. S.N. Codex Pisanus.	saec. VI
CLA III, 402: Naples Bib. naz. IV.A.8 (fol. 36–39) Palimpsest, primary script uncial, rewritten Bobbio saec. VIII.	Italy, saec. VI[2]
CLA VIII, 1221: Heidelberg, Univ.-Bibl. *Pap. 1272* Fragment of Digest from papyrus codex found in Egypt.	Uncial, saec. VI
CLA IX, 1351: Pommersfelden, Gräfl. Schönbornn'sche Bib. *Lat. pap. 1–6*	Uncial, saec. VI
Supp. 1723: Manchester, John Rylands Library Pap. 479 Fragment of Dig. XXX from papyrus codex	Uncial, saec. VI
Addenda 1858: Fragment.	Uncial, saec. VI

Novels (*Epitome Juliani*)

CLA III, 366: Milan, Bib. Trivulziana 688 Probably copied at Novara, second half of saec. VIII.	minuscule, saec. VIII–IX
CLA V, 557: Paris, Bib. nationale, lat. 4568 Also contains *Iustiniani et Iustini Constitutiones.*	minuscule, saec. VIII–IX
CLA V, 518: Paris, Bib. nationale, Baluze 270, fol. 68–69.	Uncial, saec. VIII
CLA VII, 946: St. Gall Stiftbib. 722 Also contains *Lex romana curiensis, capitula remedii.* Probably from Cher, since bishop Remedius (ca. 800) is mentioned in the *capitula remedii.*	Rhaetian minuscule, saec. VIII–IX
CLA VII, 986: St. Gall Stiftbib. 1395 Fragment of *Epitome Juliani*, probably from northern Italy.	Uncial, saec. VII–VIII

Yet the presence of the texts cannot be taken to mean that Justinianic law actually came to dominate Italian legal practice. The fourth and fifth centuries had seen a serious degradation of traditional Roman norms—what Ernst Levy termed the vulgarization of classical law. Even the boundaries between different categories of property were losing definition: a classical jurist, as Levy observed, would have been shocked by Ambrose's judgment awarding a widow a "usufruct" that consisted of a rent on a farm rather than control of it.[5] As this example shows, this erosion of understanding was not confined to minor practitioners in out of the way places, but extended to well-educated men in major centers. Even imperial legislation felt the pressure of this evolution, which Levy traced through the Theodosian Code among other sources. To the extent that the Justinianic codification rolled back many of these changes, at both the conceptual and procedural level, placing it fully in force would have required the reeducation of judges and practitioners throughout the peninsula.

A school of law in sixth-century Rome, such as that posited by Detlef Liebs, might have made an important contribution to such a project,[6] but evidence for its existence is extremely meager. No contemporary source mentions a law school in Italy. Nor, as we have seen, do the surviving manuscript evidence suggest any broad diffusion in Italy of the Institutes, although that was the work prepared specifically for use in law schools. We shall see below, in chapter four, that the Turin glosses to the Institutes, which Liebs claims as evidence for sixth-century Rome, are largely the work of eleventh-century jurists. The more sophisticated glosses to the *Epitome Juliani*, too, are evidently neither Roman nor western. Kaiser found, for example, that the *Paratitla*—a set of glosses cross-referencing the novels with the Code and Digest—probably originated in the east.[7] The glosses known as chapter summaries, though almost certainly western (and hence Italian), also seem to have little to do with teaching.[8] They are, in any case,

[5] Ernst Levy, *West Roman Vulgar Law* (Philadelphia, 1951), pp. 26–27. See also his *Weströmisches Vulgarrecht: Das Obligationenrecht* (Weimar, 1956). Cortese, *Diritto nella storia*, pp. 96–98 notes the problems inherent in the concept of "vulgar" law without, however, challenging the finding that some practices current in late antique law corresponded only approximately to classical, Theodosian, or Justinianic law.

[6] Detlef Liebs, *Die Jurisprudenz im spätantiken Italien (260–640 n. Chr.)* [Freiburger Rechtsgeschichtliche Abhandlungen, n. F. Bd. 8] (Berlin, 1987), pp. 195–282; summarized in his essay "Roman Law," in *Cambridge Ancient History*, vol. 14, ed. Averil Cameron, Bryan Ward-Perkins, Michael Whitby (Cambridge, 2001), pp. 238–59.

[7] Kaiser, *Epitome Iuliani*, pp. 306–7.

[8] Ibid., p. 326.

later than the Justinianic period, and tell us little about the efforts to make the Justinianic codification the effective law of Italy.

Law school or not, the byzantine occupation of Italy did not, it turned out, have much time. Already in the 540s, the Gothic War was sapping resources and strength, not just of the government but of what remained of late antique traditions. Writing of Rome, Supino Martini saw the interruption of book production, at least in the form of the traditional nexus between aristocratic readers and artisanal copyists, occurring as early as the late 540s.[9] Within four years of Justinian's death in 565, moreover, Lombard invaders were already in northern Italy, taking dominant positions in the Po valley and quickly pushing south to establish strong points at Spoleto and Benevento. Unlike earlier invaders, the Lombards had had little previous contact with Roman customs and showed little interest in preserving Roman culture. Roman institutions were permitted simply to collapse and the senatorial class, which had never lost its importance under the Goths, was now quickly reduced to insignificance. Ravenna, Rome and southern Italy were able to put up some resistance, at least to the extent of maintaining their independence and some contacts with Constantinople, but even these remnants of Byzantine Italy—now cut off from each other and forced to devote more and more of their resources to defense—proved incapable of sustaining the level of cultural activity they had enjoyed before.

The question to be faced in the rest of this chapter is what happened to the Justinianic *Corpus* in the four centuries following the Lombard invasions. This project is not to be confused with a history of Roman law in the early Middle Ages. In most of Europe, and often even within Italy, the written tradition of Roman law was represented by the *Codex Theodosianus* or, later, by compilations prepared especially for the Roman subjects of the Germanic kings. The most important of these was the *Lex Romana Visigothorum* or *Brevarium Alaricianum*, a derivative of the Theodosian Code, although one also occasionally finds evidence for the Ostrogothic *Edictum Theodorici* and the *Lex Romanum Burgundiorum*. Nor were written codes the only possible source of Roman law in this period. Even after the Germanic conquests, Romanized populations found it natural to perpetuate the law they

[9] Paola Supino Martini, "Aspetti della cultura grafica a Roma," *Roma nell'alto medioevo XLVIIIa Settimana di studio sull'Alto Medioevo, Spoleto 27 aprile–1 maggio 2000* (Spoleto, 2001), pp. 921–968, at p. 926.

had always known, using documents to validate legal transactions and following already well-understood rules. Indeed, by using pre-existing documents as templates for new ones, Roman legal language could easily be transmitted, generation to generation, even without ongoing contact with any of the law codes.

These multiple paths of transmission mean that generic references to Roman law, the use of Roman terminology, or the application of Roman rules cannot be taken as evidence for the influence of the Justinianic *Corpus*. In this chapter, therefore, we shall be looking for references specific to Justinian's works: quotations from them, rules original to Justinian's legislation, and (of course) manuscripts. Even so, the evidence is not without its ambiguities. Frequently it will be impossible to determine whether the author of a specific passage had acquired his knowledge of Roman law from his experience of contemporary practice, a compilation other than the *Corpus*, a collection of excerpts including some from the *Corpus*, or those works themselves. But if certainty about individual pieces of evidence will often elude us, the general picture of the circulation of Justinian's works nonetheless emerges with remarkable clarity. In particular we shall see that only the Novels in the form of the *Epitome Juliani* enjoyed any appreciable readership in the early Middle Ages, while the other works make at best brief appearances and produced no intellectual tradition of lasting significance.

Lombard Italy

Gregory the Great's familiarity with Justinian's *Corpus* is demonstrated by a letter of 603 in which he cited passages from the Novels, Code, and (once) the Digest, usually with great precision ("ut huius legis series loquitur Codicis libro primo titulo tertio constitutione undecima"). The fact that surviving sources do not cite the Digest again until the eleventh century has won this letter a certain notoriety, but it is not otherwise exceptional for Gregory. Legal citations are not rare in his correspondence, leading Conrat to suggest that he had manuscripts of the texts at hand. Elsewhere in Gregory's correspondence, moreover, Conrat believed that he could recognize phrases borrowed from Justinian's compilation even in the absence of explicit citations.[10]

[10] Conrat, *Geschichte*, p. 6, n. 5; pp. 8–13.

Yet as is often the case for Gregory, his knowledge cannot be taken as typical for the time. He himself seems to have realized the extent to which the world had changed around him. His letters reveal his effort to find ways of reaching a Christian populace—*simplicissima plebecula*—that could no longer be addressed with classical Latin prose: thus, for example, he urged upon his correspondents the selection of simple topics and texts for sermons, and he himself shifted his choice of words when writing for the widest audience. Even the circumstances surrounding the publication of Gregory's own works reflect this break with the past, for they now had to be copied, often in luxurious productions, by ecclesiastical communities rather than artisanal workshops.[11]

The principal other evidence for continuing attention to Justinian's works from around the year 600 is a considerable step down from what we see in Gregory the Great. The already mentioned chapter summaries to the *Epitome Juliani* come down to us in two manuscripts:[12] the ninth-century Vienna, Österreichische Nationalbibliothek (ÖNB) 2160, where they are given in the margin, and the eleventh-century Leipzig, Universitätsbibliothek, ms. 3503 (= Hänel 6), where they are included in the main text just before the law to which they are related. A few are also contained in Vercelli, Bib. Cap. 122, another manuscript from the eleventh century. The common thread linking the manuscripts seems to be the city of Rome. The Vienna and Vercelli manuscripts were both copied there,[13] while the Leipzig manuscript, in Beneventan, was produced by the scriptorium of Monte Cassino under Desiderius, a time when it had especially good connections with Rome.[14]

These glosses do no more than summarize the constitutions, usually in a very few words. Even so, thanks to Wolfgang Kaiser's meticulous analysis, they can give us a sense of how the period since the

[11] On book production during Gregory's pontificate, see Armando Petrucci, "L'onciale romana," in *Studi medievali*, 3rd ser. 12 (1971): 75–132.

[12] Published by Haenel, *Epitome Iuliani*, pp. 208–17. Haenel missed a few; those for cap. 424–57 were subsequently published by Conrat, "Su una più recente somma della 'Epitome' di Giuliano," BIDR, 13 (1900): 286–88. See also, Kaiser, *Epitome Iuliani*, p. 321 n. 358.

[13] AC's ascription of these manuscripts to Rome was confirmed by Supino Martini, "Aspetti," pp. 962–63.

[14] Francis Newton, *The scriptorium and library at Monte Cassino, 1058–1105* [Cambridge Studies in Palaeography and Codicology 7] (Cambridge, 1999), pp. 109, 347, and pl. 55.

Gothic Wars had undermined legal learning in Italy. To begin with, there is no effort to link the Novels to other Justinianic legislation, as had been done in the earlier *Paratitla*; even references internal to the *Epitome Juliani* do not go beyond adjacent laws. The language of the glosses, too, reveal the undertow of spoken late Latin at the expense of juristic tradition and precision. One thus finds words such as *contemptionare, incriminare, infiscare, matrimoniare, pactuare* that had been absent from the Justinianic texts and indeed from earlier written Latin. Many technical terms were simplified so that *donatio propter nuptias* becomes *sponsalia* as, indeed, does *dos*. Some Roman offices were no longer understood or were named incorrectly, and the summaries often misstate the content of the law, evidently through error.[15]

Apparently from the same environment are the chapter summaries to Justinian's Code known as the *Summa Perusina* after the manuscript, now in Perugia, that uniquely transmits it.[16] Conrat and Patetta commented upon the similarity between the *Summa Perusina* and the chapter summaries of the Novels,[17] and Kaiser has now provided a systematic comparison of the two texts. Kaiser documented a whole range of similarities:

- both use similar locutions to refer to the laws being summarized: *Haec lex loquitur* or *praesens/haec lectio dicit*;
- both incorporate a variety of words extraneous to Justinian's texts and often classical Latin generally, such as *matrimoniare, pactuare, homo* to mean "anyone";
- both make similar substitutions for classical terms and offices, using *sponsalia* for both *dos* and *donatio propter nuptias, condicionalis* for *adscripticius, iudex* for *praeses provinciae*, as well as new (or incorrect) coinages such as *fideicommissarius* and *legatarius*.[18]

Not all of these elements are necessarily unique. Words such as *matrimoniare, pactuare* or *sponsalia*, which reflect a tension between spoken and written, might well have been common usages for several centuries rather than typical only of the sixth or seventh. Yet while individual pieces of evidence may not be conclusive, Kaiser's demonstration of

[15] Kaiser, *Epitome Iuliani*, pp. 329–31.
[16] *Adnotationes Codicum Domini Justiniani (Summa Perusina)*, ed. F. Patetta, BIDR, 12 (1900); the preface is reprinted in Patetta, *Studi*, pp. 241–318.
[17] Conrat, *Geschichte*, p. 203; Patetta, pp. 283–84.
[18] Kaiser, *Epitome Iuliani*, pp. 325–46.

so many different points of congruence makes a strong argument for both works having emerged from the same environment.

The subsequent history of both works (that for the *Summa Perusina* will be discussed in the next chapter) would appear to argue for Rome as the place of origin, an inference supported by allusions to Rome in both works.[19] The date is harder to judge. Noting a reference in the summaries of the *Epitome Juliani* to the *defensor civitas*, an office that died out in the late sixth century, Liebs took that to be the date of those glosses and assigned the *Summa Perusina* to the early 600s; and he saw both of them as evidence for a survival at Rome of legal education into this period.[20] Kaiser differs with Liebs about whether these summaries had anything to do with teaching—for him they were simply glosses—and he would place both of them slightly later, in line with Patetta's mid-seventh century date for the *Summa Perusina*.[21] Apart from Liebs' observation about the *defensor civitatis*, however, there is little evidence to support any of these dates. The linguistic evidence adduced by Patetta, for example, are really no more than the hunch of a gifted reader with no particular expertise in the history of Latin; it would not be surprising if he overestimated the uniformity of Latin even before the Lombard invasions. The 590s were already a half-century later than the Gothic wars, singled out by Supino as the moment when laymen virtually disappear from the written record.[22] The scribes revealed by the documentary record were at best modestly educated and, in Petrucci's opinion, possessed of a literacy that was largely confined to reading and writing documents. Even the experts, the royal notaries who produced Rothari's *Edictum* in the 640s, wrote a Latin that was "objectively uncertain [and] incorrect."[23] They were certainly far from having the learning

[19] Liebs, *Jurisprudenz im Spätantiken Italien*, p. 271; Patetta, *Adnotationes Codicum*, pp. XLIV, XLVII; Kaiser, pp. 333, 339.

[20] Liebs, pp. 269–73; 276–82.

[21] Kaiser, *Epitome Iuliani*, p. 346. See the detailed analyis by Patetta in his preface, pp. XXII–XXXV, LXVI–LXXIII. Patetta assigned the preparation of the *Summa* to the seventh and eighth centuries generally, but more recent opinion has tended to single out the first half of the seventh century as the most likely period. See also Conrat, *Geschichte*, pp. 182–87 and, for recent historiography, H. Siems, *Handel und Wucher im Spiegel frühmittelalterlicher Rechtsquellen* [MGH, Schriften, bd. 35] (Hannover, 1992), p. 176.

[22] Supino Martini, "Aspetti," p. 926.

[23] Petrucci, "Scrittura e libro nell'Italia altomedievale," *Studi Medievali*, 3rd ser. 10 (1969): 961–1002, at p. 997 [trans. in Petrucci, *Writers and Readers in Medieval Italy*, Charles Radding ed. and trans. (New Haven, 1995), chaps. 2, 3 at pp. 54–55.]

for either the Latin or the intellectual complexities even of the *Institutes*, much less the Code. Seen in this perspective, a date of around or even before 600 could easily make sense for the glosses.

Lending strength to a comparatively early date for both sets of glosses is the difficulty of finding other evidence of interest in Justinianic law as late as the mid-seventh century. It is not surprising that we lack manuscripts of any of the Justinianic works from between the late sixth century and the late eighth. Book production itself did not entirely cease. Christian religious communities could not do without books and, in the absence of professional copyists, urban clergy learned to produce them. Some of their work, indeed, was of a high quality, suitable for lending grandeur to Roman liturgical texts intended for presentation as gifts to churchmen in distant regions. Yet this productive capacity could not easily be expanded, not least because copying books still lay outside the scope of most monasteries, and it could not be spared for purposes such as secular law.[24] The consequences of this situation can be seen in the *CLA*: no manuscripts or fragments of the Institutes, Code, and Digest survive from the seventh century and eighth centuries. Confirming that the *CLA* represents a genuine lack of interest, rather than simply losses of books over time, is the high percentage of manuscripts that were erased to be used for other texts: five of six, or all except the Florentina. Not only were the works of the *Corpus* not worth copying. They were not worth keeping.

The impression that there was little interest in the Justinianic works is confirmed by the other available evidence. The papacy may well have possessed copies of Justinian's works, for they reappear (briefly) in the ninth century, but Gregory the Great's successors in the seventh or eighth century found no occasion to cite them. Nor were Justinian's works cited in other documents from either seventh- and eighth-century Rome. Nor do they appear in any of the surviving documents from Ravenna, the other region still under Byzantine control. About the only work that can be assumed with any confidence to have originated in this period is the *De ordine ecclesiastico*, a drastic reduction of 59 chapters from the *Epitome Juliani* into 52 chapters. This

---

[24] On this general trend in Italian book production, see Petrucci, "Scrittura e libro," esp. pp. 974–76, and "Libro, scrittura e scuola," in *La scuola nell'Occidente dell'alto medioevo*, XIX Settimana di studi sull'alto medioevo (Spoleto, 1972), pp 313–37 at 318–20 [*Writers and Readers*, pp. 33–36, 62–64].

compilation survives in a single manuscript, Berlin, Staatsbibliothek, ms. Phill. 1735 and won its principal circulation as one of the sources for the collection of Benedict Levita, one of the pseudo isidorian forgeries.[25]

In part, perhaps, such findings reflect the pressure felt by both Rome and Ravenna in this period. Even in regions much closer than Italy to Constantinople, it proved difficult to keep the Justinianic codification fully in force: J. F. Haldon observed that "imperial legislation and Roman (Justinianic) jurisprudence were confined to those areas over which the imperial govenment had direct and constant supervision—effectively, Constantinople and its environs."[26] In Italy, moreover, where the focus of Byzantine government had become "fundamentally military," law could not have been a priority. "Although we still hear of *iudices* and *consules* in seventh- and eighth-century documents, these titles no longer signified distinct civil offices but instead were among the titles used to describe the civil functions accumulated by dukes and tribunes."[27] Another factor was the continued importance of the Theodosian Code. Thus, the handful of Ravennate documents citing Roman legal rules all refer to principles already found in the Theodosian Code.[28]

If Justinianic law was not to be found where in theory it still applied, it cannot surprise that it was absent from Lombard Italy where it did not. The documentary record dramatically conveys the disruption caused by the arrival of the Lombards: only two genuine documents from Lombard Italy survive from the period before 700.[29] More abundant documentation from the eighth century permits us to see a certain diffusion of literacy among lay society as well as the existence of notaries, whose handwriting reveals their continuity with late antique traditions.[30] Some documents either explicitly mention the Lombard *Edictum* or show awareness of specific laws; one apparently from the 720s refers to a rule "that Liutprand established in

---

[25] Kaiser, *Epitome Iuliani*, pp. 460–92 of which pp. 476–92 are an edition of the text.

[26] J. F. Haldon, *Byzantium in the Seventh Century. The Transformation of a Culture*, revised ed. (Cambridge, 1997), p. 267.

[27] Thomas F. X. Noble, *The Republic of St. Peter. The Birth of the Papal State, 680–825* (Philadelphia, 1984), pp. 5–6.

[28] Paolo Frezza, *L'influsso del diritto romano giustinianeo nelle formule e nella prassi in Italia, IRMA* pars I, 2, c *ee*, pp. 10–11.

[29] Luigi Schiaparelli, *Codice Diplomatico Longobardo* [Fonti per la Storia d'Italia, 62, 63] (Rome, 1929–32).

[30] Petrucci, "Libro, scrittura e scuola" [*Writers and Readers* chap. 4].

the Edict [*quam domn. Liutprand in edicto adfixeset*]."[31] But though written Lombard laws were cited in these documents, Justinian's *Corpus* was not. Two documents do include a short phrase from the *Codex Theodosianus*,[32] but even these references probably resulted from using older documents as models for new ones rather than from any direct study of that text.

Justinian's codification had never been given the force of law in Europe north of the Alps, so it is natural that when Roman law is mentioned there—for example, in the decrees of ecclesiastical councils—the references appear to have been to either the *Codex Theodosianus* or the *Breviarium*.[33] Yet the evidence for the circulation of these works provides an instructive comparison with the fate of Justinian's Corpus. The manuscript evidence for the Theodosian Code itself parallels that for the Justinianic *Corpus*: while the *CLA* lists eleven manuscripts containing the Theodosian Code, only three of these are later than 600; two of these contained brief excerpts rather than the whole book while the third (a fragment now in the Vatican) was palimpsested in the eighth century.[34] Partially compensating for the declining interest in the *Codex Theodosianus*, however, was the growing influence of the *Breviarium*. Seven manuscripts or fragments of the *Breviarium* survive from the period between the late seventh and early ninth centuries, with another three manuscripts containing excerpts of the text or shortened versions of it. Conrat remarked that the *Breviarium* ruled in the Frankish kingdoms,[35] and Ian Wood reached a similar conclusion, noting the rising number of manuscripts of the *Breviarium* over time.

The absence of any positive evidence from the seventh and eighth centuries has sometimes tempted historians to attribute to this period

---

[31] *Codice Diplomatico Longobardo* no. 81; see also CDL 96 (748), 163 (762), 293 (774). On this subject generally, see Nick Everett, "Literacy and the law in Lombard government," *Early Medieval Europe*, 9 (2000): 93–127.

[32] *CDL* nos. 198 and 222, recalling *Cod. Th.* 2.9.3, and CDL no. 62 recalling *Cod. Th.*5.9, on which see Frezza, *L'influsso*, p. 13.

[33] Conrat, *Geschichte*, pp. 13–14, for the occasional references to Roman law in the acts of ecclesiastical councils.

[34] Although Ian Wood used the *CLA* to argue that "the evidence of the manuscripts... [shows] that the Theodosian Code was at least as important as the Breviary in the sixth, seventh, and eighth centuries," he does not appear to have noticed the sharp decline in surviving manuscripts produced after 600. Jill Harries and Ian Wood, eds., *The Theodosian Code* (Ithaca, 1993), p. 159.

[35] "Es hat sich bisher das Resultat ergeben, dass von einer territorialen Einschränkung abgesehen in Frankreich während des früheren Mittelalters das Breviar herrschte und von der Justinianische Gesetzgebung lediglich Julian gekannt und benutzt wurde." *Geschichte*, p. 77. Wood, *Theodosian Code*, pp. 165–66.

odd-seeming works that seemed to fit poorly elsewhere. Two such works—very different from each other!—are the *Collectio Gaudenziana* and the *Epitome Codicis*: both appear to be from the eleventh century instead.[36] The truth appears to be simpler. The Justinianic codification simply fell from sight and from use, in Italy and everywhere else, between the end of the sixth century and the end of the eighth.

Carolingian Europe

For most of Latin Christendom, the reigns of Charlemagne and his successors transformed the conditions of higher education and learning. Systematic instruction in classical Latin rescued that language from the undertow of spoken romance and created a small but sophisticated class of readers and writers diffused throughout Europe. Nor was this advanced literacy necessarily confined to ecclesiastics. Some laymen, among them the elite northern Italian judges and notaries *sacri palatii*, could and did write accurate Latin.[37] Beyond basic language skills, moreover, Carolingian education also meant a wider diffusion of the liberal arts and a concomitant growth in the expertise to tackle other kinds of complex texts.[38] To serve this increased body of readers, finally, there came dramatically greater production of all kinds of books, with consequences for European libraries that can still be seen today.

Yet despite such favorable circumstances, it is difficult to detect any significant interest in the Justinianic codification. While manuscripts of the *Epitome Juliani* begin to appear in some number, that popularity did not extend to the Institutes, Code or Digest. Citations of the *Corpus* by clerics were still very rare, with most of them being concentrated in a handful of papal letters from a brief period in the ninth century. Not even documents, whose quantities become a flood by the tenth century, show detectable influence of Justinianic law until we approach the year 1000. We shall consider these sources in turn.

---

[36] The *Collectio Gaudenziana* is discussed in chapter three. We deal with the *Epitome Codicis* in chapter five.

[37] Armando Petrucci and Carlo Romeo, *"Scriptores in Urbibus" Alfabetismo e cultura scritta nell'Italia altomedievale* (Bologna, 1992), pp. 195–236.

[38] Rosamund McKitterick, *The Carolingians and the Written Word* (Cambridge, 1989), pp. 13–20.

Manuscripts

Coming after several centuries when book production was at a low ebb, the Carolingian renaissance represented a key moment both for preserving ancient texts and stocking libraries with manuscripts. Bischoff estimated that roughly 7,000 manuscripts survive from the late eighth and ninth centuries, a total that dwarfs the 1,800 manuscripts and fragments attributed by the *CLA* to the entire period before 800.[39] This revival of scriptorial activity extended to nearly all fields of ancient learning, including medical treatises and Quintillian, the most technical of the classical rhetorical treatises.[40] As L. D. Reynolds comments: "By the end of the ninth century the major part of Latin literature had indeed been copied and was enjoying some degree of circulation, however limited, localized, or precarious it may in some cases have been. The list of texts for which we have ninth-century manuscripts, however fragmentary, . . . [is singularly impressive]: a large part of the classical heritage had been safely gathered up and in most cases transcribed into a script which was new and elegant and a pleasure to read."[41] It was, in short, a pivotal period in the history of classical texts.

The copying of ancient sources went well beyond what Carolingian scholars were able to use. One need only read the entries in *Texts and Transmission*, Reynolds' invaluable survey of individual Latin texts, to see that many works copied during this period did not find readers until much later—sometimes as late as the fourteenth or fifteenth century. For literary texts, the most famous case is perhaps that of Tacitus. *Annales* books 1–6 survive in a single eighth-century German manuscript, books 11–16 of the *Annales* and the *Historiae* come down in a single Monte Cassino manuscript of the eleventh century, while the minor works including the *Agricola* and *Germania*, were transmitted by a single ninth-century manuscript that has apparently been lost again in the twentieth century: none of these works found a significant number of readers before the fifteenth century.[42] Many other important texts copied in Carolingian times—including Cicero's letters and

[39] Bischoff, *Latin Palaeography*, p. 208. The actual contrast between pre-Carolingian and Carolingian manuscripts is even starker than the numbers themselves indicate because the *CLA* includes many early Carolingian manuscripts.

[40] L. D. Reynolds et al., *Texts and Transmission. A Survey of the Latin Classics* (Oxford, 1983), pp. xxix–xxx.

[41] *Texts and Transmission*, pp. xxvii–xxviii.

[42] *Texts and Transmission*, pp. 406–11.

some of his rhetorical writings, the *Res Gestae* of Ammianus, and some of Ovid—similarly remained in obscurity until the fourteenth century.

This vast effort of preservation did not, however, extend to most of Justinian's *Corpus*. The *CLA* does reveal a renewed production of the *Epitome Juliani* at the beginning of the Carolingian period, with three of the five earliest manuscripts or fragments being written in minuscule from the turn of the eighth to ninth centuries; the other two, in uncial, are only slightly earlier. Scholars have long supposed that the comparatively broad circulation enjoyed by the *Epitome Juliani* was due to the clergy, who were interested in the many constitutions that bore upon the position of the church, and the manuscript evidence supports this assumption: four of these five manuscripts can be assigned to specific ecclesiastical centers. The ninth century, moreover, saw continued interest in this work, with four more manuscripts that represent a wide geographical diffusion of the work. Berlin, Staatsbib., ms. fol. lat. 269 comes from the late eighth or early ninth century, while Paris, BN 4418 was only slightly later; circulation in the second half is witnessed by ÖNB ms. 2160, perhaps from Rome, and Leipzig, Universitätsbibliothek, ms. 3493/3494 [= Hänel 8/9] (one manuscript now in two parts). The manuscripts of the *Epitome Juliani* often contain other works of juridical interest, perhaps copied right along with the *Epitome* from the same exemplar. This practice possibly also explains the appearance of short selections from the Institutes and Code in Leipzig Hänel 3493/3494.

Yet the relatively abundant evidence for the *Epitome Juliani* only serves to dramatize the very different fate of the rest of the Justinianic Corpus. The main evidence for its having been copied at all in this period comes from a fascicle preserved by having been incorporated into Berlin ms. lat. 269.[43] The fragment consists of an entire gathering

[43] On this manuscript, see Kaiser, *Epitome Iuliani*, pp. 387–415; Bernard Bischoff, *Katalog der festländischen Handschriften des neunten Jahrhunderts (mit Ausnahme der wisigotischen). Teil I: Aachen-Lambach* (Wiesbaden, 1998), no. 365; and Andreas Fingernagel, *Die illuminierten lateinischen Handschriften süd-, west- und nordeuropäischer Provenienz der Staatsbibliothek zu Berlin PK: 4.–12. Jahrhundert* (Wiesbaden, 1999), no. 51. Giovanna Nicolaj recently tried to assign this manuscript to Nonantola, although without offering any reason for her ascription and evidently overlooking the fact that the leading expert on carolingian Nonantola—Bischoff—attributed it to Provence. ("Ambiti di copia e copisti de codici giuridici in Italia (secoli V–XII in.)," in *A Ennio Cortese* (Rome, 1997), pp. 478–96 at pp. 487–88; and "Documenti e *libri legales* a Ravenna: rilettura di un mosaico leggendario," in *Ravenna da capitale imperiale a capitale esarcale. Atti del XVII Congresso internazionale di studio sull'alto medioevo [Ravenna, 6–12 giugno 2004]* (Spoleto, 2005), pp. 761–99 at pp. 779–80). It goes without saying that her corollary conclusion, that the text derived from Ravenna, is equally baseless.

containing the very end of the Institutes (from In. 4.18.5) and the very beginning of the Digest (to D.1.7.3, although with a substantial lacuna). The history of the gathering itself has been somewhat confused by marginal notes calling attention to its insertion in the middle of the *Collatio Legum*, a text that was part of the original volume containing the *Epitome Juliani*: since the much later scholar who added them imitated the original script of the manuscript, modern scholars have been misled into thinking that the extra fascicle must have been a part of this volume from an early time. Setting aside that false clue, all one can say is that the extra fascicle, like the *Epitome Juliani*, is from the early ninth or perhaps even the late eighth century; that both it and the rest of the manuscript were probably copied in southwestern France, perhaps Burgundy; and that they very possibly were the work of the same scriptorium. The top of a fascicle number—either VIIII or XIIII—remains where the gathering was trimmed to fit the current volume. A rough calculation shows that six to seven fascicles in this format would probably have been sufficient for the Institutes, so the original volume may have contained the Institutes, additional sections of the Digest, and perhaps other materials as well.[44]

The Digest fragment has attracted the most attention, most notably from Pietro Pescani and Robert Röhle,[45] as evidence of a textual tradition different from that of the Florentina. The Berlin fragment also witnesses the penetration of the Institutes and the Digest outside of Italy, the region where it had been imposed by Justinian's own authority. Yet it is hard to see what impact those works could have had there. Neither of them is cited in the region until much later, nor would the surviving fascicle have been easy to study, because (unlike the *Epitome Juliani* with which it was bound) it does not adopt a page format marking out the beginning of each law. The fascicle, in any case, contains no glosses. Like the Carolingian manuscripts of Tacitus, this book evidently found few readers and had no discernable impact on the culture of its time.

---

[44] For details see Kaiser, *Epitome Iuliani*, p. 400, whose analysis is confirmed by our own study of the manuscript.

[45] Robert Röhle, "Das Berliner Institutionen- und Digestenfragment Ms. lat. fol. 269," in BIDR, 3rd ser. 10 (1970): 129–73; Pietro Pescani, "La posizione del codice R nella tradizione della Litera Bononiensis," *La Critica del Testo. Atti del secondo Congresso internazionale della Società italiana di storia del diritto* (Firenze, 1971) II, 671–90.

One might expect the situation in Italy to have been better, but it was not. The Institutes is witnessed by a single manuscript, now reduced to two brief fragments in the Biblioteca Capitolare and the Biblioteca Comunale of Verona and numerous smaller pieces at the Beinecke Library of Yale.[46] It apparently was copied at Verona, where was preserved the sixth-century manuscript that now survives as a palimpsested fragment; it contains a few glosses, but most of them are later, from the eleventh century. For the Digest and the Code, moreover, we have no manuscript evidence at all from Italy, although the Code is represented by a brief excerpt (C.3.13.2–3.17.1) constituting the first two folios of Münich, Staatsbib. Clm. 6375, according to Bischoff a ninth-century manuscript from southern Germany. Since these folios evidently were copied only because they belonged to the archetype of the main text, Eusebius' *Historia Ecclesiastica*,[47] their appearance here reflects neither contact with the entire work nor indeed any interest in it.[48]

Modest enough in itself, this harvest of Justinianic manuscripts—four manuscripts plus two fragments (the Berlin fascicle and the Verona Institutes)—looks particularly meager when seen in the context of Bischoff's 7,000 ninth-century manuscripts. Despite a now ample capacity for producing books, the Justinianic works apart from the *Epitome Juliani* seem to have attracted virtually no attention. Nor does the situation improve in the tenth century, a period of generally

---

[46] G. Moschetti, "I frammenti veronesi del secolo IX delle Istituzioni di Giustiniano," *Atti del Congresso internazionale di diritto romano e di storia del diritto. Verona 27–28–29—IX—1948* (Milan, 1953), pp. 439–509. The Beinecke fragments belong to ms. 744, a fifteenth-century missal from Verona. R. G. Babcock and W. Cohen, "A New Manuscript from the Abbey of San Zeno at Verona," *Yale University Library Gazette*, 66 (3–4 April, 1992): 105–16. We are grateful to Anders Winroth for having called these fragments to our attention. Santini mistakenly lists a ninth-century fragment of the Institutes in Vercelli Bib. Cap. 174; "Il sapere giuridico occidentale," p. 178. For a careful description of this latter manuscript, which contains the capitulary collection of Ansegisus, see Patetta, "Sull'introduzione in Italia della Collezione d'Ansegiso," [orig. pub. 1890] repr. *Studi*, pp. 719–28.

[47] For a description of the manuscript, which does not mention the excerpt from the Code, see B. Bischoff, *Die Südostdeutschen Schriebschulen und Bibliotheken in der Karolingerzeit. Teil 1. Die Bayrischen Diözesen* 3. Auflage (Wiesbaden, 1974), p. 147; the excerpt is described in Krüger, *Codex Iustinianus*, pp. VIII–VIIII.

[48] Evidently later, however, are the two constitutions C.9.16.1 and 4 found in Modena, Bib. cap. O.I.4 of the pseudo isidorian decretals, a manuscript that should be attributed to the eleventh rather than the ninth century. Described by Patetta, *Studi*, pp. 125–26; see also G. Russo, *Tradizione manoscritta di Leges Romanae nei codici dei secoli IX e X della Biblioteca Capitolare di Modena* (Modena, 1980), p. 26 and tav.

reduced production of manuscripts and for which not even a copy of the *Epitome Juliani* survives. The preliminary conclusion must be that Carolingian Europe was simply largely indifferent to Roman law.

Letters, Collections and Treatises

Although sixth- and seventh-century writers had little direct acquaintance with Justinian's law-books, some of them had heard of them and could refer to their existence in passing. Thus, Isidore of Seville described the four parts of the *Corpus Iuris Civilis* in his *Etymologiae*, and this work was probably the source of Paul the Deacon's remarks in his *History of the Lombards*. Bede, similarly, had mentioned the Code in his history, apparently drawing on Marcellinus' history rather than Isidore. Yet even such passing references to the *Corpus* are extremely rare during the ninth and tenth centuries.[49] The principal exception is the *Historia Tripartita* of Anastasius Bibliotecarius, librarian to Popes Hadrian II and John VIII, but even this is an indirect source, deriving from the Byzantine historian Theophanes.[50]

More significant for our purposes are references to the *Corpus* in correspondence or other works. For the most part, the pattern is the same as that of the manuscripts, with citations being rare, brief, and usually to the *Epitome Juliani*. Hincmar of Reims, for example, who is often regarded as one of the Carolingian authors most interested in Roman law, turns out to have relied mainly on the Theodosian Code or the *Breviarium*. The rare citations of the *Epitome Juliani* in Hincmar's works are all from late in his career (after 865), and it is not even certain that he actually possessed the entire work: Devisse thought he was probably working from a collection of excerpts from the *Epitome* prepared for clerical use.[51] Ratramnus of Corbie, similarly, was able to cite two passages from the *Epitome Juliani* in a treatise written as part of the "filioque" controversy against the Greek church.[52] The picture is not better in the tenth century. Regino of Prüm cites

---

[49] Conrat, pp. 97–102.

[50] *Theophanis Chronographia*, ed. Carolus de Boor (Leipzig, 1883), II, p. 94; see also *The Chronicle of Theophanes Confessor: Byzantine and Near Eastern History, A.D. 284–813*, trans. by Cyril Mango and Roger Scott (Oxford, 1997); Conrat, pp. 102–6.

[51] See the careful analysis by J. Devisse, *Hincmar et la loi* (Dakar, 1962), esp. p. 63; for Savigny on Hincmar, see *Geschichte des römischen Rechts*, II, 280–83; 484–85.

[52] *Ratramni Corbeiensis Monachi Contra Graecorum Opposita Romanam Ecclesiam Infamantium Libri Quatuor*, PL 121: 330CD, citing Ep. Jul. 6, 115.49.

two chapters from the *Epitome Juliani* in his collection of canons,[53] and the father of Odo of Cluny was said, by Odo's biographer, to have known the Novels. A few passages from the *Epitome Juliani* appear in charters from late tenth-century Fleury under Abbo.[54] Finally, coming from the end of the tenth century, is the legal collection of Abbo of Fleury that includes a number of chapters taken from the *Epitome Juliani*, although here, too, as Conrat noted, there is reason to suspect that Abbo was using an intermediate collection rather than an integral text.[55]

In ninth-century Italy, epistolary references to Justinian's work come exclusively from the papacy. The correspondence of Eugenius II (824–27) provides a single reference to Ep. Jul. 119.6, dealing with lands possessed by religious foundations.[56] A larger cluster comes from the papacies of Nicholas I (858–67) and John VIII (872–82), both of whom were aggressive defenders of papal prerogatives.

- In 865, Nicholas I twice quoted from the Code in a letter to the Byzantine emperor asserting the primacy of the Roman church. One was a passage from C. 1.1.8 in which Justinian addressed Pope John II with respect (*"Petimus vestrum paternum affectum . . ."*), although that passage enjoyed a separate transmission and thus may not have been taken directly from the Code. The other was a phrase from C. 3.1.6 about judges not hearing cases where their own interests are involved—this last in a context of refuting the deposition of the patriarch of Constantinople.[57]
- In 866, in a long letter advising the King of the Bulgarians on law, Nicholas paraphrased a passage from the Institutes (In. 1.10.pr) in the context of barring marriage between god-parents and god-children, perhaps also including a phrase from the definition of *sponsalia* in D. 23.1.1; he quoted the same passage of the Institutes

---

[53] PL 132: 261, citing Ep. Jul. 7.1,2; see Conrat, *Geschichte*, pp. 258–60.

[54] P. Riché, *Enseignement du droit en Gaule du VIe au X^ie siècle*, IRMA, I 5 b bb (Milan, 1965), pp.19–20. See also J. Gaudemet, "Survivances romains dans le droit de la monarchie franque, du Ve au Xe siècle," *Tijdschrift voor rechtsgeschiedenis*, 22 (1955): 149–206.

[55] PL 139: 473–508; Conrat, *Geschichte*, pp. 259–61.

[56] PL 124: 643D.

[57] MGH, *Epist.* VI, Ep. 88, pp. 458, 461. For the separate transmission of this text, see Krüger's note to C. 1.1.8 in the *editio maior* of the Code; and Conrat, "Römisches Recht bei Papst Nikolaus I," *Neues Archiv der Gesellschaft für altere deutsche Geschichteskunde* n.s. XXXVI (1911): 719–27, at p. 721.

again later in the chapter on consanguinity. The secular lawbook he included with his letter (c. 13), however, is thought to have been of Lombard law.[58]

- In August 878, John VIII cites C. 6.57.5 in two letters on the same subject but to different recipients. Both times he attributed it (and Ep. Jul. 21, 10 cited in one of the letters) to John II in conjunction with Justinian.[59]
- In 879, John VIII cites Ep. Jul. 115.15 for a rule concerning excommunications.[60]

Although the citations of the Code and Institutes are striking, coming from a century when those works were not otherwise mentioned, one should not overstate the depth of learning represented by these letters. None of the passages are actually discussed or analyzed; instead, the letters merely quote them briefly or mention them in passing. Material such as Justinian's gracious remarks to John II or the rule on excommunications, moreover, is so specific to the church that the curia's knowledge of these passages cannot be taken as implying any detailed understanding of the Code as a whole. In this

[58] MGH, *Epist.* VI, Ep. 99, pp. 568–600, at pp. 569, 582. The rest of this letter makes frequent, unspecific references to "leges," but there is little specifically Roman about the rules the pope recommends, which show also considerable influence from the Lombard and Frankish law current in Italy. Conrat denied that the phrase "sed post sponsalia, quae futurarum sunt nuptiarum promissa," p. 570, derived from D. 23.1.1 "Sponsalia sunt mentio et repromissio nuptiarum futurarum"; "Römisches Recht bei Papst Nikolaus I," p. 720n., making the circular argument that the Digest does not seem to have been known in the early Middle Ages. Yet the relevant passage of the Institutes (In. 1.10) uses neither the term *sponsalia*—a term that by the seventh century usually referred to wedding gifts—nor any variant of the phrase *nuptiarum futurarum.* If the papacy had a copy of the Digest, moreover, it would not have required much searching in it to have located this phrase in the first law of the title *De sponsalibus.* The discussion of the reference to a book of secular law is discussed pp. 724–7; the passage itself is on p. 575 of the edition.

[59] MGH, *Epist.* VII: letter 111 (878, Aug.), pp. 102–3, to Ludwig III (also citing Ep. Jul. 21, 10) and letter 129 (878, Aug.), pp. 114–5, to the archbishop of Mainz; both letters make an unspecific reference that appears to be to Ep. Jul. 109, 1. Also mentioning Justinian is a letter attributed to John VIII that deals with the law of sacrilege in which Justinian's rule is rejected in favor of Charlemagne's; Mansi, XVII, col. 351 = Ph. Jaffé, *Regesta pontificum romanorum ab condita ecclesia ad annum post Christum natum MCXCVIII*, 2nd ed. (Lipsiae, 1885–88) no. 3180. This letter was later incorporated into Gratian's *Decretum*, C. 17, qu. 4, c. 21, but the MGH editors omitted it from their edition of John's correspondence.

[60] MGH, *Epist.* VII, letter 170 (p. 138), "in secundo novellarum Justiniani libro, ut nemo episcopus aut presbyter aliquem excommunicet, antequam cause probetur" [= E. Jul. CXV].

regard, John's attribution of the Code and Novels to both John II and Justinian is a telling error, possibly deriving from a misunderstanding of Nicholas I's letter to Emperor Michael, but in any case cautioning us against imagining that the works of the *Corpus* had received any serious attention in the papal curia of this period. Indeed, an 875 letter from John VIII to Emperor Louis II discusses Roman law without mentioning Justinian's books at all, citing instead the Theodosian Code and letters from Gregory I and Felix III.[61]

Also Italian and roughly contemporary with these papal letters are three juristic collections that represent the only substantial appearance of Justinian's Code and Institutes for the early Middle Ages. The most important of these is the *Lex Romana canonice compta*, a compilation that survives in a single manuscript, Paris, Bib. Nat., lat. 12448.[62] The manuscript is composite, breaking at f. 131v, the last page of an intact gathering. The first part of the manuscript, which includes our text on ff. 79–112, dates from the early tenth century; the second part of the manuscript is from the late ninth century. The two parts of the volume are not, however, bound together by chance, as is shown by the way the first section ends. Knowing that his text had to merge with pre-existing fascicles, the scribe of the first part wrote smaller and made other adjustments to the format of the last page so that all of his text would fit.

The name *Lex Romana canonice compta* comes from the page header used for it in the manuscript. Kaiser refers to the collection as the *Capitula legis Romanae*, a title he extracted from the incipit ("incipiunt cum sententiis suis capitula romanae legis ad canones pertinentia"),[63] but we shall use the more familiar name here. The compilation consists of 371 legal texts gathered into 324 chapters. Of these, 211

[61] MGH, *Epist.* VII, letter 52 (pp. 304–6).

[62] The text has been published in an edition by C. G. Mor, *Lex romana canonice compta. Testo di leggi romano-canoniche del sec. IX pubblicato sul ms. parigino Bibl. Nat. 12448* (Pavia, 1927). A thorough description of the manuscript and its contents can be found in Kaiser, *Epitome Iuliani*, pp. 493–501. For further details see, Antonio Ciaralli, "*Universali lex.* Il *Codex Iustinianus* nei documenti veronesi tra xi e xii secolo," *Medioevo. Studi e documenti*, 1 (Verona, 2005), pp. 111–60, at n. 9. Also arriving at a tenth-century date was Bernhard Bischoff, *Handschriftenarchiv Bernhard Bischoff* (Bibliothek der Monumenta Germaniae Historica, Hs. C 1, C 2) ed. by Arno Mentzel-Reuters (Munich, 1997). A preference for a ninth-century date is expressed by Giovanna Nicolaj, who does not, however, offer the hint of a reason for this attribution. "Ambiti di copia e copisti," p. 487.

[63] Kaiser, *Epitome Iuliani*, pp. 501–3.

passages taken from the *Epitome Juliani*, 123 from the Code, and 22 from the Institutes;[64] the remaining chapters were drawn from miscellaneous sources, including mainly scholia to the *Epitome Juliani* but also Novel 143 in the version of the *Authenticum*, an extract from the Edict of Theodoric, and a chapter from Lothar's *Capitulare Olonnense ecclesiasticum primum* (825) in the redaction of Lupus of Ferrière's *Liber legum*.[65] The compiler of the *Lex Romana canonice compta* does not appear to have had any particular expertise in Roman law. Conrat observed that he often failed to achieve a well-organized perspective of his sources, scattering laws from the same title of the Code in different places; a few excerpts even appear more than once.[66] The rare glosses to the *Lex Romana canonice compta* point to the same conclusion, for they provide references to canon law rather than any juristic analysis.[67]

The *Lex Romana canonice compta* is thought to have been prepared in northern Italy, the region where the Paris manuscript originated. As for its date, it is certainly later than the *Liber legum*, attributable to the period between 829 and 837, while a *terminus ante quem* is provided by the incorporation of some of its material into a second collection dedicated to canon law. The date of this latter work, said to have been prepared for Archbishop Anselm of Milan and known accordingly as the *Collectio Anselmo dedicata* (*CAD*), is given by the archbishop's dates (882–896). The dedication, in which the author describes himself as "the least important sheep in Anselm's flock" (*ego minima gregis ipsius ovicula*) leave no doubt that it originated in a Lombard

---

[64] Mor's appendices listing the contents of the *Lex Romana* must be checked with care, not least because he appears (bizarrely) to have taken his numbering from a pre-Krüger edition of the Code. Krüger suggested that the source text of the *Lex Romana canonice compta* might have been a version of the (hypothetical) *Epitome aucta*, but see below, chapter 5 at note 13.

[65] Kaiser, pp. 508–11. For the *Liber legum*, see Hubert Mordek, *Bibliotheca capitularium regum Francorum manuscripta: Überlieferung und Traditionszussammenhang der fränkischen Herrschererlasse* (München, 1995), p. 257. Modena, Bib. Cap. O.I.4 includes this same law of Lothar (De precariis quoque quae a rectoribus ecclesiarum . . . = *Liber Papiensis*, Lothar 21) with a title—*Cap. in lege romana*—suggesting that the passage came from the *Lex Romana canonice compta* or a similar compilation.

[66] "Systematischen Gesichtspunkten in höheren Masse gerecht zu werden ist dem Verfasser nicht gelungen." *Geschichte*, p. 207. Conrat's perplexity at the apparent disorganization of the work emerged with particular clarity in his later monograph in which he reorganized the chapters of the *Lex Romana* into an ancient/modern juristic framework for purposes of determining how much Roman legal doctrine survived in the early Middle Ages. See M. Conrat, *Die Lex Romana canonice compta. Römisches Recht im frühmittelalterlichen Italien, in systematischer Darstellung* (Amsterdam, 1904).

[67] Mor, *Lex Romana*, pp. 14–15.

center close to Milan. Horst Fuhrmann recently suggested Pavia as a possibility. Not only was Pavia the Lombard capital, and thus in possession of more legal resources (both human and archival) than most other cities, but a recently discovered early fragment of the *Collectio Anselmo dedicata* may also have been copied there.[68] Unlike the *Lex Romana canonice compta*, the *Collectio Anselmo dedicata* survives in multiple manuscripts, including four from the late ninth and tenth century.[69]

Paul Fournier doubted that the *Collectio Anselmo dedicata* derived directly from the *Lex Romana canonice compta*. His objection was based upon the fact that, while both collections include chapters from Lothar's *Capitulare Olonnense* (in both cases, it turns out, in the form of the *Liber legum*), they incorporate different chapters from it: the *Lex Romana canonice compta* has cap. 10 while *Collectio Anselmo dedicata* has cap. 1 and 5 (= *CAD* book 7, 138, 126). He therefore hypothesized that the similarities between the two collections, rather than reflecting the use of the *Lex Romana* by the compiler of the *CAD*, trace back instead to their derivation from a common source.[70] Fournier's suggestion never found wide acceptance, however, and Kaiser leaves no doubt that the *Lex Romana canonice compta* was the source of the Roman law materials in the *Collectio Anselmo dedicata*. The latter collection, he notes, echoes the *Lex Romana* in the choice and even the order of the Justinianic constitutions included. It also repeats the *LR*'s erroneous ascription of an excerpt from the *Edictum Theodorici* to C. 7.38, and even incorporates the glosses the copyist includes in Paris ms. 12448.[71]

In addition to the links between the *Lex Romana canonice compta* and the *Collectio Anselmo dedicata*, some historians have also posited a connection between the *LR* and a third compilation, known as the *Excerpta Bobiensa*.[72] (Kaiser refers to this work as the *Regulae ecclesiasticae*.)

---

[68] Horst Fuhrmann, "Fragmente der *Collectio Anselmo dedicata*," *Deutsches Archiv für Erforschungen des Mittelalters*, 44 (1988): 539–43. For the manuscript fragment, see Ugo Fiorina, "Due frammenti della «Collectio Anselmo dedicata» rinvenuti nell'Archivio di Stato di Pavia," *Athenaeum*, 60 (1982): 248–53.

[69] A partial edition is provided in Jean-Claude Besse, "Collectionis *Anselmo Dedicata* Liber Primus," *Revue de droit canonique*, 9 (1959): 207–96. The most recent and detailed discussion of these manuscripts is to be found in Russo, *Tradizione manoscritta*.

[70] P. Fournier, "L'origine de la collection «Anselmo dedicata»," in *Mélanges Girard* (Paris, 1912), pp. 475–92; E. Besta, *Le Fonti* (Milano, 1923), vol. I, 1.° p. 178.

[71] Kaiser, *Epitome Iuliani*, p. 556.

[72] F. Maasen, "Bobienser Excerpte des römischen Rechts," in *Sitzungsberichte der kaiserlichen Akademie der Wissenschaften, phil-hist. Kl.* 35 (1860): 73–108; ed. by C. G. Mor, "Bobbio, Pavia e gli 'Excerpta Bobiensia,'" *Contributi alla storia dell'Università di Pavia* (Pavia, 1925), pp. 43–114.

This work like the others evidently dates from the later ninth century and is also apparently Lombard in origin. It survives in two manuscripts: Milan, Bib. Ambr. G. 58 Sup (from late ninth-century Bobbio) and Livorno, Bib. Labronica ms. 10 from the tenth century.[73] In addition to a large collection of Novels, it contains eighteen constitutions from Justinian's Code, sixteen of them from book 1 and the rest from book 3. The connection between the *Excerpta Bobiensia* and the *Lex Romana Canonice Compta* could not be one of direct dependence because each contains materials absent from the other. The hypothesis rather was that both collections drew upon the same pre-existing compilation of Justinianic texts, making selections from this common source rather than directly from manuscripts of the Code, Novels, and Institutes. This idea, which in a preliminary form can already be seen in Conrat, was given its most vigorous exposition by Carlo Guido Mor.[74]

Although widely accepted, this hypothesis failed to survive Kaiser's examination of the chapters drawn from the *Epitome Juliani* in these works. The *Lex Romana canonice compta* and the *Collectio Anselmo dedicata* both proved, not surprisingly, to have derived from the same textual tradition of the *Epitome Juliani*—specifically the group A tradition represented most notably by two manuscripts from northern Italy ca. 800, Paris, BN lat. 4568 [= *CLA* 557] and Milan, Biblioteca Trivulziana 688 [= *CLA* 366]. The novels in the *Excerpta Bobiensia*, in contrast, turn out to derive from the group D tradition of which Vienna ÖNB 2160 is the earliest surviving representative.[75] The novels contained in the two collections could not, therefore, have come from a common source and there are few other elements in common. Both compilations, therefore, must now be seen as evidence of direct contact with the Justinianic texts themselves.

Yet the absence of a shared source for these compilations does not mean that they were entirely independent. One unresolved problem

---

[73] For the Milan manuscript, see P. Collura, *La precarolina e la carolina a bobbio* (Milan, 1943). Bischoff also dated this manuscript to the second half of the ninth century; *Handschriftenarchiv Bernhard Bischoff.* Kaiser provides detailed indices of the contents of both manuscripts, *Epitome Iuliani*, pp. 523–36.

[74] Conrat, *Geschichte*, p. 212; C. G. Mor, "Di una perduta compilazione di diritto romano ad uso del clero, fonte degli «Excerpta Bobiensia» e della «Lex romana canonice compta»," *Archivio giuridico* XCV (1926), pp. 20–26 [now in *Scritti*, pp. 271–78]. See now the summary of earlier historiography in Kaiser, *Epitome Iuliani*, pp. 562–64.

[75] Kaiser, *Epitome Iuliani*, pp. 564–76.

is the coincidence that troubled Fournier of finding different excerpts from the *Capitulare Olonnense* in both the *Lex Romana canonice compta* and the *Collectio Anselmo dedicata*. Kaiser's demonstration that both compilations drew upon Lupus' *Liber legum* only adds to the difficulties, for nothing we know about that text suggests that it was particularly common in the ninth century. Only two complete copies of it survive today, both of them later than the compilations we are discussing, nor is there any evidence of its being quoted until it appears in the *LR* and *CAD*. One possible explanation of this apparent coincidence, however, would be if both works were products of the same center. In that case the compiler of the *Collectio Anselmo dedicata* would have had available to him not only the *Lex Romana* itself but also the books from which it was originally compiled.

Regardless of how many centers there were, however, all three compilations reveal a remarkable coherence in what they regard as important. Kaiser discovered a number of points of contact between all three compilations. The *Collectio Anselmo dedicata*, for example, combines the Justinianic excerpts with selections from the Register of Gregory the Great and selections from various canon law compilations; these last include recension A2 of the pseudoisidorean decretals, the *Collectio Dionysio-Hadriana*, shortened versions of the Roman councils of Zacharias (743) and Eugenius II (826), and excerpts from the Council of Epheseus, Pseudo-Gelasius, and the treatise *De recipiendis et non recipiendis libris*. The Paris ms. 12448 contains, in addition to the *Lex Romana canonice compta*, the *Collectio Dionysio-Hadriana* of canon law and shortened versions of the Roman councils of Pope Zacharias from 743 and of Pope Eugenius II from 826, all copied by the same early tenth-century scribe; the other part of this composite manuscript contains a collection of excerpts from the register of Gregory I, the *Collectio Novariensis*, and Pseudo-Gelasius. The manuscripts containing the *Excerpta Bobiensa*, similarly, display much the same pattern, for both of them include a collection of Gregorian materials known as the *Regulae definitionum Gregorii* while the Labronica manuscript also contains other texts, notably the *Collectio Hibernensis* and Pseudoisidorean decretals, that served as source material for the *Collectio Anselmo dedicata*. Kaiser even demonstrated that the *Excerpta Bobiensa* and the *Regulae definitionum Gregorii* arrange their materials according to a similar scheme of topics.[76]

[76] Kaiser, *Epitome Iuliani*, pp. 494–99, 514–21, 523–36, 548–50, 553–54.

The link between these different sets of materials go beyond shared source materials to the techniques by which the texts were handled. For example, the Paris collection, the *Regulae definitionum Gregorii*, and the *Collectio Anselmo dedicata* all use both abbreviated and full length forms for their Gregorian excerpts, even though they do not always abbreviate the same excerpts in the same way. Sometimes the *Collectio Anselmo dedicata* gives the abbreviated text contained in the Paris collection, sometimes it gives the complete text of a passage found abbreviated elsewhere and at still other times it gives an abbreviated text where the Paris manuscript gives the integral version. The Paris manuscript and the *Collectio Anselmo dedicata* even differ in the versions they give for the papal councils of 743 and 826.[77] As with the *Liber legum*, therefore, the compiler of the *Collectio Anselmo dedicata* seems to have had at his disposal not only the already shaped materials of Paris ms. 12488, but also the source texts that had been worked over to produce the texts found in that manuscript; he was also capable of performing the same kind of textual surgery on the Gregorian excerpts as seen in the independent collections. The *Regulae definitionum Gregorii*, similarly, resembles the collection in Paris 12448 but displays too many distinctive features to have shared a common archetype.

The question for us, however, is why the compilers of these collections, all working in the second half of the ninth century, were suddenly interested in Roman law. One clue is provided by the contemporary flurry of citations of Justinianic materials in the correspondence of popes Nicholas I and John VIII. In that case, though, the invocation of Roman law seems to have been part of a general political strategy to shore up papal authority at a time when it was under attack. The weakness of the Carolingian empire left the pope without strong political support, even as the Byzantine empire was increasingly hostile to papal pretensions and as Rome itself seemed threatened by both Muslim and Lombards in southern Italy. In this context, John VIII in particular began to claim for the papacy not only the honor due the heir of St. Peter but also the respect due to the ancient seat of the Roman republic and empire. Percy Ernst Schramm long ago noted that while neither Nicholas I nor Hadrian II appear to have mentioned the Roman senate, JohnVIII mentioned it repeatedly, most notably in his claim that "the senate, the whole

[77] Kaiser, *Epitome Iuliani*, pp. 554, 588–99.

Roman people, and the *gens togata*" supported his coronation of Charles the Bald as emperor.[78] The same policy appears to lay behind the invocation of Roman law in letters to Louis II.[79] The other side of this policy, and one that was particularly important in dealing with the Greek church, is the defense of papal traditions, including a life of Gregory I written during these years by John the Deacon. Even here, however, Gregory's Roman heritage was emphasized as the *Vita* began with a reference to Romulus.[80]

Although our texts are Lombard and episcopal rather than Roman and papal, many issues were the same. The pseudo-isidorean decretals, for example, could be as useful to ninth-century bishops as they later would be to popes. Just as Roman law reminded Romans of the great classical past to which the Roman church now claimed the succession, so in northern Italy the invocation of Roman law represented an assertion of ecclesiastical independence from the dominant Lombard law.[81] There were also connections at the personal level between the two centers. Paul Fournier noted that the link between John VIII and Anselm of Milan goes back to the period while Anselm was still archdeacon, leading him to suggest that the *Collectio Anselmo dedicata* reflected, at least indirectly, many of John's own policies.[82] John himself sought the alliance of the archbishop of Milan as he

[78] "eligimus . . . et approbavimus una cum annisu et voto omnium fratrum . . . sanctae Romanae ecclesiae ministrorum amplique senatus totiusque Romani populi gentisque togatae et secundum priscam consuetudinem solempniter ad imperii Romani sceptra proveximus et augustali nomine decaravimus . . ." E. A. Eckhardt, "Das Protokoll von Ravenna 877 über die Kaiserkrönung Karls des Kahlen," *Deutsches Archiv*, 23 (1967): 295–311 at 306. Percy Ernst Schramm, *Kaiser, Rom und Renovatio* (Leipzig, 1929), p. 47

[79] MGH, *Epist.* VII, letter 111, pp. 102–3 (cited above) and *Fragmenta* no. 52, pp. 304–6. Both discussed by Schramm, pp. 48–49.

[80] G. Arnaldi, "Giovanni Immonide e la cultura a Roma al tempo di Giovanni VIII," *Bullettino dell'Istituto Storico Italiano per il Medio Evo e Archivio Muratoriano*, 78 (1956): 33–89; but see also Arnaldi, "Giovanni Immonide e la cultura a Roma al tempo di Giovanni VIII: una retractatio," in *Europa medievale e mondo bizantino : contatti effettivi e possibilità di studi comparati : Tavola rotonda del XVIII Congresso del CISH—Montréal, 29 agosto 1995*, ed. by Arnaldi and G. Cavallo (Rome, 1997), pp. 163–77.

[81] G. P. Bognetti, "Pensiero e vita a Milano e nel milanese davanti l'età carolingia," *Storia di Milano*, II (Milan, 1954), pp. 716–803, at p. 790.

[82] Fournier, "L'origine de la collection «Anselmo dedicata»," pp. 20–22. G. Arnaldi, "Papato, arcivescovi e vescovi nell'età post-carolingia," in *Vescovi e diocesi in Italia nel medio evo (sec. IX–XIII)* (Padua, 1964), pp. 27–54 at pp. 37, 45. For a letter of John VIII urging his ally to return to the obedience of the then archbishop Anspert—one of the costs, evidently, of the papal alliance with Charles the Fat, see MGH, *Epist.* VII no. 271, pp. 239–40.

tried to influence the direction of Italian politics in the years following the death of Charles the Bald.

For our present purposes, the important point is that the late ninth-century revival of Roman law must be seen as symbolic and political rather than specifically legal. Thus, the sudden appearance of references to Justinianic law in papal letters of the 860s and 870s, and in the collections from about the same time. Thus, too, the equally sudden abandonment of Roman law, even as a symbol, even before the end of the ninth century. For the tenth century, indeed, there is little to be said. Papal documents after John VIII do not appear to make use of the works of the *Corpus*; thus a letter of Benedict VI from 972–74, dealing with whether a man can marry the sister of a woman to whom he was betrothed, mentions Roman law without citing any specific text.[83] The only significant tenth-century reference we have been able to find comes from a letter of Atto of Vercelli in a letter, also on marriage, in which he cites C. 5.4.26.2, Ep. Jul. 32.1.1, and In 1.10.2 and 1.10.12, mentioning them only after Lombard and Salic law, and along with St. Paul, various popes, and (of course) the Bible.[84] Since the Justinianic materials cited were all included in the *Collectio Anselmo dedicata*—a work known to have been available at Vercelli—it is unlikely that Atto's knowledge of them reflects any direct contact with Justinian's texts.[85]

Tenth-century canon law collections, none of which went beyond the Novels, tell much the same story. The earliest of these is the *Capitula ex lege Iustiniana*, which originally made up part of the collection of ecclesiastical and canonistic materials in Rome, Biblioteca Vallicelliana, ms. T. XVIII. Although the folios that actually contained the text no longer survive, the index to the volume enumerates the contents of the collection in detail: it consisted of nearly 40 chapters of the *Epitome Juliani* drawn from eight novels, all dealing with various issues of ecclesiastical interest. The manuscript, in Beneventan and caroline script, is from the eleventh century, but

[83] Conrat, *Geschichte*, p. 25 and n. 7; the letter is Mansi XIX, p. 57 [= Jaffé, no. 3779].

[84] PL 134: 106–11; the Institutes are cited at 106D–7A, the Code and Epitome Juliani at 107CD.

[85] C. 5.4.26 was cap. 175 in the *Lex Romana canonice compta* and cap. VII.7 in the *Collectio Anselmo dedicata*; In. 1.10 was cap. 186 and VII.18; Ep. Jul. 32.1 was cap. 181 and VII.13. For the *Collectio Anselmo dedicata* at Vercelli, see Patetta, *Studi*, pp. 701–7, and Russo, pp. 48–50 with references to other bibliography.

the collection's origin in the 910s or 920s is betrayed by its interest in the issues related to the debate over the re-ordination of bishops consecrated by Pope Formosus.[86] A second collection, similarly from southern Italy and similarly marked by the re-ordination controversy, is *Collectio in IX libris* of Vatican Library, Vat. lat. 1349. This compilation is based largely on materials from the Vallicelliana manuscript, with the difference that they here are organized according to subject; the 21 chapters from the *Epitome Juliani*, in particular, were all included in the *Capitula ex lege Iustiniana* and were probably taken directly from it. Also deriving from the Vallicelliana materials is the much shorter collection contained in Rome, Bib. Casanatense 2010 (B. V. 17). This collection included only 7 chapters from the *Epitome Juliani*, but they, too, all came from the *Capitula ex lege Iustiniana.* Later, in the first half of the eleventh century, a different southern Italian compiler would combine the *Collectio in IX Libris* with the *Lex Dei*, Lombard law, and capitularies as late as Henry II's capitulary from 1014 to produce the *Collectio in V Libris.* This collection comes down to us in three manuscripts: BAV, Vat. lat. 1339, Biblioteca Vallicelliana, ms. B.11, and Monte Cassino 125. This compiler evidently had a copy of the *Epitome Juliani* available, since his version of some chapters is more accurate than those he found in the *Collectio in IX libris* even as he preserved the rubrics provided by the older collection.[87] None of these collections offers anything significant in the way of legal commentary, nor do any of them draw on the Justinianic works apart from the Novels.

All of the collections of Novels just discussed are clearly oriented toward clerical use. Different from them in this regard is the Klagenfurter fragment preserved in a single bifolium as Kärnter Landesarchiv GV-Hs. 10/2/2. This brief and partial text combines several chapters of the *Epitome Juliani*, according to Kaiser in the group B tradition,

---

[86] This collection was first described by Patetta, "Contributi alla storia del diritto romano," pp. 3–38; it was studied in more detail by P. Fournier, "Un groupe de recueils canoniques italiens des Xe et XIe siècles," in *Memoires de l'institut national de France, Académie des inscriptions et belles-lettres*, vol. 40 (Paris, 1916), pp. 95–213, at 96–123, who noted the relevance of the collection to the ordination controversy and suggested a Neopolitan provenance. Kaiser [*Epitome Iuliani*, pp. 615–37] determined that the textual tradition of this collection as well as the other two discussed in this paragraph was based on the group D version of the *Epitome Juliani.*

[87] On this, see Fournier, "Un groupe de recueils canoniques italiens," pp. 159–89; Kaiser, *Epitome Iuliani*, pp. 632–37.

with several laws taken from the *Lex Visigothorum*. The other group B manuscripts are from Skt. Gall (Stiftbib. 1395) and Burgundy (Berlin, ms. lat. 269), while the bifolium itself, according to Bischoff, originated in Nonantola in the mid-ninth century.[88] Both the Justinianic and Visigothic materials deal, broadly speaking, with inheritance, but in the absence of both the beginning and end of the piece and of the bridge between the Roman and German laws it is impossible to say more about its purpose.

It is equally difficult to imagine the environment from which this fragment emerged. Although a large quantity of documentation survives from ninth- and tenth-century Italy, most of it prepared by professional notaries, even the most general references to Roman law are exceedingly rare. Roman legal terminology, where it is used, remains uncertain and imprecise: one has the impression of phrases copied from charter to charter rather than resulting from direct contact with classical texts.[89]

Conclusion

Fifty years ago, in his classic survey of Italian legal history during the Middle Ages, Francesco Calasso entitled his chapter on Justinian *L'Italia terra di diritto giustinianeo*—Italy the land of Justinianic law. His intention was to focus on the historical circumstance, noted at the beginning of this chapter, that Italy was the only European country where the Justinianic codification had formally been given the force of law, replacing all previous enactments. Having enunciated his theme, however, Calasso immediately had to concede that it was far from clear how deeply Justinianic law had penetrated Italian society. Only fourteen years elapsed between the application of the codification to Italy by the Pragmatic Sanction and the Lombard invasion, and many pre-Justinianic norms continued in use in the seventh and eighth centuries: the Church, the Lombard king Liutprand, and Lombard

[88] H. Menhardt, "Ein Bruchstück der Lex Visigothorum aus einer dem Codex Holkhamensis 210 verwandten Handschrift," ZSS GA, 46 (1926): 360–64 (with plate); Kaiser, *Epitome Iuliani*, pp. 638–53, including edition.

[89] See Frezza's survey of the evidence in *L'influsso del diritto romano giustiniano*, pp. 10–18. For a survey of the very conflicting evidence on *convenientia*, see Giovanna Nicolaj, *Cultura e prassi di notai preirneriani. Alle origini del rinascimento giuridico* (Milan, 1991), pp. 42–57.

law frequently adhered to Theodosian norms, and notaries continued to employ terminology, such as *res mancipi* or the ancient *sollemnitas verborum* of the *stipulatio*, that had disappeared from the Justinianic codification.[90] Balanced against these problems, when Calasso wrote, stood the glossed manuscripts of the Institutes and Code that testified to the study directed toward the Justinianic codification even if the world of practical life remained untouched.

In this chapter we have seen that, once those precious glossed manuscripts are removed from the evidence for the early Middle Ages, little remains to suggest that Justinianic law played a significant role before the end of the tenth century, in Italy or elsewhere. There must have been manuscripts, at least in antique copies, for otherwise the texts probably would have been lost forever.[91] But there is scant evidence that those manuscripts were copied or read. Apart from the *Epitome Juliani*, which survives in multiple codices, the manuscript evidence for the Justinianic works is limited to two fragments, one of a ninth-century Institutes in Verona and another, not Italian, of an Institutes together with a portion of the Digest.

Other evidence leads to the same conclusion. While it is possible to collect a modest number of references to the *Epitome Juliani*, both within and outside of Italy, the principal works of Justinian's codification left almost no mark on the early Middle Ages. Direct contact with Justinian's texts Institutes and Code is suggested only by the handful of citations produced by the papacies of Nicholas I and John VIII, and by the three canonistic collections that were created at the same time: the *Excerpta Bobiensia*, the *Lex Romana canonice compta*, and the *Collectio Anselmo dedicata*. None of these indicate any particular juristic expertise or interest. Rather, they seem to reflect the use of Roman law as a symbol of the Roman past to which the papacy, and the church more generally, claimed to be heir. It is no surprise, therefore, that when the particular political circumstances of the 860s to 880s had passed, references to Roman law fell off precipitously. It could still, rarely, be invoked for polemical purposes, but our evidence shows no interest in it as law.

---

[90] Calasso, *Medio Evo del Diritto*, pp. 81–93. Cortese, *Il Diritto nella Storia Medievale*, pp. 112–23, would prefer to see vulgarization in these survivals, but either interpretation concedes a limited penetration of Justinianic law into legal practice.

[91] The Latin texts of Justinian's codification were hardly used in the late ninth-century Greek *Libri Basilicorum*. See Wolfgang Kunkel, *An Introduction to Roman Legal and Constitutional History*, trans. by J. M. Kelly (Oxford, 1973), pp. 179–80.

CHAPTER THREE

THE PERIOD OF REDISCOVERY

After centuries of indifference and neglect, the Justinianic codification in the eleventh century became the focus of intense study. A handful of references around the turn of the century gave way after 1025 to a steadily increasing flow of manuscripts and citations that extended eventually to all works of the Justinianic codification. The Bamberg and Turin manuscripts of the Institutes and the Pistoia manuscript of the Code, previously dated to the tenth century, prove to be important witnesses to this process, but they do not stand alone. Equally important is evidence that has received little attention in the past century, in particular the glosses and commentaries to the Lombard law. A few small works from before the end of the century even demonstrate the emergence of a purely Romanist jurisprudence.

While this picture of the reception of the *Corpus* might strike some readers as dangerously new, in other ways it represents a return to ideas dominant before Kantorowicz. It was Conrat, after all, who first insisted on the significance of the eleventh century, and of the Lombard jurists, in the transition between early medieval and "Bolognese" jurisprudence. The hypothesis that Justinian's works were brought back into circulation by specialists who understood their value is also consistent with what we know about eleventh-century intellectual life generally. Medieval scholars did not simply find books by chance. Generally they had to look for works whose existence they knew of only from references in their reading. For the tenth century, Guglielmo Cavallo documented the way that Gerbert, for example, wrote correspondents in many regions attempting to find books that were mentioned in his reading but that were unavailable to him.[1] Monte Cassino in the eleventh century, and the recovery of the *Logica Nova* in the twelfth,[2] provide other well-known instances of scholars seeking

[1] "Libri scritti, libri letti, libri dimenticati," in *Il secolo di ferro: mito e realtà del secolo X* [Settimane di studio del Centro italiano di studi sull'alto medioevo, 38] (Spoleto, 1991), pp. 759–802 esp. at p. 782.

[2] C. H. Lohr, "The Medieval Interpretation of Aristotle," in *Cambridge History of Later Medieval Philosophy*, ed. Norman Kretzmann, Anthony Kenny, Jan Pinborg (Cambridge, 1982), p. 83; on the translations and their translators, see George Lacombe, et al. *Aristoteles Latinus* (Bruges and Paris, 1939–76).

out manuscripts of works that were rare and unread. The Justinianic compilation, which is no less technical than advanced works in logic or science, fits the same pattern. Rather than the renewed interest in the Digest producing the juristic renaissance, it was the revived interest in legal studies generally and in Roman law that led readers to seek out the Digest and Justinian's other works.

In this chapter we shall endeavor to establish the general outlines of the circulation of Justinian's *Corpus* from the beginning of the eleventh century, when only the *Epitome Juliani* could be said to have had any appreciable circulation, to the end of the century when all parts of the codification were being read and studied. We shall take the material as chronologically as the uncertainties of dating the evidence allows. The first section of the chapter considers the period to mid-century; next we shall take up the evidence for the three decades between 1050 and 1080; and we shall treat the last two decades of the century at the end.

The Beginning of a Juristic Revival: 950–1050

The decades around the year 1000 provide a variety of evidence, much of it hard to interpret, that the Justinianic law was being read in various regions in Italy. For the area around Rome, this interest was attested by the brief emergence of the *Summa Perusina* from obscurity and the production of the Bamberg Institutes. South of Rome in the Beneventan zone, it took the form of glosses in the Florentina and the production of one, perhaps two, attempts to summarize Roman law for secular purposes. A third stream of evidence from Ravenna amounts to barely more than a handful of documents scattered over several decades, although thanks to later remarks by Peter Damian and Odofredo it has drawn more interest from historians. Later but more enduring in the long run, are citations of the Justinianic works that begin to appear from Pavia, the old capital of the Lombard kingdom and still the largest single center of legal Lombard law judges. Only here does one see an interest in Justinianic law that grows in both quantity and sophistication over time, achieving by the mid-eleventh century a self-sustaining momentum of legal studies.

Rome and the Beneventan Zone

Although the chapter summaries of Justinian's Code that make up the *Summa Perusina* probably originated in the late sixth or early seventh centuries, it is only around the year 1000 that one sees them cited. The earliest reference comes from Rome itself, in a document from 996 from Santa Maria in Via Lata; two other references, the latest from 1014, come from the monastery of Farfa.[3] (Justinianic law is also mentioned in a few other Farfa documents of the period—a fact especially notable because Farfa, though close to Rome, was itself under Lombard law).[4] Another quotation from the *Summa Perusina* occurs in a 1010 letter of Pope Sylvester II,[5] while two passages are found in Vercelli Bib. Cap. 122, a mid-century Roman manuscript of the *Epitome Juliani.*

The unique manuscript of the *Summa Perusina*, Perugia, Bib. Cap. ms. 32, also dates from this period. Despite the poor quality of the parchment, which is stiff and full of holes, the scribe managed to produce a surprisingly handsome manuscript. His minuscule has been difficult to date, owing mainly to a variety of precaroline elements that give his writing an archaic cast despite other, more modern features. The paradox is resolved, however, by the recognition that we are probably dealing with a scribe whose early graphic training was in Beneventan script; the manuscript accordingly is to be attributed to central or southern Italy in the first half of the eleventh century.[6] One does, however, wonder what his exemplar was like. The most probable hypothesis, and one consistent with how the text is cited in documents, was that the summaries were transmitted as a separate text without the Code, as one also sees done for some glosses to the *Epitome Juliani.* Even so the difference in scale is striking—a few folios for the *Epitome Juliani*, usually at the end of a manuscript

[3] Patetta, *Adnotationes codicum domini Justiniani*, pp. xliii. The documents are: *S. Maria in Via Lata Tabularium*, ed. by L. M. Hartmann and M. Merores (Wien, 1895–1913), n. 24 from 996; *Regesto di Farfa* ed. I. Giorgi and U. Balzani (Roma, 1879–1914), nos. 437 and 492 from 999 and 1014.

[4] Frezza, *L'influsso del diritto romano giustiniano*, pp. 11–12.

[5] Horst Fuhrmann, *Einfluß und Verbreitung der pseudoisidorischen Fälschungen*, MGH, *Schriften* 24, 3 vols. (Stuttgart, 1972–73), pp. 331 and 721 n. 147; see also Kaiser, *Epitome Iuliani*, p. 339.

[6] A. Ciaralli and Valentina Longo, "Due contributi a un riesame della Summa Perusina (Perugia, Bibl. Cap. ms. 32)," *Scrittura e Civiltà*, 25 (2001): 1–62.

of the work itself, compared with a long manuscript for the *Summa Perusina*.

A more important manuscript from this period and from Rome itself is Bamberg Ms. Jur. 1, the earliest intact manuscript of the Institutes. It was written by two hands, one of them in *minuscola romanesca*. Although its present location in Bamberg has given rise to speculation that it was copied for imperial use, perhaps for Otto III, the manuscript does not display any of the characteristics typical of books commissioned for royal use; it is more likely (as Bischoff suggested) that the manuscript was taken to Germany and incorporated into the imperial library during the reign of Henry III. As to its readers in Italy or later in Germany, the manuscript offers few clues. It does not appear to have been used for study because the rare marginal glosses are in the hands of the scribes and thus were probably copied directly from the exemplar. Contemporary additions to the manuscript consist of a description of the varieties of ancient palace judges on the flyleaf and two very brief extracts from C. 1.1.17 on the role of judges and, in a different hand, a law of Otto I on the last page. Although the content of these materials suggests readers who were judges, the insertions were not written in the documentary script one would expect from a legal professional but in a mediocre *minuscola romanesca* indicative of a poor graphical education.

The revival of Roman law in the Beneventan zone is in many ways similar to that in Rome and Lazio: mysterious in origin, secular in orientation, and short-lived in duration. It has long been known that a handful of Beneventan glosses in the margins of the Florentina date from this period. One of them (vol. I, 17r) provides a translation for the Greek word "ousia"—"id est substantia." Yet to this interest in the Digest, limited as it was, Wolfgang Kaiser has now juxtaposed a contemporary second witness to an interest in Roman law in the Beneventan zone. The *Collectio Gaudenziana* comes to us uniquely in British Library ms. add. 46676, a late tenth-century manuscript in Beneventan script.[7] This compilation presents a confusing mix of

[7] Augusto Gaudenzi, *Un'antica compilazione di diritto romano e visigoto, con alcuni frammenti delle leggi di Eurico, tratta da un manoscritto della Biblioteca di Holkham* (Bologna, 1886); Conrat, *Geschichte*, pp. 57, 166 ff., 277 ff.; Patetta, "Sui frammenti di diritto germanico della collezione gaudenziana e della *Lectio legum*," *Studi*, pp. 861–98; G. Vismara, *La Fragmenta Gaudenziana*, IRMA, I, 2 b *bb* ß (Milan, 1968); G. Santini, "Il sapere giuridico," p. 110; Cortese, *Il diritto nella storia medievale*, vol. I, pp. 250–53. Kaiser, *Epitome Iuliani*, pp. 655–844.The ms., now British Library Add. 46,676, is dated and briefly described in Lowe, *The Beneventan Script*, vol. 1, p. 77, vol. 2, p. 127.

Justinianic texts—some novels, selections from three titles of the Code (C. 1.3, 11.42, 11.48), and simplified versions of various parts of the Institutes—with a variety of other, mainly visigothic materials. (The combination of Justinianic and visigothic texts invite comparisons with the Klagenfurter fragment, but the two works are not related textually, and use different traditions of the *Epitome Juliani*: group B for the Klagenfurter fragment and group D for the *Collectio Gaudenziana*).[8] Part one begins with the *commonitorium Alarici*, from which, in fact, the title *Ordo mellifluus* is drawn. The text proceeds with a novel, three paragraphs of the Pragmatic Sanction, and a rare collection of Novels also found in some manuscripts of the *Epitome Juliani*; then, without indicating a shift in sources, the text continues with fourteen chapters (known as the *Fragmenta Gaudenziana*) that apparently are based on Visigothic law. The compilation returns to Roman law with C. 1.3.7, 8, 19, 20, and 33; a constitution of the Emperors Theodosius and Valentinianus also found in a handful of other manuscripts; an abbreviated version of C. 1.2.14; C. 1.3.10; and C. 11.48.7, 12. The remainder of the first part consists of excerpts from the Institutes of Justinian, omitting many chapters, giving the title only for others, and shortening those given *in extenso*, with 3 chapters of the Brevarium interspersed. These are then followed with extracts from the Visigothic law, incorrectly attributed to Justinian. The second part is given over to the *Epitome Aegidii*, a shortened version of the Brevarium.[9]

Since contact with the Code and Institutes would be notable for any period between the sixth and mid-eleventh century, it is not surprising that scholars have struggled to find a context for the *Collectio Gaudenziana*. Augusto Gaudenzi, who discovered the collection and for whom it is named, doubted that the selections from the *Epitome Aegidii* originally belonged to the Collectio. Conrat, similarly, noting the many textual corruptions, concluded that the collection must have been assembled out of multiple pieces, with "the oldest kernel being far older than the ninth century."[10] Such reasoning generally led to the collection being assigned a fairly early date, to the seventh, eighth or ninth centuries. These conclusions, however, have been recently overturned by Wolfgang Kaiser's detailed study of the text and manuscript: in reality the first detailed study ever addressed to

[8] Kaiser, *Epitome Iuliani*, p. 708.
[9] See the detailed summary in Kaiser, *Epitome Iuliani*, pp. 669–92.
[10] *Geschichte*, p. 283.

the *Collectio Gaudenziana*. Kaiser draws attention to the interventions made by a second hand to the summary of In. 2.1.25 on ff. 18v–19r, where the corrector inserts two lengthy, additional passages into a text that had made sense without them. Such corrections, which reworked the original Justinianic text in exactly the same manner as the original version had done, are what one expects of an author, not a proofreader. Yet if the British Library manuscript was prepared under the compiler's own supervision, then the place and date of the manuscript give us the place and date of the compilation: southern Italy in the late tenth century.

In addition to establishing a new, later date for the *Collectio Gaudenziana*, Kaiser also rejects the idea that it was assembled out of pre-existing materials. All of the source texts, whether Justinianic or visigothic, were subjected to similar editorial excisions: phrases are simplified or simply deleted, explanatory details are omitted, language is simplified. The compiler even made some effort to assure that the Justinianic law given in the first part did not contradict the *Epitome Aegidii* of the second.[11] Yet if he was not working with pre-existing texts, then he must actually have had access to the text he included in his collection: at minimum, the *Epitome Juliani*, Justinian's Code and Institutes, the *Lex Visigothorum*, and the *Epitome Aegidii*. How well the compiler understood these materials is another matter. Kaiser doubts that he fully grasped how great the differences were between these various sources. It is noteworthy, too, that the compiler omitted not only all passages dealing with the philosophy of law (such as the first two titles of book one of the Institutes) but nearly everything concerning the role of judges. These limitations, however, do not mitigate the originality of his objective: to produce a simplified, generally practical overview of Roman law.[12]

A third possible witness to southern Italian interest in Roman law in the Beneventan zone might be the brief text preserved in Rome, Biblioteca Vallicelliana, ms. B. 32, a Beneventan manuscript from the third quarter of the eleventh century.[13] Its portentous and not entirely accurate title—*Lectio legum brebiter facta a Leone sanctissimo papa*

[11] Kaiser, *Epitome Iuliani*, pp. 793–802.
[12] Kaiser, *Epitome Iuliani*, p. 803–5.
[13] Conrat, *Geschichte*, pp. 268–74; Patetta, *Studi*, pp. 29–38; 862–68; Cortese, *Diritto nella storia medievale*, vol. I, pp. 249–50; Kaiser, *Epitome Iuliani*, pp. 720–22. For the date of the manuscript, see Lowe, *The Beneventan Script*, p. 77.

et Constantino sapientissimo et piissimo imperatore ab institutionibus ex libro novelle magni Justiniani dispositionis ad directionem humanitatis—was borrowed from the late eighth-century Greek title of the *Ecloga* of Leo Isauro and Constantine Copronimo. In fact, the six chapters of the text as we have it come from a variety of sources, including one from the *Summa Perusina*, one from the *Edictum Theodorici*, two from the *Lex Visigothorum* (one of which is attributed to Justinian), and two that reflect Lombard law without actually quoting any specific text. Although it is impossible to date this text with any exactness, the use of the *Summa Perusina* and *Lex Visigothorum* have better parallels with the environment of the late tenth or early eleventh centuries than any earlier period. Like the *Collectio Gaudenziana*, moreover, the *Lectio legum* deals with secular topics, including the theft of animals, liability for crimes committed by a relative, and a widow's right to her husband's property.

Yet if the *Collectio Gaudenziana* and the *Lectio legum* represent a revival of secular law in the Beneventan zone, they do not suggest that this movement had gotten very far. Neither author goes beyond selecting a variety of texts from different and often incompatible compilations, then simplifying both the language and legal content of those texts to make them accessible for elementary readers. Nor is there any evidence to suggest that things got better in subsequent decades. To the contrary: apart from the canon law collection mentioned in the last chapter—the *Collectio in V libris*—no further evidence exists for southern Italian interest in Roman law until the second half of the eleventh century. It is a movement that begins, and apparently ends, with these works.

Ravenna and Pavia

Perhaps because of their brief duration, these revivals of Roman law in Lazio and the Beneventan zone have attracted little attention from historians. The situation is different for Ravenna, owing mainly to Odofredo's claim that the *libri legales* came to Bologna directly from there. Little has been found to validate the thirteenth-century legend. Although Roman law had remained in force in early medieval Ravenna, legal practice there had not been particularly influenced by Justinianic norms.[14] It is noteworthy, therefore, when a document

[14] Pier Silverio Leicht, "Ravenna e Bologna," in *Atti del Congresso Internazionale di Diritto Romano (Bologna e Roma 17–27 aprile 1933)* (Pavia, 1934), Part 1 (Bologna), vol. 1, pp. 277–90; for the survival of pre-Justinianic norms at Ravenna in the early Middle Ages, see pp. 281–83.

from 953 seems to refer to a rule on emphyteutic leases of ecclesiastical property from one of Justinian's Novels.[15] An explicit citation of the Justinianic texts is first found a generation later, in 975, when the record of a legal proceeding begins with an arenga quoting a Novel of Justinian (Epitome Juliani cap. 106 no. 370 [= Novel 113])[16] and C. 2.4.16.[17] Neither of these citations actually bear on the matter of the case, which had been waged between the two sons of a now dead Constantius and a priest named Johannes, but rather serve the essentially rhetorical purpose of supporting the principle that legal issues once decided should not be reopened again. Justinianic law continues to be cited in subsequent generations, but only rarely: a few late tenth-century documents repeat a formula paraphrased from C. 2.3.20,[18] for example, while a document from 1013 repeats the arenga already used in 975.[19]

More important for the reputation of Ravenna than any document is a 1046 letter of Peter Damian regarding the computation of the grades of consanguinity for marriage. Certain *sapientes* of the city of Ravenna, he wrote, justify their methods of calculating consanguinity by citing the principle "quod Iustinianus suis interserit Institutis: *Sed nec neptem,* intuit *fratris vel sororis ducere quis potest, quamvis quarto gradu sit.* [In. 1.10.3]."[20] Damian shows that he, too, can cite Justinian by invoking In. 1.10.1, 3.2.3, and 3.5.5, but his refutation of opposing views relies mainly on ecclesiastical authorities.[21] The significance

[15] Marco Fantuzzi, *Monumenti ravennati de' secoli di mezzo, per la maggior parte inediti* (Venice, 1801–4), I 25, cited by Frezza, pp. 11–12.

[16] Giovanna Nicolaj mistakenly cites Nov. 111.1 as the source of the passage and inexplicably rules out the *Epitome Juliani* as the version used of Novels in favor of the *Authenticum; Cultura e prassi di notai preirneriani*, p. 37. In fact, the relevant passage ["Negotia iam finita nullo modo volumus refricari"] uses exactly the same words as the *Epitome* with only a slightly different order ["finita autem iam negotia refricari nullo volumus modo"].

[17] Cited in J. Ficker, *Forschungen zur Reichs- und Rechtsgeschichte Italiens* (Innsbruck, 1868–72), vol. 4, p. 37, n. 28. Ficker cites not the document itself but C. Morbio, *Storie dei municipi italiani, illustrata con documenti inediti* (Milan, 1838), vol. I, p. 46. We have not been able to find the cited first edition, however, nor have we located the document in the much more widely available second edition.

[18] P. Federici, *Rerum Pomposianarum historia* (Roma, 1781), vol. I no. 16, from 986; Fantuzzi, vol. III no. 6, from 997; see on this Nicolaj, *Cultura e prassi*, pp. 39–40, and Ruggero Benericetti, *Le carte del decimo secolo nell'Archivio arcivescovile di Ravenna* (Ravenna, 1999–2002), vol. 2, p. xxv.

[19] J.-B. Mittarelli, *Annales Camalulenses ordines Sancti Benedicti* (Venetiae, 1755–73), vol. 1 no. XCI col. 209–12.

[20] Kurt Reindel, ed. *Die Briefe des Petrus Damiani* [MGH, *Die Briefe der deutschen Kaiserzeit*, vol. IV, part 1] (Weimar, 1983), no. 19, pp. 179–99, at p. 180.

[21] Ibid., pp. 185–87. For Damian's legal learning in general, see N. Tamassia,

of the letter, however, lies less in what it says about Damian's learning than in his characterization of those *sapientes* who were causing the trouble as both schoolmasters and judges, for Damian refers to them as holding "in gimnasio ferulam" and who argue cases "in tribunalibus."[22]

Writing in the early twentieth century, P. S. Leicht combined Damian's letter with the documentary evidence to argue for a legal revival in late tenth-century Ravenna. Although he had to concede that pre-Justinianic norms were followed in Ravenna throughout the early Middle Ages, Leicht contended that Justinianic procedures were introduced at the end of the tenth century, during the time of the Ottonians whom, he suggested, possibly sponsored a juristic center at Ravenna "like that at Pavia"; for him, accordingly, Damian's letter showed the continued survival of that school into the mid-eleventh century.[23] Subsequent scholars, however, have been largely skeptical of Leicht's reasoning.[24] To begin with, the documentary record for use of the Justinianic works is very thin: a handful of documents, often repeating the same formula, spread out over half a century. Possibly, too, these citations merely reflect the ideology of the Ottonian dynasty, who in this period began to refer to their empire as "Roman";[25] indeed, within this imperial ideology Ravenna itself was seen as a *sacra urbs* whose symbolic importance was inferior only to

---

"Le opere di Pier Damiano: Note per la storia giuridica del secolo undecimo," *Atti del Reale Istituto Veneto di Scienze, Lettere ed Arti*, 62 (1902–3): 891–908, shows that certain legal phrases were also common in the writings of Peter Damian, though he did not find any specific citations of the *Corpus Iuris Civilis*. Damian's knowledge of canon law, however, was somewhat better. See J. Joseph Ryan, *Peter Damian and His Canonical Sources* (Toronto, 1956).

[22] *Ibid.*, p. 193 ll.12; on this passage see also I. S. Robinson, *Authority and Resistance in the Investiture Contest. The Polemical Literature of the Late Eleventh Century* (Manchester/New York, 1978), p. 80.

[23] Leicht, "Ravenna e Bologna," pp. 283–86; the quoted passage occurs on p. 284. See also Leicht's earlier article, "L'exsecutor litis nel processo ravennate," *Atti del Reale Istituto Veneto di Scienze, Lettere ed Arti*, 79 (1920): 563–79.

[24] See, for example, Cortese, *Diritto nella storia medioevale*, vol. I, pp. 357–60; E. Genzmer, "Die iustinianische Kodifikation und die Glossatoren," *Atti del Congresso Internazionale di Diritto Romano (Bologna & Roma, 17–27, aprile 1931)* (Pavia, 1934), Part I (Bologna), vol. 1, pp. 345–430 at 371–72; Lange, *Römisches Recht im Mittelalter*, pp. 20–21. The evidence is surveyed in detail by Ingrid Heidrich, *Ravenna unter Erzbischof Wibert (1073–1100) Untersuchungen zur Stellung des Erzbischofs und Gegenpapstes Clemens III. in seiner Metropole* (Sigmaringen, 1984), pp. 148–56.

[25] Carl Erdmann, "Das ottonische Reich als Imperium Romanum," *Deutsche Archiv für Geschichte des Mittelalters* 6 (1943): 412–441 [reprint in C. Erdmann, *Ottonische Studien* (Darmstadt, 1968), pp. 174–203.]

the former capitals, Rome and Aachen.[26] Yet, apart from a reference to C. 4.66.2 in a diploma of 1001,[27] imperial interest in the Justinianic books seems mainly to have been for their symbolic value. Nor, finally, has it ever been possible to argue that Ravennate notaries—the men who would have been most involved in legal studies—were particularly well-educated or innovative during this period. Most of the formulas found in eleventh-century documents were very old, often dating back to the seventh century, while the quality of Latin was mediocre and continued to decline until the end of the eleventh century.[28]

The significance of Damian's letter, finally, should not be exaggerated. Writing between 1046 and 1048, Anselm of Besate tells us that he learned law as well as rhetoric from Sichelmo of Reggio, whom he describes as "liberalium artium peritissimus. Quem ut pre omnibus in suis rethoricis noster habet Tullius, sic Iustinianus pre omnibus in imperialibus suis edictis et legalibus iudiciis." Since Anselm was born about 1020, these comments would appear to refer to the late 1030s or perhaps ten years before Damian's letter. Anselm makes good on his claims to know Justinian by quoting the Code in the introductory letter, paraphrasing the beginning of the Institutes in his dedication to Henry III, and invoking the Novels twice in the *Rhetorimachia*.[29] These citations are essentially ornamental, being inserted to lend style and learning rather than to further a legal argument, but they confirm the wider circulation that was suddenly being won

---

[26] Johannes Fried, *Otto III. und Bolesaw Chrobry. Das Widmungsbild des Aachener Evangeliars, der „Akt von Gnesen" und das frühe Polnische un ungarische Königtum* (Stuttgart, 1989), pp. 36–37.

[27] *Ottonis II. et III. Diplomata*, ed. by Theodor Sickel [MGH, *Dipl.*, vol. 2], p. 392; discussed by C. G. Mor, "Una citazione del codice giustinianeo in un diploma di Ottone III," *Studi in onore di Vicenzo Del Giudice* (Milan, 1952), vol. II, pp. 201–5 [repr. Mor, *Scritti*, pp. 77–81].

[28] Benericetti, *Le carte del decimo secolo*, vol. 2, p. xxxvi.

[29] Karl Manitius, ed. *Rhetorimachia* [MGH, *Quellen zur Geistesgeschichte des Mittelalters* 2] (Weimar, 1958). The passage quoted begins on p. 99 l. 13. For Manitius' discussion of Anselm and Sichelmo, see pp. 62–65; the paraphrase of the *Institutes* is on p. 97; the quotations of the *Novels* on pp. 163, 167. A fourth reference, ostensibly to the *Code*, seems somewhat doubtful; it entails a reference to *res mancipi et non mancipi*, which was, however, also a phrase used in eleventh-century notarial documents. For a general discussion of this work, see Beth S. Bennett, "The Significance of the *Rhetorimachia* of Anselm of Besate to the History of Rhetoric," *Rhetorica*, 5 (1987): 231–50; C. M. Radding, "The Geography of Learning in Early Eleventh-Century Europe: Lanfranc of Bec and Berengar of Tours Revisited," *Bullettino dell'Istituto Storico Italiano per il Medio Evo e Archivio Muratoriano*, 98 (1992): 145–72.

by the works of the *Corpus* in the second quarter of the eleventh century. Even if Ravenna had a school where Roman law was taught in the 1040s, it would not have been especially unique.

A final objection to the claims of Ravenna, as Leicht himself realized, was the absence of juristic commentaries produced there. Leicht addressed this problem by suggesting that Ravennate legal learning might be reflected in the glosses to the Institutes and *Epitome Juliani* contained in Cologne, Historisches Archiv W. 328, although his claims about that manuscript are considerably mitigated by his concession that it reflects Lombardist usages. In fact, Leicht's specific suggestion is quite impossible: we shall see below that the Cologne glosses correspond exactly to the methods used in the *Walcausina*, one of the full-scale commentaries to the Lombard law. But he was correct in thinking that any revival of Justinianic law in Ravenna could not have been confined to the territory of the exarchate itself. Ravenna was not isolated from the rest of northern Italy in the decades around the millenium or even earlier.[30] In particular, there seems to have been the regular movement of people between Ravenna and Pavia, the traditional capital of the Lombard kingdom. Karl Leyser observed that Otto the Great's extended stays in Pavia, the legal center of the Lombard kingdom, marked a significant exception to the restless travels of that king, commenting that "[t]he institutions of the Italian kings . . . invited use."[31] Judges from the Italian kingdom can be also seen in Ravenna. A plea from 967, for example, shows judges from throughout Italy present in Ravenna for a case held jointly by the pope and emperor;[32] a later plea, from 1014, shows Roman law judges from Ferrara sitting together with Lombard law judges from Pavia, all of whom claimed the title *iudex sacri palatii*.[33] Indeed, the document mentioned above for its citation of the Novels and Code

[30] For graphic evidence suggesting contacts between Lombard notaries and Ravenna in the eighth century, see Francesca Santoni, "Palazzi vecchi e nuovi: il fenomeno grafico tra Ravenna, Pavia e Milano (sec. VIII–IX)," in *Ravenna Studi e Ricerche*, 9 (2002): 115–136.

[31] Karl Leyser, "Ottonian government," in *Medieval Germany and its Neighbors 900–1250* (London, 1982) [orig. pub. in *EHR*, 96 (1981): 721–53], p. 101.

[32] C. Manaresi, *I placiti del «Regnum Italiae»* [Fonti per la storia d'Italia, vols. 92, 96, 97] (Rome, 1955–60), no. 155; "Gaupeltus iudex domnorum regum" is probably to be identified with the man of the same name who was among the most important judges in Pavia.

[33] Manaresi, *Placiti*, no. 290 [Ferrara, 14 December 1015.] See also, Radding, *Origins*, pp. 76–77.

shares both the general organization (slightly modified to acknowledge the rights of the pope) and some specific language with *placita* prepared elsewhere in northern Italy by Lombardist judges.

Whether the judges of Pavia first encountered Justinian's works at Ravenna or found them on their own, there is no doubt that they were reading them by the first half of the eleventh century. The earliest dateable evidence of their interest comes from notes copied into a manuscript of the *Liber Legis Langobardorum* or *Liber Papiensis*, a compilation that gathered the Lombard *Edictum* into one volume with the Frankish and Ottonian capitularies in force in northern Italy. The date of this particular manuscript, now bound in two volumes as Milan, Biblioteca Ambrosiana mss. O. 53 and 55 sup., can be inferred from a regnal list written near at the end of O. 53 in the hand of one of the principal scribes: the last date given is for the coronation of Conrad II in 1028, suggesting a date for the manuscripts between that year and Conrad's death in 1039. We are fortunate to have this clue to the dating of the volumes, because the script used by the scribes could easily be mistaken for hands from the ninth or tenth century.[34] In fact, this writing seems typical of mid-eleventh-century legal professionals from the region around Milan, and the script used in this manuscript is markedly similar to the signature of an *Ambrosius iudex* who copied the text of Rothari 153 into Vercelli, Bib. cap. ms. 122, a manuscript of the *Epitome Juliani* to be discussed below.

The Ambrosian manuscript is relevant here because of a series of notes that bridge the current division between the two volumes. Known as the *Quaestiones ac monita*, these loosely organized *opuscula* deal with issues in Lombard, Frankish, and Roman law. Some items appear partially or more than once, confirming that they were copied from a pre-existing source, although how much older than the manuscript is impossible to say; a reasonable guess might be the first quarter of the eleventh century. Since the lawbook in which they are found is oriented toward practical use, it is not surprising that most items deal with issues of interest to legal professionals. Thus, there are sections addressing inheritance rules for Roman and Frankish law, who should take on the role of *tutor* for a child, which issues

[34] Thus Bischoff's notes on this manuscript show that he cancelled original attribution to the tenth century and corrected it to the eleventh—presumably when he arrived at the regnal list.

should be resolved by battle, the proper form in which oaths should be made, and the proper form for a notary to use when making an authentic copy of a document. Apart from the theoretical character of these questions—for they have no apparent link to actual cases—it is striking that the answers to them were sought in texts: the *Liber Papiensis* for Germanic law and Justinian's *Corpus* for Roman law.

The *Quaestiones ac monita* explicitly cites the Justinianic corpus twice.[35] Section 5, on succession in Roman law, is based on *Epitome Juliani* 109.1–3 (Quia sic praecipit lex Romana in libro qui vocatur Novella, quae egit Iustinianus imperator temporibus suis). Section 22, on the ages of man, quotes (somewhat inappropriately) from *Institutes* 2.23.1. (Et de aetate dicitur secundum quod hic declaratur et iuxta illud quod dicitur in lege Romana in libro qui vocatur Instituta: "De fideicommissariis," in lege quae inchoat sic: "Nunc transeamus ad fidecommissa." Et in ipsa lege quae sic incipit ut supradictum est: "Omnia fideicommissa antiquis temporibus infirma esse.") Two other items also seem to reflect knowledge of the Institutes:

> [7] Questio Romana: si homo fecerit furtum, reddat in quadruplum ad hominem Romanum et pro culpa nasum perdat et bannum regi; si evenerit quod cum ipso comprehensus non fuerit et in post inventus fuerit, in duplum componat. [In. 4.6.23,25]
>
> [13] Si homo invenerit scazo in terra aliena, medietatem habeat qui invenit ac medietatem cuius terra est, quia lex Romana dicit. [In. 2.1.39]

These chapters do not specifically cite the Institutes, but that is consistent with the normal style of the *Quaestiones ac monita*. Section 6, for example, draws on more than twenty individual Lombard and Frankish laws to explicate the rules for trial by battle, but cites none of them; section 8, on the length of time necessary to bar legal challenges to possession, similarly does not mention the four different laws employed in the answer. The practice thus seems to have been not to name a source unless a specific passage was being quoted.

The sources of two other references to Roman law are harder to determine with confidence. Sections 18 and 19 read:

> [18] Recordare: si homo mallaverit alium, quod ipse tulisset ad furtum cartulam, qua continebatur de tantis rebus, quae valebant super VI solidos? Iustum est, nihil respondeat, si non appellaverit, quod cartula ipsa

[35] The text of the *Quaestiones ac monita* is appended to Boretius' edition of the *Liber Papiensis*, MGH, Leges IV, pp. 590–94.

valebat super vi solidos. [Otto I, 6] et homo Romanus? Lex est ut, si perdiderit quidem aliter cartulam ipsam, reddere debet caput tantum rei.

[19] Quaestio: si Romanus homo ad placitum wadiam dederit, et non habet fideiussores paratos, comes prendat et faciat mittere in carcere, quia lex Romana precipit: si quis fideiussores non habuerit, non despicitur carcere. Tamen de Langobardo hoc non posuimus, quia lex precipit, ut habeat "tres dies sine culpa" [Liut. 127].[36]

Savigny suggested that cap. 18 derived from a combination of D. 48.2.7.1, C. 9.1.3 and C. 9.3.2, and that cap. 19 echoed D. 48.3.3 and C. 9.4.6.[37] None of these attributions is certain and later historians, conscious of how rare the Digest was before 1075, have understandably been reluctant to embrace them. Whatever the sources of these statements, however, the *Quaestiones ac monita* remains significant as the earliest evidence that Lombardist jurists were turning their attention to Roman law.

Antiqui and *Moderni*

The significance of Pavia for the history of the Justinianic books lies less in the *Quaestiones ac monita* itself than in what comes next. Unlike what we saw with Ravenna, Rome, or south Italy, the study of Roman law among Lombardist jurists advanced steadily for the next several generations. Although the period between the 1020s and 1050 left no free-standing work, some of its activities were preserved among the glosses preserved in the later (ca. 1070–1080) *Expositio* to the *Liber Papiensis*. Some of these early glosses can be recognized by their ascriptions to *antiqui*—a term used to distinguish scholars of a previous generation from *moderni* of the current generation. Others cite judges whose career can be traced through documents. The career of the Pavese judge Bonifilius, for example, can be traced from 1014 to 1055 in surviving documentation. The career of judge Wilihelmus cannot be much later, since multiple glosses mention his debates with Bonifilius, including one report of a debate between him,

[36] Boretius suggested that "non dispicitur carcere" may have been a scribal error for "mittatur in carcere." See also section 1, a truncated variant of this comment.

[37] These are not the only passages in the *Quaestiones ac monita* where Savigny saw the influence of the Digest: he saw cap. 9, on gifts made to a slave without the knowledge of his lord, as deriving from D. 16.3 on deposits, and cap. 25, dealing with a slave who takes something from a third party by claiming to be acting on behalf of his master, as combining various comments on noxal actions from D. 9.4. *Geschichte*, II: 247–49 nn. g,i,k,l.

Bonifilius, and an *archiepiscopus* Lanfranc—evidently Lanfranc of Canterbury, a native of Pavia who had left Italy by the late 1030s.[38] Taken together, such evidence permits us to bridge the gap between the tentative early stages represented by the *Quaestiones ac monita* and the confident control of Justinianic law apparent after 1050.

The *Expositio* contains seven glosses assigned to Bonifilius or the *antiqui* that mention the Roman law, including some citations to particular passages of the Institutes.[39] Bonifilius' perhaps somewhat younger contemporary Wilihelmus also cites the Code and the Novels.[40] These citations are notable not only for showing a continuing expansion of the number of Justinianic texts under study, but also for the fact that those works were being used, not simply as repositories of the rules of Roman law, but also as sources of principles that could be used to interpret Lombard law. For example, the gloss to Rothari 2, dealing with conspiracies against the king, reads in part:

> . . . Quod ait "nec ille nec heredes eius," dicebant antiqui causidici intelligendum esse, si non esset per iussionem regis, quod ipse et heredes eius tenerentur, quia iam rumperetur lex Romana in hoc quod dicit: penalis actio non transit in heredes nisi lis contestata fuerit [In. 2.9]. . . .

The comment to Otto I 4, attributed to Bonifilius, is even more detailed in its citation:

> Et si appellatus fuerit convictus, dicebat Bonifilius, eum debere componere debitum, sicut ille qui res alienas malo ordine tulit iuxta Liuprandi legem que est "Si quis porcos" [Liut. 150], si ipse qui deposuit Longobardus fuerit; et si Romanus fuerit, debet depositum componere pro furto, per similitudinem cuiusdam legis que est in primo Institutionum libro. Nam ibi legitur [In. 2.1.16]: "Si anseres tui vel galline turbati turbateve evolaverint, et aliquis eos vel eas rapuerit lucrandi animo, furtum committit". Quam similitudinem sapientes non laudant, . . .

In a gloss to a law (Rothari 7) establishing the penalty for having an enemy killed by an ally [*collega*] rather than doing it yourself, the

---

[38] *Expos.* to Wid. 6§23. Other glosses describing exchanges between Bonifilius and Wilihelmus include *Expos.* to Roth 12§4, Roth. 47§3, Roth. 179§3, Grim. 2§1, Liut. 12§3, Kar.M. 129, Otto I 4§4,5. For Lanfranc see Margaret Gibson, *Lanfranc of Bec* (Oxford, 1980).

[39] *Expos.* at Roth. 1§2 citing *In.* 2.9.3; Roth. 2§4 citing *In.* 4.12.1; Roth. 7§1 citing In. 3.25.5; Roth. 204§2; Grimoald 4§3; Wido 6§19 citing *In.* 2.9.3; Otto I 4§3 citing *In.* 2.1.16.—this last by Bonifiglio. A few other comments by the antiqui make general references to Roman law.

[40] *Expo.* to Roth. 221§8 citing C. 3.7.1; to Otto I 4§3 citing c. 4.34.3; and to Liut. 69§7 citing *Ep. Jul.* 104.

antiqui make a remarkable leap to the definition of *societas* found in *In.* 3.25.5:

> Dicebant antiqui iudices, quod si quis esset electus ad societatem, sicut in tertio libro Institutionum legitur in titulo *De societate*—legitur enim ibi "qui societatem contrahit, certam personam sibi eligit"—[In. 3.25.5] et si quislibet eius inimicus eum adsalierit, et alter alium dimiserit aut astalim fecerit, idem si alter eorum videns inimicum suum venientem socio dixerit: "ope et auxilio tuo eum adsalire volo," si ipse suum auxilium promiserit et postea eum pugnantem dimiserit: quod morte dignum esse. Quod dominus etiam Guilelmus affirmavit.

But elsewhere the antiqui went still further, invoking the rules of Roman law to provide for cases not covered by Lombard law, as when they cited the *Institutiones* as establishing a barrier to actions against heirs,[41] or when a Lombard rule was supported by its agreement with the Roman rule on the same subject.[42]

The principle underlying this usage of Roman law was made explicit in Wilihelmus' dictum: Roman law was *lex omnium generalis*.[43] This principle did not mean that Roman law was to govern whenever it conflicted with Lombard law, because the judges certainly understood the rule of personality of the law. Wilihelmus' idea, rather, was that the jurist should resort to Roman law whenever the Lombard law was silent or unclear, and especially when the concepts and categories of the law could not precisely be determined using Lombard texts alone. The importance of this attitude was underlined by Antonio Padoa Schioppa who noted that "such a premise, found for the first time in the *Expositio*, was essential for the entire development of juridical doctrine as it later occurred in the Bolognese tradition."[44] In fact, as we have seen, this attitude is apparent in the glosses dateable to the first half of the eleventh century.

This revived interest in the Justinianic texts led to the first citation of the Code in an imperial constitution. It was issued at Rimini

---

[41] *Expos.* at Rothari 2§4 [1.3.1.4].

[42] *Expos.* at Rothari 204§2 [2.10.1.2], regarding the age of majority.

[43] *Expos.* at Otto I 4§4 [2.55.40.3].

[44] "L'intero sviluppo della dottrina giuridica di stampo bolognese non avrebbe potuto verificarsi senza una simile premessa, della quale l'Expositio constituisce in assoluto la prima testimonianze in Europa." A. Padoa Schioppa, "La cultura giuridica," in *Storia di Pavia*, 2 (Milan, 1987), pp. 219–35 at pp. 232–33. See also the remarks of Calasso, *Medio Evo del Diritto*, pp. 338–39; and Astuti, *Lezioni di storia*, pp. 367–68.

by Henry III in April 1047 in response to a question from legal specialists [*legis periti*] on a problem that had arisen from their study of the Code. That constitution begins:

> In legibus cautum est, ut nemo clericorum iurare praesumat; alibi vero reperitur scriptum, ut omnes principales personae in primo litis exordio subeant iusiurandum calumniae. *Nonnullis legis peritis* venit in dubium, utrum clerici iusiurandum praestare debeant, aut alii personae hoc officium liceat delegare. Quia enim illud constitutionis edictum, uti clerici iurare prohibentur, a Theodosio augusto Tauro prefecto pretorio de Constantinopolitanis clericis promulgatum fuisse videtur, idcirco ad alios clerics pertinere non creditur . . .[45]

The reference is to C. 1.3.25 but with the inscription of C. 1.3.20—as in fact it is given, and subsequently corrected, in Pistoia 106, a manuscript from about this period. As to who these *legis periti* may have been, one possibility is that the query came from local jurists, for Rimini was near a region where Roman law was still in force; against this hypothesis, however, one must weigh the fact that the best efforts of historians have failed to discover even minimal evidence of their activities. It is far more likely that the query came from the same circle of Lombardist jurists whose familiarity with the Code and Institutes is documented by the *Expositio*. The Lombardist influences are readily apparent in the language of Henry's decree: the use of *praesumare* echoes the language of legislation since the time of Charlemagne, while the reference to the *Codex Justinianus* as the *edictum* takes up the term customarily applied to Lombard law. Indeed, Henry had not only visited Pavia only a few months before he issued his legislation, but he was accompanied on his travels by the distinguished and venerable judge Bonifilius. A month before this constitution was issued, it had been Bonifilius who had been honored with the request to state the law at a trial personally presided over by the emperor.[46] Finally, it must be noted that the query itself arises from attitudes toward law similar to those found in the *Expositio*. Not only is there the presumption, reminiscent of Wilihelmus' famous

---

[45] Boretius, *Liber Papiensis* Hen. II, 1; also edited in MGH, *Constitutiones et acta publica imperatorem et regum*, I (Hannover, 1893), n. 50, pp. 96–97; MGH, *Die Urkunden der deutschen Könige und Kaiser*, 5. *Heinrichs III*, ed. H. Bresslau and P. Kehr (Berlin, 1931), no. 191. Only slightly later, from 1058, comes a paraphrase of a brief passage of the *Code* in a Tuscan placitum (Manaresi no. 405) document; see Nicolaj, *Cultura e prassi*, p. 72 n. 193.

[46] *Urkunden Heinrichs III*, no. 188; Manaresi, no. 377.

dictum, that Roman law is the *lex omnium generalis* and applicable to current conditions. But there is the same alert interest in legal procedure: can clergy testify in court? can actions be brought against heirs? are thefts analogous to unlawfully retained deposits? Henry's constitution and the *Expositio* show such issues not only being noticed but debated, apparently as a result of an increasingly meticulous scrutiny of Justinian's texts.

The first half of the eleventh century thus marks an important shift in the circulation of Justinian's codification. If anything, the surviving evidence probably under-represents the significance of the 1030s and 1040s. Both the *Expositio* and the *Walcausina*—another commentary on the *Liber Papensis* from the third quarter of the century—frequently note a diversity of opinion, including now-outmoded views, in terms so vague (*secundum quosdam*) as to suggest discussions which already had been going on for some time. Yet even with the evidence we have, it is clear that a corner has been turned. By the 1020s, at the latest, the legal professionals of northern Italy were studying the Institutes—as evidenced both by the *Quaestiones ac monita* and by Bonifilius' familiarity with the Institutes. By the 1040s, if not earlier, their study had extended to the Novels and, more significantly, to the Code, which is cited in glosses dateable to this period and in which they encountered a problem they brought to the attention of Henry III. The very end of the period also even sees the Institutes being taught alongside the liberal arts, as witnessed by the quotations from Peter Damian and Anselm of Besate. Meager as it is, this evidence outstrips the aggregate of references to Justinian's works we found between the death of Gregory the Great and the end of the tenth century. Although sources become truly abundant only later, it seems likely that the real turning point in the recovery of Justinian's *Corpus* occurred in these decades leading up to 1050.

1050–1080

Although scholarly attention on the period following 1050 usually concentrates on the trickle of citations of the Digest, the real story is the torrent of evidence for the rest of the *Corpus* and especially for the Code. Documents from the period sometimes cite the *Corpus* and, what is perhaps more significant, we also have manuscripts in significant numbers for the first time. Complementing such evidence, moreover, are two full-scale Lombard law commentaries from the

1060s and 1070s, in which it is easy to recognize a knowledge of Roman law far surpassing anything seen in the West since the sixth century. (The *Corpus* will make its appearance in collections of canon law only later, toward the end of the century.) These sources bring the revival of Justinianic law out into the open, already with considerable mastery of the texts and with a momentum and enthusiasm that is almost palpable even today.

Manuscripts

Of the manuscripts dated to the second half of the eleventh century, a handful can be attributed more specifically to the third quarter of the century. (See table 5) Vercelli Bib. Cap. ms. 122 may even be somewhat earlier. In addition to the *Epitome Juliani*, it contains the *Lex Dei* or *Collatio Legum Mosaicarum et Romanarum*, a late antique work seen mainly in manuscripts of the *Epitome Juliani*, a *stemma cognationum*, some glosses, and some very brief excerpts from the Institutes and Code. Like Bamberg Jur. 1, Vercelli 122 is written in *romanesca*, suggesting again the importance of the ancient capital as a source of legal texts. In this case, however, the manuscript appears to have left the city within a short time of having been copied, because an "Ambrosius iudex" copied the Lombard law, Rothari 153 "Omnis parentela" on the folio bearing an *arbor cognationum*. Ambrosius is a name rarely found outside of Milan and such a localization is consistent with Ambrosius' own script, which bears marked similarities to that of the scribes who copied the Ambrosiana *Liber Legis Langobardorum*.[47] Also confirming the migration of the manuscript to northern Italy are the tachygraphic glosses in the margin, written in a system tied to the court judges of Pavia and not known to have been used later than 1080. Given the near coincidence in time between when the manuscript was produced in Rome and when Ambrosius possessed it in Lombardy, one can plausibly suppose that Ambrosius deliberately sought it out if he did not in fact originally commission its copying.[48]

---

[47] Patetta, *Adnotationes Codicum Domini Justiniani*, p. XLI n. 2, proposed identifying this "Ambrosius iudex" with the judge "Ambrosius qui et paganus" active in and around Milan in the last three decades of the eleventh century; but a comparison of the signatures disproves this hypothesis.

[48] For a discussion of the paleography of this manuscript, see A. Ciaralli, "Produzione manoscritta," pp. 83–90.

Table 5: *Corpus Iuris Civilis* manuscripts of the eleventh century

	XI.1	XI.2	XI/XII
Institutes	Bamb. Jur. 1	Turin D.III.13 *M. Cassino Comp. XI	Bamb. Jur. 2 Poppi 206 Rome, Bib. Naz. Sess. 110
Code		†Pistoia 106 †Paris 4516 *Vall. Carte XII,3	†Darmst. 2000
Digest (*Digestum Vetus*)		Vat. lat. 1406 Paris lat. 4450	
Novels (*Epitome Juliani*)		Vercelli 122 (mid XI) Leip. 3503 (XI^3)	Paris 4714

Similarly from the third quarter of the eleventh century are two manuscripts in Beneventan. The *Chronicle of Monte Cassio* mentions volumes of the Institutes and the *Epitome Juliani* among the books acquired during Abbot Desiderius' rule, between 1058 and 1087. Francis Newton, in his recent book on the Desiderian scriptorium, identified the second of these as Leipzig Universitätsbibliothek, ms. 3503 (Hänel 6); written in the older style Newton calls Old Angle, this manuscript is ascribed to the earlier part of Desiderius' abbacy.[49] The manuscript of the Institutes listed in the *Chronicle* apparently has not survived, although Monte Cassino does possess fragments of an eleventh-century Institutes that was rescued from book bindings (= M. Cassino Comp. XI, Iuridica, Nr. 1). This manuscript is not in Beneventan and was not produced at Monte Cassino, being rather from further south in Italy.

Not listed in the *Chronicle of Monte Cassino*, but possibly also produced by the Desiderian scriptorium, is a Beneventan manuscript of Justinian's Code that survives in two folios preserved as Rome, Biblioteca Vallicelliana, Carte vallicelliane XII, 3.[50] This fragment contains portions of book 7 in their integral, i.e., non-epitomized, form, including even subscriptions unknown to Krüger. To judge

[49] Newton, *Scriptorium at Monte Cassino*, pp. 259, 347 and plate 55.

[50] Roger Reynolds, "Gratian's *Decretum* and the *Code* of Justinian in Beneventan Script," *Mediaeval Studies*, 58 (1996): 285–88, calling attention to Bib. Vall., Carte XII, 3.

from the surviving folios, the original volume presented the text in a large script spaciously laid out on parchment of high quality. The quality of the work—and the fact that the original volume would have been 700 folios long if it contained the entire Code—leave no doubt that this manuscript was the work of an important scriptorium. For a Beneventan manuscript of this period, one thinks naturally of Monte Cassino, and although the Code is not mentioned in any of the Desiderian book lists (there are three of them), those are not exhaustive: we know of many other books produced during Desiderius' abbacy that were omitted from those lists.[51] Since other important Beneventan-zone scriptoria such as Benevento are not known to have been interested in secular books generally, and since the two scribes whose work is preserved in these folios wrote scripts consistent with books copied at Monte Cassino in the period before 1070, it remains on balance probable that this fragment originated in Monte Cassino. Whatever this manuscript's origin, however, the destruction of a volume independent from the northern tradition and possibly copied directly from an antique exemplar represents an enormous loss to the textual tradition of the Code.

The last manuscript attributable to the third quarter of the eleventh century takes us to the heart of the historical processes that revived Justinianic law. Pistoia, Bib. cap. ms. C. 106, the earliest surviving copy of the *Epitome Codicis*, is a manuscript that shows all the signs of hard use. The parchment is rather stiff and dark, and since the ink is often light in color it is difficult to get good photos of it. The text is not in the right order, because the sequence of the quires was confused when the manuscript was rebound in the fifteenth century. And the margins on many pages are full of additions and glosses: not just at the top or bottom, but also along the outer edge and sometimes in the inner margin. The complexity of the manuscript is so extreme that even the meticulous Paul Krüger—necessarily working without the benefit of photography—made significant errors enumerating the constitutions it contains.[52] Precisely for this

[51] Newton, *Scriptorium*, pp. 24–26, 261–65.

[52] For a detailed description of the paleography of this ms., including a breakdown of much of the marginal and interlinear material by hand, see Ciaralli, "Ancora sul manoscritto pistoiese del Codex (Arch. Cap. C 106). Note paleografiche e codicologiche," in *Scrittura e Civiltà*, 24 (2000): 173–226. Appendix I lists the added constitutions, and Appendix II the longer glosses (Chiappelli's *scholia*) by copyist.

reason, however, Pistoia 106 is a crucial and extraordinary witness to the intense activity involved in reviving Roman law. Looking first at the eight copyists responsible for the main text, there are several points of interest. The hands are quite varied among themselves, with some of them displaying elements that by the mid-eleventh century were more typically found in documents than in books—a factor that probably contributed to the difficulties of dating the manuscript correctly. And the copying was distributed very unevenly among the scribes, with one doing only eight lines, another a little more than a page, and with the scribes frequently switching off in the middle of a page. This certainly was not an organized scriptorium, and one may not be too far off imagining some kind of study group. In this, Pistoia 106 is reminiscent of Paris, BN lat. 9656, a roughly contemporary manuscript of Lombard law.

Confirming the impression that the manuscript was at the center of scholarly study are the additions made to it. Constitutions were added to the manuscript by at least another twenty-three copyists, all of whom are also to be attributed to the second half of the eleventh century. One of these scribes copied at least 81 constitutions, or more than half of the 145 added to the original text; ten other scribes copied multiple constitutions, with at least another twelve adding only one. The simplest hypothesis would be that every copyist represents a collation of the Pistoia ms. with a different source, but the exact number is less important than the general impression that reconstituting the integral text of the Code involved many small steps and engaged scholars in several different centers. The impression of furious activity surrounding the Pistoia manuscript also extends to the hundreds of glosses, both marginal and interlinear, which were added by at least another fifteen eleventh-century hands. A total of more than forty people working with a single manuscript in such a brief period of time has few parallels in medieval manuscripts of any subject matter or period, and attests to the interest that the Code was suddenly attracting in the late eleventh century.

A final point of interest concerns the glosses. The scale of exegetical activity was itself impressive: although Chiappelli published nearly a thousand glosses, there are several hundred more that he omitted. His edition divides the glosses into three categories. Scholia drew attention to issues of juristic interest addressed by the constitutions, usually in a very brief form but occasionally adducing definitions from other works ranging from Cicero to the Digest. Critical glosses offered variant readings; for example, a gloss to the reading *prudensque* in C. 4.34.3 notes "*aliter prudens. aliter providens*," while one to C. 6.20.12 *putet* offers *mutet* (the reading printed by Krüger) as an alternative.[53] Interpretative glosses provided explanations of specific words or phrases, often clarifying obscurities of the syntax. Chiappelli's classification is somewhat arbitrary, because the distinction between "scholia" and "interpretative" glosses had nothing to do with content: he simply treated as scholia all glosses marked *Nota*—a sign widely diffused among eleventh- and twelfth-century manuscripts and used in the Pistoia manuscript by multiple scribes. Individual readers, of course, were not limited to a single category of commentary. It is also significant to notice that early students of the Code took pains to circulate glosses, since many glosses in the Pistoiese, and not only scholia, also appear in the Darmstadt manuscript. Some of the scholia, indeed, seem to have been present in the exemplar, for they were copied by the scribes responsible for the main text.

As to who was doing this work, all available evidence points to the Lombardist jurists of northern Italy. They are the only ones known to have cited the Code in the period leading up to 1050 or even, as we shall see, 1080. Some of the paleographical elements already mentioned for Pistoia 106—the letter forms more typical of documents than books from this period, the numbers of hands involved, even the minimal writing skills of some who contributed to the marginal additions—are consistent with an environment of judges and notaries, such as the specialists in Lombard law. The glosses point in the same direction, as Cortese and others have already noted.[54] The list of similarities between the Pistoia glosses and the Lombardist tradition includes:

1. the use of the word *corrumpi* in glosses to C. 5.9.3 and C.6.56.5 in the sense of supercede, as *rumpere* was used in the *Expositio*.[55] This gloss is in the hand of the scribe who copied that section of text, an indication that it was found in the exemplar.
2. the use of the word *capitulum*, the Lombardist term for Frankish and Ottonian imperial legislation, to refer to C. 2.6.7.

[53] *Glossa Pistoiese*, nos. 358, 451.

[54] E. Cortese, "Legisti, canonisti e feudisti: la formazione di un ceto medievale," in *Università e società nei secoli XII–XVI. Nono Convegno Internazionale, Pistoia, 20–25 settembre 1979* (Pistoia, 1982), pp. 195–284 at p. 207.

[55] Chiappelli, *La Glossa Pistoiese*, scholium 97.

3. the style of citing laws, using the first words of the law. Since the order of laws varied significantly from one manuscript to another of the *Liber Legis Langobardorum* as in the *Epitome Codicis*, this method of citation was practical for both texts.

Even without such clues, however, it would be hard to doubt that this manuscript was linked to the jurists best known for their commentaries on Lombard law, because theirs are the only works from this period that display an interest in Justinian's Code, or in the rest of the *Corpus*.

Roman Law in Commentaries to the Liber Papiensis

In addition to the *Expositio*, materials from which were discussed in the previous section, this period is also represented by the *Walcausina*. This commentary must have enjoyed a substantial circulation in the late eleventh century, because two manuscripts survive from this period (Paris, BN lat. 9656 and Wien, Österreichische Nationalbibliothek 471, two other eleventh century manuscripts (Florence, Bib. Laurenziana Plut. 89 sup. 86 and London ms. add. 5411) repeat many of the same glosses found in the Paris and Vienna manuscripts, and a fifteenth-century manuscript witnesses a third copy in the same tradition, now lost.[56] For our present purposes, however, the *Walcausina* has the advantage of being securely dateable to the third quarter of the eleventh century. The commentary's name comes from prefatory verses attributing it to Walcausus (or Gaulcausus), a judge of Pavia who appears in the documentary record from the 1050s to the end of the 1070s. In addition, one of the scribes who copied the Paris and Vienna manuscripts can be identified through his handwriting as a certain *Johannes notarius sacri palatii*, author of a 1070 document from Pavia (*in suburbium Ticini*).[57] Both of these markers, therefore, suggest that the *Walcausina* may have a date as early as the 1060s, although (as with the *Expositio*) some of the material must have originated much earlier. The latest possible date would seem

[56] For a full account of the treatise itself, see C. Radding, "*Petre te appellat Martinus.*" The Paris and Vienna manuscripts are discussed in Ciaralli, "Produzione manoscritta," pp. 97–101. Additional details about the *Walcausina* will be available in the edition we are preparing for the MGH.

[57] Milan, Archivio di Stato, Diplomatico, 654/35, S. Maria Mater Dominici, 1070 Oct. 28.

to be the 1070s, not least because the text and glosses are essentially identical in the two manuscripts even though the manuscripts themselves, to judge from the evolution of Johannes's script, must have been copied some years apart.

The *Walcausina* is an intensely condensed text clearly intended to serve practical ends. In dealing with early laws that had been modified by subsequent enactments, the redactor often inserted phrases modifying the original text so that it correctly stated the current law: the inserted phrase would be marked as such by signs, while a marginal note directed the reader to the later enactment on which it was based. The *Walcausina* also provides many Lombard laws with model pleas in direct speech ("Petre te appellat Martinus . . .") to illustrate how an action under a given law would proceed in court. Yet even in such apparently purely Lombard issues, the *Walcausina* did not hesitate to draw upon Justinianic law. Occasionally, the language inserted directly into the Lombard text will be taken from the Institutes. At other times, Roman procedure will be cited as the basis for court action under Lombard law: the last model plea for Roth. 232 ends with the comment, "but none of this really matters, for things should be done as is read in Roman law."[58] The application of the principle that Roman law was "omnium generalis" could hardly have been plainer.

As table 6 shows, all four works of the *Corpus Iuris Civilis* are cited, in a variety of glosses. The two references to the Digest have attracted the most notice, and some surprise; these will be discussed in the context of the other earliest citations of the Digest in chapter six. The most significant of the citations, however, may well be those to the Code. That work, as we have seen, was virtually unknown in the early Middle Ages, but in the *Walcausina* it was cited more frequently even than the Institutes, with references taken from six of the nine books that would make up the medieval Code. The author or authors of the *Walcausina* used the Code in the form of the *Epitome Codicis*, which appears here and in the *Expositio* for the very first time. The citations in the *Walcausina*, moreover, point to manuscripts not very different from the three earliest manuscripts of the *Epitome Codicis*—Pistoia 106 and Paris 4516, which date from this period, and the slightly later

[58] "Sed tota haec altercatio paene nichil valet; debet enim esse ut legitur in Romana lege."

Darmstadt 2000. Nearly all of the laws that are paraphrased or explicitly cited by book are found in the base text of Pistoia 106, a manuscript produced at this time. (For book nine we have used Paris 4516, a daughter manuscript of Pistoia 106.) The exception to this rule—C. 9.8.5.4, which is cited in a table attached to Loth. 67—appears in Darmstadt 2000, another manuscript of the *Epitome*.[59]

Table 6: Citations of the *Corpus Iuris Civilis* in the *Walcausina*

Institutiones	
Roth. 15: Nam nomine *proximitatis* vocantur parentes *usque ad septum gradum et et sentimo a sobrino sobrinaque natus nataque . . .*	In. 3.5.5: *proximitatis* vero nomine his solis praetor promittit bonorum possessionem qui *usque* ad sextum gradum cognationis sunt, et ex *septimo a sobrino sobrinaque nato nataeve.*
Roth. 170: . . . ut legitur in Institutis "Adquiritur"	In. 2.9.1
Roth. 224: Scito, si quis Longobardus *servo communi* libertatem dederit, quod *pars adcrescit socio* non danti, ut legitur in antiquo iure Romano, quod lex Longobarda sequitur	In. 2.7.4: si *communem servum* habens aliquis cum Titio solus libertatem ei imposuit vel vindicta vel testamento, eo casu *pars* eius amittebatur et *socio adcrescebat.*
Roth. 227: . . . *si non potuerit* libellum ostendere, absque sacramento *remanet suo loco possessio.*	In. 4.15.4: . . . *si* modo actor *non potuerit* suam esse probare, *remanet suo loco possessio.*
Roth. 277: [inserted into the text of the law] *sive sit propria sive locata sive gratis concessa . . .*	In. 4.4.8: . . . domum autem accipimus, *sive* in *propria* domo quis habitat *sive in conducta vel gratis* sive hospitio *receptus sit*
Roth 309: [inserted into the text of the law] quia non fuit sua, postquam *desivit eam persequi*, per intellectum Romanae legis	In. 2.1.13: quodsi *desieris persequi*, desinere tuam esse
Roth. 354: Per Institutionum capitulum sata solo cedunt	In. 2.1.32
Roth. 367: id est *aut pure aut in diem aut sub condicione*	In. 3.15.2: Omnis stipulatio *aut pure aut in diem aut sub condicione* fit.

[59] Boretius suggested, with some uncertainty, C. 1.17.2 as the target for the vague reference in a gloss to Liut. 28 ("ut legitur in codicis"); that law is not in the manuscripts of the *Epitome Codicis*. It seems likely, however, that the law intended is actually C. 1.22.6.

Table 6 (*cont.*)

Liut. 115: *prescriptis verbis que de extimato proponitur*	In. 4.6.28: *praescriptis verbis quae de aestima to proponitur, . . .*
Liut 47: et moriatur per Romana lege de plagiariis	In. 4.14.10 or C. 9.20.16
Codex	
Roth. 1: . . . et *ex quo quis tale crimen* commiserit *nec alienare nec manumittere potest,*" ut legitur in nono libro codicis, "*nec debitor iure ei solvit,*" . . .	C. 9.8.6.3: *ex quo quis tale crimen* contraxit, *neque alienare neque manumittere eum posse: nec ei solvere iure debitorem*
Roth. 9: *exceptis servis libertinis familiaribus, nisi in crimine maiestatis,* nam hii nequeunt accusare dominum.	C. 9.1.20: Si quis ex *familiaribus* vel ex *servis . . . maiestatis* autem *crimen excipimus.* C. 9.1.21: *Liberti . . .*
Roth. 178: Similiter Iustianus precipit	C. 5.1.2 (rule is not mentioned in Institutes)
Roth. 232: aut si dicerit: *res litigiosa* fuit, non potuisti alienare, reddat caput, ita ut legitur in Romana lege.	C. 8.27.2: *rem litigiosam non videtur vendere* C. 8.36.1: Cum creditor pignus ven dit, *non potest videri litigiosae rei emptio contrahi* [the term *res litigiosa* is not found in the Institutes]
Liut. 19: Nam honus solidorum crescit etiam ultra sortem, et usurae sepe in sortem rediguntur et ita usurarum exiguntur.	C. 4.32.28.1: Quapropter hac apertissima lege definimus nullo modo licere cuidam usuras praeteriti vel futuri temporis in sortem redigere et earum iterum usuras stipulari
Liut 28: [at: . . . per legem iudicaverit] nam potestates leges sciebant, ut legitur in codice	Boretius suggested C. 1.17.2, but C. 1.22.6 is perhaps more likely.
Liut. 90: ut in secundo libro Codicis, que constitutio incipit, "Si quis in conscribendo"	C. 2.3.9
Rachis 6: ut legitur in Codice, "Si quis crimen intenderit"	C. 9.8.3
Kar.M. 33 Per hoc exemplum accusator iuret antea, et per usum tractum a Romanis legibus	C. 2.59.2
Lud.P. 16: [inserted into the text of the law] *Se vero intra id tempus reversus post intimationem suam fuerit defunctus, etsi necdum se purgaverit,*	C. 9.40.1.1: . . . *sin vero intra id tempus reversus post intimationem suam fuerit defunctus, etsi necdum se purgaverit, ad heredes proprios res transmittit.*

Table 6 (*cont.*)

tamen ad heredes proprios res transmittat. Si vero intra annum noluerit adesse iudicio, res perdat, . . .	C. 9.40.2: . . . intra anni spatium noluerit adesse iudicio, res eius fisco vindicentur
Lud.P. 16: [diagram] nam secundum nonum librum Codicis, omnes res post annum transactantur	C. 9.40.1,2
Loth. 67: [gloss to table *De conspirationibus*] Omnis alienatio quam hii fecerunt, postquam hanc inceperint, *nullius est momenti*, ut legitur in nono libro Codicis	C. 9.8.5: dotes donationes, quarumlibet postremo rerum alienationes, quas ex eo tempore qualibet fraude vel iure factas esse constiterit, . . . *nullius* statu imus *esse momenti.*
Loth 69: ut legitur in quarto libro Codicis	C. 4.20.19
Hen. II 1 . . . ut in Codice per legem que incipit "Cum clericis"	[notes that the inscription cited in the law properly belongs with C. 1.3.25]
Digesta	
Roth. 151: . . . ut Romani actores, veluti *necessitas probandi semper incumbit illi qui agit.*	D. 22.3.21: . . . *quia semper necessitas probandi incumbit illi qui agit.*
Extravag. 9 [Kar. M. 142]: . . . nisi aliud pro alio solverit consentiente creditore vel commendatore.	D. 12.1.2.1: nam in ceteris rebus ideo in creditum ire non possumus, quia aliud pro alio invito creditori solvi non potest.
Novellae	
Roth. 168: scilicet per legem "Si quis deliquerit," secundum antiqu	Ep. Iul. 34.1
Roth. 170: . . . quod videri potest ex Novella	
Wid. 6: . . . ut legitur in Novellis	Ep. Iul. 44.2
Wid. 6: . . . ut videtur in Novellis	Ep. Iul. 66.7
Hen. II 1 . . . ut in Novella omnes litigatores	Ep. Iul. 122.1
Hen. II 1 . . . ut in Novella h.c. in primo capite	Ep. Iul. 119.1

Twice the glosses bring us very close to the text found in the Pistoia *Epitome Codicis*. It has often been noticed, for example, that the erroneous inscription for C. 1.3.25 employed in Henry III's constitution of 1047 is found in the Pistoia Code, with a correction subsequently written in. The *Walcausina* provides the same correction in a marginal gloss to Henry's law. The other point of interest is a gloss to Roth. 232 that employs the term *res litigiosa*. This term rarely appears in the Justinianic codification, but its use in C. 8.36 is noticed by a gloss contained in the Pistoiese: *Nota: rem litigiosam venditam*.[60] (This gloss was copied by the scribe, suggesting that it also appeared in the exemplar from which Pistoia 106 was copied.) The appearance of this term in the *Walcausina*, therefore, represents another possible link between the *Epitome Codicis* and the Lombard law specialists of Pavia.

By being confined to direct citations from the *Corpus*, table 6 omits other evidence of the expertise in Justinianic law assumed by the *Walcausina*. Roman terminology runs throughout the commentary, with the Roman system of actions being frequently invoked to explicate Lombard procedures. Thus, the gloss to Roth. 2, concerning conspiracies to which the king is a party, comments that "penalis actio transit in heredes"; the gloss to Liut. 16 makes a similar observation about the Roman *actio mutui* ("haec actio transit in heredes"), adopting the language of In. 4.3.9. Other Roman procedures mentioned include the *actio conducti*, (Roth. 152, Liut. 95), *actio in factum* (Roth. 152), *actio in rem incorporalem* (Roth. 165), *actio propter collationem, actio communi dividundo, actio familiae hereiscundae* (Roth. 167), *actiones hereditariae* (Roth. 174), *actio concepti* (Roth. 232), *actio arbitraria* (Roth. 349), *actio mutui* (Liut. 16), *actio mandati* (Liut. 38, Liut. 116), *actio tutelae* (Liut. 74), *actio noxalis* (Liut. 96), *donatio causa mortis* (Liut. 101), and *actio ut ex venditio* (Liut. 115). Further illustrating this interest are several tables, reproduced in all of the manuscripts of the *Walcausina*, that place individual Lombard laws under appropriate Roman categories. Most of the Roman terminology mentioned above can be found in the Institutes, but not all; the action *ex venditio* is mentioned in C. 4.54.3, while *collationes* are not discussed at all in the Institutes but in C. 6.20. Whatever the source, the readers of the *Walcausina*—and we are still considering the period before 1080—evidently were expected to recognize these sources and find them on their own.

---

[60] Chiappelli, *Glossa pistoiese*, scholium 135.

These cross-references to Roman procedure should not be taken as idle displays of learning. The *Walcausina* is intensely concerned with procedure. Many of the model pleas are fairly elaborate, covering different claims and defenses, and indicating the appropriate proof for the circumstances defined by the plea; often, too, the *Walcausina* notes that the correct form was or had been debated by the jurists themselves. At Roth. 362, for example, the *Walcausina* discusses the correct form of an accusation as depending on what Roman category the case falls into—"sed si est actio in personam, ut michi videtur, aliter esse debet"—and continues on to consider which *exceptiones* can be offered in defense. The commentary to Roth. 227, similarly, offers two different versions of the procedure for reclaiming property after a lease depending on whether the process is construed as an action *in rem* or an action *locati*. The main point, however, is that Roman law was being used to explicate Lombard law rather than the other way around—and in the third quarter of the eleventh century. It follows that details of Roman procedure which untrained readers might have missed were of great interest to Lombard jurists, and we shall see in our discussion of the Marturi plea that they carried this approach over even to the Digest.

Historians have barely noticed the *Walcausina*'s remarkable grasp of Roman sources, in large part because their attention has generally been drawn to the *Expositio*.[61] The *Expositio* left a smaller footprint in the manuscript tradition than the *Walcausina*, surviving in only one manuscript, Naples, Bib. Naz. Brancacciano I.B.12, written in a Beneventan script of the early twelfth century.[62] A *terminus post quem* for the composition of the *Expositio* is provided by the reference to Archbishop Lanfranc, since his elevation to Canterbury occurred in 1070. But it may not be too much later. Boretius, who edited the text for the MGH, ascribed the composition of the *Expositio*

[61] Most notably by Enrico Besta, "L'Expositio al Liber Papiensis," *Annali dall'Università Toscana*, 30 (1911); and Giovanni Diurni, "L'*Expositio ad librum Papiensem*," *Rivista di Storia del Diritto Italiano*, 49 (1976): 1–277, and also separately (Rome, 1976). See also Radding, *Origins*, pp. 125–39.

[62] In the most recent revision of the "Handlist of Beneventan manuscripts," Lowe, *The Beneventan Script*, 2nd ed. (Rome, 1980), vol. 2, p. 105, Virginia Brown attributes this manuscript to the second quarter of the 12th century; this dating is also that of Francis Newton (personal communication). An earlier date, to the late eleventh or early twelfth century, was suggested by G. Cavallo; see A. Padoa Schioppa, "La cultura giuridica," in *Storia di Pavia*, 2 (Milan, 1987): 219–35, at p. 225 n. 46.

to the 1070s and 1080s and, as Padoa Schioppa recently observed, nothing written since then undermines this dating;[63] Enrico Besta even argued that the text was essentially complete even earlier, with the reference to Lanfranc being a late addition to it. One reason for this conclusion is that the author of the *Expositio* appears to have been a student of Wilihelmus, whose activities go back at least to the early 1030s, when Lanfranc was still in Pavia, and who cannot be supposed to have been active much after 1050. Another is the complete absence of any reference to the dispute between pope and emperor, the legal status of the church, or the election of the pope, although Lothar 37 invites discussion of that topic.[64] A third indication is the fact that the *Expositio*, although generous in incorporating material from earlier scholars, makes only a handful of references to Walcausus and none to his commentary. Given the wide circulation enjoyed by the *Walcausina*, the *Expositio*'s failure to discuss it in any detail suggests that the two commentaries were roughly contemporary in date.

Unlike the *Walcausina*, whose manuscripts display an extremely intricate integration of commentary with text, the earlier transmission of the *Expositio* was as commentary alone, in the form of a *glossa a catena*. The format takes its name from the chain of *lemmata* in the form of direct quotations (often underlined) from the base text that permit the reader to match the gloss with the passage it discusses.[65] In a legal text, the incipits of the laws provided natural *lemmata*, as can be seen in an appendix in the London manuscript of the *Liber Legis Langobardorum* in which the model pleas of the *Walcausina* are reduced to a *glossa a catena*. Apparently the scribes who copied the *Expositio* were working directly from a *glossa a catena* because they differed in their handling of the *lemmata*, the first scribe omitting them and the second reproducing them; this second scribe also occasionally copied two consecutive commentaries without inserting the relevant law. These errors also reveal that whereas the Brancacciono manuscript takes the form of the *Lombarda*, the original *glossa a catena* followed the sequence of the *Liber Papiensis*.[66]

---

[63] Padoa Schioppa, "La cultura giuridica," p. 225.

[64] See, especially, Diurni, "L'*Expositio*," pp. 53–54.

[65] On the *glossa a catena* generally, see John O. Ward, "From Marginal Gloss to *Catena* Commentary: the Eleventh-century Origins of a Rhetorical Teaching Tradition in the Medieval West," *Papergon*, ns. 13.2 (1996): 109–20.

[66] This original sequence is also revealed by internal cross-references, which assume

The often long discursive commentary of the *Expositio* cites Justinian's *Corpus* even more abundantly than does the *Walcausina*. Boretius, who edited the text for the MGH, tabulated 64 citations to the Institutes, 58 to the Code, 8 to the Digest, and 22 to the *Epitome Juliani*—several times the totals for the *Walcausina*.[67] The high degree of familiarity with the Justinianic codification that the *Expositio* supposed of its readers is itself noteworthy, and the citations were often made with sufficient precision to facilitate checking references and reading the passages in context. Whereas the *Walcausina* had often been content to cite by work and book ("ut legitur in quarto libro Codicis"), references in the *Expositio* typically provide the *incipit* of the law and often a substantial part of the text as well. Thus, for example, the *Expositio* to Roth. 270 cites C. 6.1.4 with the words: ut in Codicis sexti libri dicente lege: "Quicumque fugitivum servum in domum."[68] This method of citation by incipit was the same as that already being used for citing Lombard laws, and it would survive as the standard Bolognese form for citing Roman law for the rest of the Middle Ages.

As with the *Walcausina*, nearly all of the citations to the Code in the *Expositio* are found in the base text of Pistoia 106, which appears to have closely resembled the version available to the author of the *Expositio*. The absence of references to any of the constitutions added to the margins of Pistoia 106 provides a further indication in support of a date for the *Expositio* from the 1060s and 1070s—contemporary with or very slightly later than the *Walcausina*, and probably Pistoia 106 itself. There are, however, references to two, and perhaps three constitutions not found in Pistoia 106, Paris 4516, or Darmstadt 2000. One of them, the reference to C. 9.8.5.4 in the gloss to Loth. 67, was also known to the author of the *Walcausina*. The reference

laws are placed "above" (*supra*) or "below" (*retro*) according to the place in the *Liber Papiensis*. Besta, "L'Expositio," p. 5; and, Diurni, *L'Expositio*, p. 31 n. 6, with a complete list of citations.

[67] *Praefatio ad Librum Papiensem*, MGH, *Leges* IV, lxxxviii–lxxxix. Virtually all these are either explicit citations, where the specific law-book is named, or they contain language echoing specific passages. Diurni arrived at higher totals of more than 95 citations of the Institutes, more than 70 of the Code, 10 of the Digest, and 36 of the *Epitome Juliani*; *L'Expositio*, pp. 60–97; 221–77, but his additions are questionable because they are both imprecise in form (never more than a general ascription to "*Lex romana*" and often not even that) and without verbal parallels between the citation and the passages he sees cited; I therefore have not used them here. Padoa Schioppa, however, accepts Diurni's totals; "La cultura giuridica," p. 232 n. 101.

[68] The forms of citation are itemized by Diurni, pp. 60–70.

to C. 4.30.14, in *Expos.* to Rach. 1, would be another exception, although one must notice that here the comment is so incomplete that Boretius had to guess at the reference.[69] More interesting is the quotation in *Expos.* to Liut. 20§6 from a *Codicis nono libro capitulum* that in reality comes from the *Edictum Theodorici*. Since this law does become C. 9.16.3 in later manuscripts, its appearance in the *Expositio* links the version of the Code in use among the Lombardist jurists with the later Bolognese tradition of Justinian's Code.[70]

Notable, finally, are the citations of the Digest in both the *Walcausina* and the *Expositio*. Some scholars have wished to see these citations as drawn from a collection of extracts from the Digest, rather than from direct contact with that work,[71] the reasoning evidently being that had anything like the integral text been available, the Digest would have been employed much more extensively.[72] But that considerably underestimates the effort needed to achieve even a preliminary mastery of long, complicated texts. We have seen that roughly half a century was needed for the Institutes to go from the handful of citations in the *Quaestiones ac monita*, to the still occasional use by Bonifilius, Wilihelmus, and their contemporaries, to the deployment of the Institutes seen in the *Walcausina* and the *Expositio*. Seen in this context, the handful of references to the Digest found in these commentaries is about what one would expect, and hardly more remarkable than the multitude of references they make to the Institutes and Code. Again, this is entirely appropriate for commentaries from the 1060s and 1070s, for by 1076 study of the Digest had already reached a point where it could be cited, aptly, in the famous 1076 *placitum* from Marturi in Tuscany, which is the earliest, precisely dateable source to cite the Digest.[73] We return to this issue in our chapter on the Digest.

---

[69] Diurni, pp. 79–81, argued that there were several citations in the *Expositio* to laws not found in the earliest manuscripts of the *Epitome Codicis*; although citations of this kind would add to the weight of evidence in favor of seeing the reconstruction of the Code as growing out of the work of the Lombardist jurists, these additional citations do not withstand critical scrutiny.

[70] Diurni, p. 81 and n. 56.

[71] Diurni, pp. 93–98.

[72] Others, notably Conrat (*Geschichte*, p. 415) have used the references to the Digest, and especially the one reference to the Digestum Novum, to argue that the *Expositio* was composed closer to 1100; but we know far too little about the Novum to use it as an index for dating anything.

[73] Manaresi, *Placiti*, no. 437.

1080–1100

The evidence from the third quarter of the eleventh century comes entirely from professional jurists, and leaves little doubt of their central role in turning Justinian's codification into a field of study. By the last two decades of the eleventh century, however, the *Corpus Iuris Civilis* had diffused beyond its first readers to be taken up by both sides in the struggle between pope and emperor. Writing in 1080 or 1084 the author of the *Defensio Henrici IV. Regis* repeatedly invoked the Code and Institutes in attacking the position of Gregory VII; passages from the same works were also included in a collection of canon law that may date to the same time; and around 1100 one finds the Digest cited in the *Collectio Britannica* and the *Panormia* of Ives of Chartres, both also from the papal entourage. The juristic tradition, meanwhile, is attested to by a comparative abundance of manuscripts, many of which contain early glosses.

As the name suggests, the *Defensio Henrici IV. Regis* was a vindication of Henry IV against the efforts of Gregory VII to depose him. It was written in 1080 or 1084 (a difference that matters little to our inquiry), and has traditionally been ascribed to a Petrus Crassus, based on dedicatory verses at the end of the text. In recent decades, however, that ascription has become rather uncertain. To begin with, the verses do not give the name of the author as *Petrus Crassus*. What they say (and the text, uniquely found in a sixteenth century manuscript, is defective at several points) is:

> Petrus fidelis librum componere feci, . . .
> Henrice rex amabilis . . .
> hunc liberum nostrum accipis,
> quem vestri Crassus tradidit.

Roughly, "I, faithful Peter had this book composed. . . . King Henry, may you accept this our book which your Crassus gives you." As I. S. Robinson observed, "these words suggest a case analogous to that of the polemic which bears the title 'Bishop Theodoric of Verdun to Pope Hildebrand,' but which is known to have been composed by the *scholasticus* Wenrich of Trier. Perhaps the *Defensio* 'composed at Peter's request' was also the work of a *scholasticus*, unknown save for what his treatise reveals of his literary and scholarly personality."[74]

[74] Robinson, *Authority and Resistance*, pp. 76–77.

Indeed, the practice suggested by Robinson was quite common in this period, and one could add to it several works written by Alberic of Monte Cassino under the name of his abbot Desiderius, and one work addressed by Alberic to Desiderius but clearly intended to be presented to Gregory VII.[75] There is no certainty from this construction that *Petrus* and *Crassus* refer to the same person. Indeed, to the reasons already advanced by Fitting and Heidrich,[76] one can add that the use of the first-person plural, "nostrum," suggests that multiple people are involved, especially since Petrus has already used the first person singular in the first line.

The name matters mainly because some historians have tried to identify the author of the *Defensio* with a "Petrus Grassus" who appears in a witness list in a 1074 document from Ravenna.[77] The historiographical significance of the *Defensio*, indeed, has been used as evidence for the otherwise elusive law school at Ravenna. Yet the text itself points in a rather different direction. Noting that the places named in the treatise were Milan, Cremona, and Nonantola, in addition to Rome, Robinson concluded that it was "Lombardy and the *regnum Italiae* which engaged the author's attention, rather than the Exarchate."[78] Such an orientation is also consistent with what we have seen with the circulation of the Justinianic *Corpus* up until this period.

Although the *Defensio Henrici IV. Regis* has received attention mainly for its extensive citations of Roman law, including references to 19

---

[75] Charles Radding and Francis Newton, *Theology, Rhetoric and Politics in the Eucharistic Controversy, 1078–79: Alberic of Monte Cassino against Berengar of Tours* (Columbia University Press, 2003).

[76] H. Fitting, *Anfänge der Rechtsschule*, p. 40; Heidrich, *Ravenna unter Erzbischof Wibert*, p. 152. These arguments are accepted by Cortese, *Il diritto nella storia medioevale*, vol. I, pp. 357–58, who notes the additional confusion resulting from the attempt to link this "Petrus" to the jurist Pepo found in Tuscan pleas, the possibly not identical Pepo of Bolognese legend, Peter, bishop of Bologna, Peter the notary of Arezzo, and the author of the *Exceptiones Petri.* See P. Fiorelli, "Clarum Bononiensum Lumen," in *Per Francesco Calasso. Studi degli allievi* (Reggio Calabria, 1977); C. Dolcini, *Velut Aurora Surgente. Pepo, il vescovo Pietro e l'origine dello Studium Bolognese* [Instituto stor. ital. per il medio evo, *Studi storici* 180], (Rome, 1987); Nicolaj, *Cultura e prassi*, pp. 96–101. Since Peter was a very common name in this period, more evidence needs to be offered than has yet been presented for any of these identifications.

[77] Ficker, *Forschungen*, vol. 3, p. 113. The document is calendared in Heidrich, *Ravenna unter Erzbischof Wibert*, p. 171. Adding to the problems already mentioned with this identification is the fact that neither ecclesiastical nor judicial office is assigned to this Petrus—highly unlikely for the learned author of the *Defensio*—while other witnesses are designated "iudex" and "notarius."

[78] Robinson, *Authority and Resistance*, p. 77.

constitutions from Justinian's Code, the author's learning in ecclesiastical materials is perhaps more extensive than his knowledge of civil law: in addition to Augustine and Ambrose and the Bible, he cites Gregory I, the Rule of St. Benedict, Cassian, Leo I, and various legislation from church councils, as well as Sallust, Ovid, Terence, and Martianus Capella among classical authors. The argument itself, rather than being juristic in nature, derives instead from imperial polemics. The treatise opens with a lament for the injustices of the time (as Robinson notes, a common theme of imperial propaganda),[79] which leads directly to an attack on Gregory VII for his deposition of Henry IV. Two passages from the Code are inserted among quotations from Paul, Gregory, and Leo in the admonitions quoted against judging unjustly, and subsequent chapters further develop the theme that Gregory VII was disturbing the peace of the world and interfering in the sphere of laws that rightfully belonged to secular rulers. Driving the point home, this portion of the treatise offers numerous citations from correspondence between popes and the emperors of the time, and section 4 ends by quoting from the Code on paternal rights (C. 2.2.3) and from the Institutes on parricide (In. 4.18.6, mistakenly attributed to the Code). After section 5 develops the imperial case against Hildebrand as a false monk, section 6 offers a handful of citations from the Code and Institutes in support of the argument that the pope has unjustly deprived Henry of his inheritance; even here, however, the author mixes in passages from Paul, Josephus, Augustine, and Gregory the Great. The final sections, on other iniquities of the pope, are again based mainly on ecclesiastical sources, with Justinian being invoked only for C. 9.46.10 (mis-attributed to the Digest), a general observation on punishing those who intend crimes, and C. 1.7.5 on punishing apostates.

While the numerous citations of the Institutes and Code demonstrate that the author of the *Defensio* had access to those works—or at least to selections from them—it is by no means certain that he had any specialized learning in the law. What he has done is find the passages that could be quoted in support of the argument he wanted to make. Sometimes the references are appropriate and sometimes not;[80] and sometimes the quotation is pure fluff, as when the Code is quoted for the sentiment "that what is legitimately done should

[79] Robinson, *Authority and Resistance*, pp. 78–79.
[80] The best detailed analysis is still Conrat, *Geschichte*, pp. 606–12.

not be treated as a wrong,"[81] that it is sacrilege to break the sanctity of divine laws (C. 9.29.1),[82] or that those who enjoy the privileges of a life of religious contemplation should observe Catholic law (C. 1.5.1).[83] The impression that the author of the *Defensio* is mining his sources for texts worth quoting rather than legal principles is particularly strong when he attributes passages not to Justinian but to the original authors of the laws, in effect treating the Code as if it were a florilegium.[84]

Rather than revealing a renewed interest in the Justinianic texts, which in any case had already occurred, the *Defensio* mainly demonstrates that Roman law had acquired sufficient prestige in the 1080s to be invoked even in non-technical contexts. Confirming this trend are citations of the *Corpus* in works from the reform movement. These works have played a disproportionate role in the historiography of Justinian's *Corpus* ever since Paul Fournier proposed, in 1917, that the revival of Roman law resulted from the search by allies of the reform papacy for materials useful for collections of sacred canons.[85] Recent research, however, has arrived at a considerably more cautious estimate of the scholarship involved. It is now generally agreed that Gregory VII was neither a trained jurist nor particularly interested in law;[86] indeed, as Rudolf Schieffer observes, it is highly "doubtful" that legal science based on close reading of texts even approximated Gregory VII's intentions, while the interest of later canonists in fine distinctions and polemics would have left him perplexed.[87] Still more conclusive is the evidence provided by the earliest recension of Gratian's *Decretum*, now identified by Anders Winroth: apart from a brief discussion on whether women can bring accusations in canon law, it "contains no passages where Gratian I [the author of the first

---

[81] . . . *quod legitime factum est, nullam culpam meretur.* (C. 9.9.4) *Defensio*, p. 438 ll. 27–28. The passage was identified by Conrat, *Geschichte*, p. 609.

[82] *Defensio*, p. 439 ll. 2–3.

[83] *Defensio*, p. 452 ll. 14–15.

[84] As noticed by Conrat, p. 607.

[85] Fournier, "Un tournant," pp. 151–53; repeated in Fourier and G. Le Bras, *Histoire des collections canoniques en Occident depuis les Fausses décrétales jusqu'au Décret de Gratien* (Paris, 1931–32), vol. 2, pp. 13–14.

[86] Horst Fuhrmann, "Das Reformpapsttum und die Rechtswissenschaft," in *Josef Fleckenstein*, ed., *Investiturstreit und Reichsverfassung* (Sigmaringen, 1973), pp. 175–203; Fuhrmann, "Papst Gregor VII. und das Kirchenrecht zum Problem des Dictatus Papae," *Studi gregoriani*, 13 (1989): 281–320, esp. 127, 136–37.

[87] Rudolf Schieffer, "'The Papal Revolution in Law'? Ruckfragen an Harold J. Berman," *Bulletin of Medieval Canon Law*, n.s. 22 (1998): 19–30, at p. 30.

recension] made substantial use of Justinian's *Corpus Iuris Civilis*." Having shown that Gratian had no particular aversion to secular law, Winroth thus concluded that he was "simply... not particularly well oriented in Roman law."[88]

It is hardly imaginable that a push by Gregorian canonists into the study of Roman law vigorous enough to deserve credit for the revival of Justinianic law could have left so little mark on canon law itself. Rather, the truth seems to have been that Gregorian contact with Roman law, in addition to being significantly later than that of the Lombardist jurists, never amounted to much. A case in point is provided by the *Collectio canonum* attributed to Anselm of Lucca (d. 1086). This work is interesting to us because it includes a number of passages from the first book of the Code that were not included in the *Epitome Codicis*, as well as two novels from the *Authenticum*, a work that had not been cited for several centuries.[89] Yet the collection itself is surrounded with difficulties. The text cannot be earlier than 1082, but it continued to evolve into the twelfth century and survives in several recensions. The work of sorting out these recensions, moreover, has not yet been done: the edition is incomplete and in any case does not indicate which chapters are included in the various manuscripts. The manuscripts themselves are mostly from the twelfth century, adding to the uncertainty about Anselm's own version. Thus, BAV, Vat. lat. 1363, usually taken as the base text of the A version, is not earlier than the first half of the twelfth century.[90] Adding to the list of uncertainties is the possibility, forcefully argued by Gérard Fransen, that Anselm either was not the author of the compilation—which would allow for the possibility of a date later than 1086—or that he was responsible for only the first seven books.[91]

---

[88] Anders Winroth, *The Making of Gratian's Decretum* (Cambridge, 2000), p. 153.

[89] *Anselmi episcopi Lucensis Collectio canonum una cum collectione minore*, ed. F. Thaner (Innsbruck, 1906, 1915).

[90] On the textual problems, see Peter Landau, "Erweiterte fassungen der Kanonessammlung des Anselm von Lucca aus dem 12. Jahrhundert," *Sant'Anselmo, Mantova e la lotta per le Investiture. Atti del Convegno Internazionale di Studi (Mantova, 23–24–25 maggio 1986)* P. Golinelli, ed. (Bologna, 1987), pp. 323–38 and in Italian pp. 339–48; and the discussion of Kathleen G. Cushing, *Papacy and Law in the Gregorian Revolution. The Canonistic Work of Anselm of Lucca* (Oxford, 1998), pp. 5–8, with extensive additional bibliography.

[91] G. Fransen, "Anselme de Lucques, canoniste?," in *Sant'Anselmo vescovo di Lucca nel quadro delle trasformazioni sociali della riforma ecclesiastica*, ed. C. Violante [Istituto storico italiano per il medio evo, *Studi storici*, 13] (Rome, 1992), pp. 143–56. It is worth noting, however, that the only material from the *Corpus* in the last six books are references to C.1.5.5,2–4 and C. 1.1.2. Cushing, pp. 203–9, 192–93.

Even if these doubts about the date and contents of the *Collectio canonum* are set aside, it remains true that the work has serious limitations as a legal compilation. The first seven books, as Fransen notes, have no discernable internal order.[92] J. Rambaud-Buhot, moreover, observes that Anselm did not hesitate to delete sections of his texts, so that "certain of his canons are veritable mosaics formed out of short extracts from one or multiple works of the same author."[93] Cushing similarly concedes that Anselm "was not always entirely faithful to the intention, and perhaps ambition, of the original text or its formal source.... It is clear that he regarded his canonical texts as enduring and unassailable authorities. Yet with his rubrics, his omissions, and his excerpts, he could also most effectively distort and transform those sacred authorities."[94] The Justinianic texts in the compilation, indeed, give the impression of having been collected rather casually, with little real understanding. Excerpts from the Code, for example, were all drawn from the first book, and all from titles devoted to ecclesiastical issues, so they could easily have been located and copied by a reader not familiar with the text. Like the *Defensio*, the *Collectio canonum* usually cites not Justinian or the Code but the original authors of the legislation.

Although this *Collectio canonum* was among the most influential canonical collections to emerge from the reform papacy, we cannot even assume that Rome was the source of the Justinianic texts. Anselm was originally from a Milanese family belonging to the circle of judges and notaries: he thus came from the region where use of the *Corpus* in school is best documented and from the group engaged in studying it for professional purposes.[95] Similarly from the heart of Lombard legal studies was Bonizo di Sutri, originally from the area of Piacenza and Cremona, who cites occasionally from the Code and Novels during the second half of the 1080s.[96] Bonizo also cites Lombard and Frankish legislation, which he would similarly have known from growing up in that environment. It is only with the collection of

[92] "Anselme de Lucques canoniste?," p. 144.

[93] "La critique des faux dans l'ancien droit canonique," *Bibliothèque de l'École des Chartes*, 126 (1968): 5–62, at p. 42.

[94] Cushing, *Papacy and Law*, p. 102.

[95] Ibid., pp. 43–45.

[96] Walter Berschin, *Bonizo von Sutri. Leben und Werk* (Berlin/New York, 1972), pp. 3–6; Robinson, *Authority and Resistance*, pp. 81 and 86 n. 124; Conrat noted the influence of Lombard law in his *Decretum*; *Geschichte*, p. 370 n. 8.

Deusdedit, ca. 1083–87, that we find the *Corpus* cited (in very modest quantities) in canonical collections by an author clearly from outside the Lombard law zone.[97]

The Digest is not cited in canonistic compilations until the 1090s. The traditional view gives priority to the *Collectio Britannica*—so called because it appears uniquely in British Library ms. add. 8873. The manuscript's origins remains a puzzle, although the *Collectio Britannica* itself is believed to have been compiled in Italy. It is certainly later than September 1089, for it contains numerous enactments from the council of Melfi; and it may be later than 1094–95 or even 1100.[98] For us, the important sections of the *Collectio Britannica* are collections of excerpts from the Institutes and the Digest—this last being divided into two parts. These Justinianic materials evidently represent pre-existing collections that were apparently of eleventh-century origin and possibly prepared for secular purposes, since they were not particularly focused on ecclesiastical issues.[99] Both collections follow the sequence of the work they are excerpting; and they are unusual in that they cited passages by book and title number—*Pandectarum libro I titulo II*—unlike the citation by title name as found in Lombardist and later Bolognese citations. Ivo's *Decretum* also relied on these collections, with or without the mediation of the *Collectio Britannica*, and it also includes excerpts from the Code and *Epitome Juliani*, so that all four works of the *Corpus Iuris Civilis* are represented, as well as some passages from the *Brevarium*. Similar but not identical selections appear in Ivo's *Panormia*.[100] None of these works can be dated with complete certainty, but the earliest possible date would appear to be the mid-1090s. This is already comparatively late for the process of recovering the Justinianic *Corpus*.

We possess no Lombard law commentaries for this period, although it is impossible to say why this should be so. Possibly the *Walcausina* and *Expositio* had exhausted current lines of inquiry. Possibly, too, juris-

---

[97] On Deusdedit, see Cushing, *Papacy and Law*, pp. 95–102; Uta-Renate Blumenthal, "Falschungen bei Kanonisten der Kirchenreform des 11. Jahrhunderts," in *Fälschungen im Mittelalter* (MGH, *Schriften*, 33/1–6 [Hannover, 1988]) vol. 2, pp. 214–67. For Deusdedit's materials from Roman law see Conrat, *Geschichte*, pp. 367–68.

[98] See below, chapter 6 at n. 226.

[99] Conrat, *Geschichte*, pp. 345–47; 351–54; and Conrat, *Pandekten- und Institutionenauszug der brittischen Dekretalensammlung Quelle des Ivo* (Berlin, 1887).

[100] Conrat, *Geschichte*, pp. 378–85. Conrat doubted whether the *Decretum* and the *Panormia* were by the same author, but these attributions remain accepted today. See also R. Sprandel, *Ivo von Chartres und seine Stellung in der Kirchengeschichte* (Stuttgart, 1962).

tic energies were shifting in other directions, as indeed is suggested by the abundance of Roman law manuscripts from the period. What one does see, however, is the filtering down of Justinianic law to local specialists who placed the rules of the *Corpus* into practice. The career of one such man, the notary Pietro who was active in Arezzo from the 1070s until the early twelfth century, has been sketched somewhat speculatively by Giovanna Nicolaj.[101] Slightly earlier, and more important, are a series of documents from Verona that invoke C. 2.27.1, a constitution governing legal acts by minors. What makes these documents particularly interesting is that some of them, including the earliest (1085), were drafted on behalf of clients under Lombard law—this despite the clear statement in Liut. 57(58) that such acts were to be annulled by the courts. Nor was this simply an error: a later (1099) document in the series explicitly justifies the use of Roman procedure to override Lombard law by invoking Wilihelmus' dictum that Roman law is the *lex universalis*.[102]

A final indicator of the diffusion of Roman law at the end of the eleventh century is provided by the remarkable quantity of surviving Justinianic manuscripts for this period. The Institutes, Code, and *Digestum Vetus* all survive in multiple copies attributable to the later eleventh century or the decades around 1100; it is also noteworthy that nearly all these manuscripts were glossed, indicating a degree of engagement beyond any of the works in the canonistic tradition. Several important manuscripts are attributed to the second half or last quarter of the eleventh century: Turin, Biblioteca Nazionale Universitaria, D.III.13, the famous glossed manuscript of the Institutes,[103] and two manuscripts of the *Epitome codicis*, Bibliothèque Nationale, ms. lat. 4516 and the perhaps slightly later Darmstadt ms. 2000. A leaf of a manuscript of the Code, preserved at Stuttgart, is not only from this period but copied in a hand that closely resembles several of those in the manuscripts of the *Walcausina*. A still larger cluster of manuscripts date from the last decades of the eleventh century, or the decades

[101] Nicolaj, *Cultura e prassi*, pp. 96–101, although some of the more extravagent claims, identifying Pietro with both Pepo and the recipient of the *Exceptiones Petri*, cannot be endorsed.

[102] Ciaralli, "*Universali lex*," with editions of relevant documents and references to earlier literature.

[103] A. Alberti, *La "Glossa Torinese" e le altre glosse del ms. D.III.13 della biblioteca nazionale di Torino* (Torino, 1933), n. 543 to In. 3.7.3 makes the same error in calculating as does the *Expositio* to Roth. 15.

immediately around 1100; these include Bamberg Jur. 2, Rome, Bib. Naz. ms. sessoriano 110, and Poppi, Bib. com. ms. 200, all glossed manuscripts of the Institutes;[104] the earliest manuscripts of the complete Code, Berlin Staatsbib. mss. fol. lat. 272 and 273 and Montpellier, Bibliothèque Interuniversitaire, ms. H 82, discussed below in chapter five; and two manuscripts of the *Digestum Vetus*, Paris, BN. lat. 4550 and BAV, Vat. lat. 1406. This generous circulation makes it plain that the Justinianic *Corpus*, far from being a discovery of Gregorian canonists, could be used by them because the texts were already widely available.

The quantity of surviving manuscripts is still more impressive when one reflects that many manuscripts of these works must have perished from the centuries of active use witnessed even by those that survive. Thus, the Turin Institutes was in use at least until the fifteenth century, as is demonstrated by marginal notations on f. 16r or the rewritten passage on f. 86r; one of the two earliest manuscripts of the *Digestum Vetus*, BAV, Vat. lat. 1406, received *pecia* markings in the thirteenth century so that it could be used to follow instruction in the schools. Since many other manuscripts from this period must have been lost, destroyed, or simply worn out from such use, the original eleventh-century production of these previously obscure works must have been impressively large.

The main legal literature of the period was glosses. Except where there are sigla or other identifying marks (such as with the materials in the Cologne Institutes) dating glosses is, unfortunately, no easier than dating manuscripts: the evidence is again essentially paleographical. The oldest strata of glosses contained in the Turin Institutes are certainly eleventh-century in origin, however, as are the glosses in the Pistoia and Darmstadt *Epitome codicis*. Other glossed manuscripts of the *Institutiones*—those of Casamari (Rome, Bib. Naz. ms. sessoriano 110), and Poppi (Bib. com. ms. 200)—seem to be from the late eleventh or early twelfth century. Glosses in still other manuscripts, notably Paris 4516, were erased from the margins later in the Middle Ages and can no longer be read.

For our present purposes, however, the abundance of the manuscript evidence from the later eleventh century confirms the remark-

[104] Petrucci's eleventh-century date for the Torino manuscript is cited by Mor, *Scritti*, p. 13 n.; Nicolaj dates the Poppi manuscript "a cavallo dei sec. XI–XII," *Cultura e prassi*, p. 93 n. 266.

able transformation that had occurred in the fortunes of the Justinianic codification. From being rare books in the ninth and tenth century—seldom read or cited, almost never copied—the Institutes, Code, and Digest had won a remarkably wide circulation, with better times yet to come. It remains to consider in detail the manuscript evidence for the individual works, to determine what can be said about the process by which the texts were recovered and how those texts were studied in the earliest decades of the juristic renaissance.

CHAPTER FOUR

JUSTINIAN'S INSTITUTES

Although we possess only one manuscript of the Institutes from the early eleventh century—the already discussed Bamberg Ms. Jur. 1—several copies of that work survive from the late eleventh and early twelfth centuries. The best known of them is Turin, Biblioteca Nazionale Universitaria, ms. D.III.13, which was traditionally dated to the ninth or tenth centuries, but which is actually from the later eleventh century. Other early manuscripts include the southern Italian manuscript surviving in pieces as Monte Cassino, Compactiones XI, Iuridica Nr. 1, which perhaps is somewhat earlier than the Turin manuscript; Poppi, Biblioteca comunale, ms. 206 and Bamberg, Staatsbibliothek, Ms. Jur. 2 from the turn of late eleventh and early twelfth century; and Cologne, Historisches Archiv, ms. W 328 and Rome, Biblioteca Nazionale, Sessoriano 110 from the early twelfth century. Unlike the earliest codices of the Code and Digest, all of these manuscripts originated as integral texts, and most of them have come down to us as intact manuscripts. Of these, all except the Monte Cassino fragments clearly reflect the jurist revival. All of them originated as integral texts and, with the exception of the Turin and Monte Cassino manuscripts, all of them have survived intact.

Perhaps because the text of the Institutes poses few problems, historical discussion of these manuscripts has usually focused on their glosses. Yet apart from attesting the rapid growth of interest in Roman law in the late eleventh and early twelfth century, most of them offer little to elucidate the environment in which those studies took place. Glosses to the Institutes tend to be fairly elementary, often doing little more than explaining phrases or restating the text in simpler language: even in the eleventh century students may have lingered only briefly with the Institutes before going on to the Code, as indeed we can see from the pattern of citations to the two works in the *Walcausina* and the *Expositio*. There are also real difficulties with working with the glosses, because they were frequently added in multiple strata, often over the several centuries but sometimes in the earliest decades.[1] The Turin Institutes had glosses in sixteen different hands, by Krüger's estimate, some as late as the fourteenth or fifteenth centuries;[2] Victor Crescenzi arrived at a similar estimate of about 15 hands ranging from the late eleventh to the thirteenth centuries for Poppi 206;[3] and Alberto Alberti discerned five hands in the Sessoriano manuscript previously owned by the monastery of Casamari.[4]

Despite such problems, two Institutes manuscripts are worth careful consideration here. In part because of its mis-attribution to the ninth or tenth century, the Turin and its earliest strata of glosses have received considerable and ongoing attention from historians, although mainly as evidence for a now lost ancient commentary. Even more important for our purposes, however, is Cologne ms. 328, which apparently preserves glosses from the earliest period when Roman law was studied as a subject independent of Lombard law. We shall consider each manuscript in turn.

Turin ms. D.III.13 and Its Glosses

The Turin Institutes has suffered very substantial damage over the centuries. By the later twelfth century it had lost its first gathering, containing the text up to In. 1.12.10, necessitating the preparation of a replacement fascicle. Most of book four, from In. 4.1.16, is entirely missing, and there are also several briefer lacunae along the way. Study of the manuscript is further complicated by medieval retracing and rewriting of many passages, by reagents applied in the hope of reading sections nearly erased by wear, by smoke and fire damage suffered during the 1904 fire in the Biblioteca Nazionale of

---

[1] Overviews of Institutes glosses include F. Patetta, "Sopra alcuni mss. delle Istituzioni di Giustiniano con appendice di glosse inedite," BIDR, 4 (1891): 5–84 (repr. *Studi*, pp. 39–120) and A. Alberti, "Ricerche su alcune glosse alle Istituzioni e sulla 'summa Institutionum' pseudoirneriana," *Pubblicazioni dell'Istituto di scienze giuridiche, economiche, politiche e sociali dell'Università di Messina*, 5 (Milano, 1935): 21–94. Editions of glosses from individual manuscripts include Victor Crescenzi, ed., *La Glossa di Poppi alle Istituzioni di Giustiniano* [Fonti per la storia d'Italia, 114] (Roma, 1990). A. Alberti, *La Glossa di Casamari alle Istituzioni di Giustiniano* (Milan, 1937). Citations for editions of the Turin and Cologne glosses will be given below, in the discussion of those manuscripts.

[2] P. Krüger, "Die Turner Institutionenglosse," *Zeitschrift für Rechtsgeschichte*, 7 (1868): 44–78, at pp. 47–50.

[3] Crescenzi, *Glossa di Poppi*, pp. xxi–xxiii.

[4] Alberti, *La Glossa di Casamari*, pp. xv–xvii.

Turin, and by restorations subsequent to the fire, which required pasting protective gauze on some leaves. Although these events have seriously reduced the legibility of many of the glosses, leaving some partially or entirely unreadable, they do not impede establishing a date for the manuscript: it is from the later eleventh century, more precisely to its last quarter, and was the work of a single scribe.[5]

Although the Turin Institutes contains several strata of glosses, some as late as the fifteenth century, scholars have been principally concerned with those written in a fine caroline script with some chancery characteristics that is roughly contemporary with the manuscript itself. Sparking this interest is the fact that many of them display features that seem more appropriate for the sixth century than for the Middle Ages. One gloss (12/18) refers to Justinian as "our lord" (*nostri domini*) as if he were still alive.[6] Another (241/370) seems to refer to the *Quinquaginta decisiones*—a collection of fifty constitutions issued by Justinian after the first edition of his Code but then incorporated into the second edition,[7] while a third (297/520) mentions the "post Codicem constitutionem xxxii," apparently in reference to Nov. 84. A few glosses even provide details of pre-Justinianic practices neither discussed in the works of the *Corpus* nor of apparent utility to medieval readers. Thus, gloss 164/233 provides the historical context for a rule mentioned in In. 2.11.2 regarding the wills of deaf or mute Roman soldiers: although those infirmities would bar a man from being recruited, he might acquire them while in service.

While historians have generally agreed that these glosses were unlikely to have been composed in the tenth century—the dating current until recently—there has been less consensus about their possible origins. Fitting discussed the glosses as evidence for the existence of a law school in Rome, arguing that they drew both on pre-Justinianic materials, perhaps used for glossing Gaius' Institutes, and on the early Greek language commentary on Justinian's Institutes attributed to Theophilus Antecessor, a jurist active during the 530s.[8]

[5] As noted above in chapter one, the eleventh-century date was first established by Armando Petrucci at the request of C. G. Mor.

[6] The first number in citations to the Turin glosses refers to Savigny's and Krüger's numbering, and the second to Alberti's; where only one number is given the reference is to Alberti's edition.

[7] The gloss used the term "L. Constitutiones"; for the historiography discussing this gloss, which Conrat doubted referred to the *L. Decisiones*, see Alberti's note to it.

[8] Fitting, *Über die sogenannte Turiner Institutionenglosse*, pp. 5–38.

C. Ferrini, editor of Theophilus' *Paraphrase*,[9] doubted the direct influence of that work on the Turin glosses and suggested instead that the similarities between the two commentaries reflected common sources used by both, especially scholia to Gaius.[10] Conrat, while disagreeing with Fitting wherever possible and skeptical of his suggestion of pre-Justinianic materials, agreed that many glosses appeared to derive from Theophilus' commentary.

The hypothesis that the Turin glosses preserve a sixth-century commentary deriving from Theophilus was reasserted by H. J. Scheltema in 1970 and, with substantial additional details, by Detlef Liebs in 1987.[11] Liebs argues that the oldest stratum of glosses form a unified and integrated work, as witnessed by internal cross-references such as *superius diximus, superius exposuimus*,[12] that he ascribed to the period between 543 and 546—dates already suggested by Fitting based on his consideration of Justinian's novels. Noting the occasional references to Rome in the glosses, and the anachronisms in some references, Liebs further proposed that the glosses originated in a previously unknown law-school there rather than in the known sixth-century law schools of Constantinople or Beirut. Having made this argument in his book on Italian law, Liebs reasserted it, without further documentation, in his contribution to the *New Cambridge Medieval History*.[13] In effect, Liebs restated Fitting's case for a law-school in sixth century Rome, although without the troublesome claim that it survived throughout the early Middle Ages.

A paleographical examination of the manuscript undercuts Liebs' argument on several key points. To begin with, the author of the glosses apparently returned to the manuscript more than once, with slight alterations in his script that caused Alberti sometimes not to recognize these glosses as his work: he thus cannot have been, as Liebs supposes, simply reproducing glosses from a single pre-existing work but rather was a scholar collecting materials from multiple

[9] *Institutionum graeca paraphrasis Theophilo antecessori vulgo tributa*, ed. C. Ferrini (Berlin, 1884–97). On this commentary, see H. J. Scheltema, *L'enseignement du droit des antécesseurs* (Leiden, 1970), pp. 17–23; and J. H. A. Lokin, "Theophilus Antecessor," *Tijdschrift voor Rechtsgeschiedenis*, 44 (1976): 337–44, at pp. 340–41.

[10] C. Ferrini, "La Glossa torinese delle Istituzioni e la Parafrasi dello Pseudo-Teofilo," *Opere* (Milan, 1929), vol. 1, pp. 41–56 [orig. pub. 1884].

[11] Scheltema, *L'enseignement*, pp. 43–46; Liebs, *Jurisprudenz*, pp. 195–220.

[12] Liebs, p. 198.

[13] Liebs, "Roman Law," pp. 238–59.

sources and perhaps adding some of his own. Nor is it entirely certain that the editors of the glosses, faced with the very real difficulties presented by the state of the manuscript, have correctly identified even the supposed homogeneous nucleus added by this scribe. The editions of Savigny, Krüger, and Alberti all differ on which glosses constitute the oldest glosses, with Alberti omitting three listed by Krüger but adding another fifteen that Krüger had omitted and marking another ten as possibly belonging to the same stratum of glosses.[14] From our own examination, it is apparent that both Krüger and Alberti failed to recognize some glosses added by this *antica mano*, while also incorrectly attributing to him glosses (such as nos. 82/123, 181/260, and 212/308) that do not seem to be his work. Given the brevity of the glosses and the generic similarity to be seen in hands from the same period, such errors are not at all surprising. Yet they do mean that the editions currently available cannot substitute for studying the manuscript itself.

The re-dating of the manuscript causes even more serious problems for Liebs' argument, because he correctly regarded the tenth-century date of the Turin manuscript as an essential piece of evidence supporting his thesis. Glosses copied in the tenth century, he observed, "must have been copied by a non-jurist, who did not understand the contents and who worked from an exemplar containing the commentary."[15] Assigning this manuscript to the late eleventh century, however, renders this argument unsustainable. Rather than non-jurists, as Liebs supposed, the readers of this manuscript were certainly drawn from the juristic community: scholars who were well informed about legal procedures generally, who could write their own glosses, and who could rework existing materials into new forms. Often, indeed, the language and methods singled out by Liebs and others as evidence of the antique origin of the Turin glosses turn out to correspond exactly with what one sees in eleventh-century works such as the *Walcausina* and the *Expositio*. The use of the term *Nota*, for example, is seen throughout all kinds of manuscripts from the period, legal and otherwise. The notation of variant readings, similarly, are widely diffused through Lombard and Roman law manuscripts of the eleventh century.[16] Cross-links within glosses, noted

[14] Alberti, *La Glossa torinese*, pp. xii–xiii.
[15] Liebs, *Jurisprudenz*, p. 199.
[16] Discussed by Liebs, *Jurisprudenz*, p. 201.

by Liebs in his argument that the earliest stratum of glosses formed a coherent commentary, are found throughout the *Expositio*—whose title, indeed, recalls the use of "exposimus" in gloss 114/157 of the Turin Institutes—and in the *Walcausina*. The *Expositio* to Roth. 141 §2, for example, reads:

> Sciendum quoque, "alii" pro libera tantum intelligi, quod confirmatur per easdem rationes quibus confirmatum est superius.

The use of *sciendum* in the same gloss is reminiscent of the phrase "*extra sciendum*" (21/29) used in the Turin glosses.[17] *Queritur* and all its variants—*Questio est*, *Sed queritur*, *Hic queritur*[18]—are, of course, absolutely universal in legal and academic writing of the eleventh century.

Particularly striking, finally, is the fact that nearly all of the "awkward linguistic usages" enumerated by Liebs (p. 218) were simply normal Latin for eleventh-century Italians, being seen in prose of all kinds including the early commentaries of the Lombard laws. Locutions that fall into this category include: the frequent use of *quia* and *quando* introducing clauses with the meaning of "that"; the term *subaudis*—"understand" this word for that—which appears in the glosses of Lanfranc (educated at Pavia) as well as throughout the *Expositio*;[19] and the use of *intelligere* in almost every conceivable formulation. One even sees the occasional use of *arbitror* in the sense of "believe arbitrarily or without basis," as when the *Expositio* to Liut. 20§11 remarks: In eo quod in hac lege scriptum est: "et persona eius tradatur ad propinquos defuncti," arbitrantur quidam, ut homicida ad mortem tradendus sit. Sed non est intelligendum aliquem morti legaliter esse tradendum . . ."

The similarities go beyond linguistic practice. Two of the glosses (455/921, 456/922) attributed to the oldest set of glosses take the form of diagrammatic distinctions, to be discussed below as typical of the *Walcausina* and the Cologne glosses.[20] A different kind of link

---

[17] Remarked upon by Scheltema, *L'enseignement*, p. 44. The precise expressions: "extra sciendum" and "extra intelligendum" are not, however, found in the *Expositio* or the *Walcausina*.

[18] See the list given by Scheltema, *L'enseignement*, p. 44.

[19] For *subaudis* in the *Expositio*, see Roth. 4§1, Roth. 203§1, Roth. 340§1, Roth 372§1, Kar. M 45§7, Kar. M. 71§1—to cite only examples from book one of the Lombarda. On this usage in Lanfranc, see Radding, "The Geography of Learning," p. 157.

[20] See below at note 51.

with contemporary Lombardist commentaries comes from gloss 288/501 to In. 3.5.5. Justinian's text commented that agnatic claims can run to ten degrees of relationship, resulting in the following gloss: "Nota quia legitimis personis hereditates usque ad decimum gradum competent." This gloss, as both Fitting and Conrat agree, represents an error in that it limits inheritance to ten degrees on the male side;[21] the same error is repeated in two other glosses (310/543 and 323/570). Since Justinianic law does not differ from pre-Justinianic law on this point, it would be hard to account for this error in a truly ancient source. The mistake would make more sense in a reader who came to the Justinian's law without prior training in Roman law, as was the case with eleventh-century jurists: indeed, the same "error" occurs in a *Walcausina* gloss to Roth. 15: "Iure vero agnationis etiam usque ad x."[22] Other errors Liebs noticed in the Turin glosses might also be attributed more plausibly to eleventh-century jurists than to a school of law contemporary with Justinian himself.[23] It is even possible that the quotation from Silius Italicus' Latin version of the Iliad in gloss 396/770 was medieval rather than ancient, since the *Ilias latina* won a wide circulation only in the eleventh century.[24]

Recognizing that a large number of the oldest glosses in the Turin Institutes must have originated in the eleventh century does not, of course, mean that some of the glosses discussed by previous scholars could not have been of ancient origin. As the renewed circulation of the *Corpus* itself attests, eleventh-century jurists had direct contact with ancient manuscripts, including perhaps works that did not enter the medieval curriculum of studies and thus did not come down to us. They may, for example, have known the rare fragment attributed to Dositheus, of which an apparent paraphrase occurs in the *Walcausina*.[25] It is not even necessary to assume that all of the genuinely

[21] Fitting, *Turiner Institutionenglosse*, p. 24; Conrat, *Geschichte*, p. 117. Liebs also concedes that this is an error, *Jurisprudenz*, p. 210.

[22] Alberti mistakenly attributes this gloss to the *Expositio*; it is found in the Vienna and Paris manuscripts of the Walcausina as well as in the Laurenziana manuscript containing glosses from that tradition. The Paris manuscript appends the phrase "secundum quondam" to this gloss, expressing some doubt about its accuracy. Conrat notes (*Geschichte*, p. 117 n. 3) that this error survived in the medieval tradition.

[23] See Liebs' discussion, *Jurisprudenz*, pp. 208–15.

[24] *Texts and transmissions*, pp. 191–94.

[25] An aside at the end of the gloss to Roth. 224 reads: "Scito, si quis Longobardus servo communi libertatem dederit, quod pars adcrescit socio non danti, ut legitur in antiquo iure Romano, quod lex Longobarda sequitur." [Reading *socio* for the

ancient materials contained in the Turin glosses came from a single source. Fitting and Ferrini noted how some glosses appear to refer to pre-Justinianic law and others to Justinianic legislation as if it were still in progress. Particularly noteworthy in this regard is Ferrini's suggestion that the similarity between some of the Turin glosses and Theophilus' commentary on the Institutes might reflect the dependence of both on a common store of pre-Justinian materials already in Latin. This hypothesis has the advantage of explaining the agreement in the content between certain glosses and Theophilus' text, despite the fact that none of the glosses seems to be a literal translation of the Greek text. It also avoids the need to suppose that there existed an otherwise unattested translation into Latin of Theophilus' commentary, whose original Greek text is not known to have circulated in southern Italy before the twelfth century.

If the ancient materials in the Turin glosses are too limited and uncertain to demonstrate the existence of a sixth-century law school in Rome, the oldest stratum of glosses as a whole can now take their proper place as evidence from the earliest phases of the juristic revival. Recovering ancient glosses was only part of this process. The Turin glosses also give us a glimpse of how Justinian's works were becoming a school text by being equipped with every kind of glosses from definitions and paraphrases to *quaestiones.* A few glosses in the Turin manuscript, indeed, won sufficient diffusion to be taken up in the Accursian *Glossa Ordinaria*, while others find echoes in other early manuscripts, especially the Casamari glosses in the Sessoriano manuscript in Rome, two manuscripts in the Biblioteca Marciana of Venice, and, to a less extent, the Cologne glosses, which we consider next.

Cologne ms. W 328: Roman Law as a Field of Study

The other principal source for early study of Justinian's Institutes is Cologne, Historisches Archiv ms. W 328, whose glosses were pub-

sotio of Boretius.] The characterization of Roman law as *antiquum* is unusual, and the language is exceptionally close to Dositheus §10: "Communis servus ab uno ex sociis manumissus, neque ad libertatem pervenit et alterius domini totus fit servus iure adcrescendi." *Collectio Librorum Iuris Anteiustiniani*, vol. 2, Paul Krüger, ed. (Berlin, 1878), p. 154. The use of *adcrescere* is particularly striking, since that word is not used elsewhere in the commentary of the *Walcausina* and does not appear in the *Expositio.* Krüger knew only two medieval manuscripts of this work: a ninth or tenth century ms. in Leyden and Paris, Bib. Nat. lat. 6503, from the tenth or eleventh century.

lished by both Conrat and Fitting.[26] At 300 × 180 mm,[27] this volume is notably oblong in format, resembling in this regard the somewhat smaller Paris (263 × 165) and Vienna (255 × 165) manuscripts of the *Walcausina*. (The proportions of the three manuscripts are 0.6 for Cologne, 0.627 for Vienna, and 0.647 for Paris: very close when one allows for trimming in the process of rebinding over the centuries.) All three manuscripts also reserve comparatively wide outer margins for glosses, but the Cologne manuscript is unique for the quality of its decorations, which include some drawings of figures, several colored initials, and a beautifully decorated *arbor cognationum* that takes up nearly all of folio 32r. Six scribes participated in the copying of this manuscript, as follows:

Institutiones
A: ff. 1–22v (*minuscola romana*)
B: ff. 23r–58v
C: 59r–60r
Epitome Juliani
D: 61r–62v line 12
E: 62v line 13–line 21 *habent*
F: 62v line 21 *non etiam*—line 33 *reliquit*
E: 62v line 34–36 *vocent*
D: 62v line 37–107r *Explicit*
G and D: ff. 108r–108r (Insertion for f. 77r)

Scribe A, who copied the first 22 folios, wrote in *minuscola romanesca*, while the rest wrote an Italian caroline without regional characteristics. The three scribes who wrote each book obviously worked together, since the transitions between the parts are seamless. After the work was complete, the principal copyist of the *Epitome Juliani* was assisted by a seventh scribe in adding a missing section after the *explicit* on f. 107r and continuing until f. 108r; a tie sign marks where this passage is to be inserted into the main text. The manuscript is to be attributed to the early twelfth century.

---

[26] Max Conrat, "La glossa di Colonia alle istituzioni," *Archivio Giuridico* (1885): 105–25; and Hermann Fitting, *Institutionenglossen des Gualcausus* (Berlin, 1891).

[27] We acknowledge with thanks the help of Juliane Trede of the Staatsbibliothek of Berlin, whose description of the Cologne manuscript provided us with details of its physical structure.

Although there is a clean break between the two works in the sense that the *Epitome Juliani* begins with a new fascicle, the two parts seem to have been produced by the same workshop and bound together at an early date. The decorative initial at the beginning of the *Epitome Juliani*, for example, is longer and more refined than that of the Institutes but it is in the same style, including the lion at the top with an open mouth. The ruling of the pages, including double lateral lines, is also similar. What is certain, however, is that the two works were joined together within a short period of being finished. Thus, for example, the marginal rubrics in both parts were added by the same hand, as were the decorative letters in the margins of ff. 28r, 34r, 62v and 63r. The marginal gloss listing the divisions of the *as*, on f. 17v., also appears to have been written by D, the principal scribe of the *Epitome Juliani*. A final indicator in the same direction is the fact that the same person made corrections to the text of both works, typically adding in the margin a passage that had been omitted in the original copying.

The already mentioned *arbor cognationum* provides an important link between the Cologne manuscript and the Lombardist tradition. The Institutes (In. 3.6.9) may originally have contained such a table, which is used to calculate degrees of relationship for purposes of inheritance, but it is missing from the manuscript tradition. Sometimes the table from Isidore of Seville was used in its place, as was the case with Vercelli 122, but this particular version of it seems to have been a new composition based on the terminology of Justinian's Institutes.[28] The verses at the bottom of the *arbor* suggest that it was the work of Walcausus, who intended to use it for teaching.

> Sanguinis as metas, docuit quas nube repletas
> Grecus conventus, sapiat romana iuventus
> Hinc Gualcausus ego nullius dicta timebo.

Conrat expressed doubts about the authenticity of this reference to Walcausus, although without giving a reason for them, and they have nonetheless lingered in the historiography.[29] If Conrat's reservations

---

[28] A full discussion of the various *arbor cognationum* is provided by Conrat, *Geschichte*, pp. 631–42; he provides a transcription of the Cologne/London table on pp. 640–41, and comments on its being a reconstruction of the original on p. 636.

[29] Conrat, *Geschichte*, pp. 333–40, 583–600. Conrat's doubts were echoed, for example, by Padoa Schioppa, "La cultura giuridica," p. 233 and n. 113.

originated from the fact that the name *Gualcausus* was written over an erasure, he apparently did not notice that the erasure covers the last two lines of the verses, not just the name, and appears to result from the illuminator's correcting his own error.[30] The distinctive green ink, which would have been impossible to match, leaves no doubt that the reference to Walcausus was not a later addition, and indeed Fitting observed that one of the scribes had written the beginning of the hexameters as a reminder to the illuminator.[31]

If further confirmation were needed of the link between this arbor *cognationum* and Walcausus, it could be found from its inclusion in a eleventh-century supplement of eight folios added to the London manuscript of the *Liber Papiensis* (British Library, ms. add 5411).[32] The London version of the *arbor* retains the hexameter verses, although replacing "*Hinc Gualcausus*" in the final line with the words "*Hic sic doctus*"; in addition to their identical content, moreover, the two diagrams also share an identical decoration in the form of a feline predator (lion? tiger? panther?) animal at the foot of each diagram. The supplement as a whole is devoted to material taken from the *Walcausina*: a *glossa a catena* containing the model pleas and the table classifying Lombard laws according to the equivalent Roman actions. The copyist responsible for the supplement, moreover, also copied marginal glosses from the *Walcausina* into the main manuscript. Since all these other materials came from the Walcausina, the presence in the London supplement of this particular *arbor cognationum* confirms the claim of the Cologne hexameters that it was composed by Walcausus.

Yet Walcausus' *arbor cognationum* is not the only link between this manuscript and Lombardist traditions. Two brief treatises on Roman procedure, apparently part of the manuscript from the beginning, can also be assigned to the same environment. Both of them begin with Justinian addressing the *patres conscripti*, giving them the form of an imperial enactment: a technique that echoes the practice seen in the *Walcausina* of synthesizing several laws on the same subject into a "new law" (always graphically distinquished from the genuine ones)

[30] On this see Fitting, *Institutionenglossen*, p. 27 n. b.

[31] *Institutionenglossen*, p. 27 n. a.

[32] A third version of this *arbor* is found in Bam. Jur. 3 (formerly D.II.5), a manuscript that also contains a version of the *Quaestiones ac monita*.

that provided a direct statement of current practice.[33] The first of these Roman "false constitutions" was inserted at the beginning of the manuscript on a flyleaf (f. I) that contains, in the same hand, the very end of the Institutes (from In. 4.18.8). This page must originally have been part of the manuscript, as is shown by the fact that it shares the same incipit as f. 59r, a new gathering that was also the beginning of the work of copyist **C**: evidently this leaf was discarded for some reason and replaced with the current ff. 59–60. **H**, the copyist of this page, was also responsible for several glosses found in the manuscript, as was the scribe who copied the marginalia for the first "false constitution."[34]

The "first false constitution" is better described as a treatise meant to provide an overview of Roman judicial procedure. The Cologne manuscript is not the only place it appears, for it was included in a collection of canons from Santa Maria Novella in Florence ascribed to 1070–82.[35] It is therefore significantly older than the Cologne manuscript itself and can be attributed with confidence to the period of the *Walcausina* and *Expositio*.[36] It starts with the *apparitor*'s summoning the defendant (*reus*) to inform him that an action had been filed against him, and it continues by noting the financial limits upon amounts that can be claimed, the role of *fideiussores*, and the deadlines for both parties to appear in court. The text in the Cologne manuscript breaks off in mid-sentence at the point when plaintiff and defendant arrive in court, but to judge from the preface the original version must have continued on to discuss the role of judges and executors—in effect the process of an action from start to finish.

None of this was meant to be analytical or original. Wherever possible, indeed, the treatise incorporated actual extracts from Justinian, the longest by far being the inclusion of In. 4.11.2–5, and in general it tries to stay reasonably close to the language of Justinian's

---

[33] For stand-alone "laws," as opposed to the numerous updating achieved by inserting phrases and sentences, see the *Walcausina* at Roth. 14, 153 (after the model pleas), 351 and Rachis 8.

[34] Among the marginalia copied by the scribe of f. I are Institutes glosses 26, 107, 112, 124, 126, 178 as well as corrections to the text on ff. 18v, 28v, 33v, 50r, 51r; the hand responsible for the marginal notes on f. I also copied Institutes glosses 137, 138, 139, 167, 168, and 174, as well as several glosses to the *Epitome Juliani*.

[35] Linda Fowler-Magrel, *Ordo iudicorum vel ordo iudicarius. Begriff und Literaturgaltung* [Ius Commune Sonderhefte 19] (Frankfurt/M., 1984), p. 33.

[36] Edited by Fitting, *Institutionenglossen*, pp. 122–28.

laws. Yet it would be a mistake to think of this treatise as essentially a simple extrapolation from Justinian's works. Justinianic law, as Anders Winroth recently observed, had no special section devoted to procedure, which instead is "scattered about everywhere in the *Corpus*."[37] The synthesis achieved in this first treatise, therefore, was achieved only by collating many different pieces of the Justinianic *Corpus*. This can be seen from the density of citation. The text for an oath to be sworn by the *actor* in a case of *calumpnia*, given right before our manuscript breaks off, drew on two different Justinianic laws, one from the Code and the other a Novel, both of which had to be reworked into direct speech before arriving at words that could actually be pronounced in court.

Imprimis quidem actor ita iuret: "Hanc litem quam movi Martino, non ei movi calumpniandi animo, set extimo me bonam habere causam, nec in tota hac causa gratia dilationis aut calumpniae aut vexandi adversarii probationes a Martino meo adversario exigam, si Deus." Post reus ita: "Ego putans bona instantia uti ad contradicendum pervenio, nec causa . . .	C. 2.58.2 Et actor quidem iuret non calumniandi animo litem movisse, sed existimando bonam causam habere Ep.Jul. 44.3 (178) Omnes litigatores, postquam iusiurandum de calumnia iuraverint, hoc quoque iureiurando suo addant, quod non dilationis, nec calumniae causa, nec vexandi adversarii gratia probationes in tota causa ab adversario suo exigant.

The text as a whole, moreover, though less than two manuscript pages, cites eleven different laws from the *Epitome Juliani* and three from the Code, in addition to the Institutes.

What made this reconstruction of Roman procedures possible was a model for analyzing legal procedure that had previously been developed to study Lombard law.[38] The authors of both the *Expositio* and the *Walcausina* were working jurists—men for whom questions of how to begin actions, enforce deadlines, deal with *fideiussores*, and devise oaths were second nature. It was natural, then, that both works gave particular attention to the precise wording of accusations, with sometimes

---

[37] Winroth, *Making of Gratian's Decretum*, p. 161.

[38] In the *Walcausina*, particular detailed analysis of pleading can be found in the glosses to Roth. 9, 143 (for oaths), 146 (for proofs), Lud.P. 15, and Otto I, 3 (oaths).

several alternatives being offered, as well as to the precise wording of oaths, the deadlines governing certain pleas, and other practical issues. This same method, applied to Roman law, produced the first Cologne treatise. Even the seemingly meaningless conclusion of the oath, *si Deus*, turns out to replicate the form used in the *Walcausina* for Lombard legal oaths.[39] Conrat noted the imperfections of this effort, which did not always achieve a correct and thorough account of procedure, but he regarded it as an impressive attempt all the same, even suggesting a date for the treatise around 1100—a quarter century later than the collection from Santa Maria Novella in which it also appears.[40]

The second treatise contained in Cologne ms. W 328 is, if anything, even closer to Lombard precedents. Written by copyist **C** on fol. 59r–60r, pages left blank at the end of the Institutes, this treatise elucidates a wide variety of Roman actions through the device of the claims that would be made in court. (The same copyist, using a different ink and a smaller writing module, was also responsible for the *quaestio* on the *actio mutui* that fills the last 12 lines of f. 60r, published by Fitting as the Appendix to the second false constitution.) Both of these texts come down to us only in the Cologne manuscript.

Noting that the formula for the *actio negotiorum gestorum* used Pavia as a place away from home ("cum absens eras Papiae"), Fitting argued that the piece therefore could not be pavese in origin. He attributed it instead to Sichelmo of Reggio on the basis of the praise accorded him by his student, Anselm of Besate.[41] Yet this suggestion is open to a variety of objections. To begin with, the Latin is not unambiguous: do we have a locative case ("while you were absent at Pavia") or a dative used with *abesse* ("while you were absent from Pavia") as, for example, Conrat construed the passage? Even if we accept Fitting's understanding of the Latin, moreover, his argument proves nothing, for while it would be useful if readers or students

---

[39] See, in the *Walcausina*, the pleas for Roth. 143, Louis the Pious 15, 24, Wid. 3–6, 9, Otto I 3–6, Hen. I 2, 3. Fowler-Magerl notes that *Si Deus* is a shortened version of *Si Deus te adiuvet* given by Regino of Prüm. *Ordo iudiciorum*, p. 33.

[40] Conrat, *Geschichte*, pp. 591–92.

[41] *Institutionenglossen*, pp. 78–84. This attribution was cited by Fowler-Magerl in her discussion of this piece, *Ordo iudicicorum*, pp. 155–57, as well as the modified version of it proposed by Ugo Gualazzini, *La scuola giuridica reggiana nel medio evo* (Milan, 1952), pp. 21–30. Since the same objections apply to Gualazzini as to Fitting, we shall not discuss his suggestion in detail here.

recognize place-names used in hypothetical examples it was hardly obligatory that one's actual location be one of them. Thus, although the text and manuscripts of the *Walcausina* are certainly Pavese in origin, as was Walcausus himself, it uses Cremona, Milan, Piacenza, and even Ravenna and Rome as hypothetical place-names but never Pavia itself.[42] Nor, finally, is the learning of either Sichelmo or Anselm consistent with what we see in this treatise: we know, indeed, little more about Sichelmo than Anselm's praise of him, while the *Rhetorimachia* itself, although cast in the form of a judicial oration, displays no interest at all in the details of legal procedure.

Where one does see such learning, as Conrat recognized and most subsequent scholars have accepted, was among the Lombardist jurists.[43] Both the *Expositio* and, especially, the *Walcausina* make a common practice of glossing laws by formulating the precise words to be used in court. Not every law was provided with a model plea. Thus, for example, only two are given for the rather uninteresting seventy-nine laws (Roth. 48–126) that specify the compensation to be paid for injuries to hands, teeth, fingers, toes and other bodily parts. Yet many laws have more than one, with variations reflecting differences in the precise facts of a case and in legal interpretation. All in all, the *Walcausina* provides more than 260 such model pleas for Rothari's 389 laws alone.

The second Cologne treatise does for Roman action what the *Walcausina* and *Expositio* had done for Lombard procedures. The Roman actions are presented in the same order as in the Institutes. Conrat noted that even though names of actions were sometimes invented on the basis of remarks in the Institutes, the portrayal of them was essentially correct.[44] The form of these pleas closely follows that found in the *Walcausina* and the *Expositio*, with its ample use of direct speech and the use of P. (Petrus) and sometimes Iohannes as the names of litigants, as well as (once) Titius as a third party. For example, the *actio negotiorum gestorum* (In. 3.27.1) is explained as follows:

> Negotiorum gestorum. P.P. Olim cum absens eras Papiae, ego gerens tuum negotium preparavi vineas tuas, in quibus impendi pretium X solidorum, quos michi debes reddere. Oportet enim cuius ego. Vel:

[42] See, for example, the *Liber Papiensis* at Liut. 34, 43, and Loth. 78.
[43] Conrat, *Geschichte*, p. 588.
[44] See Conrat, *Geschichte*, pp. 583–89, p. 584.

> Olim absens eram Papie, tu negotium meum gerens ita aministrasti illud, quod inde habui dampnum X sol., quos debes emendare michi; oportet enim; cuius ego.[45]

Conrat concluded that this treatise originated with Lombard jurists working before the last quarter of the eleventh century—a judgment that still seems generally correct. Like the first Cologne treatise, the second one shows how the Lombardist jurists were coming to regard Roman law not simply as a tool for analyzing Lombard law but as a subject in its own right.

The presence in the Cologne manuscript of these Lombardist materials naturally suggests that the glosses might come from the same tradition, but it is not the only evidence. Conrat listed several other points leading to the same conclusion: the general scheme for making citations, including using the term *capitulum* to refer to laws, and, especially, the use of a definition of *dannum*, erroneously attributed to the Digest, that also is found in the *Expositio* to Kar.M. 101.3.[46] Another maxim, "ut dicit media iurisprudentia i.e. ius civile" is found both in the Cologne glosses and the *Walcausina*.[47] Fitting, more discursively, enumerated the many stylistic similarities between the Cologne glosses and in the manuscripts linked to the Walcausian tradition: characteristic phrases such as "hic videri potest" or "hic videtur"; the use of diagrammatic distinctions; a general interest in Roman actions; and even usual specific references to an "actio prescriptis verbis quae de estimatio preponitur" both in a gloss to Liut. 115 and in the Cologne gloss to In. 3.22.3.[48]

Since most subsequent scholars were satisfied by such arguments, André Gouron's recent claim that the Cologne glosses are provençal comes as something of a surprise. Gouron's evidence in favor of this attribution consists of several points: 1) the combination of Code, Institutes and *Epitome Juliani*, found in the Cologne glosses, is typical of southern France as it was for the early Lombardists; 2) provençal jurists, like those in Lombardy, referred to titles in Justinianic works as *capitula*; 3) two glosses in the Cologne glosses are repeated in the glosses in Turin ms. D.V.19, which Gouron attributes to grammarian Aubert of Béziers and dates to 1156; and 4) several linguistic parallels

---

[45] Fitting, *Institutionenglossen*, p. 133 ll. 11–18.
[46] Also mentioned by Diurni, *L'Expositio*, pp. 107–08.
[47] Conrat, *Geschichte*, p. 340 and note.
[48] Fitting, *Institutionenglossen*, pp. 31–34.

between the Cologne glosses and the southern French commentary to the Institutes *Justiniani in hoc opera*. Points 1 and 2, it will be noted, do no more than argue that those features are shared by the Lombardist and southern French schools; they provide no basis actually in favor of a French origin. Notably missing from Gouron's argument, moreover, is any effort to show that the methods and interests found in the Cologne glosses were consistent with those in southern French sources, nor even to refute Conrat's and Fitting's arguments that the glosses are consistent with Lombardist methods. Nonetheless, Gouron concluded that the Cologne glosses were "also, without a doubt, originally from the Rhône basin; a little older than [the commentary on the Institutes], they must have been drafted around 1130."[49]

This argument is, at best, disingenuous. Gouron has nothing to say about the certainly Italian provenance of the manuscript, thus sparing himself the trouble of explaining how southern French learning still largely innocent of the Digest could have transplanted itself into Italy as late as 1130s to 1150s. He does not mention the *arbor cognationum*, nor does he discuss Walcausus except in one note (n. 39) where he describes him as "mythique"—an odd characterization of someone whose career is attested by several documents, to say nothing of his role (whether with others or not) in producing the *Walcausina*. Nor does he makes any effort to exclude the possibility that his jurists themselves were drawing on materials that originated elsewhere than in southern France. This point is especially relevant since he does not himself claim that either the commentary on the Institutes or later Turin glosses were actually prior to the Cologne glosses. The parallels cited by Conrat, in contrast, are certainly from fifty years earlier than the date Gouron would propose: plenty of time for Lombardist materials to have made their way to southern France. Gouron, indeed, can hardly deny the possibility of Lombardist

[49] André Gouron, "Le traité «De actionum varietate», la version du manuscrit de barcelone (A.C.A., San Cugat 55) et la «Glossa coloniensis» aux Institutes (Manuscrit de Cologne H. A. W 328)," *Initium*, 2 (1997): 373–90, at pp. 378–79; the quotation is from p. 379. Gouron also adds that both the French commentary and the Cologne glosses cite Cicero, a phenomenon hardly so rare in the eleventh or twelfth centuries as to be worth mentioning. One might observe, however, that one of the first glosses in the *Walcausina*, the definition of *consilium* linked to Roth. 1, comes from *De Inventione* 2.31 though not identified as such by Boretius.

influence, since he himself has argued that the extracts from the Lombard law contained in the *Exceptiones Petri* and *Liber Tübingen* do not exclude the possibility that those works originated in France.

Turning to the glosses themselves, one finds these reservations amply confirmed. A number of similarities to the Lombardist tradition have long been recognized. One is the system of citing laws using the book number and incipit, noticed by Conrat. Much of the analytical terminology is also similar: *queritur, solvitur sic, hic videri potest.* Thus, gloss number 61 (in Fitting's edition) reads:

> Cum superius sit locutus de rebus que iure civili vel naturali adquiruntur, cur his loquitur de rebus que alienari possunt vel non, queritur. Solvitur sic: videtur enim facere exceptionem regule [est] "Per traditionem quoque res nobis adquiruntur; nichil enim tam conveniens est naturali equitati."

The structure of the comment, as a *quaestio* with solution, is also typical of what we saw in the *Expositio*, as is the interest in equity.[50]

Yet another link to the Lombardist tradition, and more particularly to the circle of Walcausus is provided by the thirteen distinctions in the Cologne manuscript that are laid out as branching diagrams. By no means the most complex of these distinctions is that given in the prologue to book 2 *On Things*:[51]

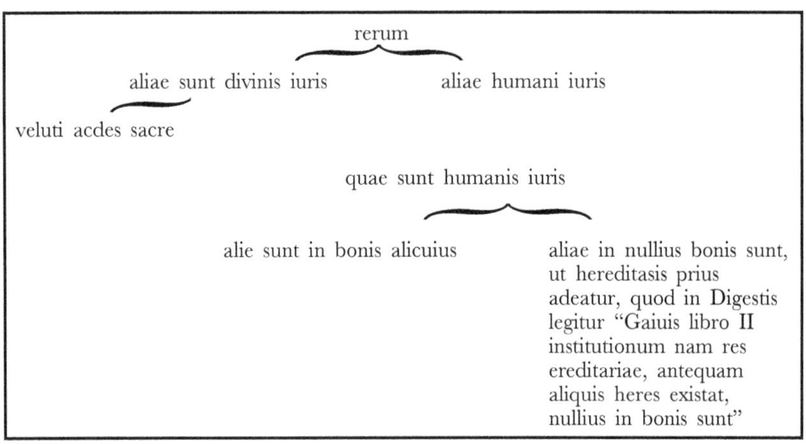

[50] On equity in the *Expositio*, see Diurni, *L'Expositio*, pp. 115–17.
[51] Fitting, *Institutionenglossen des Gualcausus* no. 35.

Diagrammatic distinctions of this kind are traditionally known as "Lombardic," but this somewhat misstates their provenance, for such distinctions are found only in manuscripts containing the *Walcausina* or its materials. The Vienna manuscript of the *Walcausina*, for example, has nearly 150 of them. Since these distinctions are linked to their specific context, none of the ones illustrating Lombard law in the *Walcausina*—even the several entitled *rerum*—are specifically repeated in the Cologne manuscript. The curving lines, sometimes decorated with little circles, sometimes (in this manuscript and in the Paris manuscript of the Walcausina) with little slashes, are closely related graphically, and quite different from other diagrams in the Roman tradition such as the *arbor cognationum* or the *arbor actionum*.[52]

Other symbols used in the Cologne manuscript provide even more conclusive links to Lombardist traditions. These are of two kinds. The first, comparatively large and standing by themselves in the margins, probably had the purpose of making it easy to find laws dealing with certain subjects, like the later "red marks" described by Dolezalek.[53] Fitting described them as resembling phi and rho, but if he had had experience with the *Walcausina* manuscripts he would have recognized them immediately. The second set of signs, much smaller and incorporated in glosses, are similarly to be found in the *Walcausina*. One of them, in the form of an inverted capital A or a capital V with a slash through it, means superseded—perhaps *vacat*? Another, perhaps best described as an oval resting on a horizontal line, seems to mean partially superseded. A *c* with a slash though it means confirmed. Knowing the code from the *Walcausina* thus permits us to understand some glosses whose sense has been elusive. Thus the character Fitting read as an *e* in gloss 55 to the *Epitome Juliani* on f. 105v is actually a slashed *c*, so that the gloss reads *i. huic c[onfirmat] K. "Laicorum," s.v.*: the capitulum "Laicorum" (Otto I 8) confirms this law, according to the best opinion (*secundum valentes*). The Cologne glosses here also adopt the convention seen throughout the *Walcausina* of qualifying some glosses as *s.a.* (*secundum asinos* or *amentes*, i.e., to be disregarded), *s.q.* (*secundum quosdam*, for positions neither proven nor disproven), or *s.v.* (*secundum valentes*, for the approved interpretations).

[52] See the examples in A. Errera, *Arbor actionum. Genere letterario e forma di classificazione delle azioni nella dottrina dei glossatori* (Bologna, 1995).

[53] G. Dolezalek and R. Weigand, "Das Geheimnis der roten Zeichen. Ein Beitrag zur Paläographie der juristischen Handschriften des zwölften Jahrhunderts," ZSS KA, 69 (1983): 143–99.

These distinctive elements would appear sufficient to extinguish any remaining doubts that the glosses in the Cologne manuscript originated with jurists schooled in Lombardist traditions. The harder question is whether they, like the *arbor cognationum* and the two "constitutions," preserve for us learning from the earliest period of Romanist origins of the Cologne glosses. Rendering judgment on this point still more difficult is the fact that the glosses are the work of several hands which cannot always be easily distinguished so that there is every reason to suspect that not all the glosses have the same age. All of the diagrammatic distinctions, however, were apparently copied by the same scribe, and his work contains other glosses—many, for example, that deal with procedural issues and the system of pleas—that are similarly consistent with Lombardist approaches.[54] A further indicator of the age of his glosses is the fact that they quote only passages from the Code that were found in the Pistoia manuscript of the *Epitome*. A handful of other glosses can be attributed to the manuscript's corrector, who was probably also the copyist for the first procedural treatise. The antiquity of other strata, unfortunately, is less certain.

We do not need the Cologne manuscript to know that Lombardist jurists had pursued their study of Justinian's *Corpus* to a considerable depth. The principle that Roman law is *omnium generalis*, articulated in the first half of the eleventh century, already meant that Roman law could freely be introduced into discussions of Lombard law, while the *Walcausina* and the *Expositio* reveal how deeply their studies had gone into the Institutes and the Code. What the Cologne manuscript shows is how these jurists were also starting to examine the legal system of Roman law for its own sake. We recognize the Lombardist origins of the *arbor cognationum* from its appearance in a Lombard law manuscript and a slight inconsistency between its terminology for relationships and that used in a passage of the Digest;[55] we recognize the Lombardist origins of the first Cologne fragment in the

[54] Allowing for the inevitable imprecisions when dealing with such brief text often written very small, the glosses that can be attributed to this hand with reasonable certainty include nos. 12, 17, 19, 32, 35, 37, 44, 47, 48, 49, 51, 54, 57, 59, 61, 62, 67, 68, 72, 74, 75, 83, 86, 87, 88, 89, 90, 99, 103, 104, 113, 114, 115, 116, 117, 120, 121, 122, 125, 132, 156, 157, 158, 171, 174, 176, 177, 189. It will be noted that glosses 176, 177, and 189 are among those Gouron notes as "extraits purs et simple du *De actionum varietate*." Gouron, "Le traité «De actionum varietate», p. 381.

[55] On this, see Conrat's discussion, p. 636, referring to D. 38. 10.3.pr.

use of the name Martinus. But references to Lombard law or practical applications are not to be found and indeed much of the matter analyzed by distinctions, such as the one just quoted on *rerum* and gloss 54 on the varieties of *peculium*, would have been of little practical use to any post-classical jurist.[56] In that sense, as Conrat stressed in the remarks quoted above in chapter one, the Cologne glosses illustrate how the study of Lombard law led to the emergence of a purely Romanist literature by the late eleventh century.

Taken together, the Turin and Cologne glosses illustrate two aspects of the juristic renaissance: the scholarly recovery of ancient learning on the one hand, and the transformation of practical learning into scholarship on the other. Yet we must not make the mistake of assuming that these different approaches represent different legal communities. Although we have here focused on the earliest stratum of glosses, other eleventh-century glosses in the Turin Institutes betray unmistakable connections with the *Expositio*, the other large-scale commentary on Lombard law,[57] confirming that this manuscript too was circulating among the practicing jurists of northern Italy. In the next chapter, we shall see how the same combination of antiquarian and practical skills combined to place into circulation the much longer and more difficult text of Justinian's Code.

[56] A complete list of the distinctions is given by Conrat, *Geschichte*, p. 385*n*.

[57] Alberti's gloss 448, for example, uses a linguistic formulation typical of *Expositio*: "Sed hoc rumpitur," while gloss 854 provides a definition—"Damnum est amissio rei nostrae sine compensatione alterius"—quoted by the *Expositio*, Kar. M. 101 §3, where it is attributed incorrectly to the Digest. These glosses are among those discussed by Luigi Chiappelli, "Il MS. torinese delle Istituzioni," ZSS RA, 11 (1890): pp. 308–10.

CHAPTER FIVE

JUSTINIAN'S CODE

Justinian's Code poses a very different set of problems from those involved in the study of the Institutes. Because the margins of some early manuscripts were erased, only Pistoia C. 106 and Darmstadt 2000 contain glosses assignable to the period before 1100 and not even these have received much scholarly attention. Yet whereas the text of the Institutes presents few difficulties, the textual tradition of the Code has defied easy understanding. Medieval readers themselves were fully aware of the problem, as evidenced by the constitutions one sees added in the margins of the oldest manuscripts and by the longer passages that were simply cancelled or erased and recopied. Such problems in early manuscripts were, inevitably, echoed in later ones, producing a textual tradition of enormous complexity even compared to other books of Justinian's *Corpus*.

The situation that posed such problems for scribes was first understood by Paul Krüger, the scholar responsible for the modern edition of the Code. Krüger argued that the manuscripts used in medieval universities did not represent an unbroken transmission going back to ancient exemplars, but rather resulted from a long process in which the Code was first shortened to a selection of constitutions, the so-called *Epitome Codicis*, and then re-expanded as omitted constitutions were reinserted into the Epitome. No text could pass unscathed through this process and, indeed, Krüger found that the medieval Code suffered from errors in organization, the result of laws being reinserted in the wrong place, as well as from the omission of all the constitutions written in Greek and the last three books of Justinian's original text.

Since Krüger's interest in the manuscripts of the Code grew out of the work for his edition, he felt no need to press his research beyond understanding the relationship between the various early manuscripts. He had little interest in studying the historical circumstances that had led to the creation of the *Epitome Codicis*, and the comments he offered about them were often very general. Yet it is somewhat surprising how little interest the problem has attracted since Krüger's edition appeared in 1877. In 1895, Patetta published a detailed description of a previously unknown manuscript of the Epitome that he found, sadly dismembered, in the Biblioteca Oliveriana of Pesaro; but this manuscript from the early twelfth century offered no clues to the early circulation of the *Epitome*.[1] Mor wrote two articles on the *Epitome*, although confessing that he had made "little headway,"[2] and in the 1980s Carmen Tort-Martorell attempted to clarify the manuscript tradition by using a computer program to compare 52 manuscripts attributed to the period before 1200. Considering as variables only the order of the laws, the inscriptions, and subscriptions in one book (the second), she arrived at no fewer than seven groups of manuscripts—three of which consisted of only one manuscript—with another sixteen manuscripts described as belonging to no particular group.[3] Such results confirm the difficult textual history of the Code without, however, saying much about what that history actually was.

In effect, therefore, this present chapter resumes where Krüger left off in the 1870s, but with a very different set of concerns. Whereas he was principally concerned with establishing the text of the Code, our objective is to explicate what happened to it during the Middle Ages. This purpose requires close attention to the manuscripts, which themselves are our main witnesses to the effort that went into acquiring and circulating the text of Justinian's Code. In undertaking this work, we took Gero Dolezalek's *Repertorium manuscriptorum veterum Codicis Iustiniani* as our point of departure, and we saw (at least in microfilm) all manuscripts ascribed by him to the first half of the twelfth century or earlier.[4] Although the examination of the manuscripts is often

---

1 Patetta, "Di un nuovo manoscritto del Codice Epitomato."

2 C. G. Mor, "Epitome Codicis: Qualche considerazione sulla sua forma originaria," [orig. pub. in 1973] in *Scritti*, pp. 25–62, at p. 25. It should be noted that Mor completely misunderstood the relationship between the surviving manuscripts, as evidenced by his attributing the Paris and Pistoia manuscripts of the Epitome to separate branches of his stemma. (p. 26) On the relationship between those manuscripts, see below. See also Mor, "Il manoscritto del Codice Giustinianeo della Biblioteca comunale di Avranches," [orig. pub. in 1968] in *Scritti*, pp. 63–76. Contrary to Mor's evaluation, this manuscript is French rather than Italian and twelfth rather than eleventh century. It was first described by André Fliniaux, "Le manuscript 141 de la Bibliothèque Municipale d'Avranches et le problème de l'introduction en France au Moyen-âge du texte des compilations de Justinien," *Atti del Congresso internazionale di diritto romano (Bologna e Roma xvii–xxvii Aprile mcmxxxiii)*. (Pavia, 1934), Part 1 *(Bologna)*, vol. 1, pp. 313–27.

3 Carmen Tort-Martorell, *Tradición textual del Codex Justinianus. Un estudio del libro 2* [Ius Commune Sonderhefte, 45] (Frankfurt/Main, 1989).

4 Gero Dolezalek, *Repertorium manuscriptorum veterum Codicis Iustiniani* [*Ius Commune*, Sonderheft, 23] (Frankfurt/Main, 1985).

tedious and repetitive, no activity that seemed so important then can fail to repay study today. We shall see that none of Justinian's other works lies closer than the Code to the revival of legal learning in the eleventh century.

Discovery and Historiography of the *Epitome Codicis*

It was a principle of the Justinianic codification, enunciated in the constitution *Deo auctore* (C.1.17.1), that "imperial constitutions need no authority beyond that by which they were enacted" (*divalium constitutionum sanctio sufficit ad eorum auctoritatem*). Unlike the Institutes and Digest which had the status of single constitutions enacted into law by Justinian's decree, the constitutions in the Code thus retained their original identity as separate pieces of legislation.[5] The compilers of the Code accordingly preserved the legislative details of the constitutions they included by prefacing each law with an inscription giving the name of the enacting emperors and providing a subscription at the end of the law with the date of the enactment.

Since medieval jurists paid scant attention to the dates of individual constitutions, copyists soon adopted the practice of abbreviating the inscriptions and omitting the subscriptions entirely. It was, therefore, in pursuit of these lost fragments of text that nineteenth-century scholars first turned their attention to the oddly truncated version of Justinian's Code preserved in the capitular library of Pistoia. Bluhme visited Pistoia on Schrader's behalf in 1822 specifically to collate the inscriptions and subscriptions, but he recognized that the manuscript was older than other known manuscripts of the Code and another scholar was sent to make a full transcription. The subsequent discovery of Paris 4516 and Darmstadt 2000 made it clear that the Pistoiese codex was one of a class of manuscripts rather than an isolated oddity.

Full recognition of the role of the *Epitome* came only with Krüger's *Kritik* of 1867. Working with other scholars' accounts of the three manuscripts of the *Epitome*, the four oldest manuscripts of the Code available to him in the Berlin national library (mss. 272, 273, 274, and 275), and the most important early printed editions, Krüger was impressed by two distinct phenomena: the lack of consistency from one manuscript to another in the order with which the constitutions

---

[5] Lokin, "Theophilus Antecessor," pp. 340–41.

were presented, and the numerous cases in which constitutions originally omitted from manuscripts were copied into the margins.[6] Such structural problems could not, Krüger recognized, be dismissed as normal copyist errors, especially when they occurred in manuscript after manuscript; indeed, none of the manuscripts he studied in this preliminary survey managed to reproduce the order of constitutions given in the *Summa Perusina*—important in this context as the only account of the contents of Justinian's Code independent of the later "Bolognese" tradition. Krüger concluded, accordingly, that the ancestors of later medieval manuscripts were not direct copies of antique exemplars, but rather must have been created by reintegrating missing constitutions into manuscripts of the *Epitome*.[7] Rather than a odd off-shoot of antiquarian interest, therefore, the *Epitome Codicis* emerged as the direct ancestor of the entire medieval tradition.

In his actual edition, Krüger used a slightly different mix of manuscripts, adding Montpellier, École de Médecine H. 82 and Monte Cassino ms. 49 to Berlin ms. 273. (He noticed that the Montpellier manuscript was largely free of the errors found in Berlin 273, but he explained this difference as resulting from corrections introduced into the Bolognese tradition.)[8] He also went further in his speculations about the textual history of the *Epitome Codicis*, working principally from his oldest manuscript of it, Pistoia, Bib. Cap., ms. C 106 (= **P**). Krüger was struck by the fact that the base text of this manuscript already contains numerous errors in the sequence of the constitutions. Some of the errors are small, such as the transposition of two laws; others involve large blocks of constitutions displaced from their correct sequence. Thus, **P** gives the first ten titles of book 1 as follows (errors in sequencing are marked with an asterisk):

1.1.1, 4
1.3.30, 33, 40, *37, 49, 50, 51, 54
1.4.2, 3, 6, 8
*1.3.32, *2, 3, 5, 6, 7, 8, 10, 11, 13, 15, 25, *16, 17, 20, 22, 24
1.4.9, 10, 12, 15, 28
1.5.1

[6] *Kritik des Justinianischen Codex*, pp. 12–18.
[7] *Kritik des Justinianischen Codex*, pp. 35–36.
[8] *Codex Iustinianus*, p. XVIIII: "In codice *M* pauca Epitomae auctae vestigia deprehenduntur."

1.7.5
*1.6.2
1.7.1
1.8.1
1.9.3, 8, *6, 15, 16
1.10.1

Similar errors also appear in the other manuscripts of the Epitome, as do other, more subtle errors of attaching inscriptions or subscriptions to the wrong laws, as occurred with the constitution cited in Henry III's legislation of 1047.[9] Krüger supposed that most of the inversions and other discrepancies resulted from errors of reintegrating individual laws and blocks of constitutions that originally had been absent from the *Epitome*. Attempting to imagine original form of the *Epitome*, he proposed that the first book may have begun as follows:

1.1.1, 4
1.3.30, 33, 37
1.4.6, 8 [16]
1.5.1[10]

Since none of the surviving manuscripts actually conveyed this original version, Krüger adopted the practice of referring to them as the "enlarged" *Epitome* or the *Epitome Codicis aucta*.[11]

As to when the *Epitome Codicis* might have been created, Krüger had little to say. Since **P** was then attributed to the tenth century, Krüger concluded that the *Aucta* was at least that old, while the apparent use of the *Aucta* in the *Lex Romana canonice compta* implied that it had already existed in the ninth century.[12] Krüger did not speculate about the date of the original form of the *Epitome*, but historians who considered the question agreed that it must have been very early. Conrat suggested the seventh or eighth centuries as the most probable period of origin, arguing that the ninth and tenth centuries were too clerical to have produced the *Epitome*; Mor and Calasso (who freely admitted his uncertainty) suggested the eighth century; while Astuti

[9] See Krüger's discussion, *Kritik*, pp. 37–39.

[10] *Codex Iustinianus*, Appendix II, pp. *56–*58. A slightly different reconstruction was proposed by C. G. Mor, "Per la storia dei libri giustinianei nell'età preirneriana," pp. 15–23; and "Epitome Codicis."

[11] *Codex Iustinianus*, pp. XXXII–XXXIII.

[12] *Codex Iustinianus*, pp. XVIIII.

thought the *Epitome* originated perhaps as early as the late seventh.[13] None of these scholars offered any evidence to support their suggestions, however, leaving them little more than guesses.

The Origins of the *Epitome Codicis*

Redating the Pistoia *Epitome Codicis* to the eleventh century significantly alters the chronological framework within which the *Epitome* has been discussed. The first casualty is the idea of an *Epitome Codicis aucta* as a distinct recension. Since the three manuscripts are not in fact identical, the concept of the *Aucta* was always something of a fiction: useful mainly as a representation of the apparently lengthy pause in restoring constitutions between the Pistoia manuscript and the Paris and Darmstadt manuscripts apparently from a century or more later. Now that all of those manuscripts are known to have originated within the space of a few decades, with the Pistoia *Epitome* receiving marginal additions almost as soon as it was finished, a very different picture emerges: rather than a long, slow development over centuries with two essentially stable recensions (the original version and the *Aucta*), the *Epitome* must be seen as a text undergoing constant and rapid evolution within the eleventh century. The importance of the manuscripts of the *Epitome*, indeed, is that they provide different snapshots of how this transformation proceeded during the second half of the eleventh century.

Also in question is the date for the origins of the *Epitome*. In reality, our conception of the *Epitome* as an early medieval text has rested almost entirely on the traditional attribution of the Pistoia manuscript to the tenth century, which excluded any later date. Yet the hypothesis that it originated in the early Middle Ages was never without problems. The works now attributable to the seventh and eighth centuries—the chapter summaries for the *Epitome Juliani* and evidently the *Summa Perusina*—are drastically abbreviated and simplified texts with frequent errors or grammar and orthography: different in every respect from the full-text extracts of the *Epitome Codicis*. Nor is it easy to imagine that a Carolingian center capable of producing this text would have left no other trace of its existence in the abun-

[13] Conrat, *Geschichte*, p. 190; Mor, *Scritti*, p. 16; Calasso, *Medio evo del diritto*, p. 291; Astuti, "Tradizione dei testi," p. 188.

dant documentation of the ninth and tenth centuries. Now that the Pistoia manuscript is securely assigned to the eleventh century, one must ask what other evidence exists for the existence of the *Epitome Codicis* in the early Middle Ages.

Except for the *Lex Romana canonice compta*, the *Collectio Anselmo dedicata*, and the *Excerpta Bobiensa*, the rare citations of the Code from the period between 600 and 1000 are far too brief (no more than a constitution or two) to permit intelligent speculation about whether they came from an integral version of the Code, the *Epitome*, or some other intermediate source. One can also exclude two of the three collections from consideration: the *Excerpta Bobiensa* because more than a third of its 18 constitutions from Justinian's Code are absent from the *Epitome*, and the *Collectio Anselmo dedicata* because all of its Justinianic materials derived from the *Lex Romana canonice compta*. The *Lex Romana* itself, however, requires some detailed discussion. Krüger thought that the *Lex Romana* must have been based on the *Epitome* because only eight of its 123 constitutions were not found in at least one of the three *Epitome* manuscripts or (as he put it) the *Aucta*. Yet looking at the manuscripts individually gives a rather different picture. The earliest version we have of the *Epitome Codicis*—although nearly two hundred years later than the *Lex Romana canonice compta*—is provided by the base text of **P**. Comparing it with the *Lex Romana*, however, yields dramatically different results from Krüger's: 25 of the 123 constitutions contained in the *Lex Romana canonice compta* are absent from **P**.[14] The discrepancies are even more marked at the level of individual titles. **P**, for example, contains laws 3, 5, 2, 6, 7 and 8 of C. 2.20; the *Lex Romana*, has laws 4, 7, 9, and 12 of the same title. The text used by the compilers of the *Lex Romana* thus cannot have looked much like **P**, or like any manuscript earlier in the tradition of the *Epitome*. It is probably safe to conclude that they were drawing on a complete copy of the Code.

Confirmation that the compilers of the *Lex Romana canonice compta* used a text different from the *Epitome Codicis* is not hard to find. When the compilers of the *Lex Romana* included a law from the Code, they

---

[14] The constitutions present in the *Lex Romana* but absent from the base text of **P** are: 2.3.6; 2.11.1, 10 [in marg. in **P**]; 2.12.6 [in marg.]; 3.12.1, 3; 3.22.4; 3.32.2 [in marg.]; 3.34.10 [in marg.]; 4.34.1; 4.42.1, 2; 4.45.3, 15, 33; 5.4.26; 6.1.1, 4; 6.22.4; 7.11.4; 7.33.1, 10, 12; 7.35.5, 6; 7.40.1, 2. (Mor's appendices listing the contents of the *Lex Romana* must be checked with care, not least because he appears to have used a pre-Krüger edition of the Code.)

generally included the number of the book, the number and sometimes the name of the title, and the number of the law. Even when they group a series of laws under one rubric, they usually provide the number of each individual law. The manuscripts of the *Epitome Codicis*, in contrast, though usually careful with books and titles, do not number the laws and evidently never did: if they had, indeed, the disorganization of the contents of the Code, so typical of all these manuscripts, could never have happened. Nor, because so many laws were omitted, even within a single title, would it be possible accurately to reconstruct the original numbering of the laws using the manuscripts of the *Epitome* alone. The compilers of the *Lex Romana canonice compta* could not, therefore, have produced their work using any imaginable variant of the *Epitome Codicis*, leading us again to the conclusion that they used a copy of the Code in its original form.

The earliest evidence for the *Epitome Codicis*, therefore, is no earlier than the mid-eleventh century—the period of the earliest manuscripts and when it began to be used by Lombardist jurists. It is, indeed, to them that the creation of the *Epitome* must be ascribed. For them, as for no other group since the sixth century, the legal language of the Code would not have posed an insurmountable obstacle: experienced in applying and teaching law, they would have understood how important it was to preserve the precise language of every enactment. As laymen who lacked access to a monastic scriptorium, and who seem often to have copied books for their own use, they also would have needed something shorter than the original. In contrast to the Institutes, Justinian's Code is an enormous work. The first nine books of the Code total roughly 340,000 words, while all twelve contain 420,000 words. Such magnitudes dwarf the other books used by these jurists: the *Liber Legis Langobardorum* without glosses is less than 60,000 words, about the size of Justinian's Institutes, while the *Walcausina* with its extensive glosses totals just under 100,000 words. Seen in this context, extracting the constitutions of the greatest interest or with the most important practical implications represented a reasonable compromise between the intellectual interests of the jurists and the resources available to them for copying books in the middle decades of the eleventh century.

Lending strength to the hypothesis that the *Epitome* was first created in the eleventh century is the fact that the juristic community had done something similar when it created the *Liber Papiensis*, at much the same time, out of scattered and unwieldy materials. What was new about the *Liber Papiensis* was not simply the combination of Lombard and Frankish laws into a single manuscript. Paris, BN ms. lat. 4613, for example, a late tenth-century manuscript from central Italy, contains the codes of the Lombard kings together with a total of nineteen Carolingian capitularies from Charlemagne, Pippin, Louis the Pious, Lothar, and Louis II king of Italy.[15] The number of texts collected in this Paris ms. 4613 is truly impressive: only a tenth of the roughly 250 manuscripts containing capitularies have as many as ten different enactments.[16] Yet no-one would mistake this manuscript for the *Liber Papiensis*. The Paris manuscript is essentially a container of pre-existing texts: each capitulary is marked off from the others by initials and page layout, and all present the text as it was enacted, including prefatory remarks and any formal language enacting it into law. The *Liber Papiensis*, in contrast, reduces the text to its practical essentials. Capitula that never had force in Italy were simply omitted, as were nearly all legislative preambles with the exception of Rothari's prologue. One would not know from the *Liber Papiensis* that Liutprand's legislation was spread out over more than 20 years, nor indeed in which of Charlemagne's many capitularies a specific law was enacted, because the only significant internal divisions were those marking the passage from one ruler's legislation to another. It is worth noticing, in this regard, that the *Epitome Codicis* similarly omitted the prefatory constitutions in which Justinian enacted the Code into law.

Like the *Liber Papiensis*, therefore, the *Epitome Codicis* represents a deliberate selection of laws—entire laws, not summaries—made by men who knew which ones mattered to them. A further parallel between the two compilations is represented by the fluid, evolving nature of both texts. We have already seen that one of the main features of the textual tradition of the *Epitome* was its steady acquisition of additional constitutions—a problem we shall shortly address. Although the variations in the tradition of the *Liber Papiensis* are less dramatic, they are nonetheless constant: virtually every manuscript of the *Liber Papiensis* contains a few laws not found in the other. The

---

[15] This manuscript was described by Bluhme, MGH, Legum vol. 1 (Hannover, 1835), p. XXVII, and most recently by Mordek, *Bibliotheca capitularium*. The text of the capitularies was reedited by Boretius, MGH, *Capit.* 1 (Hannover, 1883).

[16] Arnold Bühler, "Capitularia Relecta. Studien zur Entstehung und Überlieferung der Kapitularien Karls der Grossen und Ludwigs des Frommen," *Archiv für Diplomatik, Schriftgeschichte, Siegel- und Wappenkunde*, 32 (1986): 305–501, at p. 340. Bühler discusses this particular manuscript at pp. 375–76.

Ambrosian manuscript, for example, contains an entire set of laws not found in other codices of the *Liber Legis*, as well as marginal notations ("*Istum capitulum hic non debet esse*," "*Non debet scribere capitulo isto*") revealing an ongoing work of collation with other manuscripts. The *Epitome*, similarly, was never treated as a definitive collection. Readers of the *Epitome* moved constitutions around to correct errors, inserted rubrics that had been omitted, and incorporated additional selected laws into the text. They could act with such freedom because they understood that the *Epitome*, far from being a product of the remote past, was a living text that they had created for their own purposes. The manuscripts, indeed, reveal how those interests—and the text itself—evolved during the decades when the *Epitome* lay at the very center of juristic study.

The conclusion that the *Epitome* originated in the eleventh century is also consistent with the two explanations offered to explain its content. Krüger suggested that the *Epitome* may have omitted laws that duplicated the Institutes, a text that we know was available to eleventh-century scholars.[17] Conrat noticed that laws concerning east Roman (Byzantine) officials were consistently omitted and that the compilation was oriented to lay rather than clerical concerns.[18] His insight can be illustrated by the constitutions included in the base text of **P**, which gives only 1 of the 19 Latin constitutions in C. 1.2, dealing with the sacrosanctity of churches, and 1 of 11 constitutions of C 1.5 on Manichees, but 25 of 42 Latin constitutions of C.1.3, on the legal status of ecclesiastics; or, from book 2, 22 of 30 Latin constitutions of C. 2.3 on *pacta* and 26 of the 43 Latin constitutions of C. 2.4 on *transactiones*, but only 1 of 26 constitutions from C. 2.7 *De advocatis diversorum iudiciorum* dealing with technical details concerning ancient courts. Such selections are entirely consistent with the *Epitome* having been created by secular judges in the eleventh century, and indeed the laws selected to form the *Epitome* overwhelmingly deal with issues that would have been of immediate practical interest to them. Placing the origin of the *Epitome* in the eleventh century thus explains the aspects of its character that have struck the scholars who have studied it with the greatest care.

As to when the *Epitome* began to take shape, we cannot be far wrong in looking to the second quarter of the eleventh century. This

---

[17] *Codex Iustinianus*, p. XVIII.
[18] *Geschichte*, pp. 189–90.

is, in fact, precisely the period when one finds the earliest references to the Code—the constitution of Henry III and the citations of the Code attributed to the jurist Wilihelmus, come in the second quarter of the eleventh century, with the use of the Code in the *Walcausina* and the *Expositio* coming only slightly later. All of these citations, moreover, refer to constitutions contained in the *Epitome*, in one case even incorporating an error of ascription found in **P** itself. As already discussed, the earliest version of the *Epitome* was certainly shorter than the base text of **P**; the earliest extracts may also have been copied without their inscriptions and subscriptions because some constitutions in the *Epitome* have inscriptions from other laws attached to them—an error that could have occurred when they were added later. It may not have been long, however, before those omissions were made good and the collection as a whole augmented to arrive at the common base text of all the surviving manuscripts, with further supplemental constitutions being added later, apparently in multiple stages.

The Manuscripts of the *Epitome Codicis*

Justinian's Code in the Eleventh Century: Pistoia ms. C 106

The intensity of attention devoted to Justinian's Code in the second half of the eleventh century is vividly apparent in **P**. The main text, as already mentioned, was the work of eight scribes organizing their work in a very informal manner, with another 138 constitutions being added later. **P** is, in fact, the key manuscript for studying the supplemental constitutions, for it is the only surviving manuscript in which we can study how constitutions were added to the base text. (The handful of constitutions in the margin of **D** were added by the original scribe and thus may have resulted from oversights in the original copying—a reasonable hypothesis if the exemplar of **D** was anywhere near as complex as **P**.) This evidence was inevitably lost when **P** was copied: manuscripts based on **P** would tell us nothing about the number of constitutions in the mother manuscript, nor their location, nor how they were inserted into the sequence of the constitutions.

Although the supplemental constitutions are one of the most distinctive features of the manuscript tradition of the *Epitome Codicis*, scholars have had surprisingly little to say about them. Conrat believed that they were very early additions and that, like the base text of the *Epitome*, they were drawn from an integral manuscript of the

Code.[19] Patetta rejected this conclusion, however, preferring to see the supplemental constitutions as part of an effort to "complete the Code that lasted more than three centuries, until the school of Bologna."[20] Implicit in Patetta's interpretation is the assumption that only fragments of the original text were available until, late in the process, the "glossators" came across complete, ancient manuscripts. Patetta offered these views only as an aside, in his article on the Pesaro manuscript, but the ideas underlying them have continued to underlie the (few) modern references to the history of the *Epitome.*

We can test these ideas against the evidence of **P** itself. In that manuscript, the supplemental constitutions were copied into any available space: in the upper or lower margins or along the outer edge of the page, where they were often written at a right angle to the main text. Still others were copied onto parchment slips bound into the book, and there is reason to believe that some such slips were lost when the manuscript was rebound in the later Middle Ages. What makes these additions especially significant is that they were the work not of one or two persons but at least twenty-three different hands, all of them attributable to the eleventh century.[21] But it has not sufficiently been stressed that these supplemental constitutions are diffused throughout the entire text of the *Epitome.* Not only did all eight surviving books receive additions, but the new constitutions were distributed among several titles within each book. Never do the additions form a single, coherent block of any size.

This impression is amplified, moreover, when one breaks down the additions in the Pistoia manuscript according to which of the 23 hands inserted them in the manuscript. It may not, for example, seem surprising that hand *b* added constitutions in all eight surviving books of **P**, for his massive contribution amounted to more than half of the supplemental constitutions. But the other hands also—indeed typically—added one or two constitutions to several different parts of the text. Thus, hand *a* added 4 constitutions spread over 2 books and 3 titles; hand *c* added 2 laws in C. 2.4, 3 in C. 8.35, as well as C. 8.44.2; hand *j* copied 8 constitutions from books seven and

[19] *Geschichte,* pp. 190–91.

[20] "Di un nuovo manoscritto," p. 220 [p. 204]. Patetta implicitly rejected Conrat's position.

[21] "Ancora sul manoscritto pistoiese," pp. 19–20 and appendix I.

eight but spread out over 6 different titles. Since different copyists probably represent, at minimum, additions made at different times, these figures reveal that additional constitutions were added to **P** in very small quantities indeed.

This pattern makes no sense if the readers of the *Epitome* were actively trying to restore the Code: that is, if they were trying to reintegrate all the constitutions available to them. We can take the end of book one as an example. Following title C. 1.48 *De officio diversorum iudicum*, which it gave in its entirety, the base text contained only two constitutions of the remaining nine titles, C. 1.51.7 and C. 1.54.6. Copyists *b* and *c* both added a missing section of C. 1.54.6; *b* also added laws 3, 6, and 7 out of the ten Latin constitutions in C. 1.55; *d* added C. 1.51.14; and a possibly fourth hand added C. 1.51.1. It is unlikely that *b* (or his source) had laws 3, 6, 7 but not laws 4 and 5 of C. 1.55, or that *d* had found a slip of parchment with C. 1.51.14 but none of the surrounding materials that the base text also lacked. Such additions surely reflect deliberate choices to add these particular constitutions rather than an unsuccessful effort to restore the Code to its original form.

The same considerations apply to C. 2.3 *De pactis*. The base text of **P** contained 23 of the 30 constitutions making up this title, with laws 1, 5, 6, 10, 15, 22, and 26 missing. Five of these omissions were made good by supplementary constitutions but they were added by four different hands: C. 2.3.5 by *b*, C. 2.3.22 and 26 by *a*, and C. 2.3.15 and 22 by separate hands neither of which appear elsewhere in the manuscript. It is hard to know which is more remarkable: the gradual accretion of supplemental constitutions to the same title by four different copyists, or their continuing lack of interest in C. 2.3.1 and 6. Yet the impression again is of scholars who were adding to their manuscript the constitutions they thought useful, and only the constitutions that they thought useful.

What is most striking, however, is that the additions to the *Epitome* thus have exactly the same character as the original compilation. Put another way, the creation of the *Epitome* and its enrichment by supplemental constitutions should not be seen as two distinct stages but as belonging to a single process aimed at producing a compilation or *florilegium* of the most useful constitutions found in the Code. This conclusion, in itself, was already arrived at by Conrat, who argued that the supplemental constitutions shared the same character as the work itself and should be attributed to the same period as the original compilation;[22] what is different now is that we can date the supplemental constitutions themselves to the second half of the eleventh century. The continuity of purpose between the original compilation and the additions to it is, indeed, one of the most salient aspects that emerges from a study of **P**. Thus, of the 138 supplemental constitutions, many filled gaps in titles already containing numerous constitutions and only 4 were not from titles already represented in the base text: three laws from C. 1.55 and C. 2.33.1. Rather than attempting to incorporate every constitution available to them into their manuscripts, eleventh-century scholars deliberately chose those laws that were of particular interest for their own studies. What those sources were can only be imagined although, in the absence of any evidence that the Code was copied in the early Middle Ages, one must suppose that these eleventh-century scholars were working with partial or intact ancient manuscripts.

This ongoing contact with ancient manuscripts also accounts for a second important aspect of the work done on the text of the *Epitome*. Eleventh-century scholars were not content simply to obtain the text of additional constitutions; they also wanted to insert them in the correct position—a daunting problem that made reconstituting the Code a challenge unlike any other classical text. The earliest manuscripts of both *De Inventione* and the *Ad Herrenium*, for example, reveal lacunae that were successfully repaired by the tenth century: two passages in the case of *De Inventione*, and the beginning to 1.6.9. of *Ad Herrenium*.[23] In contrast to continuous texts such as those, whose context left little room for uncertainty as to where a recovered passage should be inserted, restoring constitutions and rubrics to the *Epitome Codicis* required that the copyist have precise knowledge of where to insert those additions into the base text. The correct sequence of laws thus had to be transmitted along with the newly retrieved constitutions, as well as incorporated into pre-existing codices.

Our analysis of the Pistoia manuscript reveals a variety of techniques adopted for this last purpose. The simplest method was the marginal notation: *hic esse non debet*: "this should not be here"; the same method was also used, as we have seen, in the Ambrosiana copy of the *Liber Legis Langobardorum*. The correct placement was then indi-

[22] *Geschichte*, pp. 190–91.
[23] Reynolds, *Texts and Transmission*, pp. 98–99.

cated by writing the incipit of the law in the margin where it belonged. The placement of additional laws, written in the margin or on slips of parchment, were similarly indicated by the incipit, but when the laws were already on the correct page the correctors also employed pairs of various tie-signs (crosses, bird's eyes, quotation marks in the form of double esses), placing one at the head of the law and the other where it should be inserted when reading or copying. A further system for correcting the organization of the text, and one that was widely diffused in this period, involved use of initials *d.h.* (*deest hic*: skip here) and *p.h.* (*pone hic*: put here).[24] The first of these notations told the reader or copyist to omit the following material, which was out of place, while *p.h.* marked the point where the original text resumed. Different methods could be combined. Thus, on f. 142v, the notation *d.h.* was followed in the margin by the incipits of the C. 8.39.3, 4, 7, 8—the laws to be added at that point.

This work of collation and correction predated the Pistoia manuscript itself. One of the original scribes, for example, copied the letters *d.h.* and *p.h.* between 2.27.2 and 2.29, where he obviously should have inserted 2.28.1; scribe H copied C. 8.35.13 in the margin of f. 164r, suggesting that it had been present in the exemplar but not in the main text. Other errors resulted from the incorporation into the text of glosses present in the exemplar, as when the copyist inserted the word *dicuntur* in C.1.45.1, after the phrase "quibus causarum merita vel fata panduntur"; a later reader, recognizing that *dicuntur* was an alternative reading to *panduntur*, corrected the error by inserting interlinear note *al[ias]*. An example of the second comes from C. 2.20.5 where an explanatory gloss to the word *immodice* mistakenly replaced that word to produce the reading "sane si lesa es *id est multum modica* liberatione."[25] Such evidence confirms the conclusion that the work of augmenting and correcting the *Epitome* had begun before **P**, and probably before 1050—a chronology entirely consistent with our other evidence for the interest in the Code in that period.

---

[24] Lowe, "The Oldest Omission Signs in Latin Manuscripts: Their Origins and Significance," collected in *Paleographical Papers*. vol. II, pp. 349–80.

[25] Ciaralli, "Ancora sul manoscritto," p. 21 and n. 61; in the case of C. 2.20.5 a *non* was evidently omitted from the gloss, compounding the error.

Justinian's Code in the Eleventh Century: Paris ms. 4516

Paris, Bib. Nat., lat. 4516, Krüger's manuscript **L**, differs from the Pistoia *Epitome* in being the work of a single scribe—glosses and the rare marginal constitutions included. It is also a far handsomer production than the Pistoiese, with good quality parchment and decorations. Krüger described the text of **L** as "almost a twin" (*gemina fere*) of **P**, but since "the manuscripts did not entirely agree in their content" he concluded that this similarity was due to their having a common archetype; he therefore used it as the base text for the end of book eight and book nine, which were missing in **P**.[26] Mor doubted the common archetype, suggesting that **P** belonged on a branch of the stemma with Darmstadt 2000 (= **D**) and separate from **L**, while Tort-Martorell thought it possible that **P** was the ultimate ancestor of both **L** and **D**.

In reality, Krüger's conclusion that the manuscripts differ in their content is almost entirely due to his own errors in recording the contents of the two manuscripts. For example, Krüger noted as absent in **P** but present in **L** a number of laws (e.g., C. 2.4.21, 2.12.6, 3.8.2) which were found as marginal additions in **P**; the incipit of another missing law (C. 7.32.12) is cited in a marginal notation in **P**, suggesting that it may have been copied on a loose and subsequently lost slip of parchment.[27] Anyone who has struggled with these manuscripts, even with the assistance of photography, can sympathize with the challenge confronting Krüger in the 1870s; even so, Krüger's account is generally far more accurate than that of Chiappelli, who claimed to correct him.[28] The differences between the two manuscripts noted by Tort-Martorell similarly evaporate when checked against the manuscripts themselves.[29]

The correspondences are significant because there is a powerful case in favor of **L** being a direct and probably unmediated descendant of **P**. To begin with, there is massive agreement between the two manuscripts, extending to the emendations in **P**, its glosses, and even linguistic deformations of orthography. Many disagreements between the two manuscripts are simply errors on the part of **L**

---

[26] *Codex Iustinianus*, pp. XVIII–XVIII.
[27] Ciaralli, "Ancora sul manoscritto," p. 35.
[28] Chiappelli, "Nuovo esame del manoscritto pistoiese."
[29] See her discussion, *Tradición textual*, pp. 172–75.

(which Krüger regarded as the inferior manuscript), or marginal comments in **P** that were mistakenly incorporated into **L**. For example, in C. 7.30.1, where **L** reads "conductori seu enfiteotecarii" instead of "conductori" the phrase "seu enfiteotecarii" can still be read in the margin of **P** with little dots serving as a tie sign linking it to "conductori" in the main text. Evidently this was a case where the explanatory glosses in **P** entered the textual tradition. Particularly interesting, finally, are three laws added to the margin of **P** but not included in **L**: all of these laws, and only these laws, were added by the same hand, presumably after **L** had been copied.

Still more decisive are the purely graphical similarities. We can indicate a passage in **L** that skips a phrase exactly the length of a line in **P**; thus

> .... iurisiurandum his
> interpositum sit etiam civiliter falso revelato eas retractari
> precipiumus

in **P** becomes

> iurisiurandum his precipiumus

in **L**, as the copyist's eye skipped a line. (The scribe later noticed his error and corrected it.) Where the corrector of **P** wrote the incipit of a law in the margin next to the constitution after which the new text was to be inserted, the copyist of **L** usually copied the new law *before* that constitution—systematically creating an error in **L**. Most important, perhaps, are the strong similarities between the first copyist of **P** and the scribe of **L**: these suggest that the same person wrote both manuscripts, with a significant passage of time dividing the copying of **L** from that of **P**.[30] Evidently he had felt the need of his own

---

[30] For details see Ciaralli, "Ancora," pp. 31–34. The proposition that these two hands are identical was accepted by Giovanna Nicolaj in a recent article, who however went on to propose a further identification with the notary Pietro active at Arezzo between 1079 and 1114/1116: "now it is evident that it was none other than Pietro of Arezzo who was the first copyist of the Code transmitted in the famous manuscript of Pistoia . . . and who also copied the Code in the entire manuscript Par. lat. 4516." ("Documenti . . . a Ravenna, p. 771). Since, however, this last identification lacks the "support of more precise elements" (Nicolaj, "Ambiti," p. 144) normally necessary to make such identifications, one must take it essentially as her own subjective impression. Our own examination of the evidence, however, revealed that the copyist of the manuscripts and the notary Pietro differed in their execution of several graphic features, arguing against the proposed identity of the two writers pending the presentation of more precise evidence in its favor.

copy of the Code, a conclusion reinforced by the fact that the manuscript remained in his possession, as demonstrated by his subsequent additions to it.

The discovery that **L** was copied from **P** has a number of important implications. In the first place, it alters the stemma of the earliest manuscripts. Believing that **L** was independent of **P**, Krüger took their agreement on specific passages as an indicator of the authenticity of that reading, but any future edition will have to operate on different principles. The difficulty of recognizing the filiation is a further point of interest. Not only was contamination between different textual traditions an intrinsic part of the process of reassembling the Code, with the sequences of the laws being borrowed as well as individual readings, but the sheer complexity of copying a heavily emended manuscript such as **P** meant that new variations and errors were constantly being introduced. Finally, and of historical significance, is what the appearance of the same hand in both **P** and **L** tells us about the chronology of the work. To the extent that the additions made to **P** appear in **L**—and nearly all of them do—they must have been made within a man's working life. Again we are reminded of the intensity of activity that surrounds the works of Justinian's *Corpus* in the later eleventh century.

Justinian's Code in the Eleventh Century: Darmstadt ms. 2000

Darmstadt 2000 was the work of two copyists both of whom wrote a rather similar non-typified caroline minuscule characterized by strongly contrasting strokes produced by the use of a pen cut short to the left. The writing of the principal scribe has a sinuous quality owing to his execution of the first stroke of low letters (*i*, *u*, *t*, etc.) with a decided turn of the pen toward the right while writing strokes detached from the line or attached to the left (again on the letters *i*, *u*, *l*, etc.) with movement to the left; similar attitudes can be seen in contemporary scripts from southern France. The juxtaposition of some advanced features (such as the form of the double *s*, the double tittles over double *i*s, and the abbreviation of *quia* with a sign like a 2) with others that are more archaic (such as the superscript semicircles to indicate a final *s*, the consistent use of the ampersand, and the system of distinctive majuscules) point to a dating for the manuscript around the turn of the eleventh to the twelfth century.

A comparison of **D** with **P** leaves little doubt that they shared a common ancestor, as Krüger supposed, although in a tradition that had diverged from **P/L** at an early date. In general, **D** presents a selection of laws very similar to **P**, and it also shares some of the more striking displacements of order. The first ten titles of book one, for example, display contents identical to **P** except for the insertion of 1.2.1—one of the marginal additions in **P**. In other books the correspondence is less perfect, because **P/L** and **D** each contains constitutions missing from the other, confirming that **D** was copied from an exemplar different from **P**. Taking book seven for particular study, one notices that ten of the eleven constitutions (C. 7.16.7; 7.21, 1, 3, 5; 7.27.3; 7.32.2; 7.33.1, 3, 5; 7.34.2) added to the margins of **D**—all by the original scribe—are missing from **P/L**; the exception, C. 7.33.5, is a marginal addition to **P**. Yet the main text of **D** contains other constitutions missing from **P/L** such as C. 7.11.4, and 7.39.9, while omitting 10 of the 18 constitutions added to **P**. The situation is somewhat better in book 2, where **D** contains 19 of the 25 additional constitutions found in **P**. The uncertain correspondence of rediscovered constitutions holds true even when one breaks down the additions made to **P** according to the copyist who added them; for example, **D** contains both 7.53. 4 and 7, added by *k*, but only 3 of the 6 additions to book seven made by *j*. **P** and **D** thus represent two glimpses of a process that must have been diffused over multiple centers communicating their discoveries somewhat imperfectly among themselves. More generally, however, the Darmstadt manuscript confirms the impression given by the Pistoia manuscript that new constitutions circulated individually or in small numbers rather than in large blocks.

The same is true for the substantive glosses to the Code, because **D** contains many of the scholia found in **P**. Some of those included in **D** were drawn from what might be regarded as the oldest strata of glosses—those that had been copied by the scribes of **P**, presumably from their exemplar; others were drawn from later strata in **P**, showing that readers of the Code were continuing to share interpretative materials. Overall, roughly two-thirds of the scholia in the first three books of **P** also appear in **D**, although the percentage is considerably lower for the remainder of the text. Since the same pattern was also seen for the supplementary constitutions, it may be that the tradition represented by **D** was more efficient or active in dealing with the first three books.[31]

---

[31] The glosses in the Darmstadt ms. are discussed by Conrat, *Geschichte*, pp. 357–59.

Other Manuscripts of the Epitome

In addition to the Pistoia, Paris and Darmstadt manuscripts of the *Epitome Codicis*, we also possess three fragments that represent that stage in the history of Justinian's Code. Two of these fragments, Stuttgart, Württembergische Landesbibliotek jur. fol. 62 from the second half of the eleventh century, and Bologna, Collegio di Spagna, 73 from the turn of the eleventh to the twelfth century are only one folio long. Even though these fragments are too brief to permit extensive textual comparisons with other manuscripts, they bring to five the total of codices witnessed from this period—a significant total in any case, and one that offers a striking contrast with the circulation of the Code before 1000. The Stuttgart fragment is also notable for its remarkable similarity to the manuscripts of the *Walcausina*. Not only does the script resemble several hands found in the Paris and Vienna manuscripts, but the decoration, impagination, and general appearance of the page leaves little room to doubt that this fragment originated in the same environment. Since those other manuscripts are known to have come from the circle of legal professionals centered in Pavia, a similar provenance is likely for this fragment.

The remaining fragment of the *Epitome*, Pesaro, Biblioteca Oliveriana ms. 26, was discovered and carefully described by Patetta in the 1890s.[32] It dates from the decades around 1100, a little earlier than Patetta thought, and was probably copied in central Italy. Although the manuscript is badly mutilated, having lost many individual leaves and even fascicles, enough of it remains to show that it lacked some constitutions contained in the Pistoia/Paris and Darmstadt manuscripts of the *Epitome* while adding others absent from those manuscripts. Taken together, therefore, these four manuscripts represent the work of three different centers where the Code was being studied. What makes the Pesaro manuscript particularly interesting, however, is the inclusion of a supplement—also mutilated—that according to Patetta contains all of the laws missing from the *Epitome*, so that the two parts together contained the complete text of the Code. The manuscript as a whole, therefore, dramatically confirmed Krüger's conclusion that the text of the Code as known in the later Middle Ages resulted from a reintegration into the *Epitome* of the Latin constitutions that had originally been omitted.

[32] Patetta, "Di un nuovo manoscritto."

Although Patetta's fine eye is apparent in, for example, his observations about how the parchment was lined (a topic not then widely studied by paleographers) he does make some errors in describing the paleography of the manuscript. To begin with, the main text was produced by a single copyist rather than two: he was, in fact, responsible not only for the text and many if not all of the rubrics, but also the laws added into the margins of the original part of the manuscript. The supplement, too, was the work of the same copyist, although this fact is disguised by the smaller module size (54 lines/page as compared with 46 in the main text) which gives his script a slightly different aspect consisting mainly of a greater regularity in the alignment of words on the line. The identity, however, is certain, and is revealed by the substantial identity in the design of the letters, including the markedly trowel-shaped ascenders, the use of a similar system of abbreviations expressed by identical signs, and the simultaneous use of the multiple, identical graphic homophones such as the *d* (upright and with curved shaft), the *u* (acute and rounded), and the conjunction *et* both as an ampersand and a tironian note. The entire manuscript, then, is the work of a single individual. Since he continued to add to his original text, first with marginal additions and then with the supplement, it is also probable that he continued to possess the manuscript after finishing it. He was, therefore, a legal professional rather than a scribe.

A further correction to Patetta's description concerns a set of tie-signs using letters of the alphabet to indicate where the constitutions in the supplement were to be inserted in the main text. The idea was an ingenious one: copying the constitutions in alphabetical order produces a correctly-ordered text of the Code, and Patetta took the accuracy of this ordering as evidence that the supplement was produced by collating the *Epitome* with an antique manuscript of the entire Code. We shall see below that Patetta went too far in asserting that the alphabetic tie-signs in the Pesaro manuscript would have reconstructed the original Code better than any surviving manuscript actually does, but the real error is concluding that the alphabetical tie-signs in the Pesaro manuscript have anything to do with the original act of collation. In fact, they are much later than the original manuscript, being from the second half of the twelfth century, and one can still see in the margins the earlier, less precise set of signs that they superseded.

Nine Books or Twelve?

Scholars have long assumed that the medieval tradition of limiting Justinian's Code to its first nine books represented a tradition going back to the *Epitome* and the early Middle Ages, but the evidence supporting this conclusion is less strong than has been supposed. Although none of the surviving manuscripts of the *Epitome* contain material from the last three books of the Code, the Pistoia and Darmstadt manuscripts both have lost fascicles at the end, with **P** ending in the middle of book eight and the Darmstadt manuscript ending in the middle of book nine. Paris 4516 finishes with the explicit of book nine and the incipit to book ten and its first title ("Explicit liber viiii. feliciter. Incipit x. de iure fisci"), written in the hand of the scribe. Noting that the final verso below the incipit was erased, Dolezalek concluded from this inscription that this manuscript originally extended to the twelfth book,[33] but the matter is less simple that it appears: not only is there a second explicit to book nine, again in the hand of the scribe, at the bottom of the last recto ("Explicit liber viiii. feliciter. Deo gratias."), but the last fascicle is longer than all of the others in the book—a quinternion instead of a quaternio—suggesting that the scribe knew that the extra folio would permit him to finish copying his exemplar. Evidently he changed his mind about continuing beyond book nine, although there is no way to be certain which was the original plan. The important point, however, would seem to be that the last three books of the Code were not automatically excluded from the collection.

The last folio of Paris ms. 4516 is not the only piece of evidence suggesting that manuscripts of the *Epitome* may have included selections from books 9 to 12. Rouen, Bib. mun. A. 537 (429) preserves a collection drawn from the Code copied, probably in France, during the first half of the twelfth century. This collection has been noticed mainly for containing a handful of constitutions from books 10–12, but these make up a very small percentage of the whole collection: roughly half a folio out of twelve and a half or 12 constitutions of

---

33 *Repertorium*, p. 343. This manuscript is discussed by E. Conte who, however, errs in stating that the incipit to book 10 was not written by the scribe who prepared the rest of the manuscript. *Tres Libri Codicis. La ricomparsa del testo e l'esegesi scolastica prima di Accursio* (Frankfurt, 1990) [Ius Commune. Studien zur Europäischen Rechtsgeschichte, 46], pp. 17–18.

a total of 580. Emanuele Conte observed that it is "natural to think that the source of this collection was a version of the *Epitome Codicis* in twelve books,"[34] and when the extracts are studied in their entirety it is easy to find evidence that this inference is correct. This filiation can be seen, for example, in occasional errors in organization, including the transposition of a group of laws from C. 1.4 into C. 1.3 characteristic of all surviving codices of the *Epitome*.[35] And it is confirmed by the close agreement between the contents of the Rouen collection and our surviving manuscripts of the *Epitome*. Only 46 of 571 constitutions in the first nine books of the Rouen collection are absent from the Pistoia and Paris manuscripts, with an exceptional concentration of new material (17 constitutions) in book 8 alone. Comparing the Rouen collection to the Pesaro *Epitome* reveals an even closer agreement: of the 46 constitutions absent from Pistoia/Paris, 21 of these, or nearly half, are found in the surviving fragments of the Pesaro *Epitome*.

Given the small selection of constitutions from the last three books in the Rouen collection, one would not assume that the manuscript from which it was drawn included extensive excerpts from the last three books of the Code—perhaps not too much more than would fit on the blank folio at the end of Paris 4516. But the definitive separation of the last three books from the first nine appears to have been a later practice—probably (as we will see) from a period well into the twelfth century.

From the *Epitome* to the Restored Code

In the eleventh century, the *Epitome Codicis* proved an invaluable device for circulating the most immediately useful constitutions of Justinian's Code among the community of professional jurists. Its readers surely understood its limitations, as attested by the additions made to the common core of constitutions in all the surviving manuscripts, but at some point such expedients were abandoned in favor of the integral text of Justinian's Code. The process by which this leap was accomplished, however, has received almost no attention from modern

[34] Conte, *Tres Libri Codicis*, p. 25.

[35] Thus, one finds at the beginning of book one in the Rouen collection the sequence: C. 1.2.1, 3; 1.3.26; 1.4.2, 3, 8; 1.3. 5, 6; CT 11.39.8; C. 1.3.13, 24. Other inversions that replicate sequences found in the *Epitomes* include C. 2.20.3, 2, 6 and C. 6.37.11, 2, 5.

scholars. Nineteenth-century historians suggested that a complete text of the Code was discovered and used to supplement the *Epitome*. This was the opinion, most notably, of Patetta, who believed that the supplement to the Pesaro manuscript was produced by collating an existing *Epitome* with a "non-epitomized pre-Bolognese manuscript, that is, one of the archetypes used by the glossators in their work of reconstitution."[36] Others, notably Conte, believe that "Irnerius and his students" must have collected many manuscripts of the *Epitome*, restoring the complete text by a process of collation.[37] Conte seems to assume that antique exemplars of the Code would have been preserved if they had existed, but he mistakes the extraordinary case of the Florentina for a general practice. In fact, the usual approach in the Middle Ages was to prefer a new copy written in a familiar script to an ancient exemplar: we possess for Tacitus (for example) the eleventh-century manuscript copied at Monte Cassino rather than the ancient codex from which the monks must have worked.[38] The circumstance that we do not now possess an antique manuscript of the Code thus tells us nothing about whether such a manuscript existed in the eleventh century.

What no-one has done is study the manuscripts themselves in any detail. Krüger himself did not systematically survey manuscripts of the integral code to determine which were the oldest—if indeed that would have been possible in the 1860s and 1870s—and no one has returned to the subject since. For such a study, however, Dolezalek's *Repertorium* provides an invaluable point of departure, especially since he seems accurately to have separated manuscripts in caroline minuscule from later manuscripts in gothic script. We began, therefore, with the 24 manuscripts and fragments of the restored Code attributed to the

---

[36] "Di un nuovo manoscritto," pp. 220–21.

[37] E. Conte, *Servi medievali. Dinamiche del diritto comune.* [Ius Nostrum: 21] (Roma, 1996), p. 38, n. 4: "Sicché sembra plausibile che i primi glossatori si siano serviti di disparate fonti altomedievali per reconstruire il Codice giustinianeo, e non di un redivivo codice completo: il fantomatico manoscritto X ipotizzato dalla critica ottocentesca non ha lasciato alcuna documenta traccia di sé. Sembra invece che le versioni epitomate pervenute nelle mani di Irnerio e di suoi allievi fossero molte e diverse fra loro; e v'è motivo di stupirsi se esse siano andate perdute dopo essere state utilizzate nella ricostruzione di un testo il più possible vicino all'originale."

[38] On the preference for new copies as late as the fifteenth century, see A. Petrucci, "Il libro manoscritto" and "Le biblioteche antiche" in *Letteratura italiana*, ed. A. Asor Rosa, vol. 2 (Torino, 1983), pp. 528–54. [trans. as "Reading and Writing *Volgare* in Medieval Italy," *Writers and Readers in Medieval Italy*, pp. 225–31]. For Monte Cassino, see now Newton, *Scriptorium and Library at Monte Cassino*.

first half of the twelfth century or earlier, all of which we have seen in person or in microfilm.

Of this group, three manuscripts emerged as the earliest examples of the integral or restored Code: Berlin, Staatsbib. Preußischer Kulturbesitz, ms. lat. fol. 272 and 273, and Montpellier, Bibliothèque Interuniversitaire, Section de Médecine, H. 82. (Krüger used Montpellier ms. H 82 and Berlin, ms. 273 in his edition, but other manuscripts included in his apparatus, such as Monte Cassino ms. 49, are somewhat later.) The paleographical characteristics of these manuscripts suggest a date for all of them between 1080 and 1120. Two folios of a fourth manuscript probably to be dated to this period survive as fly-leaves in Vienna, Österreichische Nationalbibliothek, ms. 2065.

Historical considerations also suggest that it was the late eleventh and early twelfth century that saw the transition from the *Epitome* to the integral Code. To begin with, we have no manuscripts of the *Epitome* later than the turn of the eleventh to the twelfth century. It is also this period that left us the earliest surviving manuscripts of the Digest or, at least, the *Digestum Vetus*—a text comparable in length and difficulty to the restored version of the Code. Finally, one can note the increase in energy and resources directed toward Roman law was balanced by an apparent decline in activities involving the Lombard law. Neither the *Walcausina* nor the *Expositio* were to be soon superseded, as the efforts of Italian jurists appear to have shifted the greater part of their attention to Roman law.

But the manuscripts provide other information about the transition from the *Epitome* to the Code than just the date. It is noteworthy, for example, that the three essentially intact manuscripts are all, despite their very early date, virtually complete, with few significant omissions in any of them. (The evidence will be discussed below in detail for each manuscript.) The apparent ease with which the leap was made from the *Epitome* to the integral Code thus confirms our conclusion that the use of that compilation resulted from a decision to work with a selection of excerpts rather than from the absolute unavailability of the missing constitutions: when the scholars using the *Epitome* were ready for the complete text, they achieved it without any apparent tentativeness or remaining lacunae. Further supporting this conclusion is the marked graphic diversity among the surviving early manuscripts, suggesting that they originated in different regions; their texts are also mutually independent, showing that the leap from the *Epitome* to the Code was made more than once and in multiple venues—another factor perhaps contributing to the variations among later manuscripts of the Code. This point can be explored in more detail by a more detailed discussion of these early codices.

Berlin, Staatsbib. ms. lat. fol. 273

Berlin ms. 273, Krüger's manuscript **R**, is exceptional for being laid out in two columns—all of the *Epitome* manuscripts adopt a full page format, as do most manuscripts of the Code from the first half of the twelfth century—although it differs from the double-columned legal texts typical later in its comparatively small size (240 × 190 mm). The paleography of the manuscript rivals Pistoia 106 in complexity. Although the bulk of the manuscript was the work of a single scribe, interspersed in sections he copied are contributions from twelve other copyists. Several of these copyists contributed less than a folio; some less than a page. Like the Pistoia manuscript, therefore, the manuscript must have been copied in a loosely structured environment where there were many scribes ready to take over copying, even for brief periods of time. Some aspects of decoration such as decorated initials and the overall appearance of the scripts point to Tuscany as the region of origination, although further research might be possible on this point. That it was copied by legal professionals rather than professional scribes is also suggested by the great irregularity of the script of the principal copyist (A), who wrote fluently but not with the consistency one would expect from a scribe trained specifically for the purpose of producing books.

Table 7: Berlin, Staatsbibliothek ms. fol. lat. 273

1r: hand A
17r line 4: hand B
18r: hand A
18v line 2 *cum ex tortis*: hand C
19r: hand A
74r (extra constitutions from book 5, cancelled): hand D
74v (index of book 5) hand A
75r (beginning of book 5): hand E to C. 5.1.4 *definita erat*
hand F to 77vb *in secundas nupcias sine*
77rb line 13: hand G begins C. 5.4.18 *patris sentencia* to 84v
84v: hand H to 85rb line 17 (C. 5.12.31 *ille qui dotem*)
85rb: hand I
86ra: hand A to 87ra (end of C.5.13)
87r/v: hand I to end of 87v (C. 5.14)

Table 7 (*cont.*)

88v: hand F to 89va
89v: hand A resumes with C. 5.17.5 after blank (erased) space.
95 v (back of index) hand D
132 v. hand J to 133ra
133rb lines 1–4: hand K
133rb line 4 (*et*) to 133rb r 20 *adest*: hand J
133rb line 20 *usque* to 133rb line 32: hand A
133rb line 33 to 136ra: hand J
136rb lines 1–30: hand A
136rb line 31 to 136vb: hand J
137ra to138rb line 35: hand A
138rb line 36 to end of column: hand J
138v to 146ra line 5: hand A
146ra line 6 to 146rb: hand D
147ra: hand A
147rb—148rb line 21: hand L
148rb line 21 *si ut proponit* to 152 ra line 13: hand A
152ra line 14 to 153vb line 25: hand M (very similar to hand A)
153vb line 26—163ra line 33: hand A
163ra line 34 to 166v: hand D
167r to177v: hand G

The text provided by Berlin 273 is very substantially complete, with only a few constitutions missing. Careful examination of the manuscript, however, reveals the difficulties encountered by the scribes as they worked to copy it. Although book two, for example, contains all 343 Latin constitutions, the sequence of the laws in many titles remains confused and eight constitutions had to be added to the margins.[39] Although those added constitutions have usually been explained as a fault of the exemplar, corrected at a later date when the missing constitutions were discovered, the fact that the additional constitutions are in the hand of the main scribe suggests a different interpretation. Such errors, indeed, are consistent with a scribe trying to merge multiple sources into a single text as he wrote—in this case, an *Epitome Codicis* and a separate text containing the constitutions to be added in. This kind of work naturally lends itself to the error of copying beyond the point at which one should change sources, and if the scribe did not want to discard his parchment he

[39] Tort-Martorell, p. 59 incorrectly reports the absence of 2.3.20 (f. 26v) 2.4.26 (28r), 2.21.5 (34r); the other constitutions she notes as missing are in the margins, in the hand of the original copyist.

had only two options when that happened: erasing what had already been copied (as can be seen elsewhere in this manuscript, e.g. 15v, 24r, 34v, 52r, etc.) or adding the inadvertently skipped material into the margin, as is also seen throughout the manuscript.[40] The marginal constitutions and erasures are not, indeed, the only signs that the copyists were struggling with their exemplar. Copyist A also rewrote the bottom of f. 36v, evidently to accommodate more text than he originally had, while in other places he seems to have been unexpectedly left with blank space. Thus, there is a small gap between C.2.31.1 and 2 on f. 34v, where text has been erased; blank space after C. 46.1.2 on f. 36r, with a confused text of that law; and the upper half of the first column of f. 36v has been copied leaving noticeably more white space than found in the rest of the page or the book generally. Such uncertainties are all consistent with the hypothesis that the scribes of Berlin ms. 273 were integrating a jumble of texts even as they wrote.

Although the same pattern can be found in other books, the most direct evidence for the complexity of the sources used to prepare this manuscript comes from the tortured book five. As early as the 1860s, Krüger noted that the original quire of four leaves at the beginning of that book evidently had been replaced with a longer quinternion, and that the next two quires had been truncated and partially erased.[41] Krüger did not speculate on what problems the scribe might have encountered to require such drastic interventions, but in fact the manuscript provides more evidence on this point than might be expected. Particularly interesting are folios 74 and 95, both of which were inserted into the manuscript subsequent to its original copying to provide title indices for books five and six. It is the other sides of these folios that are of interest to us: they contain a number of constitutions copied rather casually, in two columns of unequal width. These pages cannot have been taken from another book. Apart from the

[40] Combining different manuscript sources to produce a unified text was not a problem unique to the Code. The copyists of Brancacciano manuscript of the *Expositio* similarly combined the text of the Lombard laws with a catena gloss of the *Expositio*, making only rare mistakes in the form of copying too much from one source. Examples include: the omission of the first five laws of the title *De scandalis et compositionibus ad regem pertinentibus*; and on f. 4v the comment to Roth. 11 is followed immediately by that to Roth. 12, as the copyist omitted the text of Roth. 12.

[41] *Kritik des Justinianischen Codex*, pp. 14–16. See also the *editio maior*, p. VII, and Dolezalek's comments, *Repertorium*, p. 156.

informal format, the text lacks a number of constitutions: fol. 74r contains C. 5.12.24–26, 29–30 and fol. 95v contains C. 5.12.31. What these constitutions have in common is that none of them were contained in the *Epitome* or, more precisely, that they fill gaps in the epitomized version of C. 5.12. The reused pages, therefore, represent constitutions to be added into a text of the *Epitome*. Confirmation of this discovery, moreover, comes from f. 89v, a page part of the original work of copying Berlin 273 and erased for reuse. One can just make out that the original sequence of constitutions was C. 5.17.2, 4, 5—the same as in Pistoia C 106.

Making this effort still more significant is the evidence from the copyists. Copyist A, the principal scribe for the first 160 folios, is not one of the five copyists who wrote the corrected insert to book five. But copyist D, who copied the constitutions on the inserted folios, does appear elsewhere, most notably at the end of book seven, where he copied title C.73 which had been omitted from its correct position, and on f. 146, where he appears together with copyist A. Copyist G, who also participated in the replacement section, similarly appears elsewhere in the manuscript, having been responsible for the last eleven folios of the manuscript as we have it today. The corrections, therefore, resulted from the same group that had copied the original manuscript. They may, indeed, have produced other copies of the Code, for it is noteworthy that the text of C. 5.12.30, as it currently exists in the manuscript, is inferior to the text given on f. 74r by the omission of several words. Since the phrase omitted does not correspond to a line on f. 74r, one must consider the possibility of an intermediate text.

Although Krüger and Tort-Martorell both listed a number of constitutions as missing from Berlin 273, nearly all of these oversights in fact were corrected by the scribes themselves, who added the missing laws in the margins.[42] In fact, despite the obvious effort required to produce this manuscript out of disparate sources, little was missing from the final product. Getting the text of the complete Code was not, evidently, as much of a problem as the sheer mechanical difficulties of integrating two sets of sources into a single, continuous text. More

---

[42] Krüger, *Codex Iustinianus*, p. XVIIII, lists 2.20.2, 2.21.1, 2 and 4.31.8, which are found in the margins of 33v and 63v. We have not found 2.21.4, although it may be the illegible text at the bottom of the outer margin on f. 33v. Tort-Martorell lists additionally 2.3.20 (f. 26v), 2.4.26 (f. 28r) and 2.21.5 (34 v).

significant than the rare omissions of individual constitutions is the abrupt end of the text in the middle of the final title of book nine, less than one folio short of the end of book nine. Scribes who intended to stop copying at that point would normally have adapted the size of their gatherings to avoid the fragility of having a single leaf at the end—for example, by using five instead of four leaves as they had when correcting the omissions in book five. The fact they did not do so here is strong evidence that the volume originally extended beyond book nine. We shall return to this problem below.

Berlin, Staatsbib. ms. lat. fol. 272

The copyists of Berlin 272 adopted the full-page format more usual in the earliest manuscripts of the Roman law revival; it is also larger and more oblong (325 × 210 mm), with about the same proportions as the Cologne Institutes, including margins generous enough to permit glosses.[43] The manuscript is the work of two scribes, one of whom copied all but book four. Berlin 272 is the only manuscript of the three that ends cleanly at the end of book nine. Krüger did not include this manuscript in the apparatus of his edition of the Code.

Like Berlin 273, Berlin 272 was built upon a version of the *Epitome*, with the missing constitutions reintegrated into it. The scribes were less successful than those who worked on that other manuscript, however, because the original text displays several significant omissions. For example, C. 1.2 in its proper place on 6v consists only of laws 1, 11, 3, 12, 13, 19. with C. 1.2.2, 4–10, 14, and 16 displaced to f. 11rv. (A later reader cancelled the section from 1.2.11–19 and inserted an additional folio with the entire sequence of laws in correct order.) These errors are especially interesting because they cannot be blamed on the *Epitome*, whose surviving manuscripts include only the first law of C.1.2. The placement of C. 1.2.3 between C. 1.2.11 and 12 and the omission of several laws in the same title thus apparently results from errors in abstracting that material from other sources.

Possibly these errors were already present in an exemplar, since Berlin 272 does not display the constitutions copied into the margins that in Berlin 273 so vividly convey the effort involved in reconstructing the Code on the basis of the *Epitome*. Equally significant is the fact that

[43] For a detailed description of the content of this manuscript, see Dolezalek, *Repertorium*, vol. 1. pp. 148–54.

the errors apparent in Berlin 272 and 273 are so different that one cannot conceive of one as having been copied from the other. The leap from the *Epitome* to the restored Code was not, therefore, a unique event. Rather, it was one repeated multiple times, and—given the graphic diversity between the early manuscripts—apparently in multiple places as well.

One obvious question is why all this effort was invested in updating and reorganizing the *Epitomes* rather than simply working from antique manuscripts of the Code itself. "Certainly the reason must be," Patetta wrote in 1895, "that complete manuscripts of the Code were then very rare, while those of the epitomes were very numerous. The transcription of a complete copy may thus have presented serious difficulties while, on the other hand, the price of the manuscripts meant that there would have been no small difference in expense for those who owned the *Epitome Codicis* between procuring a new copy of the entire Code instead of supplementing their own copies."[44] Part of this was surely correct. The five surviving manuscripts and fragments of the *Epitome*—a text that was obsolete and scarcely worth preserving by the mid-twelfth century—testify to a very substantial circulation of the *Epitome* by the end of the eleventh century. In medieval conditions it was hardly possible to replace all those copies—which contained, by design, the legislation of greatest practical significance—with an edition deriving directly from ancient manuscripts. But it is also possible that the supplemental constitutions circulated separately during the period of transition—perhaps in a form similar to the appendix to the Pesaro manuscript with a list of incipits as a guide to the correct order. Some such method would have made it possible to use a manuscript of the *Epitome* as a basis for producing a manuscript of the complete Code—even in the absence of the manuscript of the complete Code that could simply have been copied directly.

Montpellier, Bibliothèque Universitaire, Section de Médecine, H 82

Montpellier ms. H 82, Krüger's manuscript **M**, constitutes a third version of the restored Code apparently completed in yet another geographical region. Like other legal manuscripts from this period, this codex is somewhat oblong (315 × 204 mm) with a full-page format and spacious margins that came to hold extensive glosses. It

[44] "Di un nuovo manoscritto," *Studi*, p. 220.

is correspondingly long: the surviving text occupies 263 folios, despite the fact that the text breaks off at C. 9.29.2. The copying was divided among several scribes.

Although Dolezalek describes Montpellier H. 82 as "originally having gaps in the text,"[45] this comment refers only to a few pages: the original f. 14, which was cut out and replaced for unknown reasons, and f. 27, which was erased and rewritten. In fact, our collation of the text with Krüger's edition found remarkably few omissions or errors, as Krüger himself noticed. In book 2, for example, laws 8 and 9 of the third title are reversed, C. 2.7. 26, 27 are omitted, and a rubric is given at the bottom of f. 40v that is not given in Krüger's edition. In book 5 space is left in C. 5.27.3 but no text is missing; in C. 5.44 law 4 precedes law 2; and C. 5.68 precedes C. 5.67—both titles containing a single brief law. Of all the early manuscripts of the Code we examined, Montpellier H. 82 is the one that seems to have been collated most closely with an ancient manuscript, if it was not indeed copied from one.

The care with which this manuscript was produced is also suggested by another feature that apparently has not been noticed before: it recasts the entire appearance of the page for the purpose of making it easier to find specific laws. All other medieval manuscripts of the Code adopt the format of the ancient manuscripts in which the beginning of a law is usually marked by a large initial *I* (the first letter of *Imp.* or, occasionally, *Idem*) in the left margin, followed by the rest of the inscription and then the text of the law. In contrast, **M** places the initial of the first word of the text in the left margin, shifting the inscription to a less prominent place in the right margin. It is easy to understand the reasoning behind this format. In the eleventh century, as later in the medieval tradition, laws were usually referred to by their opening words. Thus, whereas most manuscripts of the Code, whose left margins contain little except a succession of *I*'s, provide little help in finding a particular passage, the format adopted by **M** gives prominence to precisely the element that a reader would be seeking when trying to find a specific law. Nor is the model far to seek: this was precisely the format used in manuscripts of the Lombard law, a text well known to the secular jurists who had been responsible for placing Justinian's Code back in circulation.

[45] Dolezalek, *Repertorium*, vol. 1. pp. 281–91 at p. 282.

A final point of interest in this manuscript are the notes by an early reader who copied a series of excerpts from the *Digestum Vetus* on f. 62v.[46] This reader's hand is itself significant, because it is consistent with a kind of script found, for example, in a document prepared at Bergamo in October, 1085.[47] This kind of script is not unique to Bergamo—it can similarly be observed in documents prepared elsewhere in the Po Valley during the last decades of the eleventh century. But the presence of such a hand in Montpellier H. 82 supports an early date for the manuscript itself, as well as indicating the region where the manuscript circulated and was, perhaps, produced.

Other Early Manuscripts

We have already mentioned Vienna, Nationalbibliothek, cod. 2065, a fragment two folios long that survives as rear fly-leaves in another manuscript. To the extent one can judge, the text was substantially more complete than the *Epitome* so that the manuscript should be counted among those of the restored Code even though a few constitutions, omitted from the original copying, had to be added later. Other characteristics suggesting that this manuscript should be grouped with those of the restored Code are its exceptionally large size (412 × 252 mm) and generally formal layout with colored initials for each law, as well as the fact that it remained in use for a long time, even receiving some medieval constitutions as additions. This manuscript is also worth noting both as further evidence of the rapid shift to the integral version of Justinian's Code and perhaps of its geographical diffusion as well: this copyist's script has little in common with that of any of the other early manuscripts, suggesting that he learned to write in a different region.

Other evidence of the circulation of Justinian's Code comes from the slightly later manuscripts attributable to the first half of the twelfth century. It is especially noteworthy that three of them very probably came from the area in or nearby Rome. Berlin, Staatsbib., ms. fol. lat. 274 is almost entirely the work of scribes who wrote in a *minuscula romanesca* of the early twelfth century. Monte Cassino ms. 49, Krüger's ms. **C**, was not strictly speaking drafted in *minuscula romanesca*, but other

---

[46] The specific excerpts are D. 2.8.10–15.2; D. 1.3.1, 7; D. 1.1.3; D. 1.5.24, 27, 18, 20–21; D. 1.3.24. See Dolezalek, *Repertorium*, p. 289.

[47] Bergamo, Arch. di Stato, 2701.

aspects of the script leave no doubt that its scribe received his training in or near Lazio.[48] Finally, Vatican Library, Vat. lat. 11599 contains a memorandum on f. 134v noting the death in April 1157 of Ildicius Tiburtinus . . . magister et doctor"; documentary evidence reveals the presence of Ildicius as a judge at a papal plea from 1125.[49]

Manuscripts of this period also reveal ongoing uncertainty about what to do with books 9–12, the *Tres Libri.* A few of them contain excerpts from those books. Berlin 274, for example, does not end on f. 186v at C. 9.51.11, as indicated by Dolezalek: the original scribe completed that title (the last of book nine) on f. 187r and then continued on to give C. 11.48 in its entirety. Also containing material from the *Tres Libri* is Vatican Library, Vat. lat. 1427 (a French manuscript from later in the twelfth century), which continues on to C. 10.2.4, while eight lines have been erased at the end of book nine in Paris. B.N., ms. lat. 4517, from the mid twelfth century. A remarkable percentage of other manuscripts have lost their final gatherings, like **R** and **M** and the manuscripts of the *Epitome.* Thus, Berlin, Staatsbib., ms. fol. lat. 275, from the first half of the twelfth century, ends in C. 9.51, and at least four other twelfth-century manuscripts (Florence, Biblioteca Laurenziana, Redi 179; Montpellier, Bibliothèque Interuniversitaire, Section médecine, ms. H. 83; and Turin, Biblioteca Nazionale Universitaria, F.II.15) similarly have lost gatherings so that there is no way to determine where they originally ended. A scholar who knew only manuscripts of the Code might well conclude that it was normal for medieval manuscripts to lose gatherings! Rather than supposing that an amazingly high percentage of these manuscripts were poorly bound—and that it was always the gatherings at the end which were lost—it seems more probable that they were dismembered later after it had become usual to divide the Code into two parts.

Conclusion

The traditional account that saw the *Epitome Codicis* as an artifact of the early Middle Ages has always posed two historical problems: who in the early Middle Ages would have had use for a work that

[48] Ciaralli, "Produzione," pp. 95–96.

[49] José Ruysschaert, "Ildicius Tibertinus, un professeur de droit civile au XIIe siècle à la curie romaine," *Rivista di Storia della Chiesa in Italia*, 6 (1952): 384–86.

preserved Justinianic language in all its complexity? and, why, if this work was important enough to create and copy, does it leave little or no trace in early medieval evidence? The first question was barely grasped in the 1860s and 1870s, when the historiography of the *Epitome* took shape, because medievalists generally were still a long way from even a general understanding of the history of medieval culture and book production, but it has never satisfactorily been addressed since. The second question, already recognized by Conrat, has simply been regarded as perplexing, when it has even been thought about at all.

Taking a fresh look at the *Epitome* with a better understanding of the manuscript evidence has permitted us entirely to recast the issue. Rather than an early medieval compilation, the *Epitome* now must be attributed to the second and third quarters of the eleventh century. The earliest manuscripts date from this period, and it was then that the material contained in the *Epitome* begins to be cited in the works of Lombardist jurists. The work of supplementing the *Epitome* seems to have begun almost immediately, and the three manuscripts and two fragments that survive from this period attest to a remarkably wide circulation, especially for a work that was obsolete and thus of little value after the twelfth century.

The transition to the full text of the Code appears to have begun by the last decades of the eleventh century. The date alone excludes the traditional ascription of this project to the "glossators of Bologna." But it would be no improvement to attribute work obviously done more than once and in different places to any single group or region: the graphic diversity of the manuscripts compels us to recognize that the advanced study of law, and of Roman law, had become widely diffused over the northern half of the Italian peninsula. Once the complete text of the Code was thought desirable, however, it seems to have been obtained without great difficulty except in the mechanical process of reintegrating the missing constitutions into the text; this apparent ease, indeed, stands as further confirmation of the historical continuity between the earlier stage of excerpting the Code and the later stage of returning it to its complete form. The last step of all, perhaps, was the convention of dividing the Code into two parts, a practice that perhaps did not become standard before the middle of the twelfth century.

Finally, one must notice that every stage in this complex textual history was driven by the needs of the scholars who used this text.

They created the *Epitome* at a time when their resources were limited; and they progressively expanded it as their needs and expertise grew. Throughout this whole process, moreover, they displayed considerable ingenuity and skill at manipulating the text, sharing variants, and incorporating corrections into their manuscripts. This is a lesson we can now carry into our examination of the textual history of Justinian's Digest.

CHAPTER SIX

JUSTINIAN'S DIGEST

Although scholarly work on the Digest, like that on the Code, was driven by the need to establish a scholarly basis for a critical edition, the issues posed by the two works could scarcely be more different. For the Code, the longest surviving antique fragment—an unprepossessing and now unreadable palimpsest in the chapter library of Verona—preserves only a small portion of the entire text. Editing the Code, therefore, meant mainly working with the medieval manuscripts, none of which is clearly superior to any of the others. For editors of the Digest, in contrast, a central part of their work inevitably focuses on the magnificent sixth-century manuscript that is now the prize possession of the Biblioteca Laurenziana in Florence. Acquired from Pisa as a prize of war in 1406, the Pisana or Florentina (= **F**) was kept for centuries as a state treasure in the Palazzo Vecchio before being transferred to the Biblioteca Laurenziana on 14 September 1782.[1] The text of this manuscript has been widely available to scholars since it was published by Torelli in the sixteenth century, and the twentieth century saw the publication of not one but two elaborate facsimile editions (although the second facsimile may be a facsimile of the first).[2]

For modern scholars, the existence of the ancient manuscript poses two rather different kinds of problems. The first is editorial: where medieval manuscripts offer readings apparently superior to the text of the Florentina, are those passages to be taken as conjectures by medieval scholars or as evidence of an authentic tradition? We saw in chapter one that while Mommsen eventually discarded most readings in the vulgate manuscripts as conjectures, he accepted others as authentic, reflecting a manuscript tradition independent of the Florentina. Once the existence of some authentic variants had been established, of course,

---

[1] Piero Fiorelli, "Le Pandette dal palazzo vecchio alla libreria," in *Le Pandette di Giustiniano*, pp. 131–41.

[2] *Digestorum . . . ex Florentinis Pandectis*; *Justiniani Augusti Digestorum seu Pandectorum codex Florentinus olim Pisanus phototypice expressus* (Roma, 1902–10); *Justiniani Augusti Pandectarum. Codex florentinus* (Firenze, 1988).

it became a matter of judgment to decide whether or not a particular variant was genuine. Mommsen's own preference was to admit the authenticity of as few passages as possible, but scholars such as Kantorowicz have suspected that he set the bar unreasonably high. The second, historical problem flows from the first: if the medieval text of the Digest combines the text of the Florentina with another authentic source, how did that contamination or intermixing of traditions happen? Mommsen assumed that those genuine readings were added into a text deriving from the Florentina, but other hypotheses are possible and we shall explore a different scenario below. Adding to the difficulty, finally, is the enigma of how the medieval manuscript transmission of the Digest came to be divided, without apparent logic, into the *Digestum Vetus*, the *Digestum Novum*, and the *Infortiatum*—this last with the internal division of the *Tres Partes*.

In practice, study of the historical context has usually been subordinated to the detailed examination of specific manuscripts: the Florentina, other early fragments, and (less commonly) manuscripts from the eleventh and twelfth centuries. Hermann Lange thus recently had to admit that although the hypothetical archetype of the medieval Digest seemed to date to the second half of the eleventh century, the circumstances out of which the manuscript emerged—who had done the work or where the work had been done—was still a mystery.[3] Our study of Justinian's Institutes and Code, however, permits a new approach to these problems. The fact that the jurists of northern Italy put those works back in circulation in itself makes them likely candidates for having been the first to study the Digest, especially since all three works emerged from obscurity during the same decades. Indeed, we shall see shortly that there is substantial evidence to support this hypothesis. Yet identifying the earliest scholars who studied the Digest provides something we have never had before: a historical context for the revival of the Digest. Instead of treating the Digest as a unique problem, we shall be able to compare its history to the other texts used by these scholars, including the Code and the Lombard laws. We shall see that those works provide analogies to the editorial work applied to the Digest in the second half of the eleventh century, at the very dawn of its career as a medieval textbook.

---

[3] Lange, *Römisches Recht im Mittelalter*, p. 69. On Lange, see also Jakobs, "Die große Zeit der Glossatoren," pp. 228–31.

This chapter, therefore, begins by reviewing the classic problems concerning the text of the Digest—the mixed heritage of the medieval tradition and the tri-partite division of Digest manuscripts. Next it considers the evidence for the circulation of the Digest during the eleventh century, and the editorial or "philological" work applied to the Digest at this time. Finally, and pulling all of these elements together, we shall consider the earliest manuscripts in the vulgate tradition, with special attention to the earliest of them all, Biblioteca Apostolica Vaticana, Vat. lat. 1406.

The Manuscripts, Mommsen, and His Edition

As early as the twelfth century, scholars of Roman law were aware of the divergences between their own manuscripts and the Pisana, whose authority they recognized by referring to it as the *Authenticum pandectarum* and whose readings they sometimes noted in their glosses.[4] Yet it was not until the fifteenth century, with the patronage of the Medicis, that study of the ancient codex began in earnest. Poliziano offered the first detailed account of how the Bolognese tradition diverged from the text of the Florentina before the end of the fifteenth century, and the Torellis' printed edition of 1553 was, in many ways, an extension of this humanistic interest in the ancient manuscript.[5] The next several centuries then saw several, mostly unsuccessful, efforts to establish a definitive text of the Digest.[6] L. Th. Groovius planned an edition in the late 1600s, but did not finish it; nor was Henrik Brenkman more successful a few decades later, despite writing a

[4] See Savigny's extensive documentation of this point in *Geschichte*, vol. 3, appendix VII. A typical example, glossing D.28.1.20, reads: "hic 'non' Martinus addidit in suo digesto sed pisis non est." Savigny, no. 105, p. 732. For a general overview of the place of the Pisana until the sixteenth century, Severino Caprioli, "Visite alla Pisana," in *Pandette di Giustiniano*, pp. 37–98, and his earlier essay, "Per uno schedario di glosse preaccursiane. Struttura e tradizione della prima esegesi giuridica bolognese," in *Per Francesco Calasso. Studi degli allievi* (Roma, 1978), pp. 73–166, at p. 152.

[5] The work of Poliziano is discussed by Caprioli, "Visite." For the work culminating in the printed edition of the Florentina, see Gualandi, "Editio princeps delle Pandette Fiorentine."

[6] G. C. J. J. van den Bergh and B. H. Stolte, jr., "The Unfinished Digest Edition of Henrik Brenkman," *Tijdschrift voor Rechtsgeschiendenis*, 45 (1877), pp. 227–305, esp. at pp. 228–29, for the history of Digest editions in the seventeenth and eighteenth centuries. See also B. H. Stolte, jr., *Henrik Brenkman (1681–1736)* (Groningen, 1981); Brenkman's book on the Digest is *Historia Pandectarum seu fatum exemplaris florentini. Accedit gemina dissertatio de Amalphi* (Utrecht, 1722).

history of the Digest and filling the pages of his copy of Torelli with notes and alternate readings, many of which are still of scholarly interest. One consequence of the failure of these projects was that the *littera Gothefrediana*, an edition that had first been published in 1583, was still the most widely used edition of the Digest in the early nineteenth century.

The source of these problems was the remarkable number of textual variants that could be culled from the hundreds of surviving medieval manuscripts. If part of Mommsen's success in overcoming this obstacle resulted from his adoption of the Lachmann method of choosing manuscripts to study,[7] Savigny's work in documenting the medieval efforts at textual criticism was hardly less important. Writing in 1862, Mommsen argued that the readiness of twelfth-century scholars to emend their texts justified excluding all later manuscripts from the list of manuscripts to be censused—a considerable reduction in the work of collation and transcription. Those medieval readings confirmed as authentic by the *Basilica* could be explained, he believed, by the assumption that they were already present in the archetype of the Vulgate tradition—a hypothetical manuscript that he took to be distinct from the Florentina although sharing many of that manuscript's defects. "If we had a complete manuscript of the Pandects belonging to the Vulgate family and dating before the beginning of learned and literary activities, thus before the end of the eleventh century, then all the rest could probably be dispensed with."[8] In the absence of such a manuscript, however, he proposed to use instead only those manuscripts whose comparative antiquity was indicated by features such as the completeness of the inscriptions, evidence of Greek passages, and a transposition of passages in book 23 that evidently resulted from a misbound fascicle. For the *Vetus*, these criteria resulted in his using Paris, Bibliothèque Nationale, ms. lat. 4450 (= **P**), Vatican Library, Vat. lat. 1406 (= **V**), Padua, Bib. Univ., 941 (= **U**), and Leipzig, Universitätsbibliothek, 873 (= **L**).

By the time the *editio maior* actually appeared, in 1870, Mommsen could defend his exclusion of the medieval manuscript tradition in much stronger terms. Already in the sixteenth century, Torelli and Agustín had argued that some errors found in the oldest manuscripts

[7] For the Lachmann method, see the works cited in chapter one, n. 24.
[8] Mommsen, "Grundlage," p. 130.

of the *Vetus* could not be understood unless the copyist of the archetype **S** "had the Florentina before his eyes."[9] They had based their case mainly on a textual error in book fifty, reproduced in all medieval manuscripts, that resulted from an incorrect sequence of folios within one gathering of **F**. Yet that evidence was specific to the *Digestum Novum*, and it had remained an open question whether the *Infortiatum* and, especially, the *Vetus* similarly derived from the Florentina. Now, in his edition, Mommsen could point to several passages in the *Vetus* where the copyist of **S** made mechanical errors linked to the Florentina. A particularly persuasive example comes from f. 327v of the ancient manuscript where the corrector wrote a phrase omitted by the original copyist into the space between the two columns of text: although the corrector meant for the phrase to be incorporated into the right column, the earliest manuscripts of the *Vetus* mistakenly inserted it into the text on the left, into D. 23.1.9. Mommsen also discovered three cases, one each from books 5, 14, and 21, where omissions in the medieval text exactly equaled a line in the Florentina. For example, the phrase in D. 5.1.18.1 *si res non |ex maleficio veneat sed ex contractu de|beat* in **F** becomes *si res moveat* or *moneat* in **PVLU**. Such evidence persuaded Mommsen that the entire Vulgate tradition, not just books 35 to 50, derived directly from **F**. All manuscripts in the medieval university tradition thus became *codices descripti*—copies of a still existing manuscript—making their inclusion in the edition unnecessary. In the end, Mommsen made a complete collation of only one manuscript (**P** = Paris, BN ms. lat. 4450), consulting other manuscripts of the *Vetus* only when **P** and **F** disagreed.

While Mommsen's final stemma made it easier to justify excluding medieval manuscripts from his recension, it also became harder to explain how those manuscripts came to include authentic passages superior to the readings available in **F**. Previously, he had accounted for those passages stemmatically: they came from the fragment of the first 34 books from which the *Vetus* and the first part of the *Infortiatum* derived. Now, however, Mommsen had to suppose some kind of deliberate human intervention. Some early scholar, he suggested, "either Irnerius or a person unknown to us older than Irnerius," must have compared **S** with a second ancient exemplar "different from the Florentina" copying readings from this other manuscript

[9] Praefatio, p. LXVII.

into the margins or between the lines of the vulgate archetype. Mommsen backed up this position by showing how some manuscripts of the *Vetus* combine readings from **F** with an alternate tradition, as if scribes had been inconsistent or confusing in dealing with material from glosses.[10] He also documented other editorial interventions in **S**, which were later discussed at greater length by Conrat and Kantorowicz.

The discovery that the vulgate archetype derived from **F** made it more difficult to understand the medieval division of the Digest into three parts. In the classical age of Bologna, the *Vetus* went from the beginning to the second title of book 24, the *Infortiatum* from D. 24.3 to D. 38, and the *Novum* from D. 39 to the end. It was so difficult to grasp the rationale of these divisions—and the significance of the names—that the legend grew up at Bologna of the sequential discovery of the different parts.[11] Mommsen himself, as we have seen, originally accepted the gradual rediscovery of the Digest, and a similar theory has been recently proposed by Wolfgang Müller.[12] But all of these theories are difficult to reconcile with the fact that the earliest scholars to work with the Digest evidently had access to the Florentina. Mommsen himself was content to observe that **S** must have been bound in 3 (or 4!) volumes. Kantorowicz suggested that scribes simply copied to fill all available space on their folios—as if blank pages were rare in medieval manuscripts or scribes were incapable of adjusting the length of their gatherings to accommodate the text they intended to copy. Even Mommsen's simpler hypothesis of multiple volumes is contradicted by recent demonstrations that the earliest manuscripts themselves present significant variations in where they begin and end. All that seems certain is that the precise divisions of the later vulgate tradition were not fixed until the Digest had already been in circulation for decades.[13]

---

[10] Praefatio, pp. LXVIII–LXX. The value of this discussion is reduced by the fact that many of readings from the Padua (**U**) and Leipzig (**L**) manuscripts are significantly later than **S** itself, from a period when manuscripts were actively being collated against **F**, as indeed is shown by Savigny, *Geschichte*, vol. 3, appendix 7.

[11] Patetta, "Sull'introduzione del Digesto."

[12] Wolfgang Müller, "The Recovery of Justinian's Digest in the Middle Ages," *Bulletin of Medieval Canon Law*, 20 (1990): 1–29. CMR originally reached a similar conclusion (see "Vatican Latin 1406") but Mommsen's evidence on this point cannot be argued away.

[13] van de Wouw, "Textgeschichte des Infortiatum"; and two articles by Horst

With the physical characteristics of **S** now being invoked to explain the most difficult aspects of the medieval tradition of the Digest, every aspect of that hypothetical manuscript was magnified in importance. Mommsen supplemented his hypotheses about its marginal notations and multi-volume format with a few other observations. Already in 1862 Mommsen had been aware of a transposition of text in book 23 that apparently resulted from an error in ordering the inner two leaves of a gathering. Thus, instead of being producing the correct sequence of text

a b c d e f g h

the gathering reversed the position of the inner two leaves so that manuscripts copied from it contained four blocks of transposed text:

a b d c f e g h.

Beyond the fact that the earliest manuscripts all shared this error, and thus must have had a common ancestor, the size of the transposed sections tells us exactly how much text that archetype contained on the recto and verso of a single folio.

More significant for the subsequent historiography was Mommsen's observation that **S** must have been copied in "langobardic script." This inference was based on certain errors in **P**—for example, the confusion of d for cl or al—that can easily occur when scribes familiar with caroline minuscule work from an exemplar written in what used to be known as "langobardic" script. Yet Mommsen went well beyond his evidence on this point. As Sebastiano Timpanaro explains in his book on the Lachmann method, offering hypotheses on the script of lost exemplars was (and is) done for editorial purposes, specifically to permit conjectures about the original reading of otherwise unemendable passages. Such attributions, however, had to meet a high standard of proof: there should be a "notable" number of errors; those errors should appear in multiple manuscripts; and, to assure that such errors did not simply reproduce mistakes already present in the exemplar, there should be different errors in different manuscripts.[14] This last point, in particular, was underlined by Antoine

Heinrich Jakobs, "Or signori!—Die accursische Glosse als Apparatus Joannis et Azonis in Odofredus' Lectura super Digesto veteri," ZSS RA, 117 (2000): 311–423, at pp. 315–16, and "Das Ende des Digestum vetus," ZSS RA, 120 (2003): 1–41.

[14] Timpanaro, pp. 100–02, provides a detailed discussion, followed here, of the evidence necessary to venture hypotheses about script types in lost manuscripts.

Dondaine, who observed that "independent copyists do not necessarily make the same mistakes,"[15] offering as an example a text of Thomas Aquinas for which we actually have the manuscript from which the entire tradition descends.

If **S** had really been a manuscript of the entire Digest written in "langobardic" script, one would expect comparable but not identical errors to show in all other manuscripts of the Digest: in the *Infortiatum* and *Digestum Novum* as well as the *Digestum Vetus*. Mommsen's actual findings fall well short of this standard. Not only were all of the errors he mentions drawn from **P**, the only manuscript for which he actually completed a full collation, but he found only 21 errors attributable to the supposed "langobardic" script of **S**, of which only 13 involved letter shape—an insignificant number compared to the length of the *Digestum Vetus*. It also counts against his argument that, as he acknowledged, many of the errors found in **P** appear equally in **V** and **U**, since this agreement suggests that the errors were already present in the common ancestor. Short of a complete collation of the manuscripts—a task that with microfilm and modern software would be time consuming but not difficult—it is simply impossible to reach any conclusion about the script of the *Vetus* archetype. In fact, even with such evidence one should not expect a clear outcome. Eminent paleographers dealing with the famous Monte Cassino Tacitus manuscript (Florence, Biblioteca Laurenziana Mediceus 68.2) have reached no agreement about its exemplar, proposing as possibilities scripts as different as rustic capitals and ancient minuscule or semi-cursive.[16]

For Mommsen, the script of **S** was important mainly as part of his demonstration that there was an intermediate manuscript between **F** and the medieval tradition: it had no effect on his edition. It

[15] Antoine Dondaine, "Un cas majeur d'utilisation d'un argument paleographique en critique textuelle (Vat. lat. 781)," *Scriptorium*, 21 (1967): 261–76, at p. 266.

[16] See, for example, Michaela Zelzer, "Zur Frage der Vorlage des Tacitus-Codex Mediceus 68,2," *Wiener Studien*, 86 (1973): 185–95. Her suggestion that the exemplar used was written in antique minuscule or semicursive was accepted by G. Cavallo, "La trasmissione dei testi nella area beneventano-cassinese," in: *La cultura antica nell'Occidente latino dal VII all'XI secolo* (Settimane di Studi del Centro Italiano di Studi sull'Alto Medioevo 22), Spoleto 1975, pp. 357–414, at pp. 388–91. Suggesting rustic capitals, however, were E. A. Lowe and G. Andresen; see Lowe, "The Unique Manuscript of Tacitus' *Histories* (Florence Laur. 68 2)," *Paleographical Papers*, vol. 1, pp. 289–302 at pp. 300–01. It goes without saying that the paleographical expertise of all these scholars considerably exceeds that available to Mommsen in the 1860s.

became a key element in the history of the Digest only in the twentieth century, after Lowe published his description of Beneventan script and after historians applied that terminology to **S** in place of Mommsen's "langobardic" script. In fact, the identification of Mommsen's "langobardic" script as Beneventan in itself constituted a subtle error, because nineteenth-century "langobardic" script included not only Beneventan but precaroline minuscule and some northern Italian scripts as well.[17] Yet since "Beneventan"—unlike "langobardic"—indicated a particular geographical zone, historians soon came to assume that the supposed Beneventan script of **S** proved that **S** was written in southern Italy. By the 1960s, the apparently southern origins of **S** led Miquel to suggest that it must have been copied in the greatest scriptorium of the Beneventan zone, that of the monastery of Monte Cassino—effectively linking the revival of the Digest with the Church and even the Gregorian reform movement.

While Mommsen aimed for precision in describing the physical characteristics of the vulgate archetype, he was remarkably vague about when this manuscript would have been copied and been subjected to the editorial emendations attested by the later tradition. Kantorowicz believed that Mommsen had actually contradicted himself, attributing the origins of **S** variously to the ninth century, or the tenth, or the eleventh.[18] Writing recently, H. H. Jakobs expressed doubt that Mommsen could make such an error, suggesting instead that he simply had adhered to the view, implicit in his 1862 article, that the archetype of the Bolognese tradition had its origins in the tenth century.[19] Yet while Jakobs may be correct in his reading of Mommsen, few historians today would accept a date before the eleventh century. Not only are manuscripts of the dimensions of **S** unknown for the ninth and tenth century,[20] but it is impossible to imagine who in that period, when even the Code and the Institutes were essentially unknown, would have been prepared to dedicate the necessary human and material resources to copying the entire Digest.

[17] Timpanaro, pp. 101–02n.
[18] Kantorowicz, *Digestenvulgata*, p. 34.
[19] Jakobs, "Die Zeit der Glossatoren," pp. 233–34.
[20] It is also unlikely that a manuscript with the dimensions **S** must have had would have been produced in the ninth or tenth centuries. See Radding, "Vatican Latin 1406," pp. 528–29.

The Digest and Legal Learning in the Eleventh Century

The re-emergence of the Digest after its long, early medieval dormancy is announced by its citation in several different sources in the second half of the eleventh century. The earliest ones, from the third quarter of the century, came from the practicing jurists who were also the first to study the Institutes and the Code: the *Walcausina*, the *Expositio*, the Marturi *placitum*, the Cologne glosses to the Institutes, and the *Glossa Pistoiese* to the Code. Yet these references to the Digest from the circle of Lombard jurists have drawn comparatively little attention from historians. Some scholars, including Patetta, Kantorowicz, and more recently Peter Weimar, regarded their work as simply too crude or primitive to have had any lasting significance.[21] Others, such as Cortese and Nicolaj,[22] have argued that the Lombardists were too attached to Lombard law ever to have played a role in the development of Roman law.

As an alternative to the Lombardist jurists, many historians have looked to the circle surrounding the reform papacy of the late eleventh century. Almost invariably, this interpretation has looked for support to three canon law collections—the *Collectio Britannica* and Ivo of Chartres' *Decretum* and *Panormia*—that all drew on the same collection of excerpts from the Digest. None of these collections is earlier than the 1090s, the period to which they are commonly attributed,[23] but

[21] "Was die Lombardisten in Pavia an Glossen hervorgebracht haben und was in vorbologneser Zeit zum römischen Recht geschrieben wurde, ist so primitiv, daß man es getrost vergessen darf, wenn man die Anfänge der Bologneser Rechtswissenschaft zu ergründen sucht." Review of J. Fried, *Die Entstehung des Juristenstandes im 12. Jahrhundert* (Köln/Wien, 1974), ZSS RA, 96 (1979): 431.

[22] Cortese, "Legisti, canonisti e feudisti," p. 203; Nicolaj, *Cultura e prassi di notai preirneriani*, p. 15.

[23] The *Collectio Britannica* was described by P. Ewald, "Die Papstbriefe der Brittischen Sammlung," *Neues Archiv der Gesellschaft für ältere Geschichtskunde*, 5 (1880): 277–414, 505–596. Portions of it, but not those concerning the Digest, were recently edited and provided with a detailed commentary in Robert Somerville, *Pope Urban II, the* ***Collectio Britannica****, and the Council of Melfi (1089)* (Oxford, 1996); *PL* 161 contains both the *Panormia* (cols. 1043–1334) and Ivo of Chartres' later, longer *Decretum* (col. 47–1043). One vexed point for the dating of the *CB* concerns the relationship between a letter of Urban II and the Prologue to Ivo's *Decretum* and *Panormia*: Somerville, pp. 104–15, prefers the originality of the letter while Kuttner held that material in the *CB* derived from Ivo's Prologue, implying a somewhat later date for the *CB*; see Kuttner, "Urban II and the Doctrine of Interpretation: A Turning Point?," *Studia Gratiana*, 15 (1972): 53–85 [repr. in Kuttner, *The History of Ideas and Doctrines of Canon Law in the Middle Ages* (London, 1980)]. But see also the works cited in the next note.

nothing bars them from being later, from after 1100, and perhaps even significantly later, from around Ivo's death in 1115.[24] Regardless of the date, what made these works interesting was the possibility that the text of the Digest used was that of the vulgate Digest, the *littera bononiensis*—evidence of a link between that text and the reform papacy.[25] Antonia Fiori's recent study of the Digest excerpts in the *Collectio Britannica*, however, disproved this hypothesis: while some readings agreed with the Florentina against the earliest manuscripts in the vulgate tradition, others agreed with the vulgate tradition against the Florentina, and still others offered a unique reading where the Florentina and the medieval manuscripts agreed.[26] If these canonist sources do reflect direct contact with the Digest—a point that is far from certain—it may well have been with an antique manuscript different from those that produced the *littera bononiensis*. Canonist study of the Digest, in any case, seems to have been limited until somewhat later. As Winroth has shown, canon law as late as ca. 1139 had little to do with Roman law—so much so that Gratian himself, in the first edition of the *Decretum*, rarely found reason to cite it.[27]

Setting aside the *Collectio Britannica* and its related compilations leaves us again with the sources produced by the community of secular jurists. The more than twenty citations of the Digest, though dramatically more than found in the early Middle Ages, have not sufficed to convince historians that these scholars were not simply relying on collections of extracts from the Digest.[28] It is certainly true that some passages from the Digest circulated as excerpts. One example is the collection of Digest passages, mentioned in the last chapter, that was copied by an eleventh-century notarial hand on a blank page of Montpellier, H 82. Another is the brief collection of juristic fragments at the end of the manuscript containing the *Expositio* in which passages

---

[24] B. Brasington, "The Prologue of Ivo of Chartres: A Fresh Consideration from the Manuscripts," in *Proceedings of the Eighth International Congress of Medieval Canon Law* [Monumenta iuris canonici, Subsidia, 9] (Vatican City, 1992), pp. 3–22, and, in the same collection, pp. 27–46, Martin Brett, "Urban II and the collections attributed to Ivo of Chartres."

[25] Notably Ennio Cortese, *Il rinascimento giuridico medievale* (Roma, 1992), pp. 17–18; *Diritto nella storia medievale*, pp. 378–80

[26] Antonia Fiori, "La 'Collectio Britannica' e la riemersione del Digesto," *Rivista internazionale di diritto comune*, 9 (1998): 81–121.

[27] Winroth, *Making of Gratian's Decretum*, pp. 149 ff.

[28] See, for example, Besta, "L'*Expostio al Liber Papiensis*," pp. 16–17, and Diurni, "L'*Expostio*," pp. 93–97.

from the Digest are mixed with material from Cicero, the Pseudo-Isidore, and the Code.[29] Yet it would be a mistake to undervalue the significance even of collections of extracts from the Digest: given the scant interest in Justinianic texts before the eleventh century, *florilegia* that circulated in the eleventh century were probably created then as well. If most readers still had only indirect contact with the Digest, those who collected the extracts, at least, must have worked directly with ancient manuscripts. Nor were collections of excerpts necessarily brief and superficial. As the *Epitome Codicis* reminds us, a *florilegium* might well represent a viable if temporary strategy for quickly circulating the most immediately useful sections of a text too long easily to copy in its entirety.

Rather than asking whether the Digest was known as early as the 1060s to 1080s—a question, as we shall see, largely resolved by the manuscript evidence—it would be better to ask what use its earliest readers made of it. Many of these citations, as Besta observed for the *Expositio*, consist of definitions or maxims. The preface to the *Expositio* to the *Liber Papiensis*, for example, contains three quotations about the origins and purpose of law (D. 1.1.1, 1.3.1, and 1.3.18).[30] The Cologne glosses, similarly, use the Digest as a source of quotations seven times, including various definitions for *ius* (none of them overlapping with the *Expositio)* and the definitions for *contractus, res hereditaria*, and *lata culpa*. Two glosses in the Pistoia *Epitome Codicis*, finally, offer a number of definitions drawn from the Digest: duress (*metus*) and force (*vis*) as defined by D. 4.1.1, 2 and 3a, and fraud (*dolus*) as defined in D. 4.3.1.2.[31] Many of these definitions have been reworked, their language simplified into a form appropriate for glosses, but their origins remain clearly recognizable.

Other references to the Digest, however, show that jurists were also studying it with attention to details that would elude the avid collector of definitions. The *Expositio*, for example, invokes the definition of *reddendi* not for its own sake but to settle a dispute over the interpretation of Roth. 200. The gloss to Otto III, 1 notes that this law annulled the Roman law forbidding legal actions to proceed during

[29] Described by Patetta, "Contributi."

[30] MGH, *Leges* IV, p. LXXXIX provides a list of references to the Digest; Conrat, *Geschichte*, p. 406, and Kantorowicz, *Digestavulgata*, p. 86 n. 12 propose some revisions to this list but generally accept it.

[31] Chiappelli, *Glossa Pistoiese*, Scholia nos. 19, 20.

Table 8: The Digest in the *Expositio* to the *Liber Papiensis*

Expos. Praef.: . . . Intentio legis est *facere homines bonos, non solum tantum metu penarum, sed etiam exhortatione premiorum.* [D. 1.1.1] . . . *Lex est commune preceptum, virorum prudentium consultum, delictorum quæ sponte vel ignorantia contrahuntur coercitio, communis reipublicæ sponsio;* [D. 1.3.1] . . . *Benignius leges interpretande sunt, ut voluntas earum adimpleatur.* [D. 1.3.18]	D. 1.1.1.1: . . . iustitiam namque colimus et boni et aequi notitiam profitemur, . . . *bonos non solum metu poenarum*, verum *etiam praemiorum* quoque *exhortatione* efficere cupientes . . . D.1.3.1: *Lex est commune praeceptum, virorum prudentium consultum, delictorum quae sponte vel ignorantia contrahuntur coercitio, communis rei publicae sponsio.* D. 1.3.18: *Benignius leges interpraetandae sunt,* quo *voluntas* earum conservetur.
Expo. to Roth. 200 §5. Multi iudices dicunt, quod, si maritus uxorem suam occiderit, non vadit morgincap ad parentes, ideo quia ibi legitur: "revertatur"; cum morgincap non potest reverti ad parentes, quia ab illorum parentibus non venit. Sed eorum sententia a multis legibus reprehenditur; legitur enim in Digestis: "*reddendi verbum, licet retro dandi habet significationem, tamen et per se dandi significationem recipit.*" Per legem quoque Longobardam videri potest, quod "revertatur" aliquando in sua propria significatione non ponitur, immo pro "deveniat," . . .	D. 31.21: etenim *reddendi verbum quamquam significationem habet retro dandi, recipit tamen et per se dandi significationem.* D. 50.16.94: *Verbum "reddendi" quamquam significatum habet retro dandi, recipit tamen et per se dandi significationem.*
Expo. to Roth. 260 §1. Notandum, quod, licet hec lex dixisset: "rem in via invenerit", tamen idem intelligendum est, si alibi invenit: sed de via tantum ideo dixit, quia ad ea quae sepius accidunt aptatur regula iuris.	D. 1.3.4: Ex his, quae forte uno aliquo casu accidere possunt, iura non constituuntur: D. 1.3.5 Nam ad ea potius debet aptari ius, quae et frequenter et facile, quam quae perraro eveniunt.
Expo. to Liut. 71 §1. Eum, qui de alia re quam in hac lege precipitur alicui consilium dederit, ille qui passus est iuxta Romanorum legem, ex eius "dolo factum esse" appellare potest.	D. 4.3.1.1: Verba autem edicti talia sunt: "quae dolo malo facta esse dicentur, si de his rebus alia actio non erit et iusta causa esse videbitur, iudicium dabo."
Expo. to Otto I, 5 §1. et si appellatio fuerit facta post annum, illud debet emendare in simplum, id est illam tantum perdere, ut lex Romana precipit. Videlicet si infra annum conventus visus restituere contumax extiterit, in quadruplum condempnandum est; si vero post annum convenietur et iussu iudicis restituere noluerit, in lite iurabitur.	D. 4.3.18pr. Arbitrio iudicis in hac quoque actione restitutio comprehenditur: et nisi fiat restitutio, sequitur condemnatio quanti ea res est. ideo autem et hic et in metus causa actione certa quantitas non adicitur, ut possit per contumaciam suam tanti reus condemnari, quanti actor in litem iuraverit . . .
Expo. to Otto III 1 §1. In hoc quod dicit: "toto anni tempore liceat iudicibus causas agere, lites dirimere, tumultus questionum" et cetera, rumpit legem Romanam, que vetat iudicibus causam agere, lites dirimere *tempore messium vel vindemiarum.*	D. 2.12.1: Ne quis *messium vindemiarumque tempore* adversarium cogat ad iudicium venire, oratione divi marci exprimitur, quia occupati circa rem rusticam in forum compellendi non sunt.

Table 9: The Digest in the Cologne glosses to Justinian's Institutes

Gloss 3 [Fitting ed.] to In. 1 pr.: . . . et diffinitio iuris hec est: ius est ars boni et equi. ut in principio Digestorum legitur.	D.1.1.1pr. . . . ius est ars boni et aequi.
Gl. 4 to In. 1.2.1: "Ius civile est quod neque in totum a iure naturali vel gentium recedit nec per omnia ei seruit."	D.1.1.6pr. Ius civile est, quod neque in totum a naturali vel gentium recedit nec per omnia ei servit.
Gl. 5 to In. 1.2.2: Quibus modis ius dicatur, queritur. Ius enim plurimis modis dicitur. Ius enim ius naturale dicitur, de quo hic tractat. Altero modo ius dicitur ius civile. Nec minus recte ius dicitur ius pretoris, scilicet ius honorarium. Alia vero significatione ius dicitur locus in quo ius redditur, apellatione collata ab eo quod fit, in eo ubi fit, ut in Digestis legitur.	D.1.1.11 Ius pluribus modis dicitur: uno modo, cum id quod semper aequum ac bonum est ius dicitur, ut est ius naturale. altero modo, quod omnibus aut pluribus in quaque civitate utile est, ut est ius civile. nec minus ius recte appellatur in civitate nostra ius honorarium. praetor quoque ius reddere dicitur etiam cum inique decernit, relatione scilicet facta non ad id quod ita praetor fecit, sed ad illud quod praetorem facere convenit. alia significatione ius dicitur locus in quo ius redditur, appellatione collata ab eo quod fit in eo ubi fit.
Gl. 19 to. In. 1.10.12: Vulgo concepti sunt qui patrem non agnoscunt vel agnoscunt quem eis habere non licet.	D.1.5.23 Volgo concepti dicuntur qui patrem demonstrare non possunt, vel qui possunt quidem, sed eum habent, quem habere non licet.
Gl. 35 to In. 2.1.pr.: [diagram distinction: Rerum] aliae in nullius bonis sunt, ut hereditas prius quam adeatur, quod in Digestis legitur: "Gaius libro ii. Institutionum: nam res ereditariae, ante quam aliquis heres existat, nullius in bonis sunt."	D.1.8.1pr. Gaius 2 inst. . . . nam res hereditariae, antequam aliquis heres existat, nullius in bonis sunt.
Gl. 106 to In. 3.13.2: Est enim contractus, ut in Digestis legitur, duorum pluriumue consensus in idem, quo alter alteri obligatur.	D. 2.14.1 . . . Et est pactio duorum pluriumve in idem placitum et consensus.
Gl. 114 to In. 3.18.1: veluti si post contractum venditionis emtor de dolo stipulatus sit iubento iudice.	D. 4.3.7.3. qui servum mihi debebat vel ex venditione vel ex stipulatu, venenum ei dedit et sic eum tradidit: . . . ait Labeo, sive cavit de dolo sive non, dandam in eum de dolo actionem
Gl. 115 to In. 3.18.1: veluti si stipuletur de servo empto, ut, si fugerit, reddatur vel pretium restituatur.	D. 4.21.1.21.3 Idem ait futuri temporis nomine cautionem ei, qui sciens vendidit, fieri solere, si in fuga est homo sine culpa emptoris et nihilo minus condemnatur venditor: tum enim cavere oportere, ut emptor hominem persequatur et in sua potestate redactum venditori reddat, . . .
Gl. 131 to In. 131: "dolum": et latam culpam. "Culpa": desidiae atque neclegentiae.	D. 11.6.1.1: . . . lata culpa plane dolo comparabitur. D. 17.2.72 Socius socio etiam culpae nomine tenetur, id est desidiae atque neglegentiae. D. 50.16.227: Magna neglegentia culpa est: magna culpa dolus est.
Gl. 193 to In. 4.18.5: Set non eos qui telum gerunt causa tuendae salutis, ut Paulus dixit v. Responsorum	Dig.48.6.11.2 Paulus 5 sent. . . . Qui telum tutandae salutis suae causa gerunt, non videntur hominis occidendi causa portare.

harvest or grape-gathering—a reference to D. 2.12.1. Evidently the Digest was being read (or excerpted) with an attention to Roman court procedure that no non-jurist would share. Still more evidence of attention to the Digest's account of Roman procedure comes from the *Walcausina*, a work with a special interest in Lombard procedure. The first reference occurs in a distinction entitled *litigatorum* linked to Roth. 15. This diagram compares Lombard and Roman procedures, and among the latter one finds a passage from D. 22.3.21: [*Veluti*] *necessitas probandi semper incumbit ille qui agit.* The same phrase is also quoted in a gloss to Roth. 151 concerning the procedure for proving ownership. The second distinction, linked to the phrase, "non tibi respondeo" in the last model plea illustrating Otto I, 3, is headed "Utitur iis reus exceptionibus."[32] The purpose of this distinction is to list cases in which the accused can refuse to answer an accusation; it begins with the instance of an actor sentenced to death and ends with a broad reference to the many cases (*innumerabilibus modis*) contained in the "sacred constitutions" and in the Digest (*in Digestis*). This comment appears to refer to the many laws in book forty-four of the Digest that deal with the *exceptio rei iudicatae* and, especially, the rule enunciated in D. 2.11.4.1 that exempts a person sentenced to death from the obligation to answer a claim.

This evidence of attention to Roman procedures serves as the background of the most famous single piece of evidence for the revival of the Digest: the record of a court case held at Marturi (Poggibonsi) in Tuscany in March 1076.[33] Present at this proceeding, among others, were Nordilus, *missus* of duchess and marquess Beatrice of Tuscany, Guillielmus *iudex*, and Pepo *legis doctor*. They had to deal with the validity of a charter of donation made to a monastery roughly eighty years earlier by marquis Ugo (d. 1001); shortly after the donation, the property had been seized by a third party, and the current possessor now claimed that long possession barred the suit. Normally this response would have been sufficient, but someone inserted into the discussion a law of the Digest (*lex Digestorum*) "per quam copiam magistratus non habentibus restitutionem in integrum pretor pollicetur." The reference is to D. 4.6.26.4, where Ulpian attributes to

[32] MGH, *Leges* IV: 571.

[33] Manaresi, *Placiti*, no. 437. On the circumstances of this case, see Frank Theisen, "Die Wiederentdeckung des römischen Rechts im Alltag des 11. Jahrhunderts. Dargestellt an einer Urkunden von 1076," *Revue d'histoire du droit*, 62 (1994): 127–43.

Labeo the statement that where no magistrate was available (*et si magistratus copia non fuit*) right to an action does not lapse—a principle relevant to this case because the monastery had not ceased to appeal to authorities to rectify its dispossession. The language of the *placitum*, in fact, combines Ulpian's phrase with D. 4.1.5, which promises: *Nemo videtur re exclusus, quem praetor in integrum restituturum polliceatur.* The court found the argument persuasive and Nordilus directed that the property be restored "in integrum."

Discussion of this *placitum* has normally focused on two issues: whether this Pepo *legis doctor* was the same Pepo later remembered at Bologna as the predecessor to Irnerius, and whether the text quoted from the Digest was really appropriate to the case. The first question is impossible to answer, not least because the rare glosses mentioning Pepo date from a period several generations after when he would have lived.[34] On the issue of the appropriateness of this passage from the Digest to the case in hand, Kantorowicz argued that the text of the Digest cited in the Marturi plea was "grossly misunderstood,"[35] while Cortese regarded it as "extraordinarily adapted to the case."[36] Frank Theisen, moreover, was able to link the Marturi plea to current trends among Italian jurists, including the *Walcausina*, the *Expositio* and the first "false constitution" contained in the Cologne manuscript of the Institutes.[37]

Whether or not the citation was appropriate to the case, however, it certainly demonstrates that by 1076 study of the Digest had gone deep into details of the text. The particular passage quoted was far from prominent—little more than a phrase, and not an especially memorable one—in a long excerpt near the end of a rather technical title. That this passage had been noted at all, much less remembered, tells us that the Digest was being read with special attention to its description of Roman procedure. Such mastery could not have been

---

[34] Among the contributions on Pepo, not all of which have to do with the Marturi plea, see H. Fitting, "Pepo zu Bologna," ZSS RA, 23 (1902): 31–45. The systematic mining of later anecdotes began with the article by H. Kantorowicz and Beryl Smalley, "An English Theologian's View of Roman Law: Pepo, Irnerius, Ralph Niger," now in Kantorowicz, *Rechtshistorische Schriften*, pp. 231–44; Ludwig Schmugge, "'Codicis Iustiniani et Institutionum baiulus'—Eine neue Quelle zu Magister Pepo von Bologna," *Ius commune*, 6 (1977): 1–9.

[35] Kantorowicz and Smalley, "An English Theologian's View of Roman Law," p. 234.

[36] Cortese, "Legisti, canonisti e feudisti," p. 200.

[37] Theisen, "Wiederendeckung," pp. 133–34.

achieved quickly, nor for the specific occasion of this one case, but only after many years of careful study by experienced jurists. Understood in these terms, the Marturi plea, and some of the references to the Digest in the *Walcausina* and *Expositio*, leave little room to doubt that Lombardist jurists had been engaged in the serious study of the Digest for a considerable time before 1076.

Creating the Vulgate Archetype

Conjectural Emendations

The Lombardist juristic community were the first readers of the Digest in Middle Ages, and even Kantorowicz conceded that the text they possessed was related to the vulgate tradition.[38] Does knowing this help explain what happened to the text of the Digest during the period when it was first being studied? The two traditional problems, as we have seen, are the creation of **S**, a manuscript based on the Florentina yet containing readings from a second authentic source, and the origins of the tripartite division of the Digest. No less significant, however, is the tradition of textual conjecture. The evidence on this point was brought together by Kantorowicz, often building on suggestions contained in Mommsen's preface and a few suggestive pages of Conrat's *History*.[39]

Some of the emendations Kantorowicz attributed to **S** could be seen as grammatical corrections or, indeed, as scribal errors. One category consists of changes in word order: for example at D. 5.3.13.6, where **F** reads *quia pecunia hereditaria est*, **PVLU** read *quia pecunia est hereditaria*. A second category consists of various kinds of "grammatical" corrections. These range from filling out elliptical phrases (in D. 5.3.13.14, **F**: *in corporibus et fructibus* becomes **PVL**: *in corporibus et in fructibus*), to substituting synonyms (**F**: *tractat* becomes **PVU**: *scribit* [D. 5.3.13.14], but this is surely to be seen as an error), to changing the case of some prepositional objects from accusative to ablative, to changing the modes of verbs, and introducing medieval word forms. Some of the phrases incorporated into the vulgate tradition, finally, must represent glosses erroneously taken into the main text, as when

[38] *Digestenvulgata*, p. 87 [§16] n. 12.

[39] Many of the suggestions given by Kantorowicz are borrowed from the notes to Conrat, *Geschichte*, pp. 348–49.

the oldest vulgate manuscripts add a superfluous second reference to the Twelve Tables in D. 9.4.2.1. Similar errors, in fact, can be seen in the Paris manuscript of the *Epitome Codicis*, where glosses from Pistoia ms. 106 were incorporated into the main text.

As Kantorowicz himself noted, changes to word order and corrections to grammar are found in many texts. So, too, are corrections to what must have seemed obvious errors—obvious to jurists, at least—as when *sine* was omitted from D. 23.2.25 to have it that an emancipated son can marry with (rather than *without*) his father's approval, or when *non* was inserted to convert to a negative the statement in D. 23.2.3 that a grandfather could arrange the marriage of two of his grandchildren when both were offspring of sons of his still under his *potestas*.[40] Other deliberate modifications brought the Digest into line with parallel passages in the Institutes, as when **F**'s *coniuntio* in D. 1.1.1.3 is altered to *coniugatio* in **PVL** to agree with In. 1.2pr., or when a *non* is inserted in D. 1.8.6.4 in accordance with the reading given for In. 2.1.9 in the Bamberg and Turin manuscripts.[41] This last category of interventions has the additional significance of confirming that we are dealing with men who were already expert in legal texts.

Such emendations may well have seemed, in the eleventh century, simply straightforward corrections of a flawed exemplar. Yet the editorial work on the Digest did not stop there. Take, for example, D. 9.3.5, where the end of the text as given in **F** (*Haec autem actio, quae competit de effusis et deiectis, perpetua est et heredi competit, in heredem vero non datur. quae autem de eo competit, quod liber perisse dicetur, intra annum dumtaxat competit, neque personis nam est poenalis et popularis.*) is obviously confused. **PVU**, in contrast, offer a reading that makes legal and logical sense: *quae autem de eo competit, quod liber perisse dicetur, intra annum dumtaxat competit, neque* ***in heredem sed nec heredi similibusque*** *personis* ***datur****: nam est poenalis et popularis.* Mommsen eventually rejected this passage as an emendation, citing the infelicity of the *sed nec* and also the improbability that a copyist could have retained the word *personis* while skipping words immediately before and after. His own solution (intra annum dumtaxat competit, *neque in heredem datur neque heredi*

[40] Both of these examples are from Conrat, *Geschichte*, p. 349 n. 3.

[41] Kantorowicz, *Digestenvulgata*, pp. 39–41 [§10–11]; p. 45 [§12] contains other emendations drawn from the *Institutiones*. Preliminary conclusions in this area were presented by Mommsen, Praefatio, p. LXVIII and repeated by Conrat, p. 349 n. 1.

similibusque personis) avoids these problems, but it also reveals how skillful the eleventh-century emendation actually was. Similarly, in D. 19.1.13.3,

> *Quid tamen si ignoravit quidem furem esse, adseveravit autem bonae frugi et fidum et earum vendidit? videamus, an ex empto teneatur. et putem teneri. atqui ignoravit: sed non debuit facile quae ignorabat adseverare. Inter hunc igitur et qui scit* **inter-est: quoniam quit scit** *praemonere debuit furem esse, hic non debuit facilis esse ad temerarium indicationem.*

Mommsen (and Savigny) originally took the phrase, "interest: quoniam qui scit" to be an instance where the medieval Digest preserved an authentic text missing from the Florentina; he later omitted the phrase from the *editio maior*, however, in part because a previously un-noticed translation of this passage in the *Basilica* revealed the additional phrase to have been an editorial intervention.[42]

Kantorowicz described the redactor of **S** as a philologist and jurist—a characterization that may go back to Odofredo's account of Irnerius as a master of arts.[43] Kantorowicz's view, and apparently Mommsen's as well, was of a solitary genius who applied his expertise in the language arts to the famously difficult legal text. And although Kantorowicz's attempt to identify the redactor of **S** with Irnerius has found little support,[44] the idea that "philology" was somehow involved has held on among legal historians. Cortese, for example, argued that the philological activities applied to the Digest had parallels among the canon lawyers in the circle of the reform papacy: "the reforms were based on the rediscovery of the normative patrimony, on the verification of the authenticity of wording of every piece, on the elimination of apocrypha—what one might call a subtle

[42] Kantorowicz, p. 60 [§14].

[43] Kantorowicz, *Digestenvulgata*, pp. 39–40 [§10–11]. Odofredo's text is edited in G. Cencetti, "Studium fuit Bononie," *Studi medievali*, 3rd ser. 7 (1966): 781–833, and in Kantorowicz and Smalley, "An English Theologian's View of Roman Law." On the reliability of Odofredo, see the discussion in Johannes Fried, *Die Entstehung des Juristenstandes im 12. Jahrhundert: zur sozialen Stellung und polit. Bedeutung gelehrter Juristen in Bologna und Modena* (Köln, 1974) pp. 105–07. For the survival of this idea among legal historians, see, for example, Cortese, "Legisti," p. 207: "Insomma, la ricerca filologica entra come componente essenziale del rinnovamento della scienza."

[44] The central difficulty, of which Kantorowicz was fully aware, is that while Irnerius' career is documented only for the twelfth century, extending at least until the late 1120s, citations of the Digest resume by the 1070s; Kantorowicz himself conceded that the work on **S** had to have been finished by 1085 at the latest, when Irnerius would have been extremely young.

philological operation."[45] Yet those who actually study the early canonists offer little support for Cortese's position. Horst Fuhrmann notes that active study of even canon law began relatively late among church reformers, with Gregory VII personally being neither a trained jurist nor particularly interested in law; thus, it was not until the 1080s that the principal Gregorian canon law collections were gathered.[46] This is already comparatively late for the reception of the Digest. Nor is it possible to describe the work that went into early collections such as those of Anselm of Lucca or Deusdedit as either critical or philological. The earliest Gregorian collections drew heavily on spurious sources, such as the pseudoisidorean decrees, frequently omitting phrases or combining passages from multiple works.[47] The somewhat later *Collectio Britannica*, similarly, simply incorporated a passage for Ivo of Chartres into a letter of Urban II, showing that critical standards were still shaky as late as the first decade of the twelfth century.[48] Fuhrmann, Rambaud-Buhot and Kuttner agree that one cannot see much real criticism in the area of canon law until well into the twelfth century, and the important role later played by Ivo of Chartres—a French scholar trained in the liberal arts[49]—adds further doubt to claims about a strong early critical tradition centered in Rome. One can claim for the Gregorians a major role in the reception of the Digest only by arguing that they were capable of doing better work on Roman law in the 1060s, 1070s, or 1080s than they did in dealing with canon law itself.

Nor is it easy to find emendations comparable to those worked on the Digest in other branches of eleventh-century scholarship. One might, for example, expect to find parallels to the textual criticism applied to the Digest in biblical scholarship, especially since scholars had been aware since the eighth and ninth centuries that variant readings were abundant in the Bible. In practice, however, emendation had consisted mainly of correcting grammar and choosing the best of available readings.[50] Thus, an independently minded scholar

[45] Cortese. "Legisti," p. 206.
[46] Fuhrmann, "Reformpapsttum," and "Papst Gregor VII."
[47] See the remarks of Rambaud-Buhot, quoted above, chapter three at n. 79.
[48] Kuttner, "Urban II."
[49] For Ivo, see Sprandel, *Ivo von Chartres.*
[50] F. L. Ganshof, "Alcuin's Revision of the Bible," in *The Carolingians and the Frankish Monarchy*, trans. Janet Sondheimer (Ithaca, 1971), pp. 28–40; B. Fischer, "Bibeltext und Bibelreform," in B. Bischoff, ed., *Karl der Grosse* (Dusseldorf, 1967), pp. 156–212; Laura Light, "Versions et révisions du texte biblique," in Pierre Riché and Guy Lobrichon, *Le Moyen Age et la Bible* (Paris, 1984), pp. 55–94, at pp. 59–65.

of the early twelfth century such as Gilbert of Poitiers could devote a long commentary to the Psalms without suggesting emendations to the text.[51] It was not until late in the twelfth century—or nearly a century after the events we are discussing—that one sees much effort to restore Jerome's Latin text, and even then the work was usually done by having recourse to the Hebrew text rather than through conjecture,[52] and Jacques Verger notes that theology continued to display a "philological weakness" well into the thirteenth century.[53]

The trivium was another area where scholarship generally took the form of commentaries on authoritative works: Priscian on grammar, Cicero on rhetoric, and Porphyry, Boethius, and Aristotle on logic. Many of these texts were written originally in Latin, thus avoiding the problems associated with the Bible and other works translated from other languages; they also received detailed, passage-by-passage commentaries of ever-increasing complexity by specialists in the language arts. But so far as editing those texts, the situation does not appear to be appreciably different from that of the Bible. For example, Thierry of Chartres' commentary on Cicero's *De Inventione* certainly shows sensitivity to the language of his text; thus Thierry notes a variant reading at one point, and at others called attention to unusual and possibly confusing locutions.[54] But he does not emend his text, an indication that emending texts was not a routine or usual part of the scholarship of northern Europe. In Italy, moreover, the classical manuals were rarely even glossed after the mid-eleventh century; rather, in the trend that culminated in the formation of *ars*

---

[51] CMR would like to express his appreciation to Theresa Gross-Diaz for this information. See now her book, *The Psalms commentary of Gilbert of Poitiers: from lectio divina to the lecture room* (Leiden/New York, 1996).

[52] Light, pp. 73–80; for Nicola Maniacutia, not a scholar but a Roman Cisterican monk who wrote on the textual criticism of the Bible sometime after 1140, see Vittorio Peri, "'Correctores immo corruptores.' Un saggio di critica testuale nella Roma del XII secolo," *Italia medioevale e umanistica*, 20 (1977): 19–123; but Maniacutia did not believe that the Hebrew text was the standard for establishing Jerome's translation. For some glosses from the late twelfth or early thirteenth century commenting on variant readings, see N. Haastrup, "Zur frühen Pariser Bibel—auf Grund skandinavischer Handschriften," *Classica et Medievalia*, 24 (1963): 242–69.

[53] "Pour l'essentiel, les exégètes du xiiie siècle s'en sont tenues aux recensions dont ils disposait courment, c'est-à-dire, en particulier, celle dite de l'université de Paris; recension notoirement assez fautive, ce dont les contemporains eux-mêmes eurent bientôt conscience mais sans parvenir à y porter substantiellement remède malgré la production au long du siècle de divers correctoires." Jacques Verger, "L'exégese de l'Université," in *Le Moyen Age et la Bible*, pp. 199–232, at p. 214.

[54] K. M. Fredborg, ed., *The Rhetorical Commentaries of Thierry of Chartres* (Toronto, 1988), glosses to 2.2.4, 2.47.138 and 2.57.172.

dictaminis, Italian interest in the language arts turned strongly toward composition.[55] The results of such study could be impressive in the hands of a master such as Alberic of Monte Cassino,[56] but it had little to do with the kind of word-by-word analysis involved in emending an authoritative text.

In reality, the editorial work done on the Digest is virtually unknown before the thirteenth century and it remains rare until the humanists of the fourteenth century. The one area of eleventh-century scholarship where textual criticism was used routinely, in fact, was among the same Lombardist jurists who we found to have been the first readers of the Digest. Perhaps because their professional lives were spent dealing with secular texts, they had less hesitation than other scholars in applying some basic principals of the textual criticism in their work.[57] The *Walcausina* and the *Expositio* both suggest that it was a common practice to expound each law, often phrase by phrase;[58] and while most glosses focus on legal sense as the basis for interpreting a specific passage, many others combine legal analysis with what might be called textual criticism. The opening verses of the

[55] See, generally, Radding, "Geography of Learning," and Ronald Witt, "Medieval Italian Culture and the Origins of Humanism," in Albert Rabil, Jr., ed. *Renaissance Humanism. Foundations, Forms, and Legacy* (Philadelphia, 1988), vol. 1, pp. 28–71, at 40–44, esp. pp. 41–42. For examples, see the excerpts of Alberic's *Breviarium de dictamine* in L. Rockinger, ed. *Briefsteller und Formelbücher des elften bis vierzehnten Jahrhunderts. Quellen und Erörterungen zur bayreischen und deutschen Geschichte* 9,1 (Munich, 1863), pp. 3–46; and the *Flores Rhetorici*, ed. Don Mauro Inguanez and H. M. Willard in *Miscellanea Cassinese*, 14 (Monte Cassino, 1938).

[56] See, for example, the analysis of Alberic's treatise against Berengar of Tours in Radding and Newton, *Theology, Rhetoric and Politics*, chapter three.

[57] The principal and perhaps the only other case is provided by Lanfranc's glosses to patristic texts. See Margaret Gibson, "Lanfranc's Notes on Patristic Texts," *Journal of Theological Studies*, n.s. 22 (1971): 435–50. Although these emendations are for the most part very cautious, the project itself is unusual enough to have been noticed by Lanfranc's twelfth-century biographer Milo Crispin and more recently in the scholarly literature; see Light, "Versions et révisions du texte biblique," p. 73. Lanfranc himself, of course, received most if not all of his education at Pavia, where he belonged to the community of judges. See Radding, "Geography of Learning."

[58] See, for example, Roth. 226 §1: Haec littera que est: "legibus dominorum suorum et benefactorum vivere debent" secundum Gualcosum ita est exponendum: legibus, id est in conditionibus, quas ipse asserebat, per hoc quod dicit inferius: "secundum quod a dominis suis fuerit concessum," scilicet ut ille qui aldius factus fuerit ea condicione vivat quam suus patronus ei inposuerit, et de ceteris manumissionum rebus fiat similiter. Sed Wilihelmus, quod melius est, eandem litteram sic exposuit, scilicet ut, si patronus Longobardus fuit, qui manumittitur Longobarda lege utatur; ita tamen condicio a domino ei inposita servetur ab eo. Other instances include Liut. 59 §4; Karl. M. 106 §1.

Walcausina, notably, attribute to "Walcausus meritus" the achievement of having corrected the previously erroneous Lombard *Edictum*,[59] and the text itself—virtually identical in the two manuscripts—does seem to have been subjected to a process of standardization and emendation. What was done silently in the *Walcausina*, moreover, was discussed explicitly in the glosses of the *Expositio*, some of which debate the merits of proposed emendations of the legal text itself.

> Expo. to Roth. 186. §1. Notandum, quod hic violentia tantum pro raptu ponitur; quod videri potest per litteram huius legis quae est: *et invitam tulit*. Sepe enim *et* pro *id est* ponitur. Per legem Liuprandi que est. . . .
>
> Expo. to Liut. 89: §5. . . . Notandum est quoque, quod antiquissimorum sententia ab hac in eo tantum dissonet, quod iuxta illorum sententiam hic legebatur *in* loco *ab*; quod non est laudandum, quia fere contingere posset, scilicet quod in illa die, qua manifesta compellatione possessor victus et expulsus fuit, quantum retroacto tempore possessionis rei domino perveniret, reddi posset.
>
> Expo. to Liut. 146: §2. Secundum quosdam, ponentes *i.* pro *id est*, littera huius legis quae est: *et habeat eos sibi in transacto cui furtum fecerit* est expositura *fegangi*; secundum vero alios ita exponitur, scilicet ut dicamus: sint fegangi, id est 40 solidorum culpabiles. Et secundum ultimam expositionem *fegangi*, quod inferius habetur: *componat dominus sicut lex est et edictum continet*, ad sibi nonum tantum referendum est.
>
> Expo. to Karl. M. 129: §2. Notandum est, secundum Wilihelmum hic talem litteram esse debere: *aut sine dampno restituat*, secundum vero Bonifilium: *ut sine dampno restituat*.
>
> Expo. to Grim. 2: §1. Hec lex, in hoc quod precipit, in libertate illum permanere qui 30 annis in libertate permansit, a Lodoyci capitulo rumpitur quod est "Placuit nobis de illis hominibus qui se liberos per 30 annos," in hoc quod dicit: *placuit nobis, ut per hanc possessionem—subaudis 30 annorum—liberi non sint;* et secundum hanc sententiam sequens littera ita legitur, scilicet ut dicatur: *sed si de ingenuo patre et matre sunt nati, liberi erunt, aut cartam ostendant*. Quam sententiam Bonifilius firmabat. Et dicitur etiam, quod edicta antiqua hanc litteram habuerunt: *nisi de ingenuo patre aut matre*, sed Bonifilius dicitur apposuisse *et* loco *aut*, ut sua melior esset sententia quam litterata; et quam sententiam Wilihelmus bonam esse confirmat. . . .[60]

In these glosses, the judges appear to have had some basic sense of critical principles: for example, they do not completely recast sentences,

[59] Est error spretus quo longobarda iuventus / Errabat. Verum loquitur tunc pagina sensum / Edicti rectis quod strinxit rethor habenis / Walcausus meritus quem laudat scriba disertus /Nostrorum regum sunt hinc exordia legum / Rothar iura dedit, quae lector prima videbit.

[60] Other examples include glosses to Roth. 41, 47 and 349.

but instead propose to emend only the word or phrase where copyist errors could most easily have produced a text that made no legal sense.

Not all of this editorial work is sound by the measure of modern textual criticism, not least for having contributed to the thicket of readings that sometimes obscured what was the text of the law. But what is unique is that these jurists were prepared to substitute their understanding of what a text *should* mean for what the manuscripts actually said. Since these debates often date to the first half of the eleventh century—as we know from the mention of Bonifilius and Willihelmus—the practice must have been a normal part of juristic scholarship by the time attention turned to the Digest. These emendations also seem sometimes to have been incorporated into manuscripts, because several of them appear to have been incorporated into manuscripts of the *Liber Legis Langobardorum*. It is, in short, precisely the kind of work that was done to the Digest: presumptively in the case of **S** and (as we shall see) demonstrably in the cases of **P** and **V**. Put another way, the search for the "philologists" capable of emending the Digest leads us back precisely to the eleventh-century jurists who would have had the greatest professional interest in doing so.

The Authentic Emendations and Their Origin

It goes without saying that scholars who could emend faulty texts through conjecture were also capable of improving their texts through collations, just as Mommsen supposed had happened. Indeed, the vigor with which Lombardist jurists pursued variant readings is apparent in every work they touched. Occasionally, the *Expositio* mentions alternate readings found in older or different manuscripts, sometimes described as the *edicta antiqua* or *edicta antiquorum*.[61] Virtually all of their manuscripts, moreover, contain copious notations of alternate readings. One reader of London, ms. add. 5411, for example, added all of the Walcausina's textual emendations between the lines and in the margins. For Roman law, Pistoia 106 contains hundreds of collations, edited by Chiappelli as "glosse critiche"; collations are also found in the Turin manuscript of the Institutes.

For the Digest, however, the problem is less why there are collations than why there are so few of them. Kantorowicz persuasively argued

[61] For example, *Expo.* to Roth. 193§1 comments: Notandum est, quedam edicta habere hanc litteram: *ambo penam luxurie iuxta legem sustineant* et quedam: *ambo penam sustineant iuxta legem.* See also, Roth. 41§1; Grim. 2.§1.

that Mommsen's list of collations was too short, and that they could be seen, to some extent, in all parts of the Digest. Yet even allowing for more collations than Mommsen accepted, scholars have been puzzled for centuries over why the total number seems so low, and why some gross errors in the vulgate archetype—the transposition of pages in book 23, the omission of material at the end of D. 48.3—were left uncorrected. Brenkman suggested that the redactor of the vulgate archetype had only scraps available to him; Mommsen that the second ancient exemplar was somehow "imperfectum"; Kantorowicz that the redactor had available to him only a collection of extracts comparable, perhaps, to the *Epitome Codicis*. Kantorowicz was thinking of an "epitome" of ancient origins, analogous to the *Epitome Codicis*; but as with the Code the most probable period for its creation was the eleventh century.[62] Although earlier periods lacked either the interest or the competence to deal with the Digest, a collection of excerpts from the Digest would clearly have found readers among the jurists who used the *Walcausina*, the *Expositio*, or the Cologne glosses. We have already seen, finally, that the pattern of the earliest citations of the Digest is consistent with the use of the Digest in some kind of *Epitome Digestorum*.

Positing an *Epitome Digestorum* as the source of the vulgate's authentic textual variants leads to another question. Rather than the extracts being used later, after a transcript of the Florentina was in hand, could it have been used like the *Epitome Codicis*, as a base text into which previously omitted materials were restored? Evidence in support of this hypothesis is not hard to find. For example, while Mommsen correctly called attention to the three places where text omitted from the vulgate tradition was exactly equal to a line in the Florentina—a common mechanical error in copying, he has almost nothing to say about the very unusual errors of skipping or transposing entire laws found in both early manuscripts of the *Digestum Vetus*. What is particularly interesting, moreover, is that the two manuscripts share some errors and differ in others. For example, while both the Vatican (**V**) and Paris (**P**) copies of the *Vetus* omit D. 5.3.18 and 5.3.38, **P** also omits D. 6.1.10 and 11, 6.1.80, and 10.2.46, none of which are missing in **V**, while **V** omits D. 6.1.35 not missing in **P**. Similarly, while both **V** and **P** transpose D. 5.3.43–44 and

[62] *Digestenvulgata*, pp. 51–55.

23.3.35–36, **P** alone transposes D. 1.5.6–7.[63] None of these errors are routine copying errors, like skipping a line. Where they do occur, as Tort-Martorell demonstrated, is in manuscripts of the Code. We saw in the last chapter how errors in the process of reintegrating constitutions omitted from the *Epitome* often meant placing skipped constitutions in the margin, such as one sees in Berlin ms. 273. Since scribes copying such manuscripts had to remember to include such constitutions and might insert such marginal constitutions incorrectly, exemplars as complex as these produce an even wilder patchwork of omissions and transpositions of laws in the next generation—exactly as one sees with these two manuscripts of the *Vetus*. It is noteworthy in this regard that while **L** contains the two laws in D. 6.1 omitted in **P**, it does so out of order (D. 6.1.8, 10, 11, 9, 12) just as one sees in the manuscripts of the Code. **V** in some ways even resembles early Code manuscripts, with omitted laws later inserted in the margin and even lines left blank at several places as if the scribe thought that text might be missing—a practice also seen in Berlin 273.

Also notable is the absence from the earliest *Vetus* manuscripts of the constitutions associated with the enactment of the Digest: *Deo auctore*, *Omnem*, and *Tanta*. These constitutions would have been included in a complete transcription of the Florentina, so their omission from the early vulgate tradition reveals, at minimum, a conscious decision on the part of the scribe. What makes these omissions more significant, however, is that they mirror the exclusion of the comparable constitutions from the earliest manuscripts of the Code and, indeed, the *Liber Papiensis*. Not only are we dealing with the same attitude as to what to include, but one has again the impression that whoever transcribed materials from the *Florentina* was making selections rather than simply copying the entire manuscript.

Although these points may not provide decisive proof that the reception of the Digest followed the same path as the Code, none of them are easily reconciled with Mommsen's idea that a descendent of **F** received marginal or interlinear emendations from a (partial)

[63] Our account of **V** may not be exhaustive, since Mommsen's account of this manuscript is defective and we did not attempt a complete collation of it. Not included in our list of laws omitted are a number of very short laws whose omission may have been little more than skipping a line. For a complete list of the laws restored to the text by medieval collators, see the description of **V** in the appendix.

second source. Nor is his own evidence for that procedure as strong as it may have seemed. A trivial example is provided by D. 5.3.13: **F** gives *tractat*, **PV** give scribit, and **L** gives *scribit tractat*.[64] Mommsen took this as evidence that **S**, the archetype of the vulgate tradition, had interlinear glosses treated differently by different scribes. Mommsen is certainly correct that scribes often incorporated glosses into their texts, for this process is amply apparent in the Pistoia and Paris manuscripts of the *Epitome Codicis*. But **L**, the manuscript in this case, is simply too late (from the middle of the twelfth century) for its readings to be taken as deriving directly from the *Vetus* archetype. In this particular case, the combination of readings is more likely to have resulted from transverse collations between later manuscripts, perhaps after the influence of the Pisana began to be felt once again. What is particularly striking about Mommsen's examples, however, is the absence of comparable examples from the **V** or **P**, the two manuscripts closest in time to the *Vetus* archetype. If that manuscript had, indeed, contained numerous interlinear collations, one would expect such errors to be more common than they seem to be in those manuscripts closest to it.

Fuller exploration of this point will require a more complete knowledge of **V** and **P**, and even of other early manuscripts, than can be obtained from Mommsen's edition. For now it suffices to show the question is more open than it has seemed, and that the history of the Code offers more insights into the Digest than has previously seemed the case.

The *Digestum Vetus*

Vaticanus Latinus 1406

Vatican Library, Vat. lat. 1406, Mommsen's manuscript **V**, is a codex that measures roughly 345 × 225 mm—large but not unwieldy by the standards of medieval Digest manuscripts. Although the

[64] Praefatio, p. LXVIIII. Given that Mommsen was working mostly from transcriptions of medieval manuscripts, often dating back to Schrader, all his examples need to be re-examined. Not only are **U** and **L** comparatively late, but his account of **V** does not distinguish consistently between the original copying and various strata of later additions and corrections.

calligraphic skill of the scribe who copied it is obvious in his regular and elegant caroline minuscule, the Vatican Digest is by no means a "display" manuscript, for it has little decoration of any kind apart from initials at the beginning of some books. It is, rather, a volume intended for reading and consultation that provides a variety of graphic devices—notably the larger-sized initials both in the margins, for the inscriptions, and at the beginning of laws and internally at important paragraphs to assist in locating specific passages—to help readers make their way through a long, complex, and tightly written text. (Red paragraph marks and some capitals in blue, black, and other colors—often overwriting the capitals of the original scribe—were added later.) The margins, though now reduced from rebinding, could also have accommodated glosses and apparently did, although many of them were subsequently erased. The earliest ones that remain are slightly later than the manuscript itself.

One of the most immediately striking aspects of Vat. lat. 1406 are the layers of correction and adjustment added to the manuscript during the twelfth and thirteenth centuries, which permit us to glimpse the efforts of medieval scholars to improve the text of the Digest as it was studied in the medieval university.[65] A first set of corrections, in the second half of the twelfth century, seems to have resulted from renewed contact between the vulgate tradition and the Pisana. The transposition error in book 23 was corrected at this time, and a number of laws omitted from **V** were inserted in the margin. One reader of the Pisana, indeed, appears also to have left graphically similar notations in **V**, suggesting the intriguing possibility that **V** was corrected against **F** at this time. A second set of corrections was introduced in the thirteenth century, when the manuscript was corrected with extreme care. Some of the alterations were minute—often a single letter; others involved erasing and entirely rewriting passages equal to several lines. This meticulous work probably was part of an effort to prepare **V** for use as an exemplar for copying *pecia*, if such indeed was the meaning of notations instructing copyists

[65] Although Brenkman was aware of these corrected and erased passages (*Historia Pandectarum*, p. 275), Mommsen evidently was not and his edition rarely notes when a reading from **V** is by a later hand. Pescani was the first in the modern era to call attention to this problem: "La posizione del V 1406 nella riconstruzione della prima parte del Digesto," in *Studi in onore di Giuseppe Grosso* (Torino, 1972), vol. 5, pp. 81–111, at p. 83. We wish to acknowledge Robert Röhle, who called our attention to Brenkman.

exactly where to finish one folio and start the next.[66] Although these corrections pose problems for reconstructing the early history of the vulgate text, this preparation of an older manuscript for use as an exemplar reveals an aspect of book production for medieval universities that had not previously been suspected.

Like Paris, Bib. Nat., ms. 4450 (= **P**), the manuscript on which Mommsen centered his study of the *Digestum Vetus*, and unlike any other early Digest manuscript, the Vatican Digest adopts a full-page format. Indeed, when trying to imagine the physical appearance of their common archetype, we may not be far wrong in thinking of **V**. The point of departure here is the transposition error in book twenty-three, which gives us the quantity of text of the misbound folios.[67] In **V**, the mis-ordered sections occupy space that is just slightly more than a folio, but they fall into the most spaciously-written section of the manuscript. A page written in the manner of the more closely-written fascicles of **V** would easily have borne each transposed section on a separate leaf, just as we know from the binding error that they must have been written in the manuscript from which the text of the *Vetus* descends.

Mommsen (p. XXXXVIII) described **V** as contemporary with **P**—which he thought was from the late eleventh or early twelfth century—and similar to it in every way, being presumably copied from the same archetype. In fact, as Armando Petrucci was the first to recognize, **V** is certainly older than **P**: he dated it to the eleventh century, most probably the third quarter.[68] This dating to a period some decades earlier than 1100 has found general approval recently,[69] although for our purposes here it is not necessary to insist on a date

[66] The insertion of *pecia* marking was noticed by G. Battelli, "Ricerche sulla pecia nei codici del 'Digestum Vetus,'" in *Scritti Scelti* (Rome, 1975) [orig. pub. 1953]. Battelli's conclusions, however, have been doubted by F. Soetermeer, *Utrumque ius in peciis. Aspetti della produzione libraria a Bologna fra Due e Trecento*, Giuffrè Editore, Milano 1997 (Orbis Academicus. Saggi e documenti di storia dell'università, VII), pp. 27, notes 21 and 247.

[67] Pescani computed it to have equaled something over 9000 characters a folio—4500 characters a side—but this does not take account of abbreviations. "La posizione del V," p. 88.

[68] The authors wish to express their gratitude to Armando Petrucci for consulting with us about this manuscript. His judgment was first published in Radding, "Vatican Latinus 1406," p. 523, although the analysis provided in that article, partially repeated below, depended on a comparison of Vat. lat. 1406 and Paris, BN, ms. lat. 4450, treating both simply as from the later eleventh century.

[69] Francesca Santoni, concurs with the earlier date of **V** as compared to **P**, suggesting a date for **V** in the 1070s or 1080s, barely different from that arrived at

for **V** more precise than the second half of the eleventh century. It is, however, earlier than the similarly dated **P**, and thus closer in time to the vulgate archetype than any other manuscript. As we shall see, it also offers clues about the early circulation of the Digest not to be found in any other manuscript.

Some observers have thought that **V** was the work of two scribes, one responsible for the first part, and the other copying the section from fascicle XVIII (f. 125) to the end.[70] Petrucci, however, concluded

---

by Petrucci. Santoni, "Copisti-editores di manoscritti giuridici: 1. Il codice Vaticano latino 1406 del Digestum Vetus e l'edizione del testo fra copisti e glossatori," *La Collaboration dans la production de l'écrit médiéval*, ed. by Herrad Spilling (Actes du XIIIe Colloque international de paléographie latine [Weingarten, 22–25 septembre 2000]) (Paris, 2003). Giovanna Nicolaj previously had challenged Petrucci's attribution of this manuscript to the third quarter of the eleventh century with the observation that "queste datazioni secche al quarto di secolo (senza il supporto di elementi più precisi), oggi tanto di moda, mi lasciano assai sconcertata" ("Ambiti," p. 495), but evidently she now accepts it. Indeed, although she formally describes this manuscript as dating from the second half of the eleventh century, in practice she frequently insists on a more narrow date, within the lifetime of Mathilda of Canossa's judge Nordilo, basing this claim on a suggestion of Santoni; in one passage, moreover, she even suggests that it was this particular manuscript which was present at Marturi in March, 1076. ("il Digesto Vecchio, con il ms. Vat. lat. 1406, arriva . . . a Marturi, in Toscana, nel 1076," ("Ravenna," p. 773). In short, she dates this manuscript to the same period as does Petrucci.

70 Although Santoni asserts the two halves were copied by different persons on account of the different letter size and slant of the writing, she was not able to identify a single graphic element that was different between the two parts of the manuscript, instead producing a rather extensive list of features shared thoughout in both halves. One can only assume that, not having noticed the structural features discussed below, she permitted herself to be fooled by the last page. In any case, her reasoning runs directly contrary to paleographical doctrine that emphasizes the minute details of letter formation—which are a matter of unconscious muscle memory—rather than letter size and slant that are under the conscious control of the writer. The most recent theoretical discussion of this point was generated in response to Léon Gilissen, *L'expertise des écritures médiévales. Recherche d'une méthode avec application à un manuscrit du XIe siècle: Le lectionnaire de Lobbes (codex Bruxelensis 18018)* (Gand, 1973); see Emmanuel Poulle, "Paléographie et Méthodologie vers l'analyse scientifique des écritures médiévales," en *Bibliothéque de l'Ecole des Chartes*, CXXXII (1974): 101–10, and two essays in *Scriptorium*, 29 (1975) accompanied by a response by Gilissen. Despite using different terminology (ductus vs. morphology) all authors, including Gilissen, would agree with the opinion expressed by Malcolm Parkes in 1976: Rejecting aspect, duct and alignment as useful for anything other than preliminary analysis, he concluded that "[f]or proof of identity we need criteria such as peculiarities in the formation of letters, and, better still, the presence of the same distinctive habits." "The Handwriting of St. Boniface: A Reassessment of the Problems," in *Beiträge zur Geschichte der deutschen Sprache und Literatur*, 98 (1976): 161–79. [reprinted in Parkes, *Scribes, Scripts and Readers. Studies in the Communication, Presentation and Dissemination of Medieval Texts* (London and Rio Grande, 1991), pp. 121–42; the passage quoted is on p. 123].

that both halves were the work of a single copyist, and our own careful examination found nothing to contradict this conclusion. The script in both halves is identical: the same letter forms, the same abbreviations, even minute details such as the *ri* and *st* ligatures or the abbreviations for *modo* or *vero*. (The catalog entry for this manuscript includes a full account of this hand.) The difference in superficial appearance resulted not from a change in copyists but rather an alteration in the inclination and size of the writing, with the script of the second part being more upright and written in a darker ink with a larger module—this last the result of a format with fewer lines per page (46/47 instead of 50) and fewer letters (68 instead of 83) per line.[71] The same copyist added the rubrics, apparently all at once; he also inserted a tantalizing fragment of D. 24.3.1, although in the ink and script used in the first half of the manuscript. This important manuscript was therefore the work of a single scribe, from northern Italy, except for a few places where entire gatherings were later replaced.

One begins to grasp the reasons why the same scribe's handwriting could have a different appearance in the two halves of the manuscript when one moves from the paleography to the codicology of the manuscript. Although most of the fascicles are quarternions of eight folia, the scribe departed from this pattern at three different points: fascicle VI (ff. 44–46), fascicle X (ff. 71–72), and XVII (ff. 122–24).[72] Some variation in the size of fascicles is not uncommon in medieval manuscripts, normally to join smoothly with a previously copied section or, at the end of a manuscript, to avoid leaving a short gathering that would be weak and susceptible to damage or a

[71] For an example of how different page format can alter the appearance of a scribe's handwriting, see Newton, *Scriptorium*, where he observes that the script of the famous Mediceus Tacitus (see above, ch. 6 n. 16) seems at first glance very different from the same hand's work in the Register of Gregory the Great (Monte Cassino, ms. 71) because the latter has 47 lines to the page rather than the 35 of the Tacitus. "As a result, ascenders and descenders are drastically curbed in the Gregory, and the initial appearance of the page is distinct from that of the Mediceus. Close examination, however, shows that the hands are the same." See also his plates 53 and 86.

[72] It does not alter the argument that the current fascicles X and XVII are replacement gatherings, since the quantities of text they contain fall well short of that needed to fill a quaternion. A rough calculation indicates that the text in fascicle X would have needed a single folio (recto and verso) to contain that of the replacement leaves, while fascicle XVII would have required a few lines, perhaps, more than 3 leaves. Santoni evidently gave no thought to the structure of the manuscript, which she incorrectly describes as being entirely composed of quaternions.

loss. The second case can have no bearing here, since these fascicles are all internal to the manuscript, so the short gatherings suggest that we are dealing with a manuscript copied in blocks rather than in a continuous effort from start to finish. Confirmation of the hypothesis that the shorter fascicles were meant to join sections that were already copied can be found on f. 46v—the last page of the fascicle VI, the only one of the shorter fascicles to survive—where half a page is left blank. Although it is possible that he had simply lacked the text that came next and began with a new page when it came to hand, the undersized gathering makes it more likely that this space was left blank because the text from this point on had already been copied, on what is now f. 47r.

Table 10: The structure of Vaticanus latinus 1406 by fascicles and book

Fasc.	Folios	Books	Format of transition between books
I	2–9	Book 1, 2r	10 blank lines; titles listed
II	10–17	Book 2, 11v	1 blank line; titles not listed
III	18–25	Book 3, 22r	4 blank lines; titles listed
IV	26–33	Book 4, 31r	5 blank lines; titles listed
V	34–43		
VI	44–46		Half page left blank at end of gathering
VII	47–54	Book 5, 47r	New folio; titles not listed
VIII	55–62	Book 6, 57r Book 7, 62v	No blank lines; titles not listed 1 blank line; titles not listed
IX	63–70		
X	71–72	*replacement*	
XI	73–80	Book 8, 73r Book 9, 79v	New folio; titles listed 1 blank line; titles listed
XII	81–88	Book 10, 86v	4 blank lines; titles listed
XIII	89–96	Book 11, 94r	titles at bottom of previous folio
XIV	97–105	*replacement*	
XV	106–13	Book 13, 108v	4 blank lines; titles listed
XVI	114–21	Book 14, 115r Book 15, 120v	4 blank lines; titles listed
XVII	122–24	*replacement*	
XVIII	125–32	Book 16, 127r	Part 2 of ms. begins with D. 15.3 Incipit: no blank space, titles not listed

Table 10 (*cont.*)

Fasc.	Folios	Books	Format of transition between books
XIX	133–40	Book 17, 133r	"
XX	141–48	Book 18, 143r	Incipit: 2 lines left blank
XXI	149–56	Book 19, 153r	Incipit: no blank space, titles not listed
XXII	157–64	Book 20, 164r	"
XXIII	165–72	Book 21, 171r	
XXIV	173–78		
XXV	179–86	Book 22, 197r	"
		Book 23, 185v	"
XXVI	187–94		
XXVII	195–202	Book 24 201r	"

Using the shorter fascicles as a guide, we can see that the manuscript is formed of four blocks of text copied separately, each of them containing groups of entire books of the Digest. Thus, fascicles I to VI contain the first four books; fascicles VII to X contain books 5–7; fascicles XI to XVII runs from book 8 to D. 15.2; and fascicles XVIII to XXVII originally ran from D. 15.3 to D. 24.2. The most common reason for such divisions or breaks in the copying would be where multiple copyists were working simultaneously on the same manuscript, but that cannot be the case here. A more complicated story, however, is revealed when one takes a third element into consideration: the format applied to divisions between the books of the Digest. Although the rubrics were all done later, at once, evidence of an evolving conception of page layout is revealed by examining how the scribe dealt with the end of one book and the beginning of the next at the original moment of copying: specifically, how much space he left between books for the eventual rubric. (This material is summarized in Table 10.)

The original, simplest format is found in the second part of the manuscript, from folio 125 to the end. In this section, the scribe left no blank space at all for 8 of the 9 book divisions, making it impossible later to enumerate the titles. The only variation from this pattern is for book 18, where 2 lines were left blank. This original treatment of book transitions is also found in the second block of fascicles (VII–X); there, too, no space is left at book 6, although a line was left blank between the end of book 6 and the beginning of book 7 and again at the transition between books 8 and 9. Yet though thrifty with space, this method had the disadvantage of making it difficult to locate transitions between books. Apparently realizing this, the scribe left more space in the last books to be copied. Thus, he left several lines between books in the next set of fascicles (XI–XVII), using the additional space to insert a list of titles, as he also did for book 9. This same strategy of leaving sufficient space to list the titles also adopted in fascicles I–VI for first four books except for book 2, where only one line was left blank and the title index, of necessity, was omitted. It is not, however, necessary to suppose that any great period of time separated the copying of all three blocks, for the scribe's script shows no significant variation and his ink is barely different, with the second block being perhaps slightly darker than that used in the first and third.

Several factors thus converge on the conclusion that fascicles XVIII to XXVII were a separate and older part of the manuscript: the obvious difference in script, the shortening of fascicle XVII, and the space allotted for the incipits of books. A final confirmation of the original autonomy of this section is revealed by ultraviolet light, with which one can read gathering signature numbers iii, iv, v, vi, and viii that had been erased from the versos of folios 148, 153, 164, 178, and 186. The numeration thus began from the current fascicle XVIII—the beginning of the second part—rather than from fascicle I. The second part, therefore, originally stood on its own and could have had an independent existence for some period of time. The next block of gatherings to be copied, and the earliest of those in the first part of the manuscript, were fascicles VII–X comprising books 5 to 7 of the Digest. Then, apparently not much later, the scribe copied the first and third blocks, comprising books 1 to 4 and books 8 to 15.2—thus effecting the link to the second half of the manuscript. Finally, when all the fascicles were ready, he added the rubrics and the few lines from D. 24.3.1 at the end of the manuscript in the ink and with the fluidity of script most apparent in the opening books. This conclusion also, incidentally, solves the problem of how the same scribe could write differently when adding D. 24.3.1 on the final folio than he did on the rest of the page.

We have discussed this evidence in detail here because it reveals an important, previously unimagined aspect of the earliest transmission of the Digest: the scribe did not have, when he began his work, a complete manuscript of the *Digestum Vetus*. Apparently, he had only the last part, and acquired the early sections, again in parts, most probably (given the evolution of his script) over a period of time. Put another way, our earliest witness to the medieval Digest—**V**—was copied not from a bound or complete exemplar but in smaller units corresponding to groups of books or, for the second part, divided between one title and another. (It should be noticed that, because of the divisions internal to the first part, this conclusion does not depend on the ascription of the entire work to one scribe.)

If the situation with **V** was typical—and we have no reason to believe that it was not—it helps solve one of the enduring mysteries of the vulgate tradition: the medieval division of the Digest into three parts. Mommsen hypothesized that the medieval division originated in the structure of **S**, which he supposed must have been divided into three or four volumes, but this view has not won much support from recent scholars. Two recent articles have, in a way, reverted to the theory of the progressive acquisition of the Digest. James Whitman, assuming that the Digest was originally in the hands of canonists, suggested that the *Infortiatum* was essentially suppressed for years because it contradicted the canon law on marriage.[73] Wolfgang Müller essentially revived the theory that the *Vetus* and the first half of the *Infortiatum* derived from a manuscript independent of **F**, evidently having overlooked the key passages—especially D. 23.1.10—that demonstrate that the vulgate tradition of the *Vetus* repeats an error that could only have come from **F** itself.[74] In effect, both these scholars abandon Mommsen's conclusion that the entire Digest must both have derived from the Florentina and have been the object of substantial editorial manipulation, but without offering a comprehensive theory that explains the evidence Mommsen discovered.

A more nuanced suggestion came from Hans van de Wouw's study of the *Infortiatum*. He noted that four manuscripts of the *Digestum Vetus*, including **V**, **P**, and **U**, continue into D. 24.3, breaking off in the middle of the inscription to D. 24.3.2, while Turin, Biblioteca Nazionale Universitaria, ms. F. II.14 continues to D. 25.3.5.13, while the contents of the earliest manuscripts of the *Infortiatum* varied

[73] James Whitman, "The Medieval Division of the Digest," *Tijdschrift voor Rechtsgeschiedenis*, 59 (1991): 269–84. On this argument, see also Radding, "Vatican Latin 1406," p. 547 n. 129.

[74] Müller, "Recovery of Justinian's Digest"; see especially the stemma on p. 28.

significantly among themselves. He concluded that the early manuscripts of the *Infortiatum* lacked the end of book 24 and book 25 and also stopped abruptly in mid-title at the words *tres partes* in D. 35.2.82. He cited as evidence manuscripts lacking the *Tres Partes* (as the last section was known at Bologna), including Leipzig, Universitätsbibliothek, ms. 874, Paris Bibliothèque Nationale, ms. lat. 4458, and Monte Cassino 120; manuscripts such as Paris, Bibliothèque Nationale, ms. lat. 4452 and Vatican Library Vat. lat. 1407 where the *Tres Partes* constitutes a separate section, possibly by a different hand; and manuscripts of the *Novum* that apparently had originally included the *Tres Partes*, such as Cambridge, Gonville and Caius College, ms. 271/671 and Edinburgh, University Library, ms. 154. This variation led him to propose that the vulgate archetype was divided into 2 volumes (like the Florentina), but that these volumes became defective soon after entering circulation. Thus, he suggested that the first volume had lost its final fascicle, resulting in the truncation of the *Vetus* to D. 24.2, while the second broke up into multiple parts that the earliest copyists combined to form different combinations.[75]

The evidence of Vat. lat. 1406 points to a process that is somewhat the reverse of that proposed by van de Wouw: rather than large volumes breaking up into smaller pieces, the earliest circulation of the *Vetus*, at least, was in small groups of books. Possibly this was only a temporary expedient, adopted to make a long text rapidly available to readers functioning outside institutions equipped with scriptoria and libraries; but it is also possible that the archetype of the vulgate tradition itself was not actually bound into a book, at least not right away. The main point, however, is that the precise boundaries of the *Vetus* appears to have been arrived at somewhat by chance—linked to the content of the fascicles rather than any plan—and the evidence assembled by van de Wouw suggests that the same was true of the other parts of the Digest. In particular, knowing that the Digest first circulated as fascicles makes it easier to understand how the *Tres Partes*, which begins mid-law, could have had an early life separate from the rest of the later *Infortiatum*.

---

[75] van de Wouw, "Textgeschichte des Infortiatum"; see also Gero Dolezalek, "Index manuscriptorum veterum Infortiati," *Ius Commune*, 11 (1984): 281–87. A more complete survey of how *Vetus* manuscripts end, with additional observations on the problem generally, is provided by Jakobs, "Or signori!," pp. 315–16, and Jakobs, "Das Ende des Digestum vetus."

Paris ms. 4450

Closest in age to **V** is **P**, Paris, Bib. Nat., ms. 4450, a manuscript traditionally and correctly ascribed to the late eleventh/early twelfth century. Like **V**, **P** was copied in a single-column format. [Plate 32] Although several scribes participated in the copying of **P**, none of them wrote as elegantly as the scribe of the Vatican *Vetus*. The manuscript is composed of quaternions, without any trace of the stopping and starting of copying that was so evident in **V**. Changes from one scribe to another often occur within a single gathering. **P** thus gives the impression of having been the work of an organized group, although—since we know of legal manuscripts copied by groups of notaries—we should not assume that it was the work of a traditional scriptorium. The script used is suggestive of northern Italy, but no more precise localization is possible.

P traces back to the same ancestor as **V**: it lacks the introductory constitutions, omits the same laws, and contains the same, revealing, transposition of text in book 23. Whereas **V** gives the impression of being very close to the shared archetype of the *Vetus*, the somewhat later **P** is already too distant from it to add much to what we learned from **V**. The main codicological point of interest, perhaps, is that like **V** it contains a portion of D. 24.3.2—indeed, a significantly longer section than **V** does—confirming that the abrupt ending of the *Vetus* was by no means intentional. The shared ancestry of the two manuscripts, however, makes other divergences between the two of them still more significant, as evidence of the ongoing attention the text of the Digest was receiving even as it was first winning a readership.

Credit for comparing the two early *Vetus* manuscripts goes to Pietro Pescani, who cites 65 passages where **V** and **P** offer significantly different readings, apparently as a result of deliberate interventions into the text.[76] What makes these variants important, however, is that deviations from the text given in **F** are found sometimes in one manuscript and sometimes in the other. Thus, there are several cases where **V** gives the text found in **F** while **P** emends. For example, in

[76] Pietro Pescani, "La posizione del V 1406"; see also his other articles on the Digest: "La *litera Florentina* e *Bononiensis* e la futura edizione del Digesto," *Annali della Facoltà giuridica dell'Università di Camerino*, 32 (1966): 299–336; "Ancora sui manoscritti del Digesto," BIDR, 82 (1978): 169–83; "Studi sul 'Digestum Vetus,'" BIDR, 84 (1981):159–250; "Origine delle lezioni della litera Bononiensis superiori a quella della litera Florentina," BIDR, 85 (1982): 205–82; "La Scoperta del 'Bononiensis': sue forme," BIDR, 88 (1985): 383–96.

D. 17.2.83 (line 21 in the *editio maior*), where **V** and **F** have *massis duorum dominorum flatis*, **P** gives *conflatis* instead of *flatis*; this latter reading also appears in other manuscripts of the Vulgata tradition and was even added back into **V** by a later corrector. In D. 2.14.7, both **F** and **V** provide a text that is readily susceptible to misunderstanding if not punctuated (as most medieval manuscripts were not): *utrumque itaque recte placet, et quod Iulianus et quod Pomponius. Ait praetor* . . .; **P** and the later corrector of **V** avoided ambiguity by a simple transposition of the last two words, making it clear that the praetor, not Pomponius, is the speaker of the passage that follows. In D.17.1.57 (l.35), **P** corrects the sense of the reading given in both **F** and **V**, *Publiciana actione non utiliter acturum*, by changing *utiliter* to *inutiliter*, the reading accepted by Mommsen. Other passages show **P** agreeing with **F** while **V** offers a variant. For example, in D. 4.8.8 (l.19), where **F** and the original copyist of **P** agree in reading *sed si ita compromissum sit, ut vel alterutrius sententia valeat, Titium cogendum*, **V** inserts the words *Ulp. scribit* between *valeat* and *Titium*, evidently to provide a verb to govern the final phrase. In this case, both **V** and **P** were later further emended to read *Iulianus scribit*—possibly, Pescani suggests, in recognition of the fact that the author of this passage (Paulus) never cited Ulpianus. **V** and **P** diverge from **F** and each other, finally, in D.1.14.3(27–28). Whereas **F** reads:

> atquin verum est eum praetura functum. et tamen videamus: si servus quamdiu latuit, indignitate praetoria functus sit, quid dicemus?

V replaces *indignitate* with *dignitate*—the reading accepted by Mommsen—and **P** with *indempnitate*.[77] Pescani's list (only partially summarized here) is not exhaustive. For example, Kantorowicz's examples of changing nouns from accusative to ablative appear in **P** but not in **V**, suggesting that those emendations, too, were later than the shared archetype **S**.

What is significant for our purposes is the evidence that the emendation of the Digest was an ongoing process rather than a one-time effort. Indeed, one could argue that the two surviving eleventh-century manuscripts document three different sets of emendations from the late eleventh century: one set shared by **P** and **V** that we can provisionally assign to their ancestor manuscript, and two further

---

[77] Pescani notes that Mommsen accepted **V**'s reading of this passage despite the fact that repunctuation would save the reading of **F**. "Ancora," pp. 170–71.

sets of emendations witnessed by only one of the two manuscripts. If we say that each set of emendations reflects the work of only one scholar, we have a minimum of three scholars, all active before 1100, with the learning to correct the Digest and the interest in doing so. This is already an environment with multiple scholars rather than Kantorowicz's solitary genius. But it is hard to see what reason there could be for drawing a line at three scholars rather than four or six or nine, especially since the evidence points to five different manuscripts: **P** and **V**, their two immediate exemplars, and the common ancestor of those exemplars. We cannot be far wrong if we assume an intellectual community that at any time numbered six to ten scholars—not large, certainly, but not smaller than the number of scholars making serious contributions to the study of the liberal arts in late eleventh-century France.[78]

The *Infortiatum* and the *Digestum Novum*

Apart from **V** and **P**, only two other manuscripts appear to be notably earlier than the mid-twelfth century. Both are fragments. In 1971, Robert Röhle called attention to a fragment of the *Digestum Novum* now preserved as Kassel, Stadtbibliothek 2° Mss. iurid. 100,11.[79] Although Röhle noted an attribution of this manuscript to the mid-twelfth century, we believe that it is somewhat earlier and thus the earliest known example of the *Novum*. Similarly from the first half of the twelfth century, but probably later than the Kassel fragment, is the earliest surviving fragment of the *Infortiatum*. Two bifolia of this manuscript, which can be no later than the early twelfth century, are preserved as guard pages for Vatican Library, Pal. lat. 772.[80] The leaves, which contain portions of D. 28, adopt the two-column format that was

[78] Radding and Clark, *Medieval Architecture*, pp. 27–33.

[79] Robert Röhle, "Digestorum fragmentum Casellanum, 2° Mss. Iurid. 100,11" ZSS RA, 88 (1971): 356–76; see also the description in Marita Kremer, ed., *Die Handschriften der Murhardschen Bibliothek der Stadt Kassel und Landesbibliothek*, band 2, *Manuscripta Iuridica* (Wiesbaden, 1969).

[80] Some aspects of the script of the fragment in BAV, Pal. lat. 772 are comparatively modern, especially the overlapping of curves facing in opposite directions. Other elements, however, point to a dating earlier than that reported by Röhle: the use of the ampersand for *et* including at the end of a word, the alternation of upright and inclined shafts for the letter *d*, and an apparatus of majuscule letters that usually conserves characteristics typical of an earlier period.

already on the way to becoming the standard layout for Roman law manuscripts. It is, finally, worth noting that the text into which these leaves were bound is a *Lombarda*—indeed, a *Lombarda* into which was bound a leaf containing a long commentary to Roth. 153 from the *Expositio*.

While these fragments are too brief to offer help for studies of the text of the Digest, they do confirm that all parts of the Digest were in circulation by the beginning of the twelfth century. But the Palatine fragment tells us a little more. To begin with, a *probatio pennae* shows that it was already a part of Pal. lat. 772 no later than 1174, at which time it was in Florence. This manuscript thus must have been dismembered and converted into binding material only a few decades after it was originally copied. Such a short useful life makes a dramatic contrast with the centuries of use enjoyed by **V**, and perhaps explains why we have no early Digest manuscripts except from the two *Vetus* manuscripts. Van de Wouw's hypothesis that the sections which later became the *Infortiatum* had their earliest circulation as smaller sections offers one possible explanation for this early obsolescence: lacking the *Tres Partes*, the manuscript from which the Palatine fragment came had been rendered valueless by the standardization of the parts of the Digest. Even if this were the case, however, one might have expected that the second part would simply have been added. Another possibility is suggested by the serious lacunae equivalent to 38 lines in Mommsen's edition between D. 28.3.19 *adhuc altero omittente* . . . and D. 28.4.2 . . . *licet unus inductionis causam praebuit* (f. 93r). Though the gap is not as smooth as one might expect if the Palatine fragment were meant to fill in missing laws in an *Epitome Digestorum*, it does offer additional evidence that the earliest textual tradition was more difficult than one would expect from a straightforward copy of the Florentina.

Conclusion

It is easy to see why the reception of the Digest has been such a troublesome topic. Historians have naturally assumed that the textual tradition of the Digest was governed by the same practices that affected other texts of comparable importance and antiquity—essentially those of monastic scriptoria. Yet the errors in the Digest went beyond those seen in other manuscripts, such as skipping a line, replacing obscure terms or mistakenly improving a difficult syntax. Not only had the text been cut up into large blocks, only gradually stabilizing in the three parts known by the mid-twelfth century, but the text deriving from the Florentina had been contaminated in some places with readings from a second source and in others places corrected with such intelligence that it was difficult always to be confident which readings were authentic and which were emendations.

The Digest's first readers were not priests or monks whose principal intellectual experiences came from the study of sacred works—texts it would be presumptuous to improve beyond correcting the most obvious linguistic errors—but laymen and jurists: just the men for whom the Digest would have been of the greatest interest. Their intellectual experiences were therefore different from what historians have commonly assumed about the first readers of the Digest. Accustomed to documents and books that required no particular reverence, and that perhaps had not been copied with the greatest skill, they were already adept at using textual criticism of a kind not seen until much later in ecclesiastical texts or the liberal arts. These traditions of emending texts, indeed, survived into the Bolognese period of legal studies, where their effects have complicated the lives of editors ever since. These early jurists also had to contend with limits on their resources very different from what priests or monks would have encountered. In particular, since they lacked ready access to organized scriptoria and large numbers of trained copyists, they had to find ways to circulate new—and very long—texts within the limits of what they could accomplish individually or in groups.

Apart from a few fragments, only two surviving manuscripts are early enough to bear witness to the first phases of the Digest's medieval history: Paris, BN., ms. 4450, meticulously studied by Mommsen, and the significantly earlier (and far less studied) Vatican Library, Vat. lat. 1406. For a manuscript copied by a single scribe, the Vatican manuscript is an extraordinarily complex artifact. It alone permits us to glimpse a phase when scribes were working, not with pre-existing manuscripts, but with text circulating in fascicles—an obvious compromise between the eagerness of readers to get their hands on the Digest and their limited means of copying it. Through the additions and meticulous corrections it acquired over time, moreover, Vat. lat. 1406 even reveals efforts to correct and standardize the text of the Digest that went into the thirteenth century.

As for the text itself, the Paris and Vatican manuscripts agree on the main points: the omission of some laws, notably all of Justinian's prefatory constitutions, and the occasional inversion of the order of others. These characteristics are so unlike the errors one sees in monastic manuscripts that one must consider the possibility that the Digest, like the Code, was first reduced to a collection of extracts and then restored to its full length on the basis of that epitome. What gives this hypothesis particular importance, of course, is that such a history would also explain how the vulgate Digest came to include readings from a manuscript other than the Florentina. But the extensive manipulation of the text, even in this early period, is also demonstrated by the divergences in readings between these two oldest manuscripts of the *Digestum Vetus*.

None of this can be readily imagined looking at manuscripts from the mid-twelfth century—the period from which come the earliest complete manuscripts of the *Infortiatum* and *Digestum Novum* and even the Leipzig and Padua manuscripts used by Mommsen for the *Digestum Vetus*. Conventions, perhaps arrived at through teaching,[81] were already standardizing the text by then, while copies made earlier were now rendered obsolete by an apparent abundance of manuscripts that met the new norms. And it is only by returning to the eleventh century—to the men and their manuscripts—that we can hope further to unravel the mysteries of the medieval Digest.

---

[81] For observations on the role of masters in stabilizing the divisions of the Digest, see Jakobs, "Das Ende des Digestum Vetus," pp. 31 ff.

CONCLUSION

The manuscripts discussed in this book include several that rank among the most challenging of all medieval manuscripts. Written by multiple scribes, some of whom had elementary abilities or wrote with documentary scripts, manuscripts such as the Pistoia *Epitome*, Berlin 273, or even—in other ways—the Vat. lat. 1406 pose exceptional problems to anyone attempting to understand when, how, and by whom they were produced. One cannot be surprised that nineteenth-century scholars made mistakes dealing with them. It is less easy to understand how their errors came to be perpetuated so long. The absence of citations should have been a warning to anyone who thought about it: works that are studied are cited, even in the Middle Ages. In fact, as we have seen, the works of Justinian's *Corpus*—with the exception always of the Novels—were virtually unknown between the sixth and the eleventh centuries. Early medieval manuscripts of these works amount to no more than two fragments of the Institutes, one of which also contained an unknown quantity of the Digest; not even that much survives for the Code. Evidence that these works were discussed at all is hardly more substantial, consisting mainly of a few unsystematic collections and a handful of elementary citations, mainly in papal letters from the third quarter of the ninth century.

This situation began to change only in the late tenth and early eleventh century. Indications that the Justinianic books were starting to find readers come from a number of directions: a few *arengae* from Ravenna, the *Summa Perusina* in and around Rome, the Bamberg Institutes, again from Rome. A different level of engagement, however, is apparent in the increasingly expert references to the *Corpus* found in the works of the professional jurists centered on the old Lombard capital of Pavia. One sees the use of the Institutes already in the generation of Bonifilius, whose first appearance in the documentary record comes from the 1010s; by the 1040s the Code had also been taken up; and while it is harder to be certain about the Digest a date around mid-century could not be far off. To judge from citations of the *Corpus*, such as the Marturi plea or the glosses in the *Expositio* and *Walcausina*, these studies went beyond collecting maxims and definitions to a systematic examination of Roman rules and procedures.

The role of these legal professionals in the history of Justinian's works goes a long way toward explaining some of the most unusual features of the manuscripts. As laymen lacking ready access to organized scriptoria and large numbers of trained copyists, these early jurists often had to copy books themselves—either individually or in groups. The longest of Justinian's texts, the Code and the Digest, were several times longer than the Lombard laws even with their commentaries: so long that they may simply have overtaxed the means for producing books for study. In response to this problem, the judges contented themselves with the *Epitome Codicis*, a collection of the laws most important to them that was expanded over time as new materials were extracted by return visits to the ancient manuscripts. We saw in chapter six that something similar may also have been done with the Digest.

The key text in this early period seems to have been the Code. Although it is a text that can seem sterile to us, eleventh-century jurists seem to have found endless fascination in it, perhaps in part because as a compendium of legislation it corresponded so closely to their manuscripts of Lombard law. It is the most cited work in the *Expositio* and the work for which we possess the greatest number of early manuscripts. The manuscripts also capture the intensity of scholarly work applied to the Code: the layers on layers of supplements and glosses that upwards of 40 hands applied to the Pistoia *Epitome Codicis* within a few decades; the multiple reconstructions of the integral Code, witnessing the efforts of groups in different regions; the fifteen copyists of Berlin ms. 273; the daring recasting of the entire format of the text represented by Montpellier ms. 82. The lack of interest in the history of the Code in the eleventh century must therefore be counted among the most serious failures of historians dealing with the juristic renaissance.

Given the feverish study of Justinian's texts in the third quarter of the eleventh century, it is not surprising the discipline itself soon underwent a significant transformation. The restoration of the Code and the first manuscripts of the Digest both seem to date from the 1070s and 1080s. No less significant, perhaps, is the absence of work dedicated to the Lombard law that can be attributed to the 1080s or later. Taken together, these trends suggest that the energy, expertise, and personnel which had developed in previous decades was turning more exclusively to Roman law, the "hot topic" of the moment. As is typical with anything concerning the history of legal studies, too little narrative evidence survives for us to be able to trace this process in any detail: these were not men who wrote about themselves or each other, and the earliest surviving efforts to tell the story of these events were the self-serving and mythologizing comments of thirteenth-century Bolognese masters. Yet for our more limited purpose of tracing the history that created the medieval texts of Justinian's books, the decades around 1100 marks an appropriate conclusion. Later scholars continued to suggest emendations and note collations, and it may not have been until the mid-twelfth century that the separation of the *Tres Libri* from the Code and the divisions of the Digest were completely stable. But they were working with texts that derive directly from manuscripts similar to those discussed in this book, and within a disciplinary context that had largely taken shape in the second half of the eleventh century.

APPENDIX

Vatican City, Biblioteca Apostolica Vaticana, Vat. lat. 1406

Digestum Vetus

Italian, Sec XI, second half, with replacement leaves, fascicles, and rewritten passages from the XII, XIII, and XIII/XIV centuries.

mm 345 × 225

The lining, done with drypoint on the verso of the first folio with the fascicle assembled and open, frames a full-page writing with the number of lines and lines written ranging between 45 and 50. Pricking for the lining was accomplished with the fascicle assembled and folded. Mediocre parchment, yellowish and occasionally greyish in color, with a mostly moderate contrast between flesh and skin sides and with frequent defects (holes) in preparation. Occasionally the fascicles include smaller than normal membranes or inferior sheets that have worn badly in margins (e.g., ff. 84–85, 144–45).

Pages: ii + 202 + ii. Numbering, which begins with the second, parchment guard page, is in arabic numbers in ink by a modern hand, with corrections of occasional errors by the same hand.

Fascicles: I quat. (ff. 2–9); II quat. (ff. 10–17); III quat. (ff. 18–25); IV quat. (ff. 26–33); V quint. (ff. 34–43, the bifolium 36/41 is composite); VI three singletons (ff. 44–46); VII quat. (ff. 47–54); VIII quat. (ff. 55–62, the bifolium 57/60 is composite); IX quat. (ff. 63–70); X bifolium (ff. 71–72, inserted in the first half of sec. XIII; f. 72v is blank); XI quat. (73–80); XII quat. (ff. 81–88, the bifolium 83/86 is composite); XIII quat. (ff. 89–96); XIV quat. plus a singleton (ff. 97–105, inserted in sec. XIII/XIV, agg. f. 97); XV quat. (ff. 106–113); XVI quat. (ff. 114–121); XVII bifolium plus a singleton (ff. 122–124, inserted in sec. XIII, agg. f. 122); XVIII quat. (ff. 125–132); XIX quat. (ff. 133–140); XX quat. (ff. 141–148); XXI quat. (ff. 149–156); XXII quat. (ff. 157–164); XXIII quat. (ff. 165–172, the bifolium 167/170 was inserted in the second half of the sec. XII); XXIV quat. less a bifolium (ff. 173–178, lacks leaves between ff. 173/174 and 177/178); XXV quat. (ff. 179–186); XXVI quat. (ff. 187–194); XXVII quat. (ff. 195–202). The fascicles begin with the hair side and respect the alternation hair and flesh sides except in the second fascicle where ff. 12–15 are irregular; in that fascicle, red ties signs alert the binder to the correct order of the pages.

There are at least three sets of signatures for the fascicles. The oldest, contemporary with the copying and perhaps done by the copyist, has been erased. Consisting of roman numbers, in one case accompanied by the siglum *qr* in a nexus) it can be read under ultraviolet light centered on the last verso of fasc. XX (numbered .III.), XXI (.IIII.), XXII (.V.), XXIII (.VI.), XXIV (qr .VII.), XXV (.VIII.). Signatures in roman numbers, perhaps from the thirteenth century, are visible at the center of the verso of the last folio of fasc. I (only partially visible owing to subsequent trimming of the margin) to IV and VII–XIII. Retraced more than once with darker ink, they show a skip in the numbering because from fasc. VII (numbered VI) the numbers are reduced by one. Signatures from sec. XIV in roman numerals can be seen in the lower outside corner of the *recto* of the first page of fasc. II–IV, VI–IX, XI–XIII, XVI–XXVI, and run from .II. to .XXVI. Bifolium signatures in roman numerals, not contemporary with the manuscript, are placed in the lower right corner of the recto of the first four folios of fasc. XXI. In the lower margins of ff. 158v, 159v and 161v a twelfth-century hand wrote the catchword for the following page. Catchwords in the hand of the copyist are placed in the internal corner of the lower margin of the verso of every page.

The original decoration of the manuscript, sober and essential, did not extend beyond decorative initials at the beginning of each book employing plant or (in one case) animal motifs. Some kind of decorations were part of the original plan of the book, as witnessed by the spaces left blank to accommodate it, some of which were filled in only during the thirteenth century; but there is a noticable disparity in the implementation between the first series of initials (books I–VII, to f. 62v, book VII, *P*) in which the design of the letter was drawn in pen in the same ink as the text and then crudely traced over and partially colored in red; and a second series in which the letters were executed directly in red, giving a more elegant impression. Marking the transition between the two schemes are the initial *M* and *U* of, respectively, books VIII (f. 73r) and IX (f. 79v) that, although accomplished directly in red ink, are less accomplished. The second series of initials can be seen in books X, XVI (*P*, the only initial to portray an animal and to be *full-shaft* retouched with ochre), and XVIII–XXIII; these are all effected with precision and accuracy, using a rich variety of acanthus and geometric forms as well as nodal weavings. Except for the initial on f. 73r (in reality a simple majuscule initial), which is certainly in the hand of the copyist, it is impossible to tell whether the scribe or someone else was responsible for the decorations, although it does seem that the red-lead ink used was of the same tonality as that in which the rubrics were written; some decorative motifs, moreover, are reused in apparently different letters, such as those on f. 79v, f. 143v, and 185v. From f. 79v onwards the list of titles that begins the books is highlighted in red ink, although these do not go beyond book XV. The initials of the *inscriptiones* alternate more or less regularly between red and black (that is, the yellow-brown ink used for the text); an analogous alternation was applied to subsections (roughly red-red/black-black). The scribe often left space for letters to be inserted in red, writing the letter to insert small enough for it to be concealed by the rubrication. Except for later corrections, rubrics are in the hand of the copyist and were applied subsequent to the writing of the text, as evidenced by the frequency with which they had to be written in the outside margins. Subsequently, probably in sec. XIII, all the apparatus initials were retraced (and sometimes corrected) with filigrane letters alternating in red and blue (or black). Some modest decorative interventions in blue into the older series of letters (e.g., f. 73r and 79v) belong to this phase.

There are running titles in red, contemporary with the manuscript, from f. 73r to f. 88r; the same hand, writing in ink, continued them to f. 96v. They resume between ff. 128–134 and 144–148, but only for the number of the book and written on the recto. Elsewhere there are running titles in ink, perhaps from the thirteenth century and not always visible, alternating on both faces, *l*(ibro) on the *verso* and the book number on the recto *recto*.

There are at least ten hands present in the manuscript. The oldest, (**A**), was responsible for the original and largest part of the manuscript: ff. 2r–70v, 73r–96v, 106r–122v, 125r–166v, 168r–169v, 171r–202v. **A** wrote a regular, very elegant Italian caroline minuscule, lacking in any regional characteristics; his script inclined slightly to the right and manifests occasional variations in letter size, in the rigidity of the letters, and in the color of the ink which shifts progressively from the yellow-brown in the first fascicles to the brown of the last; changes in the tonality of the ink are particularly apparent between ff. 46v and 47r, 70v and 73r, 121v and 125r, all of which correspond to the beginning of a new fascicle, as well as on ff. 137v l. 14 *adversus te | venditori competit*, and 172v l. 20 *extimandum. Idem Iulianus ait | si* ‹*a*› *magistro*). The characteristics of **A**'s script, found in both halves of the manuscript, include: use of both forms of *d* (with straight and inclined shaft); use of both *et* as a nexus and as a tironian note; use of *æ* as a nexus and the *e* with cedilla; the enclitic particle *-que* abbreviated with *q7* and the pronoun with *q˜*, with the cedilla added to the eye of the letter when needed to indicate the dipthong; the nexuses *qd* and *qs* for *quod* and *quis*; the ligature *ri*, short and elegant, along with untied forms; a high and narrow ligature *st* along with the rarer but still found *ct* (e.g. f. 86r, l. 27 from the top *delicti*; f. 132v, l. 32 from the top *facta*; f. 142r, r. 8 from the bottom *redacte*); an acute *u* used, by preference, at the end of the line but also to save space; the insular symbol for *enim*. An entirely singular usage of this scribe is the execution of the top of the ligature *ct* in a way that leaves it divided between the *c* and *t*, both of which preserve a portion of the stroke of the ligature (see, for example, f. 79r, ll. 13/14 from the top *nocturnam*; f. 140r, ll. 20/21 from the top *deduc|to*; f. 145v, ll. 26/27 from the top *redacte*); the same treatment, with loss of part of the ligature, can be seen in the assimilation of *cs* (see f. 89r, ll. 17/18 from the top *accione*). Finally, special mention must be given to the rich variety of his upper-case alphabet, including at least two kinds of *A*, with a minuscule form of greater size and a capital form with triangulation at the base and the right-hand stroke full or redoubled and hollow (a model also found for the verticle strokes of the *M*); two kinds of *M* each executed in two different ways: an uncial model with either rounded or cuspid strokes, and a capital model with full or hollow strokes; of the *U* in two forms (acute with little triangular strokes completing the shaft, or following the minuscule model with four strokes but enlarged). Significant, finally, is the letter *Q* executed with three strokes and two motions with the stroke on the line elongated toward the right. All these characteristics, even the most distinctive, are present throughout the manuscript, disproving the hypothesis offered by Pescani and Santoni that the work was divided between two scribes. The superficial difference between the first and second parts, rather, is to be explained by the fact that the copying was done in stages, with the second half copied first. Supporting this hypothesis, moreover, is the circumstance that the numbering of the original signatures apparently began with the present fasc. XVIII.

Following **A** in chronological order are the four caroline hands from the second half of the twelfth century present in the replacement bifolium ff. 167/170 (**B**, **C**, **D** e **F**). The last of these, **F** (f. 170v), notable for its hesitant and inelegant execution and limited familiarity with the calligraphy of book hands, is also the hand responsible for restoring some rubrics elsewhere in the ms. (e.g., f. 83v, 9.3r). Two hands from the first half of sec. XIII (**G** and **H**, respectively ff. 71r–72r to the words *heredem rem vendicare* of D. 7.9.7, and the rest of f. 72r) are responsible for the replacement fasc. X. Both wrote a non-typified Italian gothic, with **G** using an average module and greater regularity and **H** writing smaller and with less elegance. Also belonging to the thirteenth century is the little non-typified Italian gothic belonging to hand **I**, responsible for all of fasc. XVII. Last chronologically are the two hands **J** (ff. 97r–101r) and **K** (ff. 101v–105r), from late sec. XIII or the early fourteenth century, that were responsible for fasc. XVII. Of the two, the former wrote a mixed gothic minuscule with chancery elements while the second, writing a larger module, wrote an inelegant, rigid gothic with contrasting strokes and serrated lines.

Apart from the replacement fascicles, several passages omitted from the original text were later added to the margins. These additions consist of:

1) f. 24r, 3.2.16
2) f. 44r, 4.8.22
3) f. 53v, 5.3.18
4) f. 56v, 5.3.38
5) f. 59v, 6.1.35
6) f. 85r, 9.4.13
7) f. 87r, 10.1.9 e 10.1.13 (in Latin)
8) f. 174r, 21.1.31.24
9) f. 184r, in pencil 22.3.29 (cfr. Mommsen, p. 649, nt. 1)
10) f. 184v, 22.5.5
11) f. 192r, 23.3.70
12) f. 196r, 23.4.16 and l'*inscriptio* di 23.4.17

Of these, only the first can be described as contemporary with **A**; all the rest are later. Two different hands from the second half of sec. XII were responsible for nos. 4 and 7. No. 2 was first added by a glossator, from the second half of sec. XII) adding the law in his usual tiny script; subsequently a hand of sec. XII/XIII—the same as appears on f. 56r—erased and rewrote the addition, although making an error in the *inscriptio* that he then had to erase and correct.

The glosses offer a rather rich panorama of hands. Some were written in a minuscule so reduced in size as to lose any geographical or datable characteristics; others, that is the apparatus of *loci paralleli*, almost all of which was erased except for fasc. XV, and the stratum of glosses (including some *a grappolo*) were copied by a single hand from the end of sec. XII or the early thirteenth century.

Fascicle XIV is a palimpsest. Almost all of the *scriptio prior* is entirely erased, but a documentary matrix is apparent and with ultraviolet light one can read in the upper margin of f. 100r: «In Christi nomine. Millesimo [ducentesimo] octuagesimo primo, ind(ictione) nona», as well as the names «Symone syndico» and «Rudolfinus procurator». The parchment probably belonged to a court register, possibly of a city (the term *iudex* recurs frequently.)

In the lower margin of f. 2r one can see the remains of an almost entirely erased notation of ownership. With the aid of ultraviolet light one can make out a notarial *signum* of probably late date and a series of references to books of the Corpus iuris: «(S) C[. . . . . .] .XIIII., [in]d(icione) .VII., die marcii .XI. int(rante) sete(m)b(r)e [.] Digestu(m) e(st) d(omi)ni [. . . . . .] d(e) [. . . . . .] | [.]e ‹*forse la prima lettera è una* c, *al di sopra si osserva un segno abbr. generico per lineetta orizz.*› mur(?) ‹*le lettere sono sovrastate da un segno abbr. generico per lineetta orizz.*› con[. . . . . .] ‹*lettura dubbia*› et iudice et Digestum novum et Infortiatum et Tres partes et su[(m)]a [. . . . . . | . . . .]tu(m) d(enarios) p(arvos)».[1] On f. 4r Francesca Santoni read an erased ownership mark as «. . . çardus de Pançano,» whom she suggested could be the Wizardus or Guizardus of the modenese family of Ruberia (*Erberia*) who was elected consul of Modena in 1187;[2] unfortunately for this hypothesis, however, ultraviolet light leaves no doubt that the correct reading is «Raçardus de Pan[ç]an(o)», written in a hand of sec. XIII. On f. 6r, in the upper right margin, a partially erased note in a hand of sec. XIV reads: «Dominus Petrus debet dare d. [. . . . . .] de tassas, ‹*così*› .X. d. [. . .]». On f. 112, in the lower margin, the same hand had written «Dominus Pe.». On f. 152 r, in the upper margin, partially washed-away note in a hand of sec. XIV reads: «Dominus ‹*segue* i *principiata*› Iohannes Bonus de B[. . .] ‹*lac. non determinabile*›».

---

1 Santoni, "Copisti editores," p. ** argues that the end of the note reads *p(ro) centu(m) l(ibris)* and probably refers to the purchase price of the manuscript, perhaps including the *Infortiatum* mentioned on the previous line.

2 Santoni, "Copisti editores," p. **

Also belonging to the history of the manuscript are some notations that Giulio Battelli described as indications of *pecia*[3]—an interpretation challenged, however, by Frank Soetermeer who suggested that they simply had to do with copying.[4] These notations are found on *16v,* 29r (2), 39r, 41r, *44r, 52r, 53v, *57v, *59r, *59v, 61r, 62v, *70r, *70v, *98v, 148r, 170r, and *174r (asterisks mark those not noticed by Battelli and Soetermeer). In all of these cases, the writer accompanied their insertion by first inserting in the text, at the point indicated by the note, a sign in the form of a circumflex with a dot inside; sometimes the word is divided by a vertical bar (sometimes the bar is placed in the space between two words) as if to indicate a precise break point. In the margin, usually one of the lateral margins, he repeated the same sign as accompanied the note. Sometimes, as can be seen in the above examples, the sign is omitted in the text; in such cases, the word to notice is added in the margin. Elsewhere the same hand frequently places the same "circumflex" above other words, with or without the division bar; in such cases, the marginal notations are often missing, or are more meager. Examples of such interventions can be seen on ff. 11r (3), 51r, 57r, 58r, 60v, 73v, 74r (2), 74v, 75r (2), 76r (2), 93r (2), 171r, 172, 174r. The precision of such notes, which indicate exactly where a break is to occur, as well as a reference on f. 29r ("hic debeo complere folium Thomaxini") indicating multiple scribes at work, lend a high degree of probability to Battelli's original suggestion that *pecia* markings are involved. An indication of the date of this work, moreover, results from the appearance of such signs in fasc. XIV—as already noted a palimpsest whose earlier strata of writing can be dated to 1281.

A final point to notice with regard to the history of the manuscript is found on f. 133v where one finds a reference suggesting that the text had been collated with the ancient manuscript of the Digest now in the Biblioteca Laurenziana. At the text «si tibi mandavero quod mea non intereat» of 17.1.6.4, the Vatican manuscript omits «mea non»—a lacuna that a later corrector fills with an interlinear note. Subsequent to this intervention, another hand found at several points in the manuscript, including a citation of the *Infortiatum*

---

[3] «Che si tratti d'indicazioni di *pecie* è fuori di dubbio, specialmente considerando quelle ai fogli 39, 41v, 53v e 61, che sembrano appartenenre ad una stessa numerazione progressiva», Battelli, *Ricerche sulla pecia* cit., p. 31.

[4] Soetermeer, *Utrumque ius* cit., p. 247.

on f. 139r, inserted a tie-sign here, writing in the margin: «Pisi(s) v(idendum) e(st) no(n)».

The binding is from the eighteenth century with paper boards covered with marocco. The mosaics on the spine are impressed with the family crest of Pope Pius VI as well as of the cardinal librarian Francesc saverio de Zelada. The pastedowns as well as the first and last flyleaves are marblized.

BIBLIOGRAPHY

Primary Sources

Adnotationes codicum domini Justiniani, ed. F. Patetta, BIDR, 12 (1900).

Albericus Casinensis, *Brevarium de dictamine*, in L. Rockinger, ed. *Briefsteller und Formelbücher des elften bis vierzehnten Jahrhunderts. Quellen und Erörterungen zur bayreischen und deutschen Geschichte* 9,1 (Munchen, 1863).

——. *Flores Rhetorici*, ed. Don Mauro Inguanez and H. M. Willard in *Miscellanea Cassinese*, 14 (Monte Cassino, 1938).

Alberti, A. *La "Glossa Torinese" e le altre glosse del ms. D.III.13 della Biblioteca Nazionale di Torino* (Torino, 1933).

——. *La glossa di Casamari alle Istituzioni di Giustiniano* (Milano, 1937).

Anselmi episcopi Lucensis Collectio canonum una cum collectione minore, ed. F. Thaner (Innsbruck, 1906, 1915).

Anselmus de Besate. *Rhetorimachia*, ed. Karl Manitius [MGH, *Quellen zur Geistesgeschichte des Mittelalters* 2] (Weimar, 1958). *Aristoteles Latinus* ed. Lacombe, George et al. (Bruges and Paris, 1939–76).

Benericetti, Ruggero. *Le carte del decimo secolo nell'Archivio arcivescovile di Ravenna* (Ravenna, 1999–2002).

Besse, Jean-Claude. "Collectionis *Anselmo Dedicata* Liber Primus," *Revue de droit canonique*, 9 (1959): 207–96.

Capitularia regum francorum 1, ed. A. Boretius, MGH, *Capit.* 1 (Hannover, 1883).

Chiappelli, Luigi. *La glossa pistoiese al Codice giustinianeo tratta dal manoscritto capitolare di Pistoia* (Torino, 1885).

Chronicle of Theophanes Confessor: Byzantine and Near Eastern History, AD 284–813, trans. by Cyril Mango and Roger Scott (Oxford, 1997).

Codex Iustinianus, ed. Paul Krüger (Berlin, 1877).

Collectio Librorum Iuris Anteiustiniani, ed. Paul Krüger (Berlin, 1878).

Conrat, Max. "La glossa di Colonia alle istituzioni," *Archivio Giuridico*, (1885): 105–25.

Constitutiones et acta publica imperatorem et regum, ed. L. Weiland, vol. I [MGH, *Leges*, sectio 4] (Hannover, 1893).

Corpus iuris civilis. Ad fidem codicum manuscriptorum aliorumque subsidiorum criticorum recensuit, commentario perpetuo instruxit Eduardus Schrader. (Berlin, 1832).

Corpus Iuris Civilis, editio stereotypa (Berlin, 1877).

Crescenzi, Victor. *La glossa di Poppi alle Istituzioni di Giustiniano* [Fonti per la Storia d'Italia, 114] (Roma, 1990).

Digesta Iustiniani Augusti, ed. Th. Mommsen. (Berlin, 1870).

Digestorum seu Pandectarum libri quinquaginta ex Florentinis Pandectis repraesentati (Florentia, 1553).

Fantuzzi, Marco. *Monumenti ravennati de'secoli di mezzo, per la maggior parte inediti* (Venezia, 1801–4).

Federici, P. *Rerum Pomposianarum historia* (Roma, 1781).

Fitting, Hermann. *Institutionenglossen des Gualcausus* (Berlin, 1891).

Institutiones, ed. Paul Krüger (Berlin, 1867).

Institutionum graeca paraphrasis Theophilo antecessori vulgo tributa, ed. C. Ferrini (Berlin, 1884–97).

Iuliani Epitome latina Novellarum Iustiniani, ed. Gustav Haenel, (Leipzig, 1873).

Justiniani Augusti Digestorum seu Pandectarum codex Florentinus olim Pisanus phototypice expressus (Roma, 1902–10).

Justiniani Augusti Pandectarum. Codex florentinus. (Firenze, 1988).

Krüger, Paul. "Die Turner Institutionenglosse," *Zeitschrift für Rechtsgeschichte*, 7 (1868): 44–78.

Lex romana canonice compta. Testo di leggi romano-canoniche del sec. IX pubblicato sul ms. parigino Bibl. Nat. 12448, ed. C. G. Mor (Pavia, 1927).

Liber Papiensis, ed. A. Boretius, *Liber Legis Langobardorum Papiensis*, MGH, *Leges* IV (Hannover, 1868), pp. 289–585.

Manaresi, C. *I placiti del «Regnum Italiae»* [Fonti per la storia d'Italia, vols. 92, 96, 97] (Rome, 1955–60).

Mittarelli, J.-B. *Annales Camalulenses ordines Sancti Benedicti*, (Venetiae, 1755–73).

Quaestiones ac Monita, ed. A. Boretius, *Liber Legis Langobardorum Papiensis*, MGH, *Leges* IV (Hannover, 1868), pp. 590–94.

Ratramni Corbeiensis Monachi Contra Graecorum Opposita Romanam Ecclesiam Infamantium Libri Quatuor, PL 121: 225–346.

Regesto di Farfa, ed. I. Giorgi and U. Balzani (Roma, 1879–1914).

Petrus Damianus. *Die Briefe des Petrus Damiani*, ed. Kurt Reindel, *Die Briefe der deutschen Kaiserzeit*, vol. IV, part 1] (Weimar, 1983).

S. Maria in Via Lata Tabularium, ed. L. M. Hartmann and M. Merores (Wien, 1895–1913).

Schiaparelli, Luigi. *Codice Diplomatico Longobardo* [Fonti per la Storia d'Italia, 62, 63] (Roma, 1929–32).

Theophanis Chronographia, ed. Carolus de Boor (Leipzig, 1883).

Die Urkunden Heinrichs III., ed. H. Bresslau and P. Kehr [MGH, *Diplomata. Die Urkunden der deutschen Könige und Kaiser*, 5] (Berlin, 1931).

Secondary Sources

Alberti, A. "Ricerche su alcune glosse alle Istituzioni e sulla 'summa Institutionum' pseudoirneriana," *Pubblicazioni dell'Istituto di scienze giuridiche, economiche, politiche e sociali dell'Università di Messina*, 5 (Milano, 1935): 21–94.

Arnaldi, G. "Giovanni Immonide e la cultura a Roma al tempo di Giovanni VIII," *Bullettino dell'Istituto Storico Italiano per il Medio Evo e Archivio Muratoriano*, 78 (1956): 33–89.

——. "Giovanni Immonide e la cultura a Roma al tempo di Giovanni VIII: una retractatio," in *Europa medievale e mondo bizantino: contatti effettivi e possibilità di studi comparati: Tavola rotonda del XVIII Congresso del CISH—Montréal, 29 agosto 1995*, ed. Arnaldi and G. Cavallo, (Rome, 1997) pp. 163–77.

——. "Papato, arcivescovi e vescovi nell'età post-carolingia," in *Vescovi e diocesi in Italia nel medio evo (sec. IX–XIII)* (Padua, 1964), pp. 27–54.

Astuti, G. "Tradizione dei testi del Corpus Iuris Civilis nell'alto medio evo", in *Tradizione romanistica e civilté giuridica europea*, pp. 171–236.

——. *Tradizione romanistica e civilté giuridica europea*, ed. Giovanni Diurni [Ius Nostrum. Studi e testi pubblicati dall'Istituto del Diritto Italiano dell'Università di Roma, 2a serie, 1] (Roma, 1984).

Authenrieth, J. "Die Münchener Schule. Ludwig Traube-Paul Lehmann-Bernard Bischoff," in *Un secolo di paleografia e diplomatica (1887–1986). Per il centenario dell'Istituto di paleografia dell'Università di Roma*, ed. A. Petrucci and A. Pratesi (Roma, [1988]), pp. 99–130.

Babcock, R. G. and Cohen, W. "A new manuscript from the Abbey of San Zeno at Verona," *Yale University Library Gazette*, 66 (3–4 April, 1992): 105–16.

Battelli, G. "Ricerche sulla pecia nei codici del «Digestum vetus»," in *Studi in onore di Cesare Manaresi*, (Milano 1953), pp. 309–330; also in Battelli, *Scritti Scelti* (Roma, 1975).

Bellomo, Manlio. *The Common Legal Past of Europe 1000–1800*, trans. by Lydia G. Cochrane (Washington, D.C., 1995).

Benjamin, W. "Das Kunstwerk im Zeitalter seiner technischen Reproduzierbarkeit" [orig. pub. 1936] in Benjamin, *Illuminationen. Ausgewählte Schriften I*, (Frankfurt/M., 1977), pp. 136–169 and *Kleine Geschichte der Photographie* (1931).
Bennett, Beth S. "The Significance of the *Rhetorimachia* of Anselm of Besate to the History of Rhetoric," *Rhetorica*, 5 (1987): 231–50.
Berschin, Walter. *Bonizo von Sutri. Leben und Werk* (Berlin/New York, 1972).
Besta, Enrico. "Il diritto romano nella contesa tra i vescovi di Siena e di Arezzo," in *Archivio storico italiano*, 5th ser. 37 (1906): 61–92.
——. "L'Expositio al Liber Papiensis," *Annali dall'Università Toscana*, 30 (1911): 3–87.
——. *Le Fonti* (Milano, 1923).
Bischoff, Bernhard. *Handschriftenarchiv Bernhard Bischoff* (Bibliothek der Monumenta Germaniae Historica, Hs. C 1, C 2) ed. Arno Mentzel-Reuters, München, 1997.
——. "Italienische Handschriften des neunten bis elften Jahrhunderts in frühmittelaterlichen Bibliotheken ausserhalb Italiens," in *Il libro e il testo. Atti del convegno internazionale. Urbino, 20–23 settembre 1982*, ed. by C. Questa and R. Raffaeli, (Urbino, 1984), pp. 169–194.
——. *Katalog der festländischen Handschriften des neunten Jahrhunderts (mit Ausnahme der wisigotischen). Teil I.: Aachen-Lambach* (Wiesbaden, 1998).
——. *Latin Paleography. Antiquity and the Middle Ages*, trans. by D_ibh_ _ Cr_in_n and David Ganz (Cambridge, 1989).
——. *Die Südostdeutschen Schriebschulen und Bibliotheken*, 3. Auflage (Wiesbaden, 1974).
Bluhme, Frederick. "Bemerkungen über einzelne Handschriften und Urkunden," *Archiv der Gesellschaft für ältere Deutschegeschictskunde*, 4 (1824).
——. *Iter Italicum* (Berlin, 1824).
Blumenthal, Uta-Renate. "Falschungen bei Kanonisten der Kirchenreform des 11. Jahrhunderts," in *Fälschungen im Mittelalter*, (MGH, *Schriften*, 33/1–6 [Hannover, 1988],) vol. 2, pp. 214–67.
Bognetti, G. P. "Pensiero e vita a Milano e nel milanese davanti l'età carolingia," *Storia di Milano*, (Milano, 1953–62), vol 2., pp. 716–803.
Boyle, Leonard E. "Optimist and Recensionist: 'Common Errors' or 'Common Variations'?," in *Latin Script and Letters AD 400–900*, ed. John J. O'Meara and Bernd Nauman (Leiden, 1976), pp. 264–74.
Brasington, Bruce. "The Prologue of Ivo of Chartres: A Fresh Consideration from the Manuscripts," in *Proceedings of the Eighth International Congress of Medieval Canon Law* [Monumenta iuris canonici, Subsidia, 9] (Vatican City, 1992), pp. 3–22.
Brenkman, Henrik. *Historia Pandectarum seu fatum exemplaris florentini. Accedit gemina dissertatio de Amalphi* (Utrecht, 1722).
Brett, M. "Urban II and the Collections attributed to Ivo of Chartres," in *Proceedings of the Eighth International Congress of Medieval Canon Law* [Monumenta iuris canonici, Subsidia, 9] (Vatican City, 1992), pp. 27–46.
Bühler, Arnold. "Capitularia Relecta. Studien zur Entstehung und Überlieferung der Kapitularien Karls der Grossen und Ludwigs des Frommen," *Archiv für Diplomatik, Schriftgeschichte, Siegel- und Wappenkunde*, 32 (1986): 305–501.
Calasso, Francesco. *Medio Evo del Diritto. Le fonti* (Milano, 1954).
Caprioli, Severino. "Per uno schedario di glosse preaccursiane. Struttura e tradizione della prima esegesi giuridica bolognese," in *Per Francesco Calasso. Studi degli allievi* (Roma, 1978), pp. 73–166.
——. "Visite alla Pisana," in *Pandette di Giustiniano*, pp. 37–98.
Cavallo, G."Libri scritti, libri letti, libri dimenticati," in *Il secolo di ferro: mito e realtà del secolo X* [Settimane di studio del Centro italiano di studi sull'alto medioevo, 38] (Spoleto, 1991), pp. 759–802.
——. "La trasmissione dei testi nella area beneventano-cassinese," in: *La cultura antica nell'Occidente latino dal VII all'XI secolo* (Settimane di Studi del Centro Italiano di Studi sull'Alto Medioevo 22) (Spoleto 1975), pp. 357–414.

——. and Magistrale, F. "Libri e scritture del diritto nell'età di Giustiniano," *Index*, 15 (1987): 97–110.

Cencetti, G. "Studium fuit Bononie," *Studi medievali*, 3rd ser. 7 (1966): 781–833.

Chiappelli, Luigi. "Il MS. torinese delle Istituzioni," ZSS RA, 11 (1890): 308–310.

——. "Neue Bemerkungen über die pistoieser Glosse zum Justinianischen Codex," ZSS RA, 8 (1887): 86–99.

——. "Nuovo esame del manoscritto pistoiese del Codice giustinianeo," in *Studi e documenti di storia e diritto*, 6 (1885): 189–244.

Ciaralli, Antonio. "Ancora sul manoscritto pistoiese del Codex (Arch. Cap. C 106). Note paleografiche e codicologiche," in *Scrittura e Civiltà*, 24 (2000): 173–226.

——. "Produzione manoscritta e trasmissione dei testi di natura giuridica tra XI e XII secolo: due esempi," in *Juristische Buchproduktion im Mittelalter, Kolloquium 25. bis 28. Oktober 1998*, ed. by Vicenzo Colli (Frankfurt/Main, 2002), pp. 71–104.

——. "*Universali lex.* Il *Codex Iustinianus* nei documenti veronesi tra xi e xii secolo," *Medioevo. Studi e documenti*, 1 (Verona, 2005): 111–60.

—— and Longo, Valentina. "Due contributi a un riesame della Summa Persuina (Perugia, Bibl. Cap. ms. 32), *Scrittura e Civiltà*, 25 (2001): 1–62.

Collura, P. *La precarolina e la carolina a bobbio* (Milano, 1943).

Conrat, Max. *Geschichte der Quellen und Literatur des römischen Rechts im frühen Mittelalter* (Leipzig, 1891).

——. *Die Lex Romana canonice compta. Römisches Recht im frühmittelalterlichen Italien, in systematischer Darstellung* (Amsterdam, 1904).

——. *Pandekten- und Institutionenauszug der brittischen Dekretalensammlung Quelle des Ivo* (Berlin, 1887).

——. "Römisches Recht bei Papst Nikolaus I," *Neues Archiv der Gesellschaft für altere deutsche Geschichteskunde*, n.s. 36 (1911): 719–27.

——. "Su una più recente somma della "Epitome" di Giuliano," BIDR, 13 (1900): 286–88.

Conte, E. *Servi medievali. Dinamiche del diritto comune.* [Ius Nostrum: 21] (Roma, 1996).

——. *Tres Libri Codicis. La ricomparsa del testo e l'esegesi scolastica prima di Accursio* (Frankfurt, 1990) [Ius Commune. Studien zur Europäischen Rechtsgeschichte, 46].

Cortese, Ennio. *Il diritto nella storia medievale. I. L'alto medioevo* (Roma, 1995).

——. "Legisti, canonisti e feudisti: la formazione di un ceto medievale," in *Università e società nei secoli XII–XVI. Nono Convegno Internazionale, Pistoia, 20–25 settembre 1979* (Pistoia, 1982), pp. 195–284.

——. *Il rinascimento giuridico medievale* (Roma, 1992).

Cushing, Kathleen G. *Papacy and Law in the Gregorian Revolution. The Canonistic Work of Anselm of Lucca* (Oxford, 1998).

d'Alverny, Marie-Thérèse. "Translations and Translators," in *Renaissance and Renewal in the Twelfth Century*, pp. 421–62.

Devisse, J. *Hincmar et la loi* (Dakar, 1962).

Diurni, Giovanni. "L'*Expositio ad librum Papiensem*," *Rivista di Storia del Diritto Italiano*, 49 (1976): 1–277.

Dolcini, C. *Velut Aurora Surgente. Pepo, il vescovo Pietro e l'origine dello Studium Bolognese*, [Instituto stor. ital. per il medio evo, *Studi storici* 180], (Roma, 1987).

Dolezalek, Gero "Index manuscriptorum veterum Infortiati," *Ius Commune*, 11 (1984): 281–87.

——. *Repertorium manuscriptorum veterum Codicis Iustiniani* [*Ius Commune*, Sonderheft 23] (Frankfurt/Main, 1985).

——. and Weigand, R. "Das Geheimnis der roten Zeichen. Ein Beitrag zur Paläographie der juristischen Handschriften des zwölften Jahrhunderts," ZSS KA, 69 (1983): 143–199.

Dondaine, Antoine. "Un cas majeur d'utilisation d'un argument paleographique en critique textuelle (Vat. lat. 781)," *Scriptorium*, 21 (1967): 261–276.

Eckhardt, E. A. "Das Protokoll von Ravenna 877 über die Kaiserkrönung Karls des Kahlen," *Deutsches Archiv*, 23 (1967): 295–311.
Erdmann, Carl. "Das ottonische Reich als Imperium Romanum," *Deutsche Archiv für Geschichte des Mittelalters*, 6 (1943): 412–441 [reprint in C. Erdmann, *Ottonische Studien* (Darmstadt, 1968), pp. 174–203.]
Everett, Nick. "Literacy and the law in Lombard government," *Early Medieval Europe*, 9 (2000): 93–127.
Ewald, P. "Die Papstbriefe der Brittischen Sammlung," *Neues Archiv der Gesellschaft für ältere Geschichtskunde*, 5 (1880): 277–414, 505–596.
Ferrini, C. "La Glossa torinese delle Istituzioni e la Parafrasi dello Pseudo-Teofilo," *Opere* (Milan, 1929), vol. 1, pp. 41–56 [orig. pub. 1884].
Ficker, J. *Forschungen zur Reichs- und Rechtsgeschichte Italiens* (Innsbruck, 1868–72).
Fiesoli, Giovanni. *Le genesi del lachmannismo* (Firenze, 2000).
Fingernagel, Andreas. *Die illuminierten lateinischen Handschriften süd-, west- und nordeuropäischer Provenienz der Staatsbibliothek zu Berlin PK: 4.–12. Jahrhundert.* (Wiesbaden, 1999).
Fiorelli, Piero. "Clarum Bononiensium Lumen," in *Per Francesco Calasso. Studi degli allievi* (Reggio Calabria, 1977), pp. 426–54.
——. "Le Pandette dal palazzo vecchio alla libreria," in *Le Pandette di Giustiniano*, pp. 131–41.
Fiori, Antonia. "La 'Collectio Britannica' e la riemersione del Digesto," *Rivista internazionale di diritto comune*, 9 (1998): 81–121.
Fiorina, Ugo. "Due frammenti della «Collectio Anselmo dedicata» rinvenuti nell'Archivio di Stato di Pavia," *Athenaeum*, 60 (1982): 248–53.
Fischer, B. "Bibeltext und Bibelreform," in B. Bischoff, ed., *Karl der Grosse* (Dusseldorf, 1967), pp. 156–212.
Fitting, Hermann. *Die Anfänge der Rechtsschule zu Bologna* (Berlin and Leipzig, 1888).
——. "Pepo zu Bologna," ZSS RA, 23 (1902): 31–45.
——. *Questiones de iuris subtilitatibus des Irnerius* (Berlin, 1894).
——. *Über die sogenannte Turiner Institutionenglosse und den sogenannten Brachylogus. Ein Beitrag zu der Geschichte des römischen Rechtes vom sechsten bis zum elften Jahrhundert* (Halle, 1870; repr. 1967).
——. "Über neue Beiträge zur Geschichte der Rechtswissenschaft im früheren Mittelalter," ZSS RA, 7 (1886): 1–26.
Fliniaux, André. "Le manuscript 141 de la Bibliothèque Municipale d'Avranches et le problème de l'introduction en France au Moyen-âge du texte des compilations de Justinien," *Atti del Congresso internationale di diritto romano (Bologna e Roma xvii–xxvii Aprile mcmxxxiii). Bologna*, vol. 1 (Pavia, 1934), pp. 313–27.
Fournier, Pierre. "Un groupe de recueils canoniques italiens des Xe et XIe siècles," in *Memoires de l'institut national de France, Académie des inscriptions et belles-lettres*, 40 (Paris, 1916): 95–213.
——. "L'origine de la collection «Anselmo dedicata»," in *Mélanges Girard* (Paris, 1912), pp. 475–92.
——. "Un tournant de l'histoire du droit, 1060–1140," *Nouvelle Revue historique de droit français et étranger*, 41 (1917): 129–80.
—— and Le Bras, G. *Histoire des collections canoniques en Occident depuis les Fausses décrétales jusqu'au Décret de Gratien* (Paris, 1931–32).
Fowler-Magrel, Linda. *Ordo iudicorum vel ordo iudicarius. Begriff und Literaturgaltung* [Ius Commune Sonderhefte 19] (Frankfurt/M., 1984).
Fransen, G. "Anselme de Lucques, canoniste?," in *Sant'Anselmo vescovo di Lucca nel quadro delle trasformazioni sociali de della riforma ecclesiastica*, ed. C. Violante [Istituto storico italiano per il medio evo. Studi storici, 13] (Roma, 1992), pp. 143–56.
Fredborg, K. M. ed., *The Rhetorical Commentaries of Thierry of Chartres* (Toronto, 1988).
Frezza, Paolo. *L'influsso del diritto romano giustiniano nelle formule e nelle prassi in Italia*, IRMA I, 2, c *ee* (Milano, 1974).

Fried, Johannes. *Die Entstehung des Juristenstandes im 12. Jahrhundert: zur sozialen Stellung und polit. Bedeutung gelehrter Juristen in Bologna und Modena* (Köln, 1974).
——. *Otto III. und Bolesaw Chrobry. Das Widmungsbild des Aachener Evangeliars, der „Akt von Gnesen" und das frühe Polnische un ungarische Königtum.* (Stuttgart, 1989).
Fuhrmann, Horst. *Einfluß und Verbreitung der pseudoisidorischen Fälschungen*, MGH, *Schriften* 24, 3 vols. (Stuttgart, 1972–73).
——. "Fragmente der *Collectio Anselmo dedicata*," *Deutsches Archiv für Erforschungen des Mittelalters*, 44 (1988): 539–43.
——. "Papst Gregor VII. und das Kirchenrecht zum Problem des Dictatus Papae," *Studi gregoriani*, 13 (1989): 281–320.
——. "Das Reformpapsttum und die Rechtswissenschaft," in *Josef Fleckenstein*, ed., *Investiturstreit und Reichsverfassung* (Sigmaringen, 1973), pp. 175–203.
Ganshof, F. L. "Alcuin's Revision of the Bible," in *The Carolingians and the Frankish Monarchy*, trans. Janet Sondheimer (Ithaca, 1971), pp. 28–40.
Gaudemet, J. "Survivances romains dans le droit de la monarchie franque, du Ve au Xe siècle," *Tijdschrift voor rechtsgeschiedenis*, 22 (1955): 149–206.
Gaudenzi, Augusto. *Un' antica compilazione di diritto romano e visigoto, con alcuni frammenti delle leggi di Eurico, tratta da un manoscritto della Biblioteca di Holkham* (Bologna, 1886).
Genzmer, Ernst. "Die iustinianische Kodifikation und die Glossatoren," *Atti del Congresso Internazionale di Diritto Romano (Bologna e Roma 17–27 Aprile 1931)* (Pavia, 1934), Part I (Bologna) vol. 1, pp. 345–430.
Gibson, Margaret. *Lanfranc of Bec* (Oxford, 1980).
——. "Lanfranc's Notes on Patristic Texts," *Journal of Theological Studies*, n.s. 22 (1971): 435–50.
Gilissen, Léon. *L'expertise des écritures médiévales. Recherche d'une méthode avec application à un manuscrit du XIe siècle: Le lectionnaire de Lobbes (codex Bruxelensis 18018)* (Gand, 1973).
Gouron, André. "Le traité «De actionum varietate», la version du manuscrit de barcelone (A.C.A., San Cugat 55) et la «Glossa coloniensis» aux Institutes (Manuscrit de Cologne H. A. W. 328)," *Initium*, 2 (1997): 373–90.
Gualandi, Giovanni. "Per la storia della *Editio Princeps* delle Pandette fiorentine di Lelio Torelli," in *Le Pandette di Giustiniano*, pp. 143–98.
Gualazzini, Ugo. *La scuola giuridica reggiana nel medio evo* (Milan, 1952).
Haastrup, N. "Zur frühen Pariser Bibel—auf Grund skandinavischer Handschriften," *Classica et Medievalia*, 24 (1963): 242–69.
Haldon, J. F. *Byzantium in the Seventh Century. The transformation of a Culture*, revised ed. (Cambridge, 1997).
Harries, Jill and Wood, Ian, eds., *The Theodosian Code* (Ithaca, 1993).
Heidrich, Ingrid. *Ravenna unter Erzbischof Wibert (1073–1100) Untersuchungen zur Stellung des Erzbischofs und Gegenpapstes Clemens III. in seiner Metropole* (Sigmaringen, 1984).
Jacobi, Klaus. "Logic: the Later Twelfth Century," in *A History of Twelfth-Century Western Philosophy*, ed. by Peter Dronke (Cambridge, 1988), pp. 227–51.
Jaffé, Ph. *Regesta pontificum romanorum ab condita ecclesia ad annum post Christum natum MCXCVIII*, 2nd ed. (Lipsiae, 1885–88).
Jakobs, H. H. "Das Ende des Digestum vetus," ZSS RA, 120 (2003): 1–41.
——. "Die große Zeit der Glossatoren," ZSS RA, 116 (1999): 222–58.
——. "Or signori!—Die accursische Glosse als apparatus joannis et azonis in Odofredus' Lectura super Digesto veteri," ZSS RA, 117 (2000): 311–423.
Kaiser, Wolfgang. *Die Epitome Iuliani: Beiträge zum römischen Recht im frühen Mittelalter und zum byzantinischen Rechtsunterricht* (Frankfurt/Main, 2004).
——. "Schreiber und Korrektoren des Codex Florentinus," ZSS RA, 118 (2001): 133–219.
Kantorowicz, Hermann. "Die Epochen der Rechtswissenschaft" (1914) repr. in *Rechtshistorische Schriften.*
——. "Max Conrat (Cohn) und die mediävistische Forschung," ZSS RA, 33 (1912) 417–73.

——. *Rechtshistorische Schriften*, ed. by Helmut Coing and Gerhard Immel (Karlsruhe, 1970).
——. *Studies in the Glossators of the Roman Law*, (Cambridge, 1938).
——. *Über die Entstehung der Digestenvulgata* (Weimar, 1910), [originally published as a two-part article in ZSS RA, 30 (1909): 183–271 and 31 (1910): 14–88].
——. and Smalley, Beryl. "An English Theologian's View of Roman Law: Pepo, Irnerius, Ralph Niger," now in Kantorowicz, *Rechtshistorische Schriften*, pp. 231–44.
Kleinheyer, Gerd and Schneider, Jan. *Deutsche Juristen aus fünf Jahrhunderten*, 3. Auflage (Heidelberg, 1989).
Kremer, Marita, ed. *Die Handschriften der Murhardschen Bibliothek der Stadt Kassel und Landesbibliothek*, band 2, *Manuscripta Iuridica*, (Wiesbaden, 1969).
Krüger, Paul. *Kritik des Justinianischen Codex* (Berlin, 1867).
——. review of Chiappelli, *La Glossa Pistoiese*, in *Kritischen Vierteljahresschrift für Gesetzgebung und Rechtswissenschaft*, 28 (1886): 220–26.
Kunkel, Wolfgang. *An Introduction to Roman Legal and Constitutional History*, trans. by J. M. Kelly (Oxford, 1973).
Kuttner, Stephan. "The Revival of Jurisprudence," in *Renaissance and Renewal in the Twelfth Century*, p. 299–323.
——. "Urban II and the Doctrine of Interpretation: A Turning Point?," *Studia Gratiana*, 15 (1972): 53–85 [repr. in Kuttner, *The History of Ideas and Doctrines of Canon Law in the Middle Ages* (London, 1980)].
Landau, Peter. "Erweiterte fassungen der Kanonessammlung des Anselm von Lucca aus dem 12. Jahrhundert," *Sant'Anselmo, Mantova e la lotta per le Investiture. Atti del Convegno Internazionale di Studi (Mantova, 23–24–25 maggio 1986)* P. Golinelli, ed. (Bologna, 1987), pp. 323–38.
Lange, Hermann. *Römisches Recht im Mittelalter* (München, 1997).
Leicht, Pier Silverio. "L'exsecutor litis nel processo ravennate," *Atti del Reale Istituto Veneto di Scienze, Lettere ed Arti*, 79 (1920): 563–79.
——. "Ravenna e Bologna," in *Atti del Congresso Internazionale di Diritto Romano (Bologna e Roma 17–27 aprile 1933)* (Pavia, 1934), Part I (Bologna), vol. 1, pp. 277–90.
Levy, Ernst. *West Roman Vulgar Law* (Philadelphia, 1951).
——. *Weströmisches Vulgarrecht: Das Obligationenrecht* (Weimar, 1956).
Leyser, Karl "Ottonian government,"in *Medieval Germany and its Neighbors 900–1250* (London, 1982) [orig. pub. in *EHR*, 96 (1981): 721–53].
Liebs, Detlef. *Die Jurisprudenz im spätantiken Italien (260–640 n. Chr.)* [Freiburger Rechtsgeschichtliche Abhandlungen, n. F. Bd. 8] (Berlin, 1987).
——. "Roman Law," in *Cambridge Ancient History*, vol. 14, ed. Averil Cameron, Bryan Ward-Perkins, Michael Whitby (Cambridge, 2001), pp. 238–59.
Light, Laura. "Versions et révisions du texte biblique," in Pierre Riché and Guy Lobrichon, *Le Moyen Age et la Bible* (Paris, 1984), pp. 55–94.
Lohr, C. H. "The Medieval Interpretation of Aristotle," in *Cambridge History of Later Medieval Philosophy*, ed. Norman Kretzmann, Anthony Kenny, Jan Pinborg, Cambridge, 1982, pp. 80–98.
Lokin, J. H. A. "Theophilus Antecessor," *Tijdschrift voor Rechtsgeschiedenis*, 44 (1976): 337–344.
Lowe, Elias Avery. *The Beneventan Script* (Oxford, 1914). 2nd ed. prepared and enlarged by Virginia Brown (Roma, 1960).
——. *Codices Latini Antiquiores*, 1–11 and Suppl. (Oxford 1934–71); 2^2 (ibid. 1972). Addenda by B. Bischoff and V. Brown, *Mediaeval Studies* 47 (1985): 317–66, with 18 plates.
——. "Greek Symptoms in a Sixth-Century Manuscript of St. Augustine and in a Group of Latin Legal Manuscripts," in *Paleographical Papers*, vol. 2, pp. 466–74.
—— "The Oldest Omission Signs in Latin Manuscripts: Their Origins and Significance," collected in *Paleographical Papers*. vol. 2, pp. 349–80.
——. *Paleographical Papers. 1907–1965*, ed. L. Bieler (Oxford, 1972).

——. "The Unique Manuscript of Tacitus' *Histories* (Florence Laur. 68 2)," in *Paleographical Papers*, vol. 1, pp. 289–302.

Maasen, F. "Bobienser Excerpte des römischen Rechts," in *Sitzungsberichte der kaiserlichen Akademie der Wissenschaften, phil.-hist. Klasse*, 35 (1860): 73–108.

Manoscritti medievali della provincia di Pistoia, ed. G. Murano, G. Savino, S. Zamponi, (Tavernuzze, 1998).

McKitterick, Rosamund. *The Carolingians and the Written Word* (Cambridge, 1989).

Martí, Encarnació Ricart. "La tradicion manuscrita del digesto en el occidente medieval, a traves del estudio de las variantes textuales," *Anuario de Historia del derecho español*, 57 (1987): 5–206.

Menhardt, H. "Ein Bruchstück der Lex Visigothorum aus einer dem Codex Holkhamensis 210 verwandten Handschrift," ZSS GA, 46 (1926): 360–64 (with plate).

Miquel, Juan. "Mechanische Fehler in der Überlieferung der Digesten," in ZSS RA, 80 (1963): 233–86.

Mommsen, Theodor. "Über die kritische Grundlage unseres Digestentextes," in *Gesammelte Schriften*, vol. 2 (Berlin, 1905) [orig. pub. 1862], pp. 107–140.

——. "Zeitfolge der Verordnungen Diocletians und seiner Mitregenten," [originally published in 1860] in *Schriften*, vol. 2, pp. 195–298.

Monumenta graphica medii aevi ex archivis et bibliothecis imperii Austriaci collecta (Wien, 1858–82).

Mor, Carlo Guido. "Bobbio, Pavia e gli 'Excerpta Bobiensia'," *Contributi alla storia dell'Università di Pavia* (Pavia, 1925).

——. "Una citazione del codice giustinianeo in un diploma di Ottone III," *Studi in onore di Vicenzo Del Giudice* (Milan, 1952) vol. 2, pp. 201–5 [repr. Mor, *Scritti*, pp, 77–81].

——. "Epitome Codicis: Qualche considerazione sulla sua forma originaria," [orig. pub. in 1973] in *Scritti*, pp. 25–62.

——. "Il manoscritto del Codice Giustinianeo della Biblioteca comunale di Avranches," [orig. pub. in 1968] in *Scritti*, pp. 63–76.

——. "Per la storia dei libri giustinianei nell'et_ preirneriana," as revised in Mor, *Scritti di storia giuridica altomedievale* (Pisa, 1977), pp. 11–23.

——. "Di una perduta compilazione di diritto romano ad uso del clero, fonte degli «Excerpta Bobiensia» e della «Lex romana canonice," *Archivio giuridico*, 95 (1926): 20–26 [repr. Mor, *Scritti*, pp. 271–78].

——. *Scritti di storia giuridica altomedievale* (Pisa, 1977).

Mordek, Hubert. *Bibliotheca capitularium regum Francorum manuscripta: Überlieferung und Traditionszussammenhang der fränkischen Herrschererlasse* (München, 1995).

Moschetti, G. "I frammenti veronesi del secolo IX delle Istituzioni di Giustiniano," *Atti del Congresso internazionale di diritto romano e di storia del diritto. Verona 27–28–29–IX–1948* (Milano, 1953), pp. 439–509.

Müller, Wolfgang. "The Recovery of Justinian's Digest in the Middle Ages," *Bulletin of Medieval Canon Law*, 20 (1990): 1–29.

Muscheler, Karlheinz. *Hermann Ulrich Kantorowicz. Eine Biographie*, (Berlin, 1984).

Newton, Francis. *The Scriptorium and Library at Monte Cassino, 1058–1105* [Cambridge Studies in Palaeography and Codicology 7], (Cambridge, 1999).

Nicolaj, G. "Ambiti di copia e copisti de codici giuridici in Italia (secoli V–XII in.)," in *A Ennio Cortese* (Roma, 1997), pp. 478–96. [Also in *Le statut du Scripteur au Moyen Age, actes di XIIe colloque scientifique du Comité international de paléographie latine (Cluny, 17–20 juliette 1998)*, ed. M.-C. Hubert, H. Poulle, M.H. Smith (Paris 2000) (*Matériaux pour l'histoire publiés par l'École des chartes*, 2), pp. 127–144.]

——. *Cultura e prassi di notai preirneriani. Alle origini del rinascimento giuridico* [Ius Nostrum, vol. 19] (Milano, 1991).

——."Documenti e *libri legales* a Ravenna: rilettura di un mosaico leggendario," in *Ravenna da capitale imperiale a capitale esarcale. Atti del XVII Congresso internazionale di studio sull'alto medioevo [Ravenna, 6–12 giugno 2004]* (Spoleto, 2005), pp. 761–99.

Noble,Thomas F. X. *The Republic of St. Peter. The Birth of the Papal State, 680–825* (Philadelphia, 1984).

Nouveau trait_ de diplomatique, o_ l'on examine les fondamens de cet art . . . par deux religieux b_n_dictins de la Congregation de S. Maur, (Paris, 1750–1765).

Ottonis II. et III. Diplomata, ed. by Theodor Sickel [MGH, *Dipl.*, vol. 2].

Padoa Schioppa, A. "La cultura giuridica," in *Storia di Pavia,* 2 (Milano, 1987): 219–35.

Pandette di Giustiniano. Storia e fortuna di un codice illustre. Due giornate di studio Firenze 23–24 giugno 1983 [Accademia Toscana di Scienze e Lettere « La Colombaria», Studi LXXVI] (Firenze, 1986).

Parkes, Malcolm. "The Handwriting of St. Boniface: A Reassessment of the Problems," in *Beiträge zur Geschichte der deutschen Sprache und Literatur,* 98 (1976): 161–79.

Patetta, F. "Contributi alla storia del diritto romano," BIDR, 4 (1892): 249–86 [repr. *Studi,* pp. 121–58].

——. "Di un nuovo manoscritto del Codice Epitomato," BIDR, 7 (1895): 203–24 [repr. *Studi.* pp. 219–240].

——. "Note supra alcuni mss. delle Istituzioni di Giustiniano," BIDR, 4 (1891): 5–84 [repr. *Studi,* pp. 39–120].

——. *Studi sulle fonti giuridiche medievali,* G. Astuti, ed. (Torino, 1967).

——. "Sui frammenti di diritto germanico della collezione gaudenziana e della *Lectio legum,*" *Archivio giuridico,* 53 (1894): 3–40 [repr. *Studi,* pp. 861–98].

——. "Sull'introduzione del Digesto a Bologna e sulla divisione bolognese in quattro parti," *Rivista italiana per le scienze giuridiche,* 14 (1892): 3–20 [repr. *Studi,* pp. 201–18].

Peri, Vittorio. "'Correctores immo corruptores.' Un saggio di critica testuale nella Roma del XII secolo," *Italia medioevale e umanistica,* 20 (1977): 19–123.

Pescani, Pietro. "Ancora sui manoscritti del Digesto," BIDR, 82 (1978): 169–83.

——. "La *litera Florentina* e *Bononiensis* e la futura edizione del Digesto," *Annali della Facolta giuridica dell'Universita di Camerino,* 32 (1966): 299–336.

——. "Origine delle lezioni della litera Bononiensis superiori a quella della litera Florentina," BIDR, 85 (1982): 205–82.

——. "La posizione del codice R nella tradizione della Litera Bononiensis," *La Critica del Testo. Atti del secondo Congresso internazionale della Società italiana di storia del diritto* (Firenze, 1971) vol. 2, 671–690.

——. "La posizione del V 1406 nella riconstruzione della prima parte del Digesto," in *Studi in onore di Giuseppe Grosso* (Torino, 1972), vol. 5, pp. 81–111.

——. "Studi sul 'Digestum Vetus'," BIDR, 84 (1981): 159–250.

——. "La Scoperta del 'Bononiensis': sue forme" BIDR, 88 (1985): 383–96.

Petrucci, Armando. "Il libro manoscritto" and "Le biblioteche antiche," in *Letteratura italiana,* ed. A. Asor Rosa, vol. 2 (Torino, 1983), pp. 528–54.

——. "Libro, scrittura e scuola," in *La scuola nell'Occidente dell'alto medioevo,* XIX Settimana di studi sull'alto medioevo (Spoleto, 1972), pp. 313–37.

——. "L'onciale romana," in *Studi medievali,* 3rd ser. 12 (1971): 75–132.

——. "Scrittura e libro nell'Italia altomedievale," *Studi Medievali,* 3rd ser. 10 (1969): 961–1002.

——. *Writers and Readers in Medieval Italy,* C. Radding ed. and trans. (New Haven, 1995).

——. and Romeo, Carlo. *«Scriptores in Urbibus» Alfabetismo e cultura scritta nell'Italia altomedievale* (Bologna, 1992).

Poulle, Emmanuel. "Paléographie et Méthodologie vers l'analyse scientifique des écritures médiévales," in *Bibliothéque de l'Ecole des Chartes,* 132 (1974): 101–110.

Radding, Charles M. "The Geography of Learning in Early Eleventh-Century

Europe: Lanfranc of Bec and Berengar of Tours Revisited," *Bullettino dell'Istituto Storico Italiano per il Medio Evo e Archivio Muratoriano*, 98 (1992): 145–72.

——. *The Origins of Medieval Jurisprudence: Pavia and Bologna, 850–1150* (Yale University Press, 1988).

——. "*Petre te appellat Martinus*. Eleventh-century judicial procedure as seen through the glosses of Walcausus," in *La Giustizia nell'Alto medioevo II (secoli IX–XI), XLIVa Settimana di studio sull'Alto Medioevo, Spoleto, 11–17 aprile 1996* (Spoleto, 1997), pp. 827–61.

——. and Clark, William W. *Medieval Architecture, Medieval Learning* (New Haven, 1992).

——. and Newton, Francis. *Alberic of Monte Cassino, Berengar of Tours: Rhetoric and Politics in the Eucharistic Controversy, 1078–79* (New York, 2003).

Rambaud-Buhot, J. "La critique des faux dans l'ancien droit canonique," *Bibliothéque de l'Ecole des Chartes*, 126 (1968): 5–62.

Renaissance and Renewal in the Twelfth Century, ed. by Robert L. Benson and Giles Constable, (Cambridge, Mass., 1982).

Reynolds, L. D. et al., *Texts and Transmission. A Survey of the Latin Classics* (Oxford, 1983).

Reynolds, Roger. "Gratian's *Decretum* and the *Code* of Justinian in Beneventan Script," *Mediaeval Studies*, 58 (1996): 285–88.

Riché, Pierre. *Enseignement du droit en Gaule du VIe au X^{ie} siècle*, IRMA, I 5 b bb (Milano, 1965).

Robinson, I. S. *Authority and Resistance in the Investiture Contest. The Polemical Literature of the Late Eleventh Century* (Manchester/New York, 1978).

Röhle, Robert. "Das Berliner Institutionen- und Digestenfragment Ms. lat. fol. 269," in BIDR, 3rd ser. 10 (1970): 129–73.

——. "*Digestorum Editio Maior* und Theodor Mommsen," BIDR, 73 (1970): 19–34.

——. "Digestorum fragmentum Casellanum, 2° Mss. Iurid. 100,11," ZSS RA, 88 (1971): 356–76.

Rudorff, Adolf August. "Mommsen's Pandektenausgabe," ZRG, 6 (1867): 418–47.

Russo, G. *Tradizione manoscritta di Leges Romanae nei codici dei secoli IX e X della Biblioteca Capitolare di Modena* (Modena, 1980).

Ruysschaert, José. "Ildicius Tibertinus, un professeur de droit civile an XIIe siècle à la curie romaine," *Rivista di Storia della Chiesa in Italia*, 6 (1952): 384–86.

Ryan, J. Joseph. *Peter Damian and His Canonical Sources* (Toronto, 1956).

Santoni, Francesca. "Copisti-editores di manoscritti giuridici : 1. Il codice Vaticano latino 1406 del Digestum Vetus e l'edizione del testo fra copisti e glossatori," *La Collaboration dans la production de l'écrit médiéval*, ed. by Herrad Spilling (Actes du XIIIe Colloque international de paléographie latine [Weingarten, 22–25 septembre 2000]) (Paris, 2003).

——. "Palazzi vecchi e nuovi: il fenomeno grafico tra Ravenna, Pavia e Milano (sec. VIII–IX)," in *Ravenna Studi e Ricerche*, 9 (2002): 115–136.

Santini, G. "Il sapere giuridico occidentale e la sua trasmissione dal VI all'XI secolo," *Rivista di Storia del Diritto Italiano*, 67 (1994): 91–205.

Savigny, Friedrich Karl von. *Geschichte des römischen Rechts im Mittelalter* 2nd ed. (Heidelberg, 1834).

Scheltema, H. J. *L'enseignement du droit des antécesseurs* (Leiden, 1970).

Schieffer, Rudolf " 'The Papal Revolution in Law'? Ruckfragen an Harold J. Berman," *Bulletin of Medieval Canon Law*, n.s. 22 (1998): 19–30.

Schmidt, P. L. "Lachmann's Method: On the History of a Misunderstanding," in *The Uses of Latin and Greek*, ed. by A. C. Dionisotti, A. Grafton, and J. Kaye, [Warburg Institute Surveys and Texts, 16] (London, 1988), pp. 227–36.

Schmugge, Ludwig. " 'Codicis Iustiniani et Institutionum baiulus'—Eine neue Quelle zu Magister Pepo von Bologna," *Ius commune*, 6 (1977): 1–9.

Schrader E. et al., *Prodromus corporis iuris civilis* (Berlin, 1823).

Schramm, Percy Ernst. *Kaiser, Rom und Renovatio* (Leipzig, 1929).

Schulz, Fritz. "Paul Kruger," in ZSS RA, 47 (1927): IX–XXXIX.
Seuffert, L. Review of Conrat, *Geschichte der Quellen und Literatur des römischen Rechts* in ZSS RA, 13 (1892): 366–76.
Siems, Harald. *Handel und Wucher im Spiegel frühmittelalterlicher Rechtsquellen* [MGH, *Schriften*, bd. 35] (Hannover, 1992).
Somerville, Robert. *Pope Urban II, the* Collectio Britannica, *and the Council of Melfi (1089)* (Oxford, 1996).
Sprandel, R. *Ivo von Chartres und seine Stellung in der Kirchengeschichte* (Stuttgart, 1962).
Stein, Peter. *Roman Law in European History* (Cambridge, 1999).
Stolte, B. H., *Henrik Brenkman (1681–1736)* (Groningen, 1981).
——. "The Partes of the Digest in the Codex Florentinus," *Subseciva Groningana*, 1 (1984): 69–91.
——. "*Finium regundorum* and the *Agrimensores*," *Subseciva Groningana*, 5 (1992): 61–76.
Supino Martini, Paola. *Roma e l'area grafica romanesca (secoli X–XII)* [Biblioteca de Scrittura e Civilté, 1] (Alessandria, 1987).
——. "Aspetti della cultura grafica a Roma," *Roma nell'alto medioevo. XLVIIIa Settimana di studio sull'Alto Medioevo, Spoleto 27 aprile–1 maggio 2000*] (Spoleto, 2001), pp. 921–968.
Tabacco, Giovanni. *The Struggle for Power in Medieval Italy. Structures of Political Rule*, trans. by Rosalind Brown Jensen (Cambridge, 1989).
Tamassia, N. "Le opere di Pier Damiano: Note per la storia giuridica del secolo undecimo," *Atti del Reale Istituto Veneto di Scienze, Lettere ed Arti*, 62 (1902–3): 891–908.
Theisen, Frank. "Die Wiederentdeckung des römischen Rechts im Alltag des 11. Jahrhunderts. Dargestellt an einer Urkunden von 1076," *Revue d'histoire du droit*, 62 (1994): 127–43.
Timpanaro, Sebastiano. *La genesi del metodo del Lachmann*, 2ª ed., (Padova, 1985).
Tjäder, J.-O. "Ein Verhandlungsprotokol aus dem J. 433 n. Chr.," *Scriptorium*, 12 (1958): 3–43.
Tort-Martorell, Carmen. *Tradición textual del Codex Justinianus. Un estudio del libro 2* [Ius Commune Sonderhefte 45] (Frankfurt/Main, 1989).
Traube, Ludwig. "Geschichte der Paläographie," in *Vorlesungen und Abhandlungen*, ed. by Franz Boll, vol. 1, (München, 1909, repr. 1965), pp. 1–80.
Troje, Hans Erich. *Graeca Leguntur. Die Aneignung des byzantinischen Rechts und die Entstehung eines humanistischen Corpus iuris civilis in der Jurisprudenz des 16. Jahrhunderts* [Forschungen zur Neueren Privatrechtsgeschichte, Bd. 18] Köln/Wien, 1971.
van den Bergh, G. C. J. J. and Stolte, B. H. jr., "The Unfinished Digest Edition of Henrik Brenkman," *Tijdschrift voor Rechtsgeschiendenis*, 45 (1977): 227–305.
van de Wouw, Hans. "Zur Textgeschichte des Infortiatum und zu seiner Glossierung durch die frühen Bologneser Glossatoren," *Ius Commune*, 11 (1984): 231–80.
Verger, Jacques. "L'exégese de l'Université," in *Le Moyen Age et la Bible*, pp. 199–232.
Vismara, G. *La Fragmenta Gaudenziana*, IRMA, I, 2 b *bb*, (Milano, 1968).
Wallinga, T. "The Continuing Story of the Date and Origin of the Codex Florentinus," *Subseciva Groningana*, 5 (1992): 7–20.
Ward, John O. "From Marginal Gloss to *Catena* Commentary: the Eleventh-century Origins of a Rhetorical Teaching Tradition in the Medieval West," *Papergon*, ns. 13.2 (1996): 109–20.
Wattenbach, Wilhelm. *Anleitung zur lateinische Palaeographie* (Leipzig, 1869).
Weimar, Peter. "Die legistische Literatur der Glossatorenzeit," in *Handbuch der Quellen und Literatur der neueren europäischen Privatrechtsgeschichte, I. Mittelalter (1100–1500).Die Gelehrten Rechte und die Gesetzebung*, ed. by Helmut Coing, (München, 1973), 129–260.
——. Review of J. Fried, *Die Entstehung des Juristenstandes im 12. Jahrhundert* (Köln/Wien, 1974), ZSS RA, 96 (1979): 431.
Whitman, James Q. *The Legacy of Roman Law in the German Romantic Era* (Princeton, 1990).
——. "The Medieval Division of the Digest," *Tijdschrift voor Rechtsgeschiedenis*, 59 (1991): 269–84.

Wieacker, Franz. "Mommsens Digestorum Editio Maior: Aspekte und Aporien," in *Le Pandette di Giustiniano*, pp. 199–214.

Wickham, Chris. *Courts and Conflict in Twelfth-Century Tuscany* (Oxford, 2003).

Wilson, N. G. "A Greek Palaeographer looks at the Florentine Pandects," *Subseciva Groningana*, 5 (1992): 1–6.

Winroth, Anders. *The making of Gratian's Decretum* (Cambridge, 2000).

Witt, Ronald. "Medieval Italian Culture and the Origins of Humanism," in Albert Rabil, Jr., ed. *Renaissance Humanism. Foundations, Forms, and Legacy* (Philadelphia, 1988), vol. 1, pp. 28–71.

Zacharia von Lingenthal, Karl Eduard. Review of Mommsen's Digest edition in ZRG, 10 (1872): 165–78.

Zelzer, Michaela. "Zur Frage der Vorlage des Tacitus-Codex Mediceus 68,2," *Wiener Studien*, 86 (1973): 185–95.

PLATES

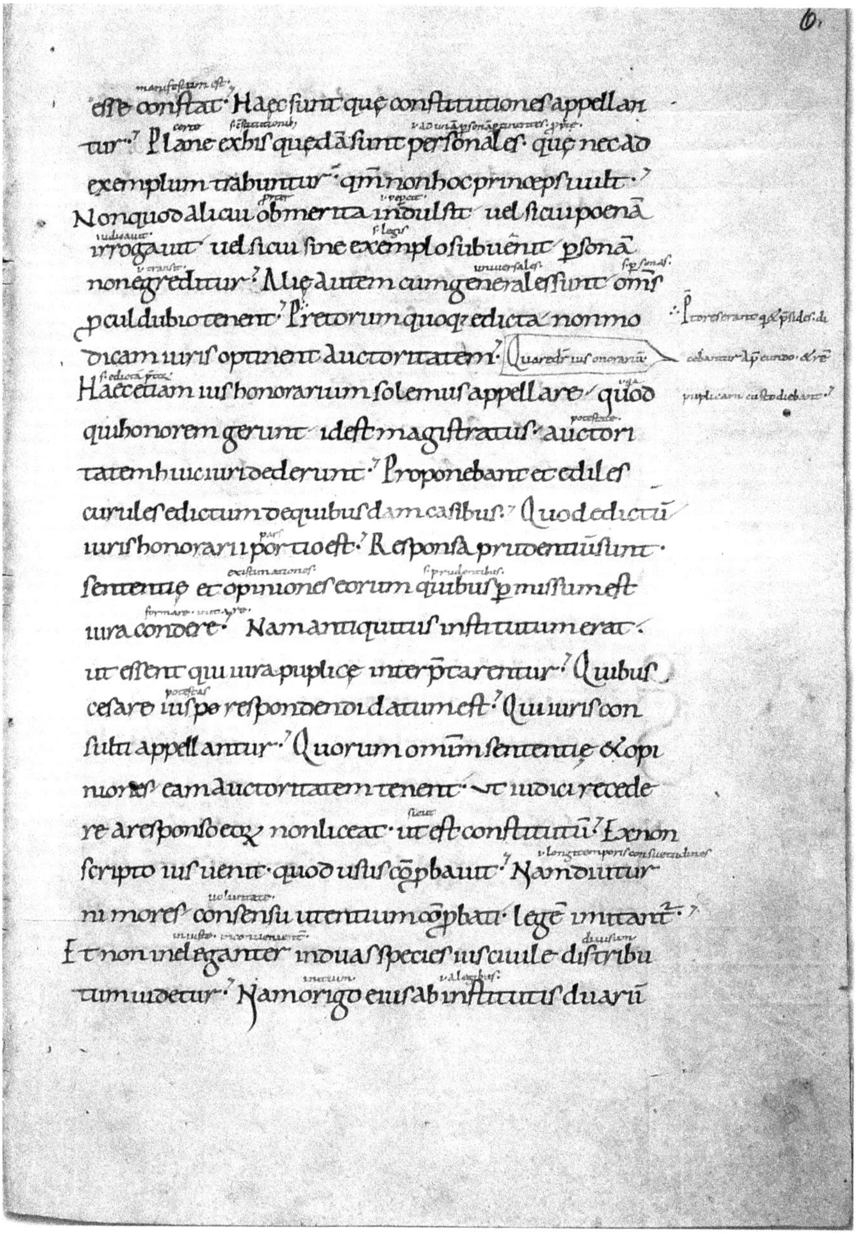

esse constat. Hęc sunt quę constitutiones appellan-
tur. Plane ex his quędā sunt personales. quę nec ad
exemplum trahuntur. qm̄ non hoc princeps uult.
Non quod alicui ob merita indulsit uel si cui poenā
irrogauit uel si cui sine exemplo subuenit psonā
non egreditur. Alię autem cum generales sint omīs
pcul dubio tenent. Pretorum quoq; edicta non mo-
dicam iuris optinent auctoritatem. Quare dr̄ ius onorariū.
Hęc etiam ius honorarium solemus appellare. quod
qui honorem gerunt id est magistratus auctori
tatem huic iuri dederunt. Proponebant et ediles
curules edictum de quibusdam casibus. Quod edictū
iuris honorarii portio est. Responsa prudentium sunt
sententię et opiniones eorum quibus pmissum est
iura condere. Nam antiquitus institutum erat.
ut essent qui iura puplice interp̄tarentur. Quibus
cesare ius respondendi datum est. Qui iuris con
sulti appellantur. Quorum omnium sententię et opi
niones eam auctoritatem tenent. ut iudici recede
re a responso eorum non liceat. ut est constitutū. Ex non
scripto ius uenit. quod usus cōpbauit. Nam diutur
ni mores consensu utentium cōpbati legē imitantur.
Et non ineleganter in duas species ius ciuile distribu
tum uidetur. Nam origo eius ab institutis duarū

Plate 1. Bamberg, Staatsbibliothek, Ms. Jur. 1, f. 6r.

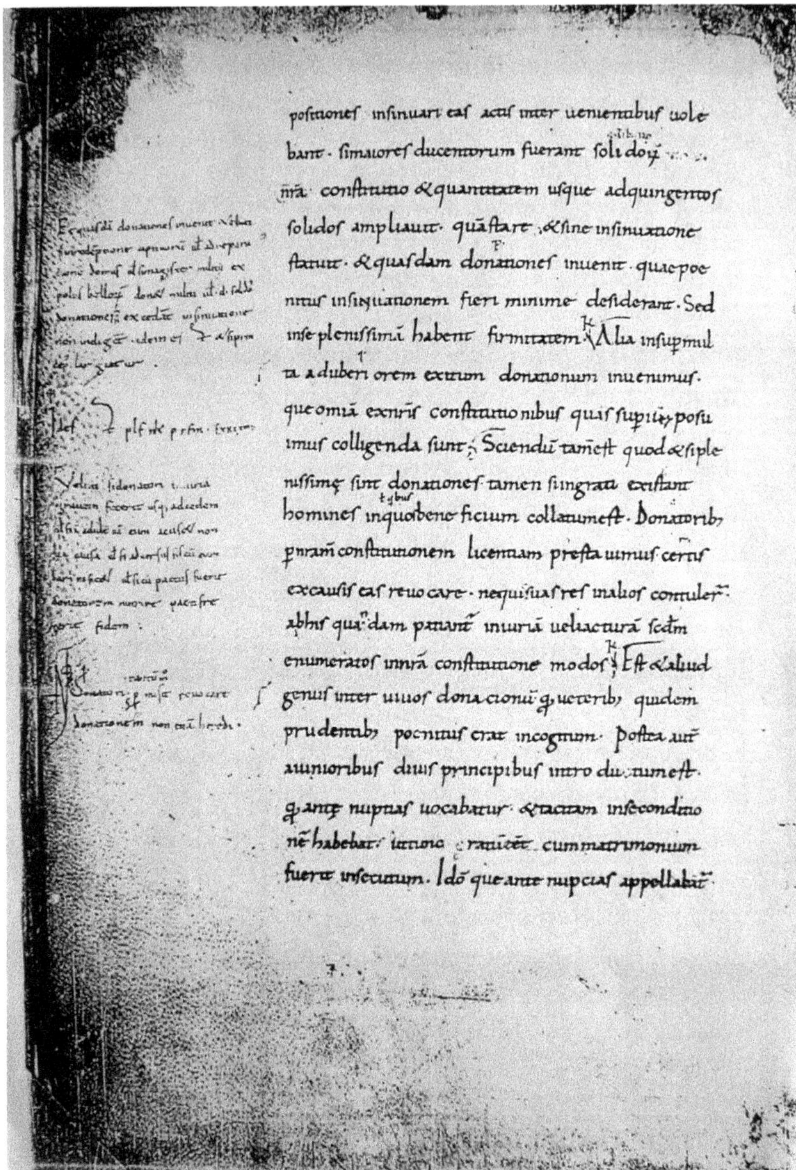

Plate 2. Turin, Biblioteca Nazionale Universitaria, D.III.13, f. 30v.

Plate 3. Florence, Biblioteca Laurenziana, s.n., f. 327v.

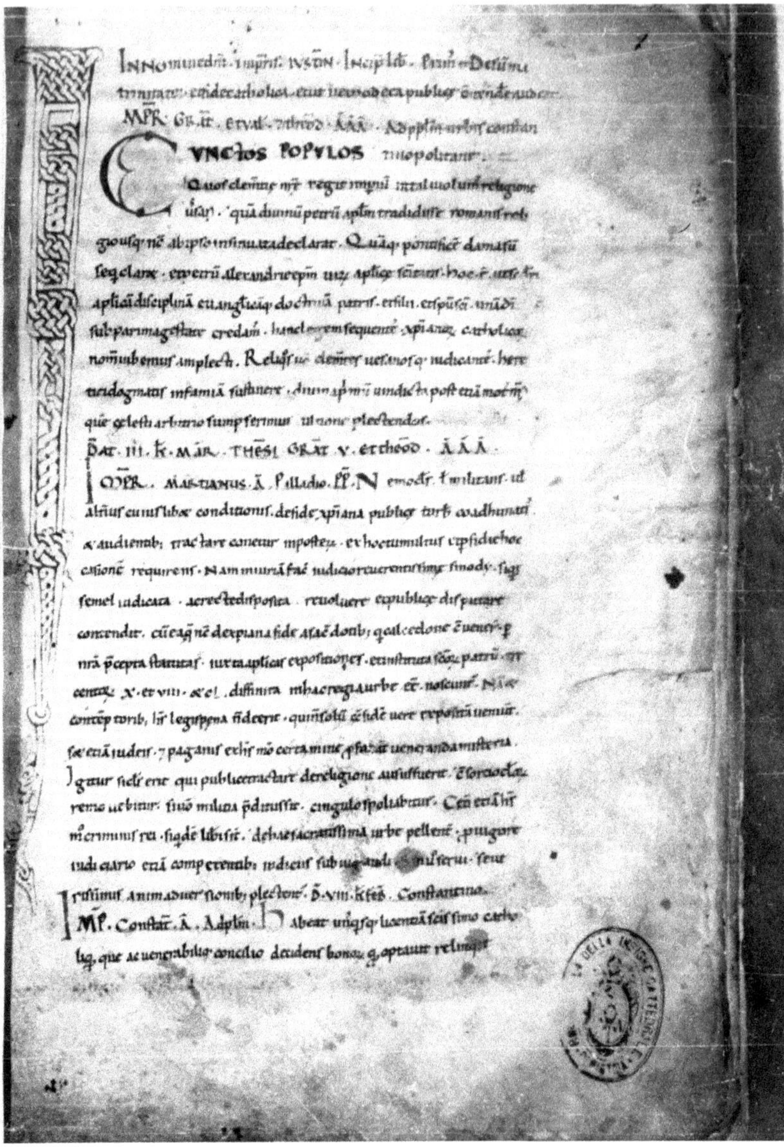

Plate 4. Pistoia, Archivio Capitolare, C 106, f. 1r.

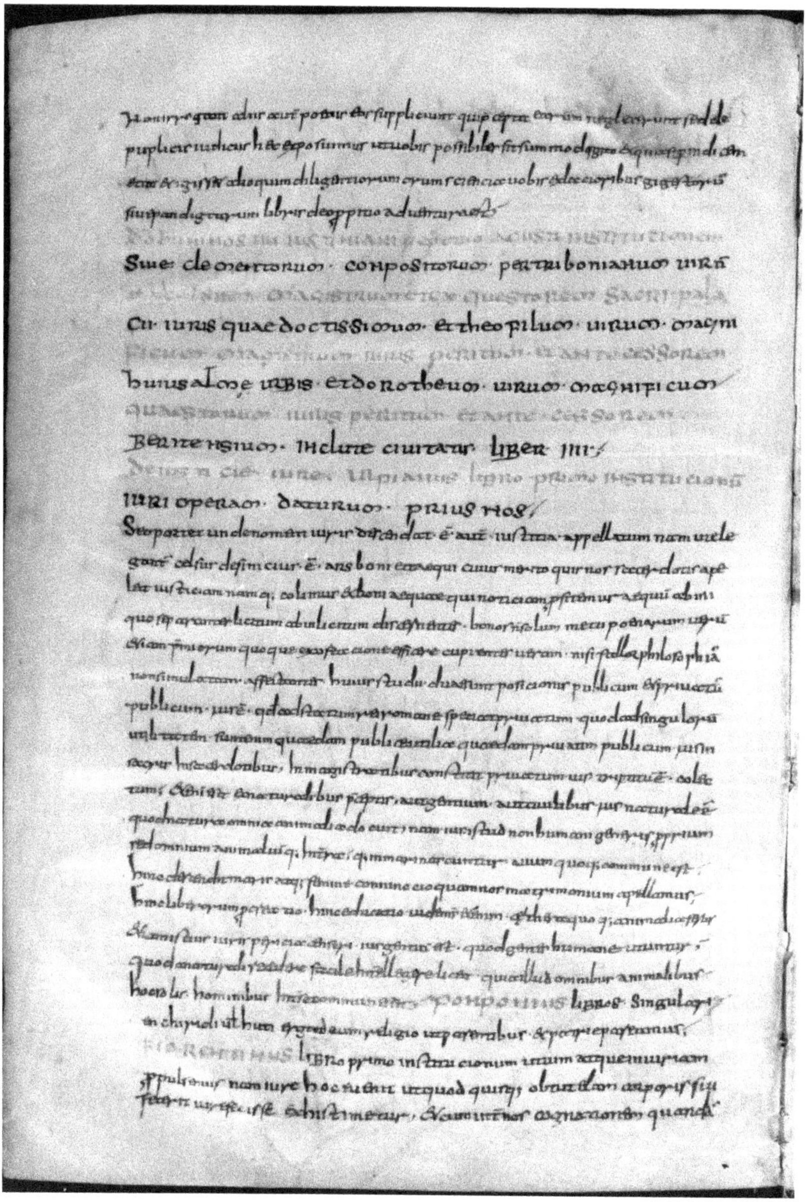

Plate 5. Staatsbibliothek zu Berlin—Preußischen kulturbesitz, ms. fol. 269, f. 183v.

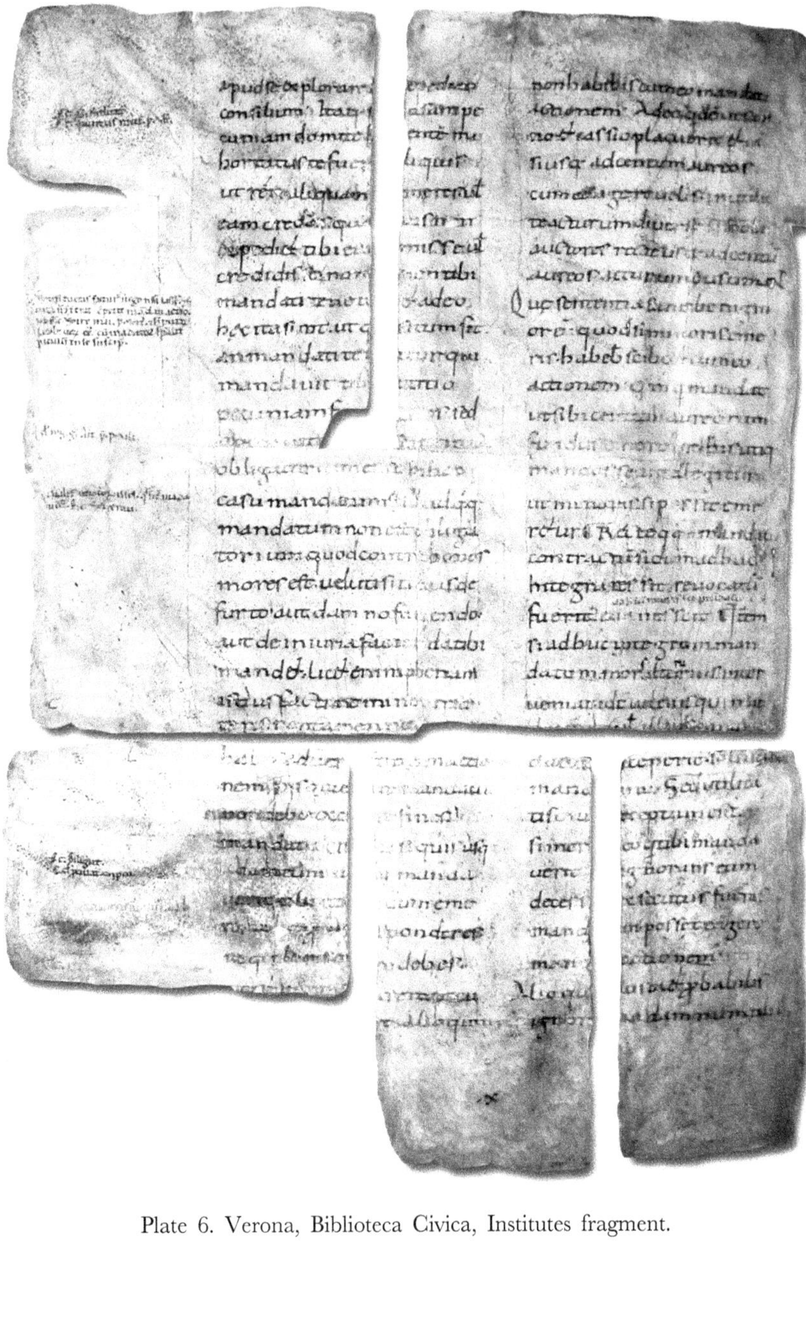

Plate 6. Verona, Biblioteca Civica, Institutes fragment.

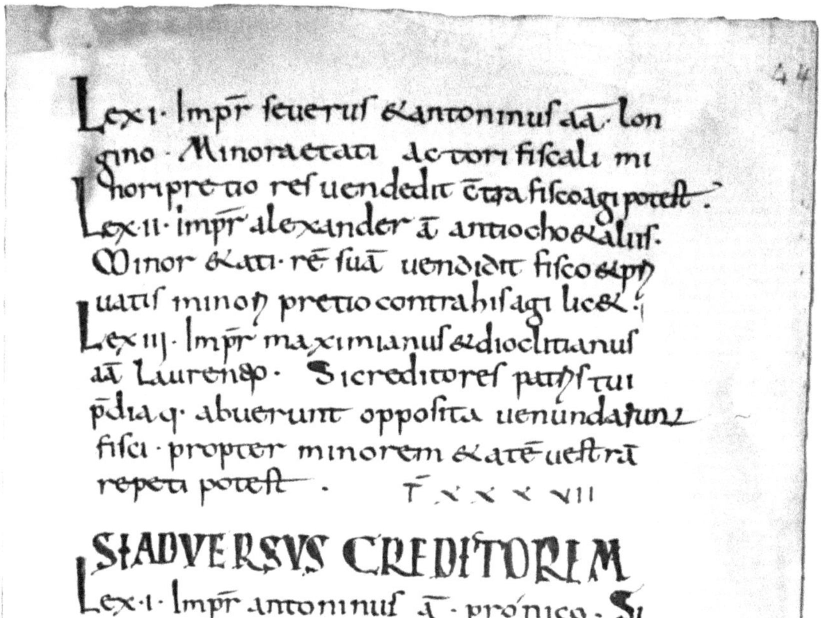

44

Lex I. Impr seuerus et antoninus AA. Lon
gino. Minori aetati actori fiscali mi
noris pretio res uendedit contra fisco agi potest.
Lex II. impr alexander A. antiocho et aliis.
Minor etati re suā uendidit fisco et pri
uatis minoris pretio contrahis agi licet.
Lex III. Impr maximianus et diocletianus
AA. Laurentio. Si creditores patris tui
prdia q abuerunt opposita uenundatum
fisci. propter minorem etatē uestrā
repeti potest. T XXXVII

SI ADVERSUS CREDITOREM
Lex I. Impr antoninus A. pronico. Si
non minor aetate se debitum con
traxit solbet.
Lex II. Impr gordianus A. galano. Si
minor etati pro acceptas pecunias
te obligasti absoluetris. T XXXVIII

SI UT SE HEREDITATE ABSTINEANT
Lex I. Impr seuerus et anthoninus AA.
florentio et aliis. Si in bonis patris te
non miscuisti conueniri illū debiss[illegible]
uellis accedere etatis beneficiū tibi
subuenit.

Plate 7. Perugia, Biblioteca Capitolare, ms. 32 f. 44r.

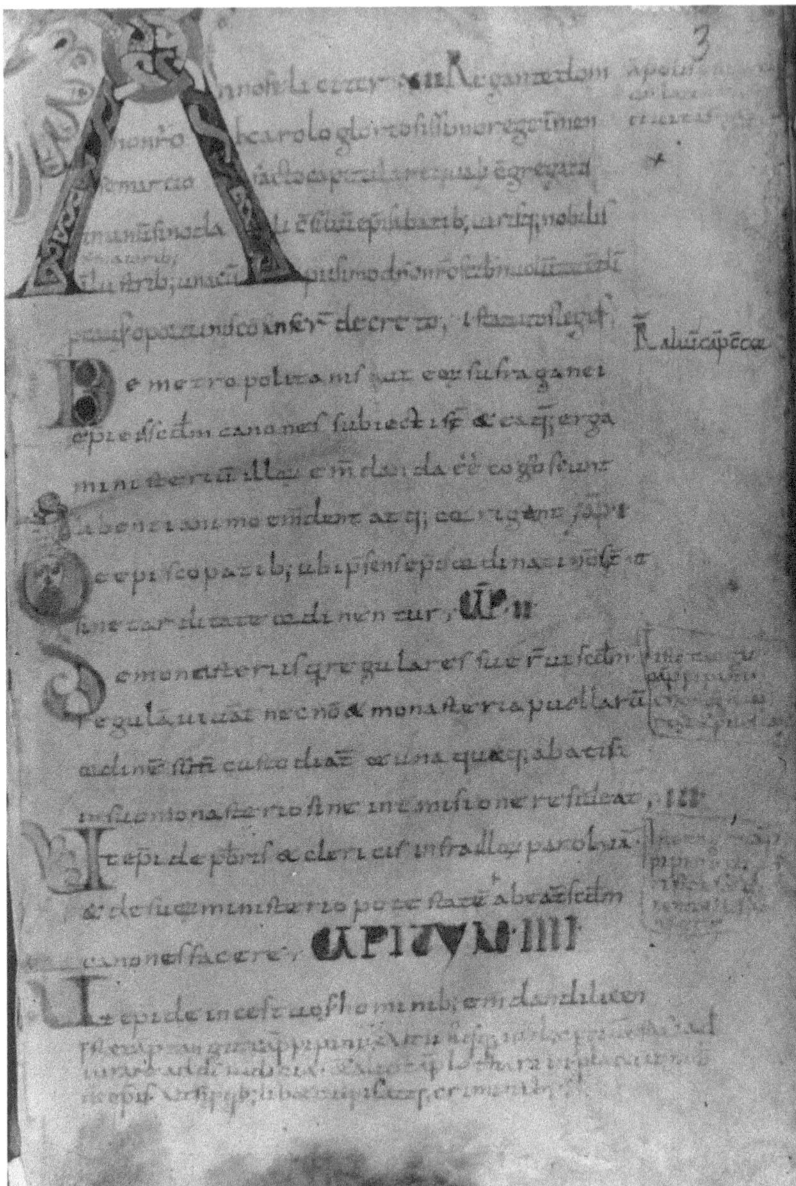

Plate 8. Milan, Biblioteca Ambrosiana, O. 55 Sup., f. 3r.

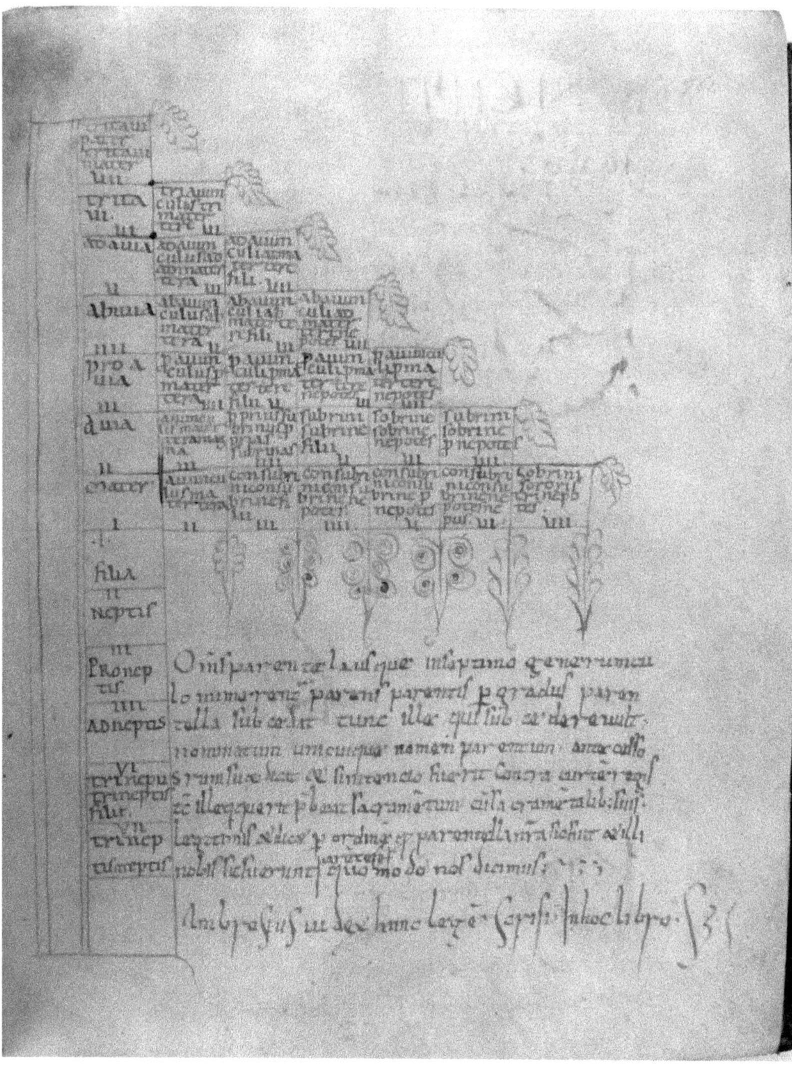

Plate 9. Vercelli, Biblioteca Capitolare, ms. 32, f. 44r.

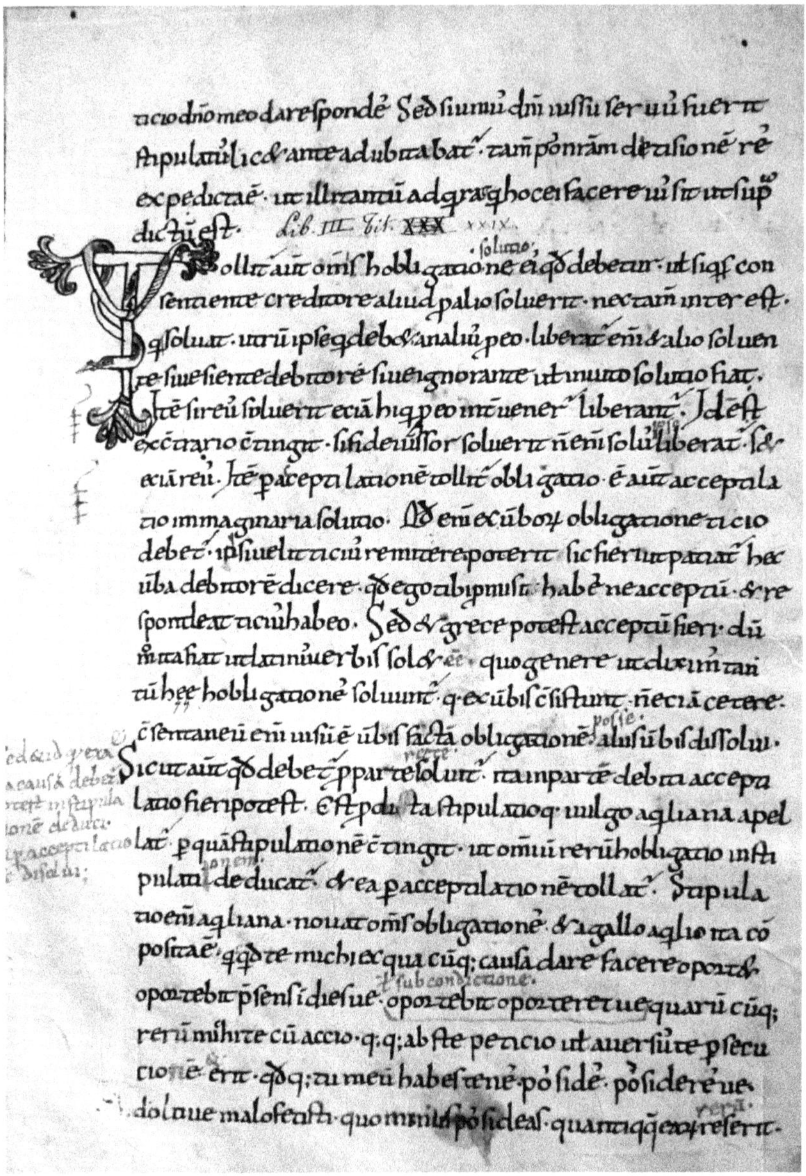

Plate 10. Montecassino, Biblioteca del Monumento Nazionale, Compactiones XI, Iuridica no. 1.

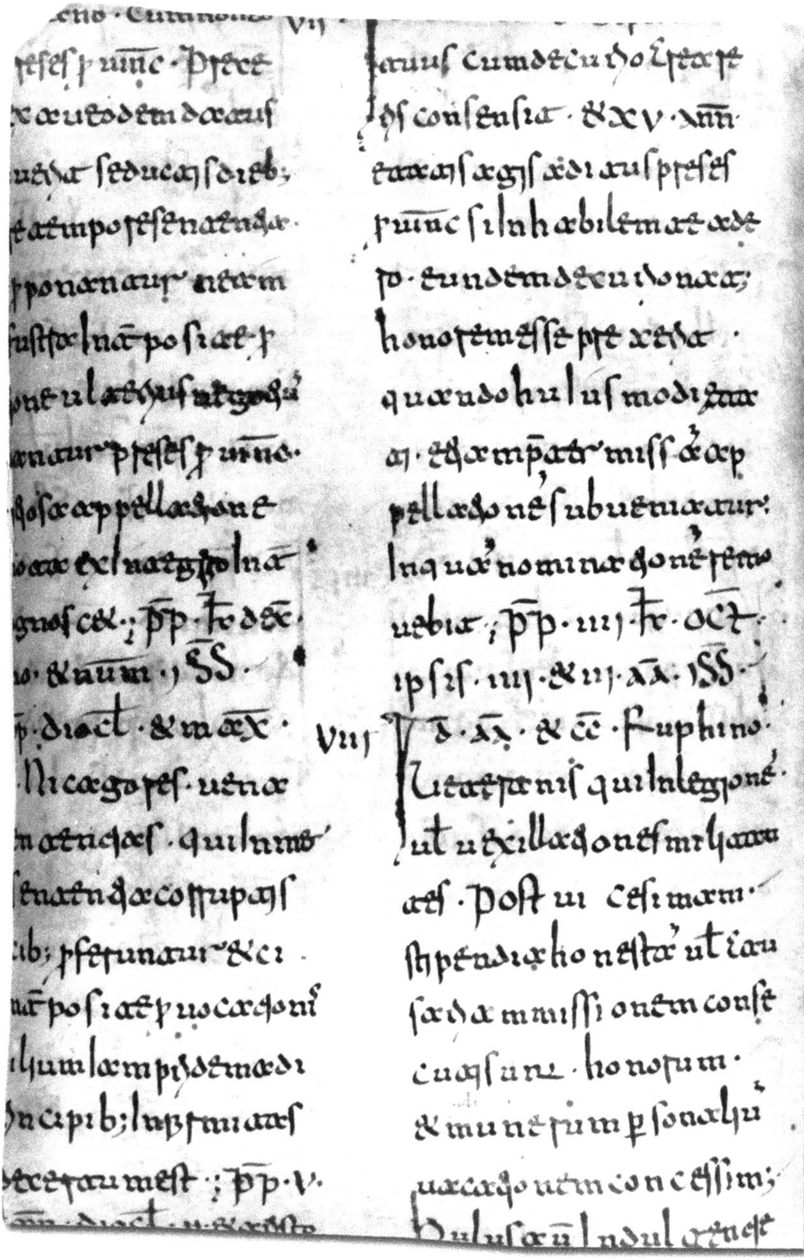

Plate 11. Rome, Biblioteca Vallicelliana, Carte vallicelliane, XII, 3.

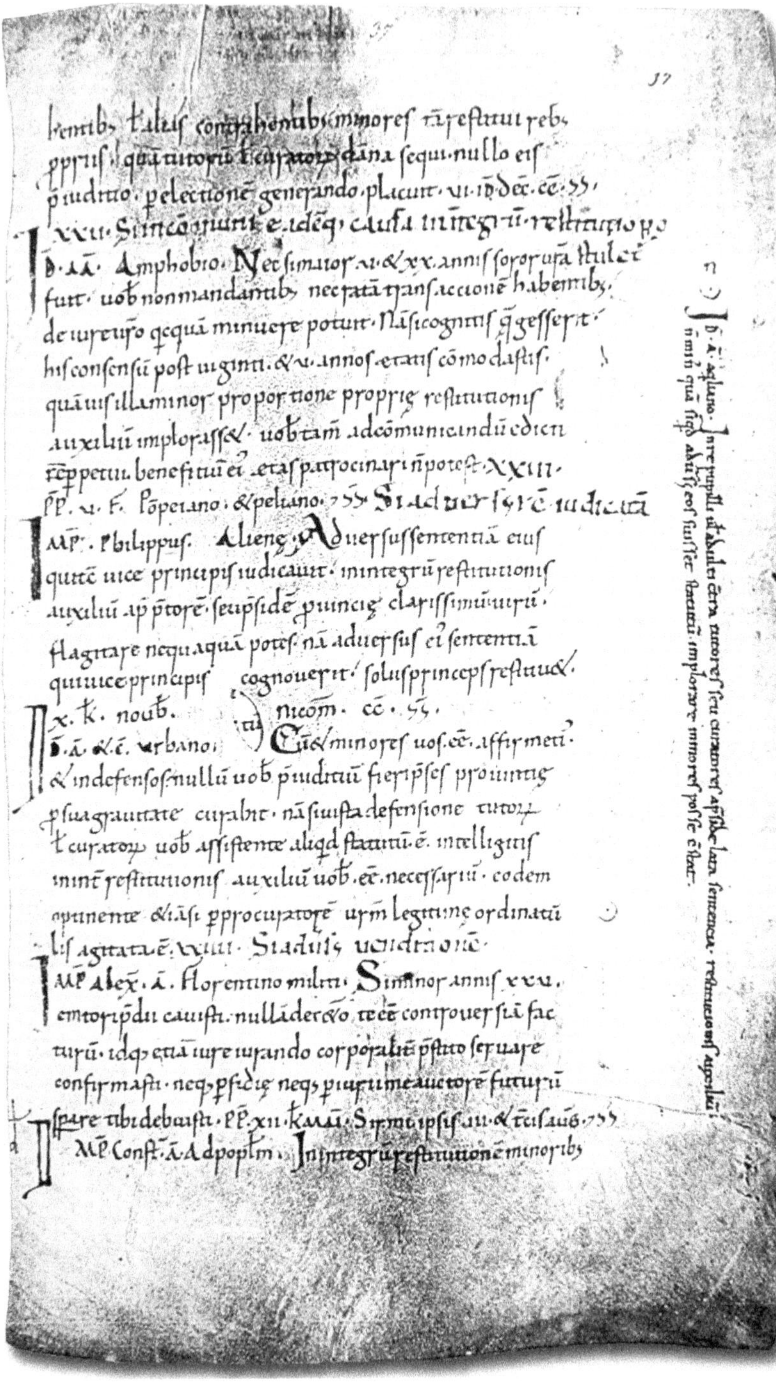

Plate 12. Pistoia, Biblioteca Capitolare, C. 106, f. 37r.

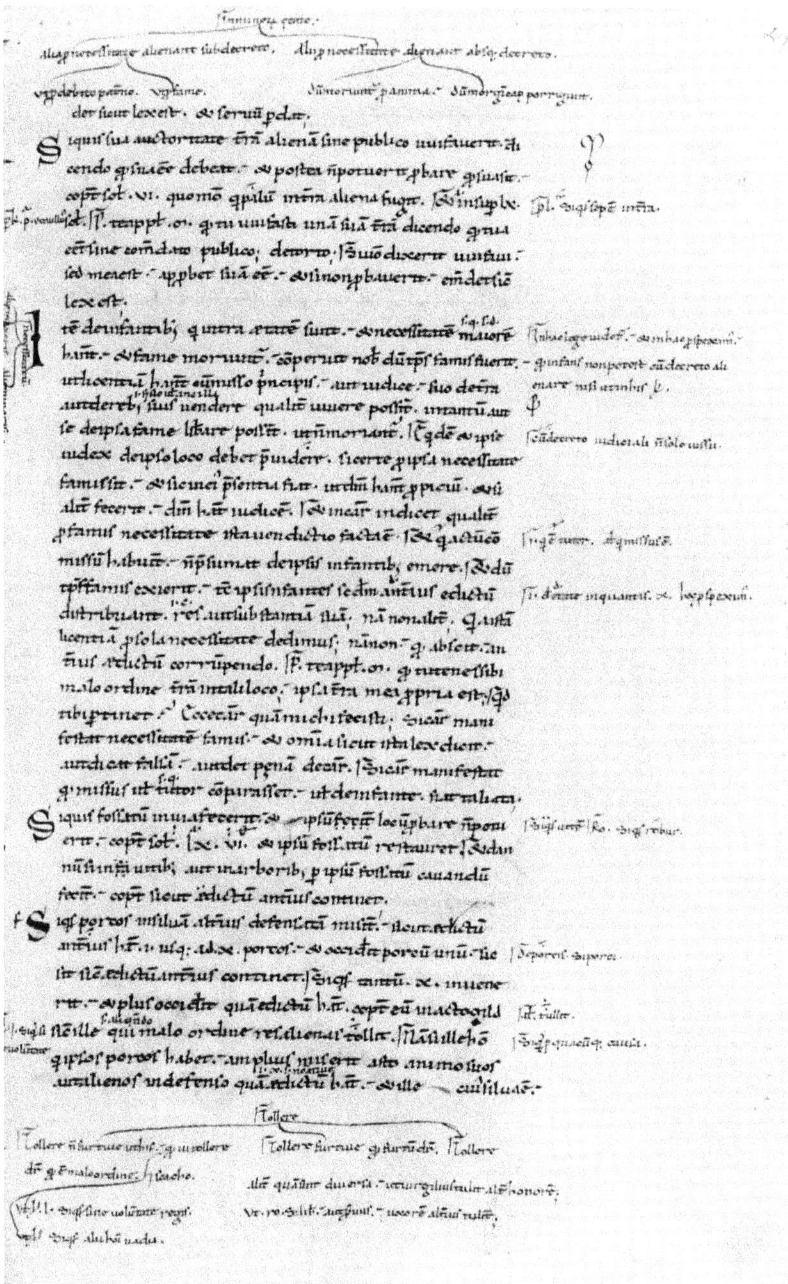

Plate 13. Vienna, Österreichische Nazionalbibliothek, cod. 471, f. 84r.

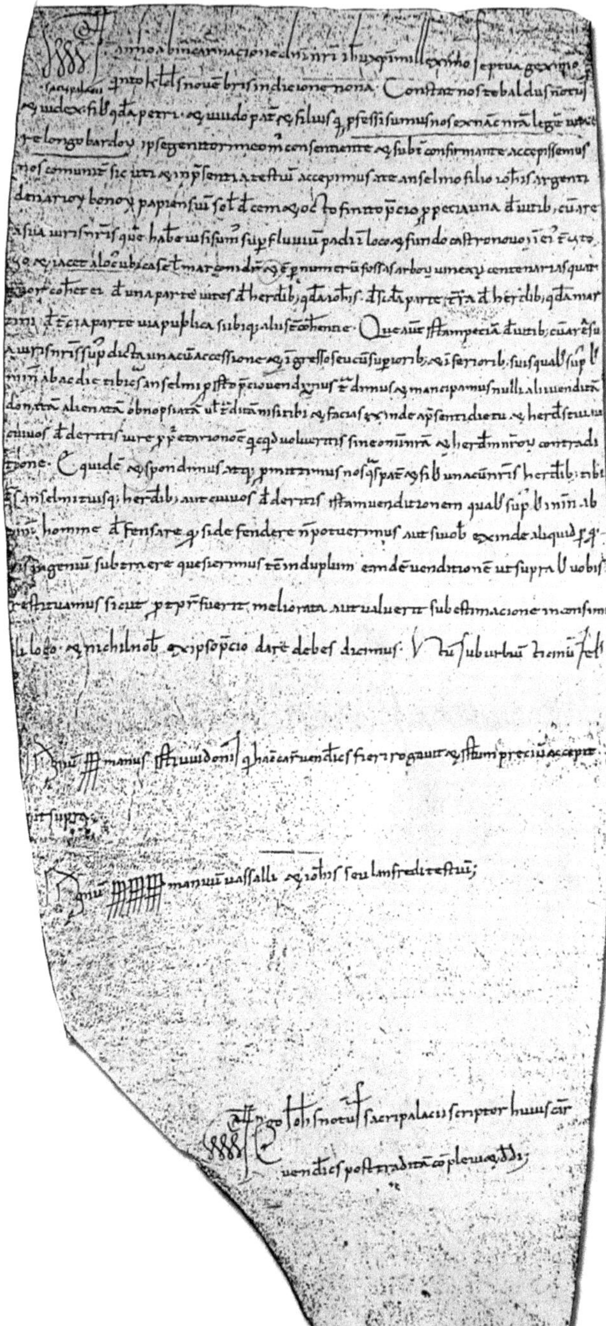

Plate 14. Milan, Archivio di Stato, Diplomatico, 654/35, S. Maria Mater Dominici, 1070 Oct. 28.

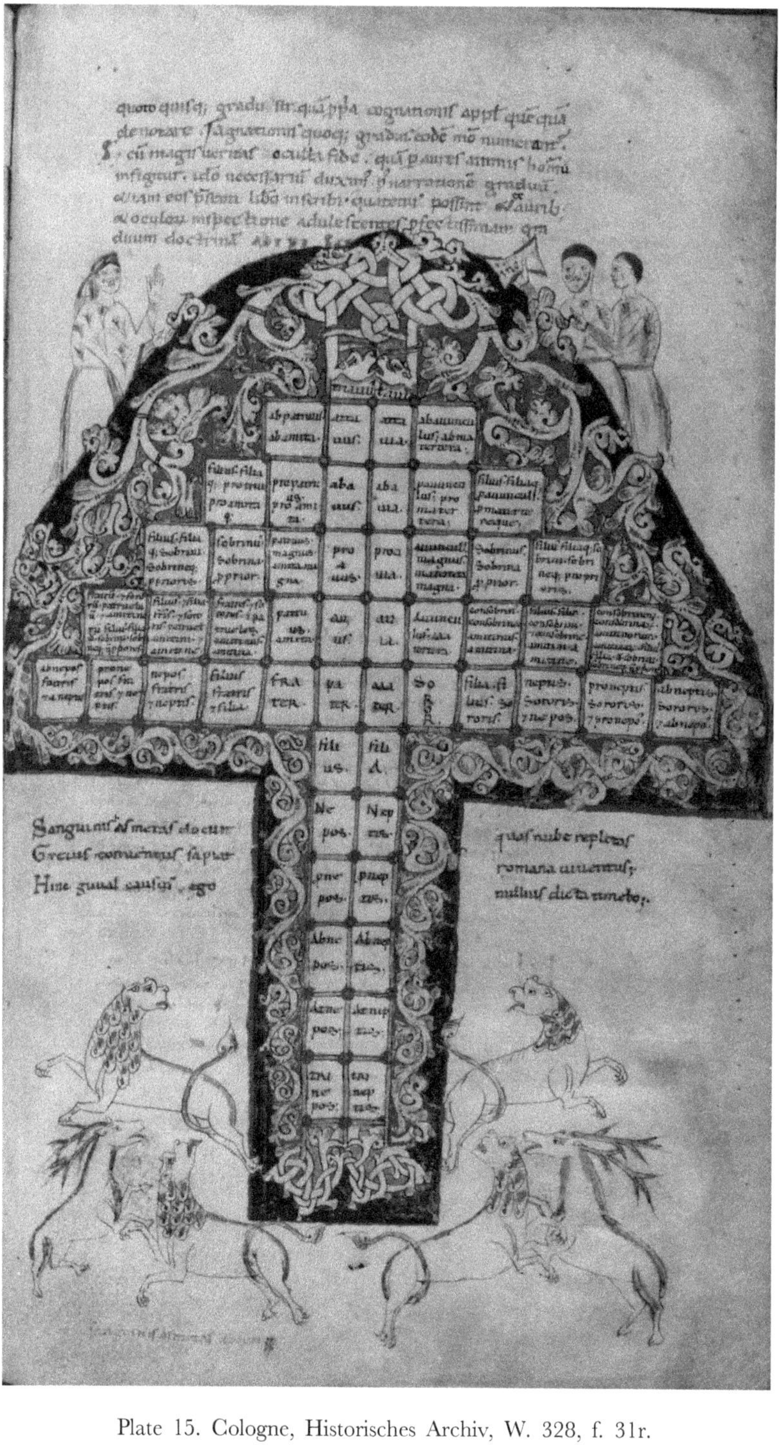

Plate 15. Cologne, Historisches Archiv, W. 328, f. 31r.

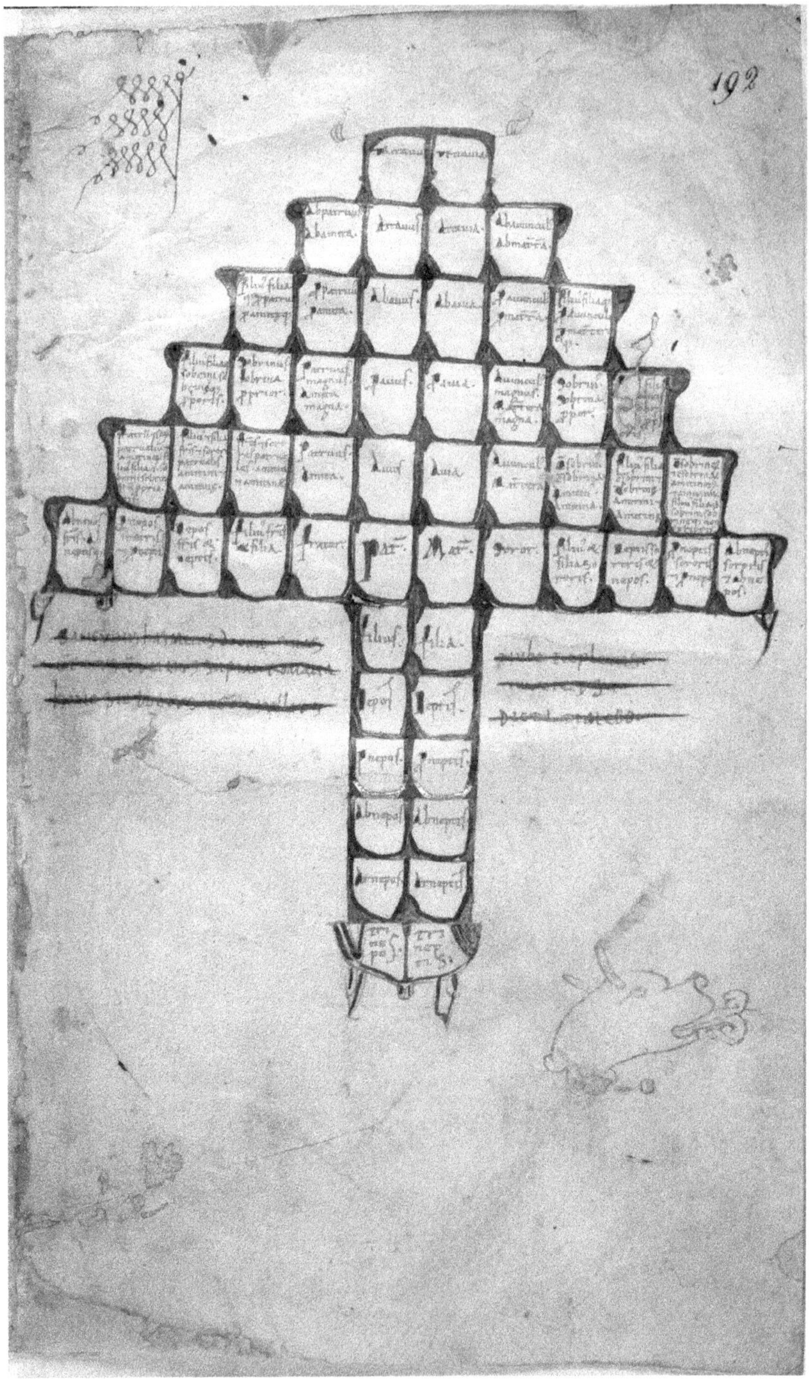

Plate 16. London, British Library, ms. add. 5411, f. 192r.

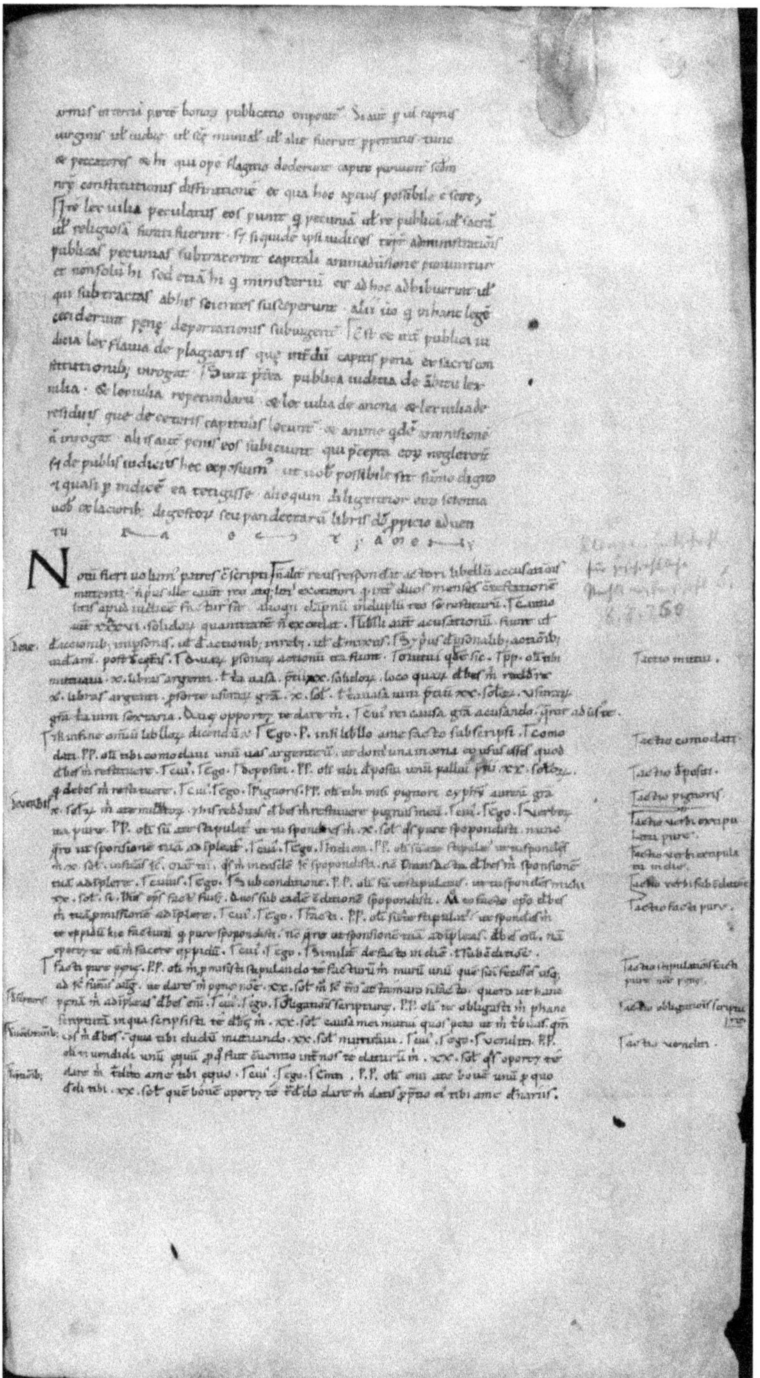

Plate 17. Cologne, Historisches Archiv, W. 328, f. 59r.

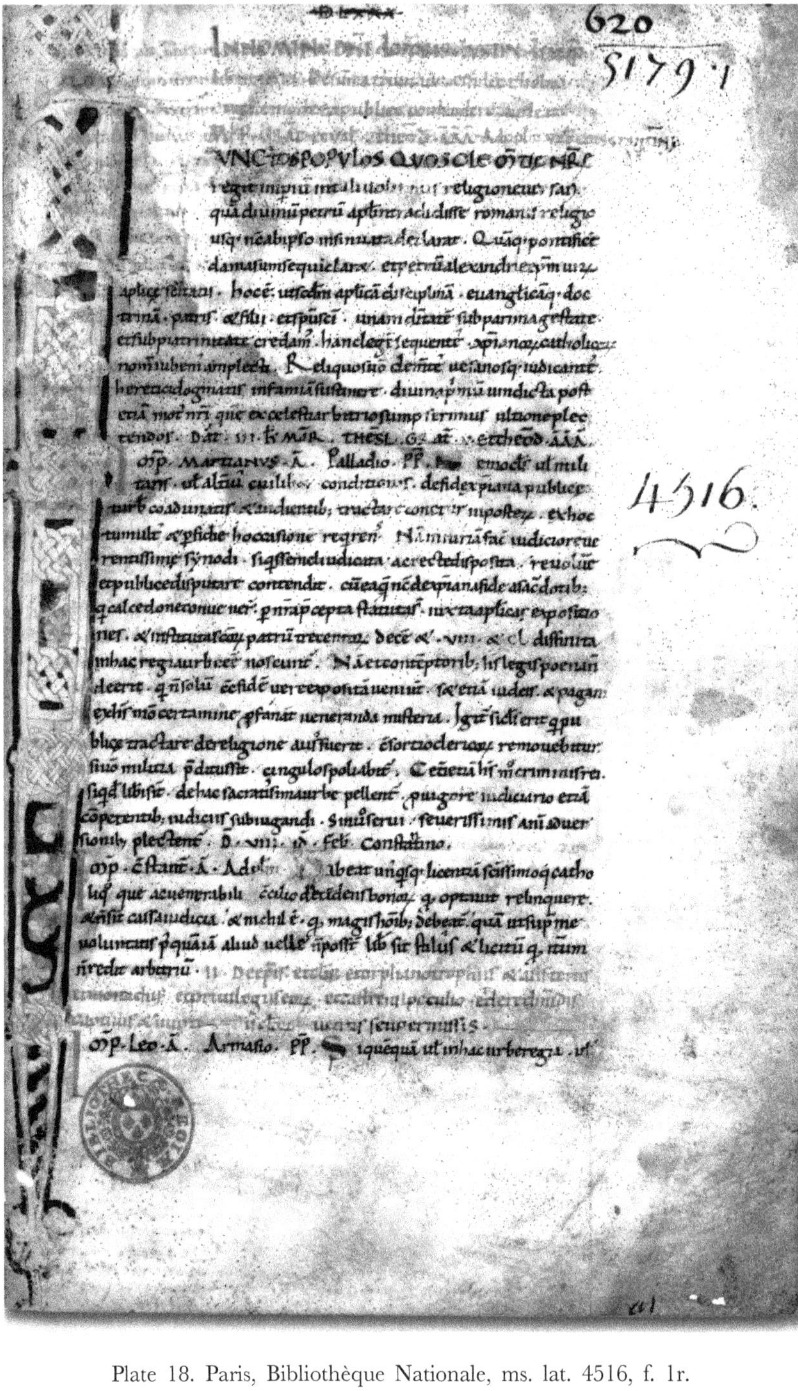

Plate 18. Paris, Bibliothèque Nationale, ms. lat. 4516, f. 1r.

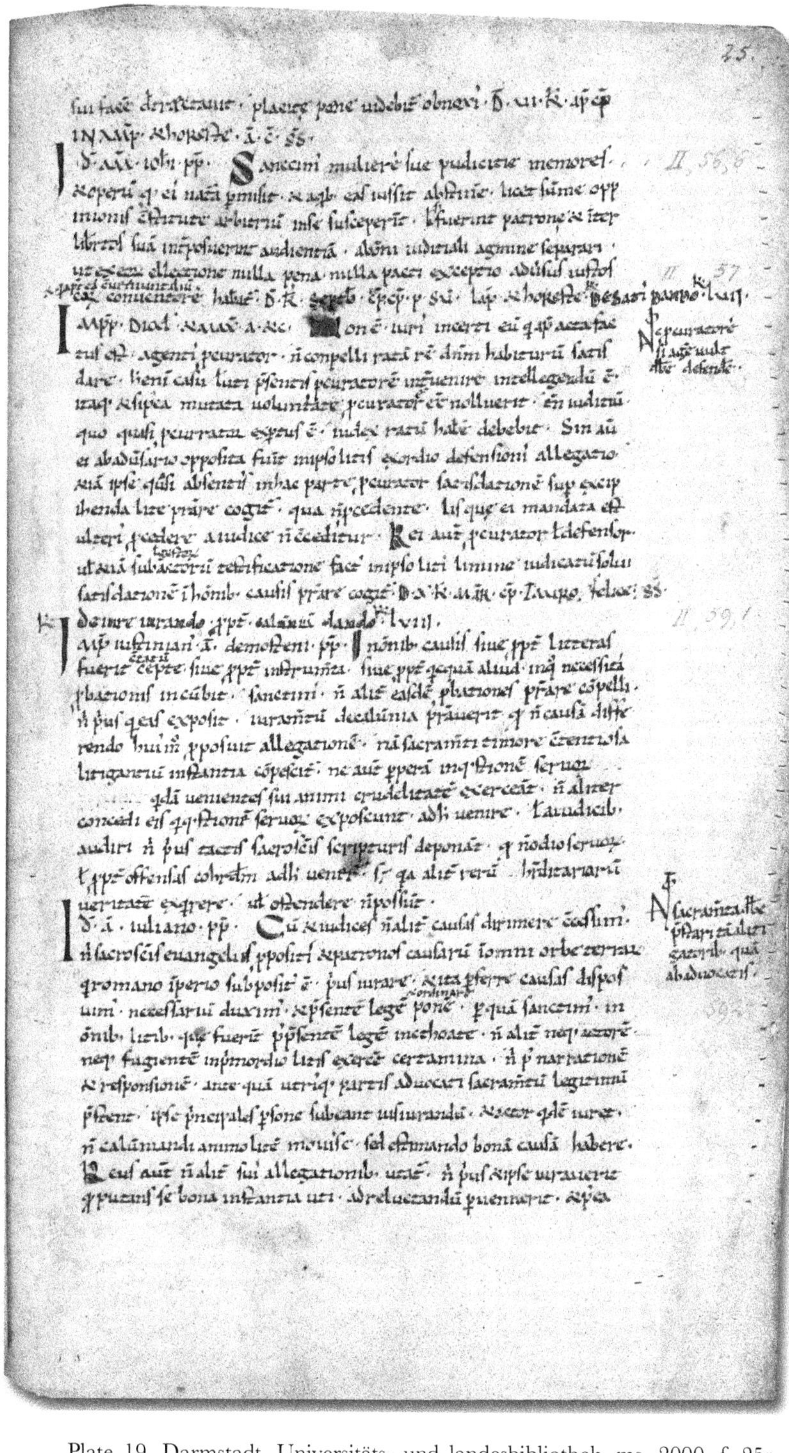

Plate 19. Darmstadt, Universitäts- und landesbibliothek, ms. 2000, f. 25r.

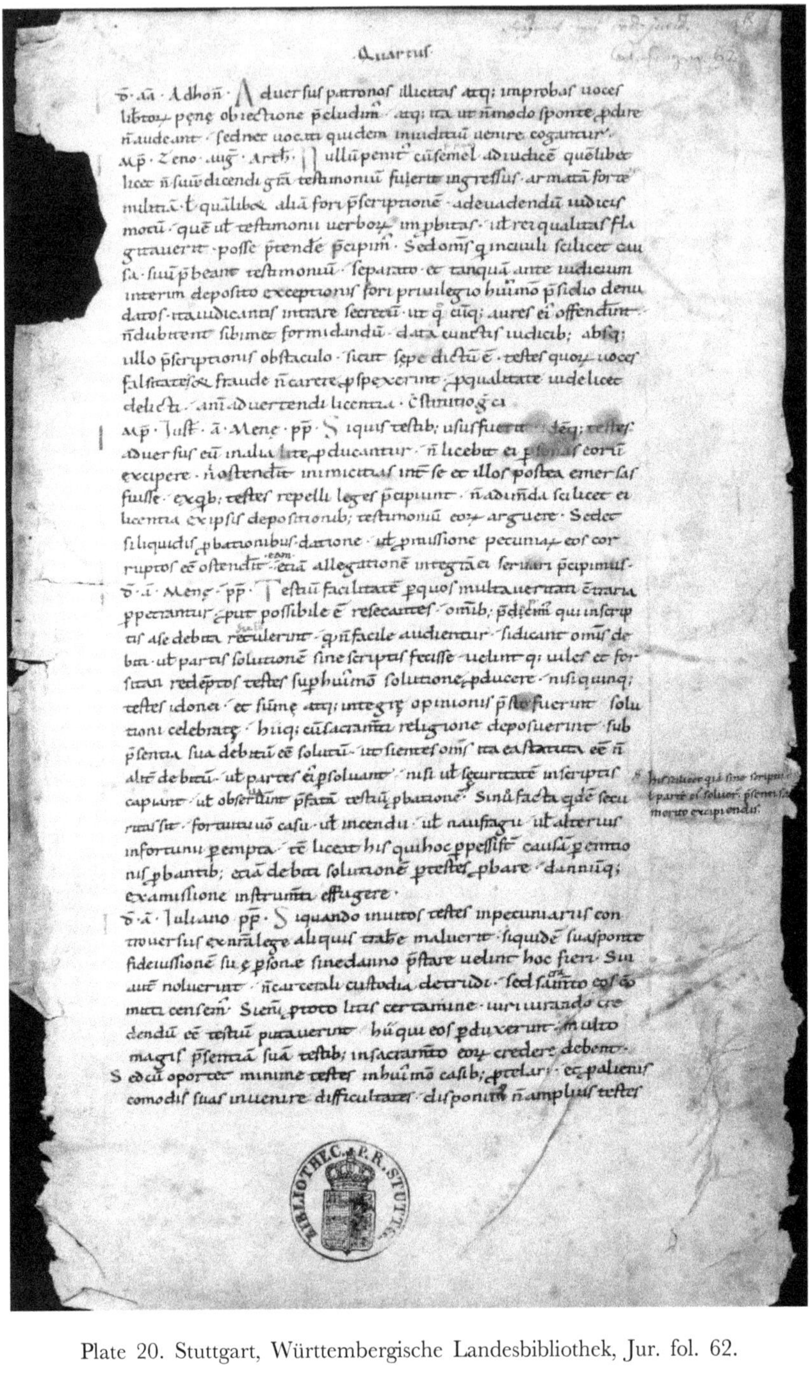

Plate 20. Stuttgart, Württembergische Landesbibliothek, Jur. fol. 62.

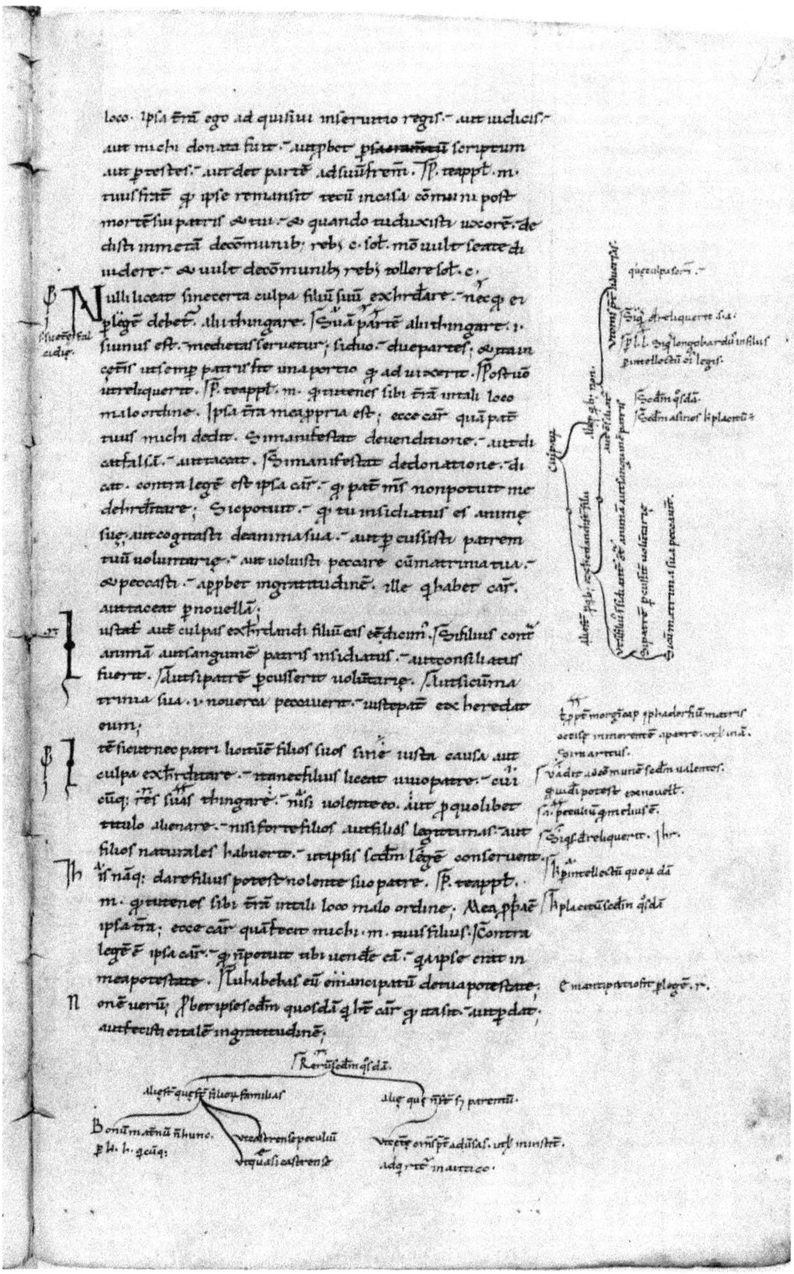

Plate 21. Vienna, Österreichische Nazionalbibliothek, cod. 471, f. 18v.

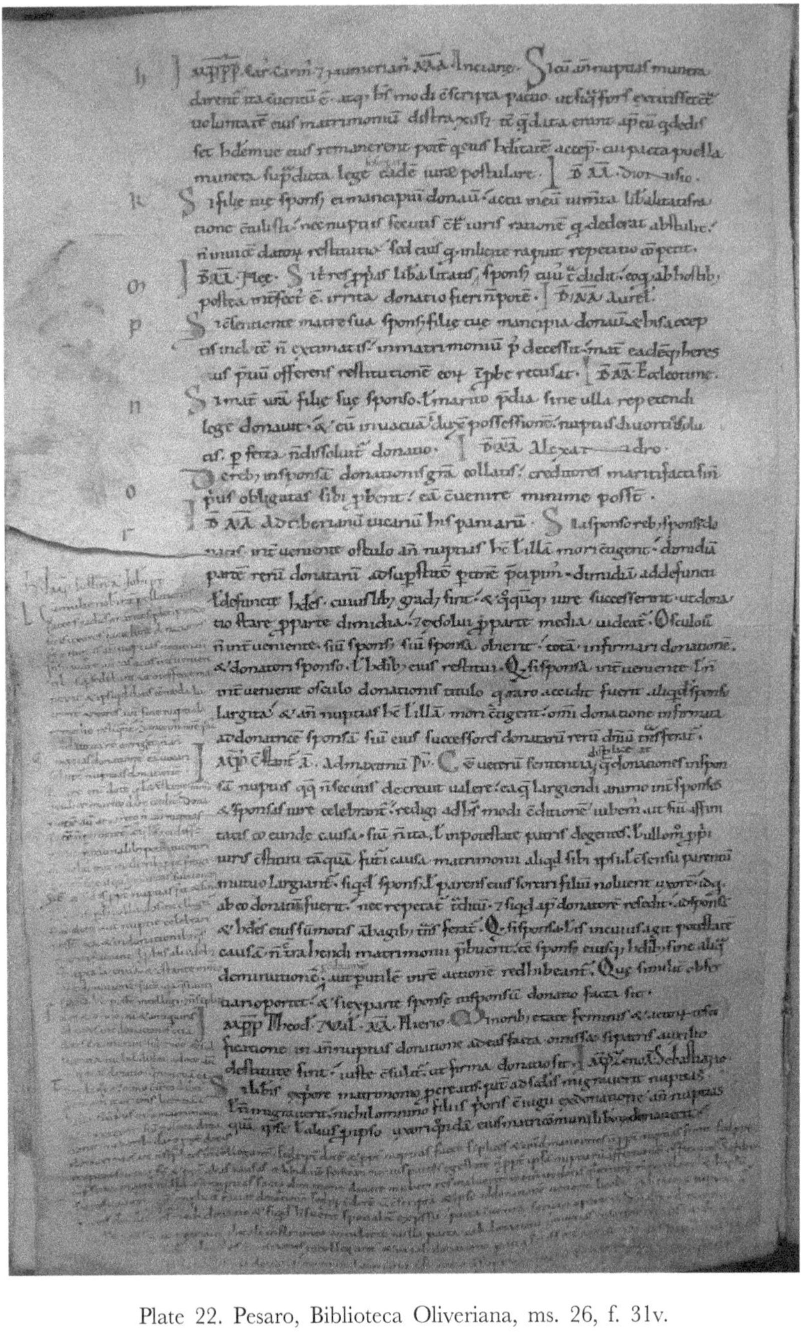

Plate 22. Pesaro, Biblioteca Oliveriana, ms. 26, f. 31v.

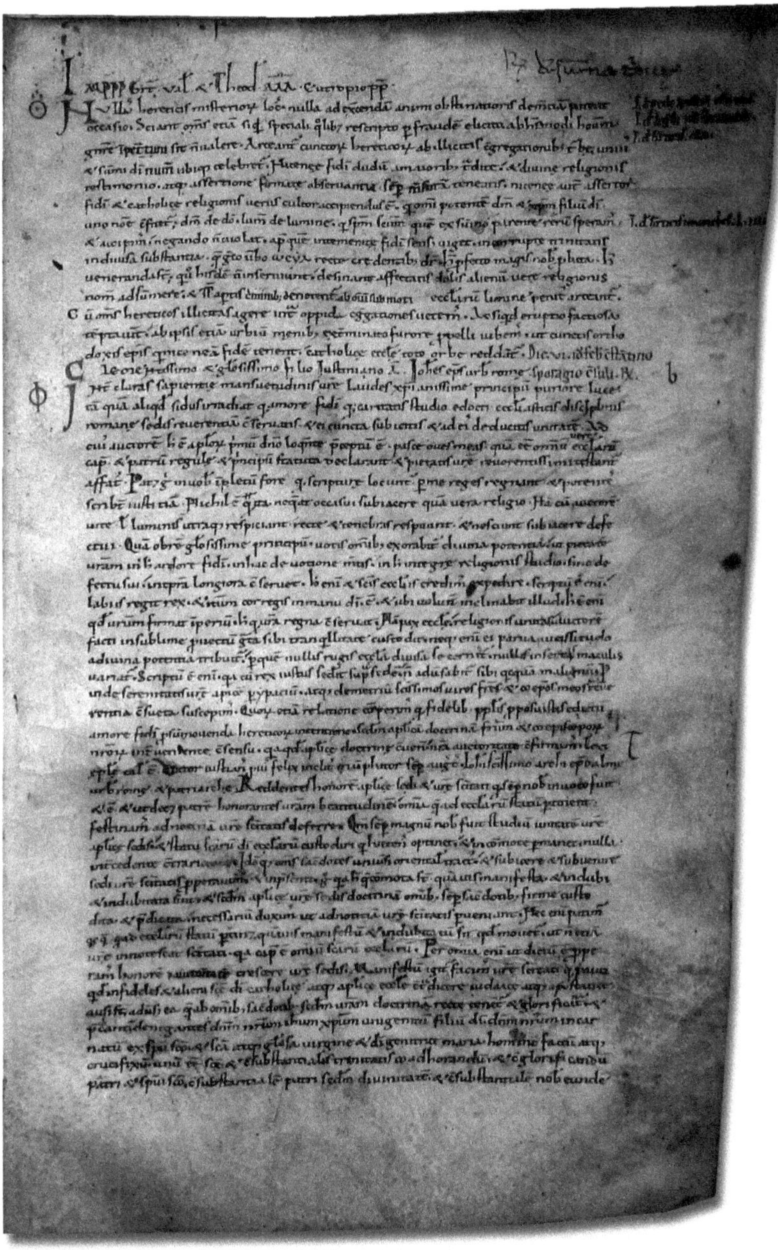

Plate 23. Pesaro, Biblioteca Oliveriana, ms. 26, f. 71r.

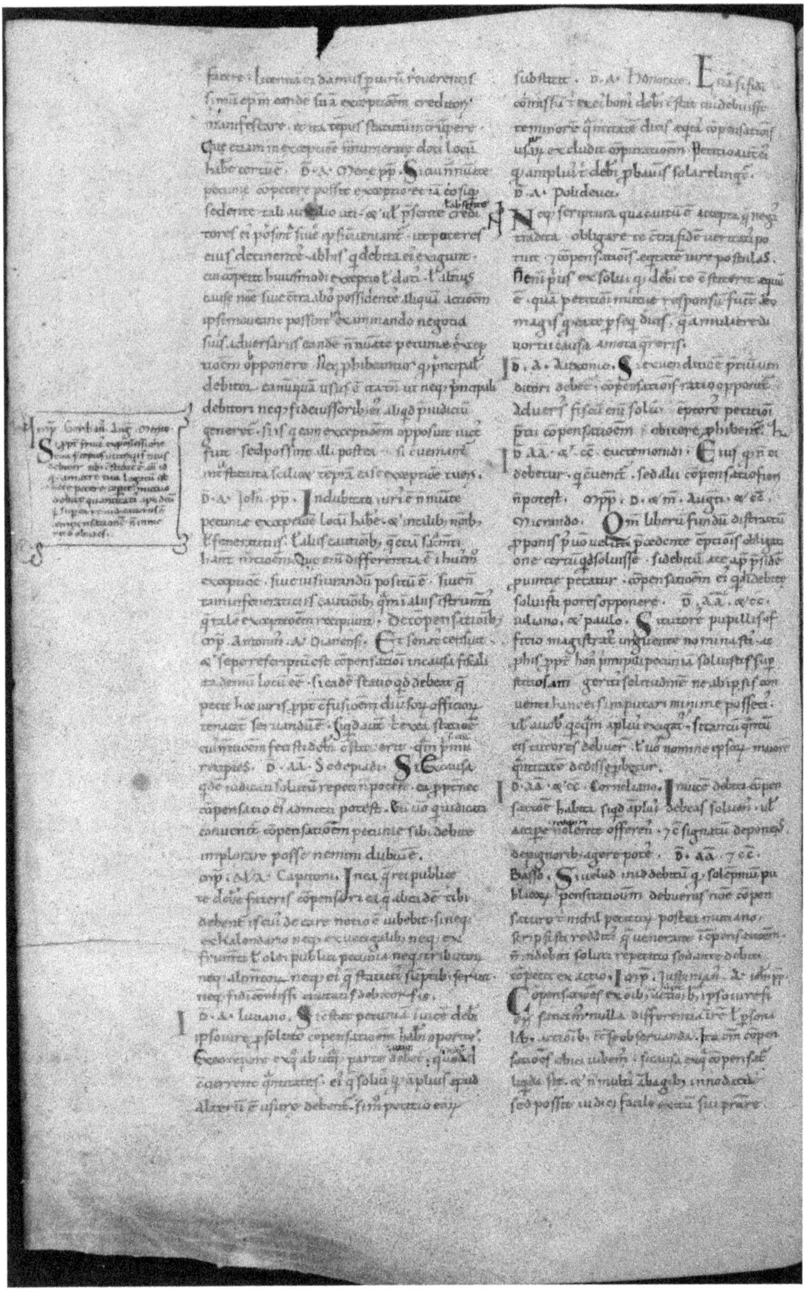

Plate 24. Staatsbibliothek zu Berlin—Preußischer Kulturbesitz, lat. fol. 273, f. 63v.

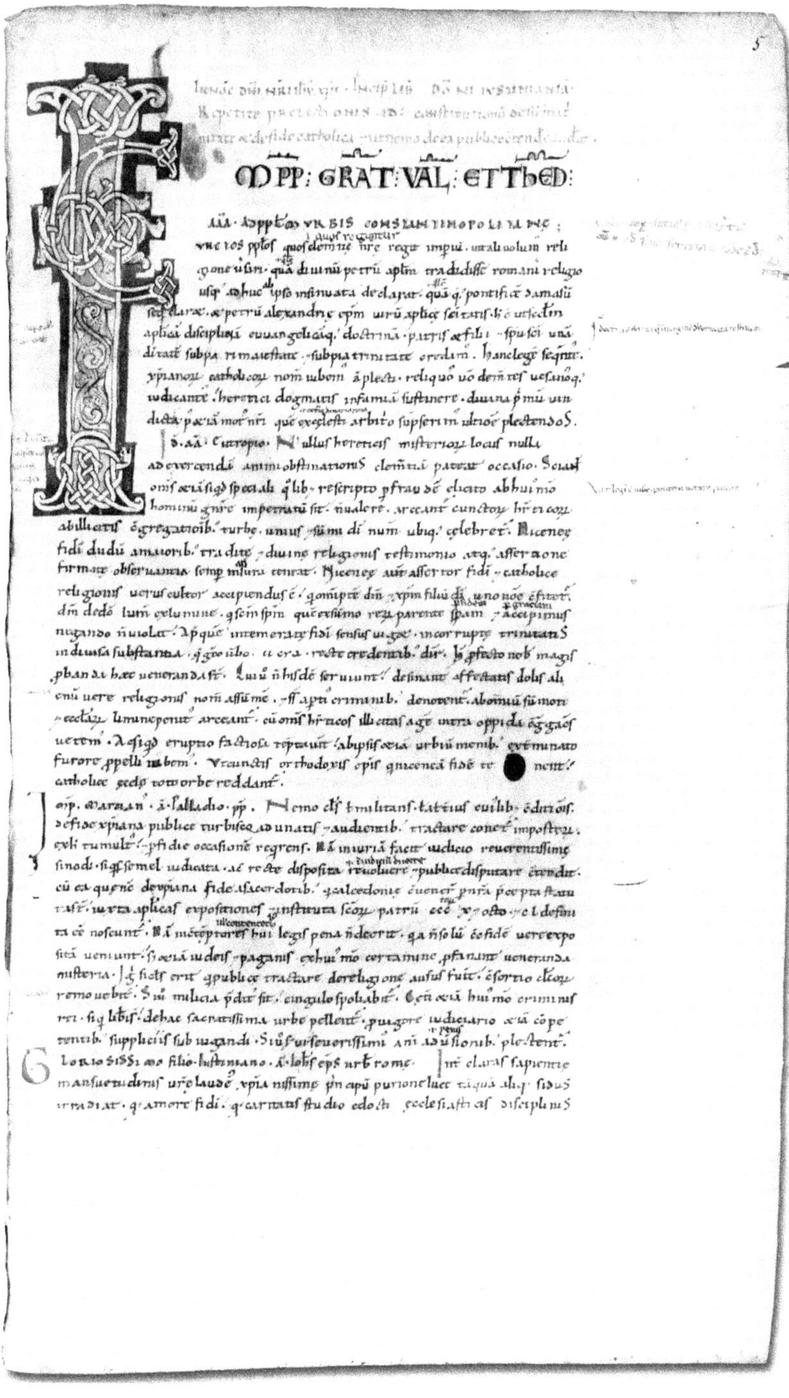

IMPP. GRAT. VAL. ET THEOD.

Plate 25. Staatsbibliothek zu Berlin–Preußischer kulturbesitz, lat. fol. 272, f. 5r.

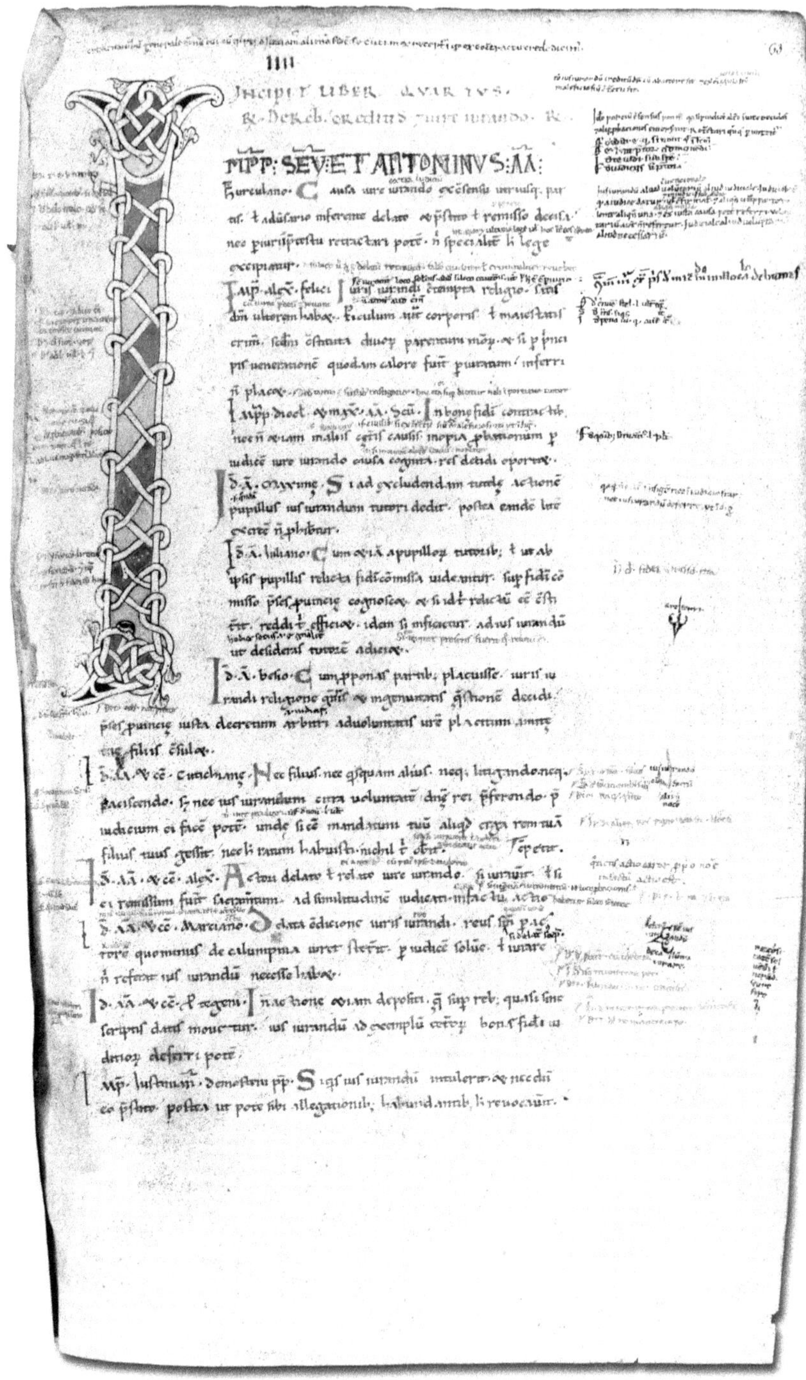

Plate 26. Staatsbibliothek zu Berlin—Preußischer kulturbesitz, lat. fol. 272, f. 63r.

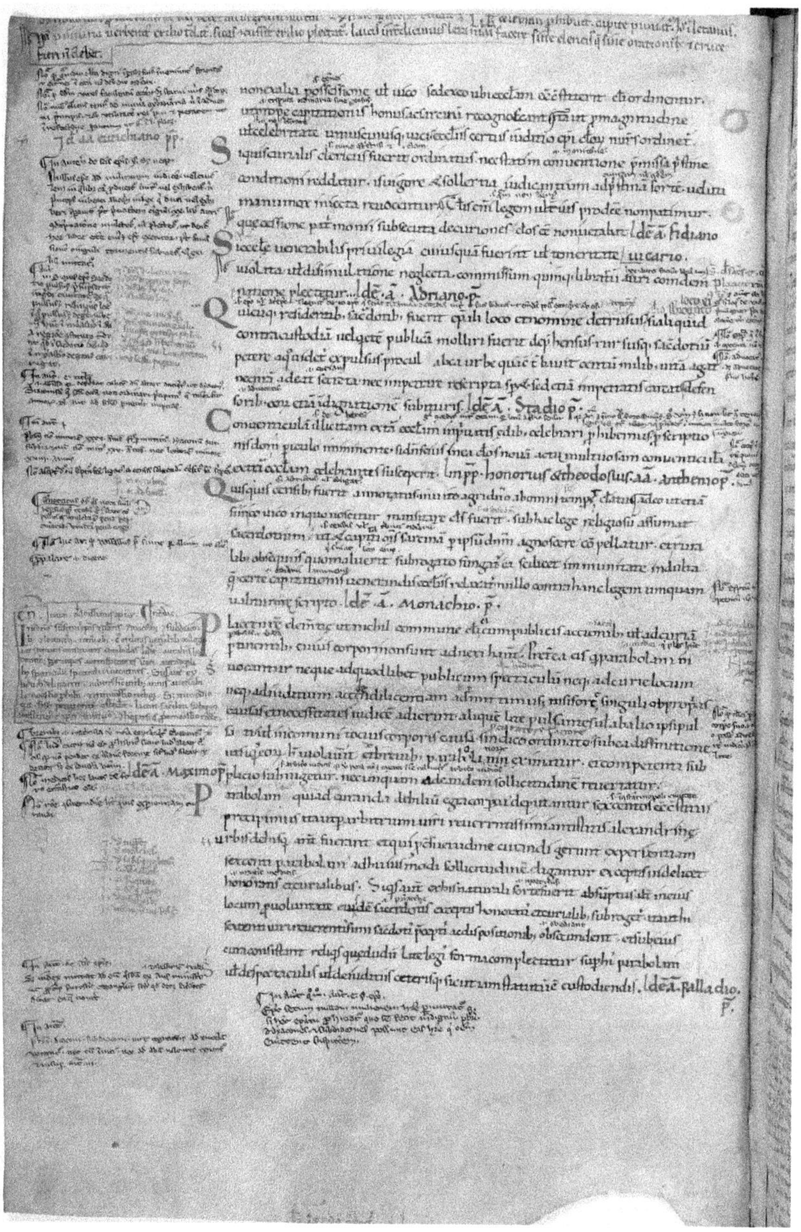

Plate 27. Montpellier, Bibliothèque Universitaire, section médecine, ms. H. 82, f. 7v.

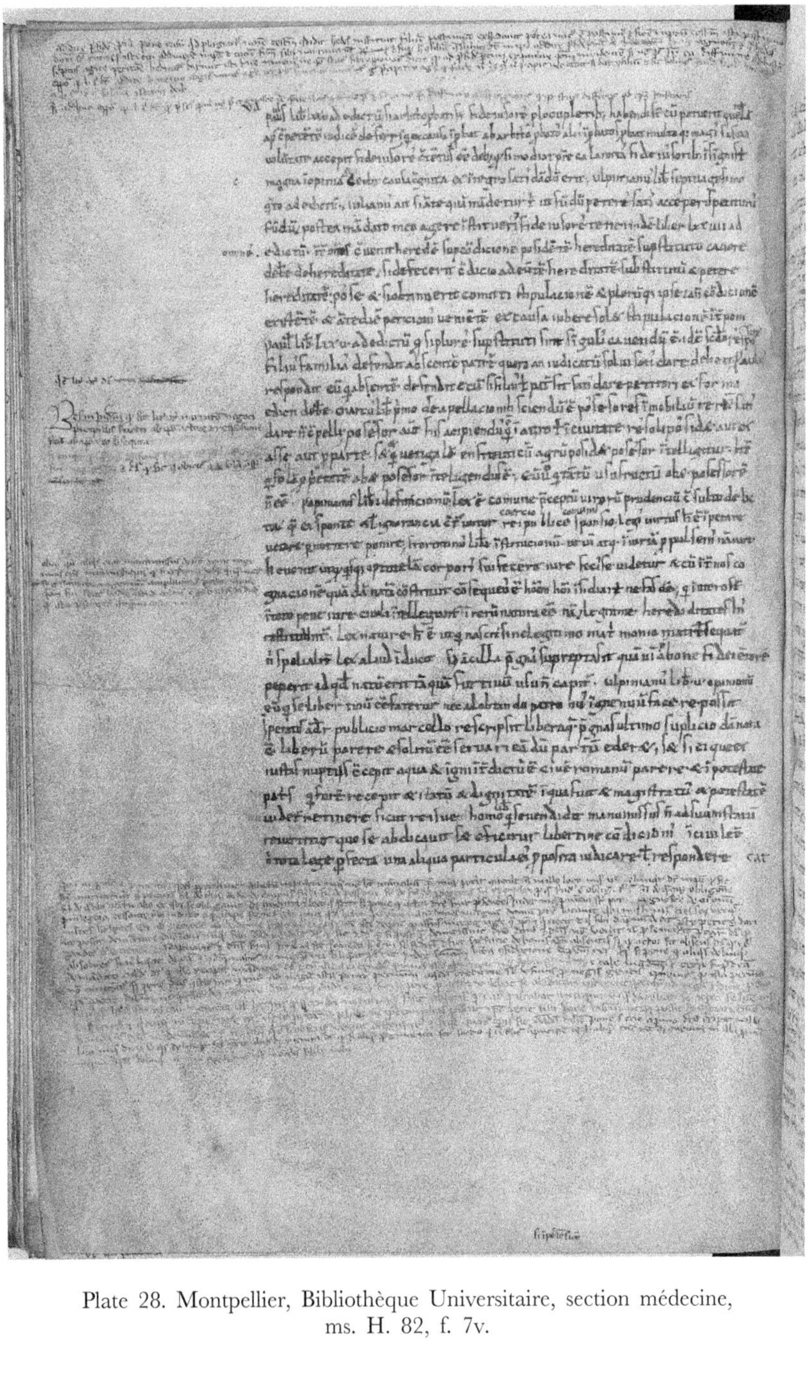

Plate 28. Montpellier, Bibliothèque Universitaire, section médecine, ms. H. 82, f. 7v.

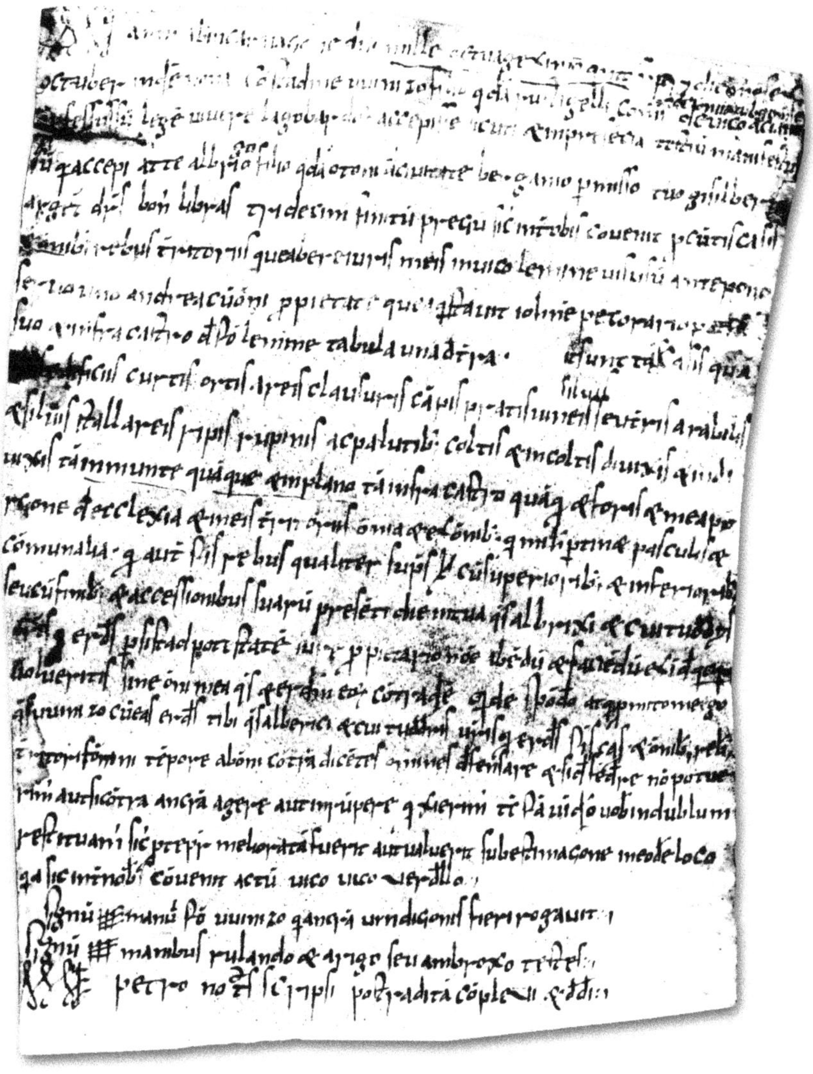

Plate 29. Bergano, Archivio di Stato, 2701, October, 1085.

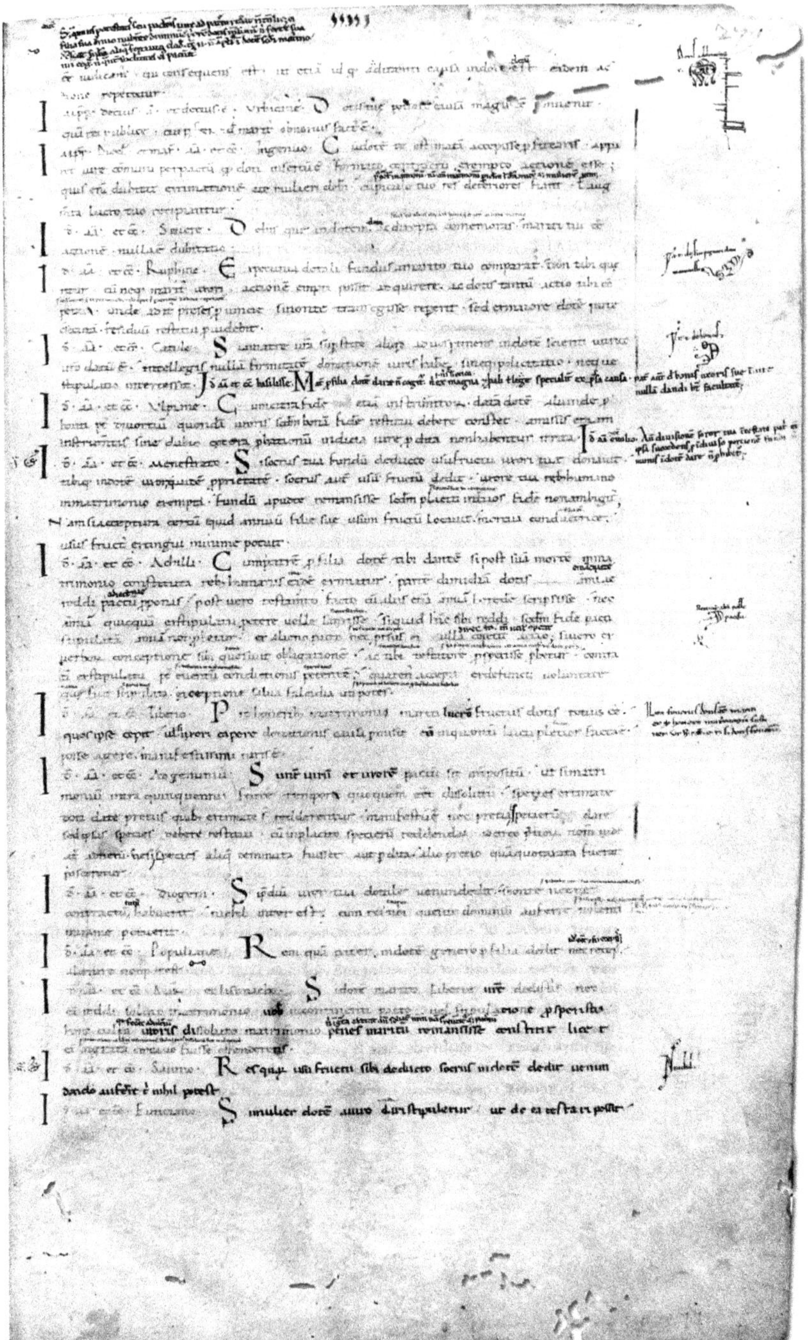

Plate 30. Vienna, Österreichische Nazionalbibliothek, ms. 2065, f. 279r.

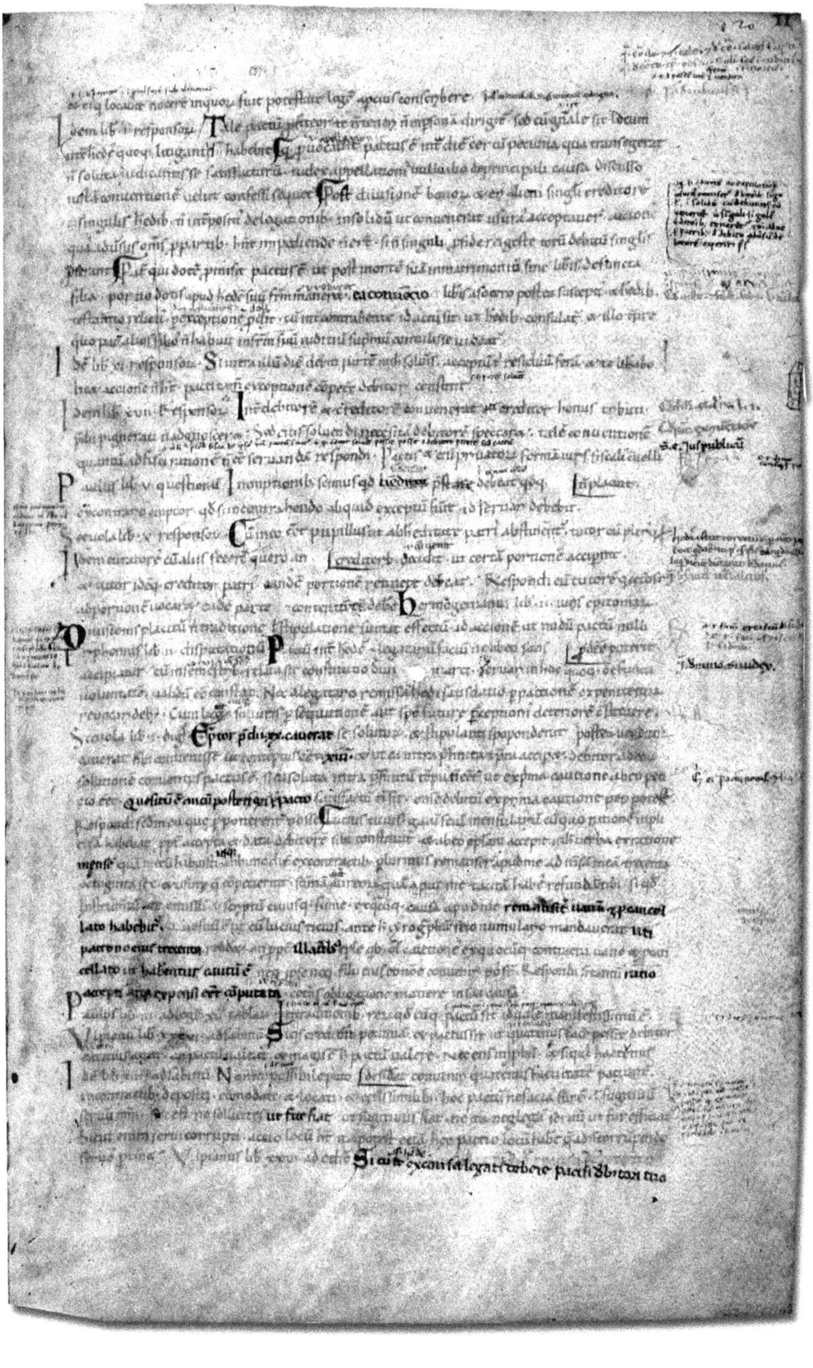

Plate 31. Biblioteca Apostolica Vaticana, Vat. lat. 1406, f. 53r.

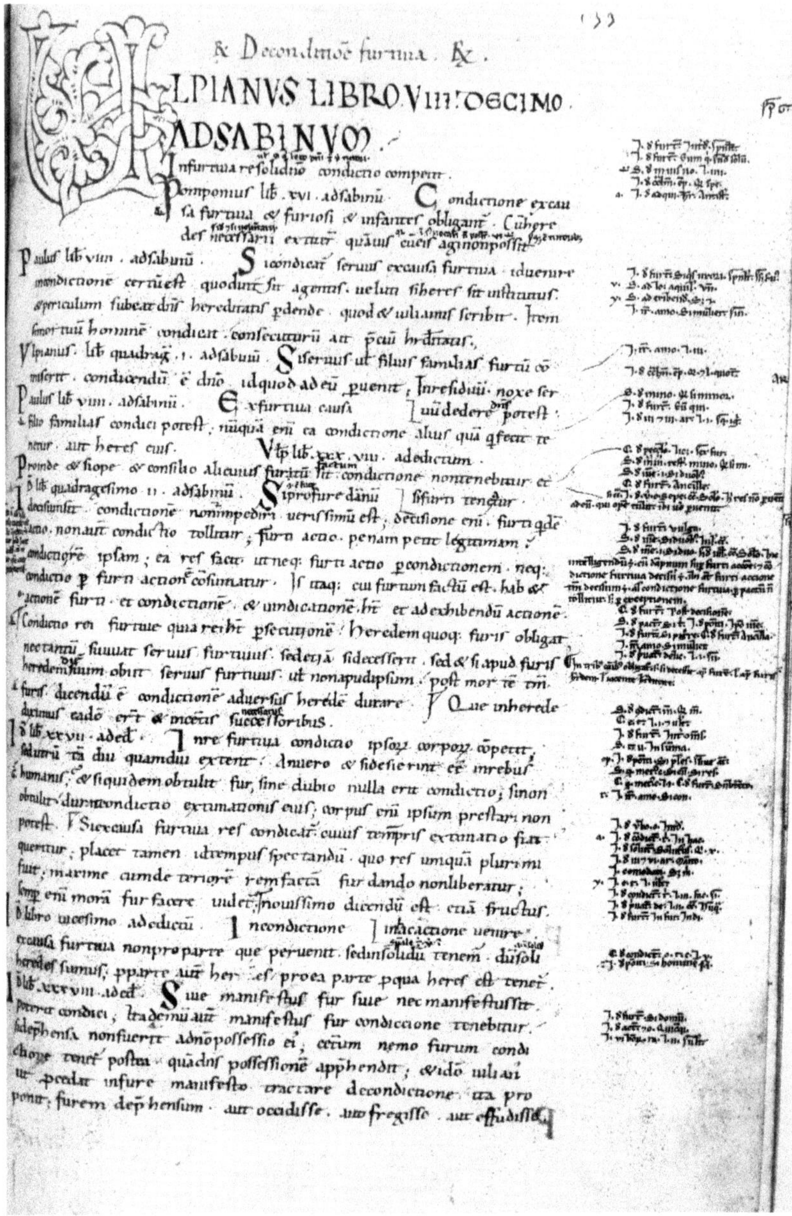

Plate 32. Paris, Bibliothèque Nationale, ms. lat. 4450, f. 133r.

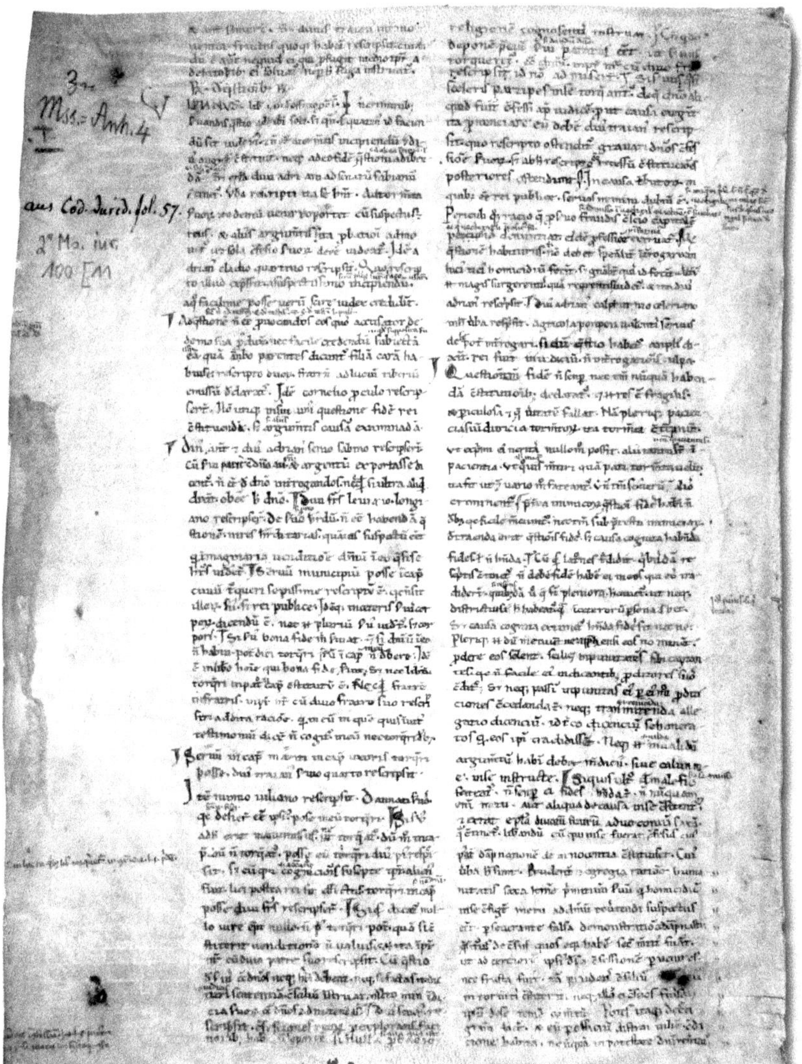

Plate 33. Kassel, Stadtbibliothek, 2° Ms. iurid. 100, 11.

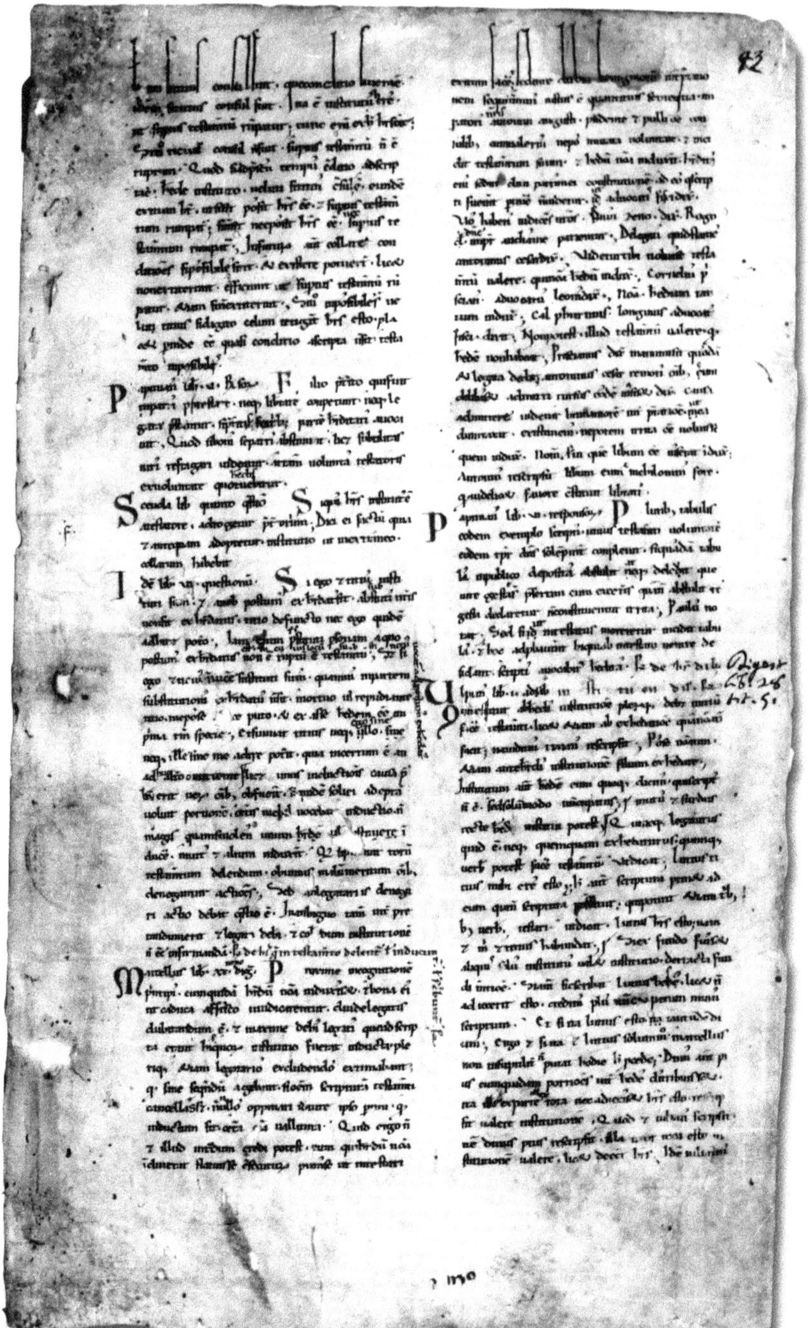

Plate 34. Biblioteca Apostolica Vaticana, Pal. lat. 772, f. 93v.

GENERAL INDEX

INDEX OF MANUSCRIPTS CITED

www.ingramcontent.com/pod-product-compliance
Lightning Source LLC
Chambersburg PA
CBHW071409230926
51613CB00015B/26